FIFTH EDITION

Educational Governance and Administration

Thomas J. Sergiovanni
Trinity University, San Antonio

Paul Kelleher
Trinity University, San Antonio

Martha M. McCarthy
Indiana University, Bloomington

Frederick M. Wirt
Professor Emeritus
University of Illinois, Urbana-Champaign

PEARSON

Boston ■ New York ■ San Francisco
Mexico City ■ Montreal ■ Toronto ■ London ■ Madrid ■ Munich ■ Paris
Hong Kong ■ Singapore ■ Tokyo ■ Cape Town ■ Sydney

Senior Editor: *Arnis E. Burvikovs*
Editorial Assistant: *Christine Lyons*
Marketing Manager: *Tara Whorf*
Editorial-Production Administrator: *Annette Joseph*
Editorial-Production Service: *Colophon*
Electronic Composition: *Omegatype Typography*
Composition Buyer: *Linda Cox*
Manufacturing Buyer: *Andrew Turso*
Cover Designer: *Joel Gendron*

For related titles and support materials, visit our online catalog at *www.ablongman.com*.

Between the time Website information is gathered and then published, it is not unusual for some sites to have closed. Also, the transcription of URLs can result in typographical errors. The publisher would appreciate notification where these occur so that they may be corrected in subsequent editions.

Library of Congress Cataloging-in-Publication Data

Educational governance and administration / Thomas J. Sergiovanni ... [et al.].—5th ed.
    p. cm.
  Includes bibliographical references and index.
  IBSN 0-205-38086-7 (alk. paper)
    1. School management and organization—United States. I. Sergiovanni, Thomas J.

LB2805.E346 2003
371.2′00973–dc21

                                   2003046382

Printed in the United States of America

10 9 8 7 6 5 4 3 2 1 HAM 08 07 06 05 04 03

CONTENTS

PART THREE   Teachers, Principals,
and Superintendents

PREFACE

Being successful in the complex worlds of school leadership and school improvement requires that teachers, administrators, and even parents be able to bring together, in some coherent way, the worlds of politics and policy and the worlds of policy and practice. These worlds provide the historical background and the realistic context that is needed to understand where we now are in school leadership and improvement, to decide where we want to go, and to craft strategies that will get us there. In the end, these worlds provide the framework and substance needed for crafting new images and practices of the policy process and of management and leadership that will better serve schools and students.

This book introduces readers to governance and administration in education. Its main audience is those who aspire to be educational administrators and supervisors. For them, the book provides an overview of the field and a preview of the more specialized courses and experiences they are likely to encounter later in their professional lives. In addition, the book is designed to help administrative aspirants assess the suitability of their own capabilities, dispositions, and interests to a career in educational administration. Other audiences include teachers and teacher-organization leaders, legislators and legislative assistants, and nonprofessionals who want to be better informed about the nature and structure of administration and governance in education. Prior knowledge of this field is not assumed of readers.

We believe that it is best to view the issues of educational administration as connected to those of educational governance. Educational administration is involved not only with the process of administering schools, but also with the execution of public affairs in educational organizations; the performance of executive functions; the guiding, controlling, and directing of educational organizations; and the judicious use of means to accomplish educational ends. Educational governance is concerned with the organization and machinery through which political units such as federal agencies, state departments, and local school districts exercise authority and perform functions and the complex political institutions, laws, and customs that are the basis of the performance of administrative functions and responsibilities. In practice, the two are dynamic and interdependent.

The Context for Schooling in the United States

Demands, constraints, and choices have always shaped the decision-making character of educational administration. Only the content of demands, constraints, and choices changes with the times. Chapters 1 and 2 of this book examine the environment in which schooling in the United States exists. Enduring public values such as equity, efficiency, choice, and excellence are examined historically and currently as prime influences on school policy. The expression of these values changes with the times, but the values themselves are both formidable and stable. Indeed, conflicts among the four values are responsible for much of the current debate about the adequacy of U.S. schools and the reforms needed to improve them. The values are examined within the context of several issues now influencing administrative practice: school autonomy and governmental control; the influence of state-legislated learning on teaching as a profession; balancing democratic and professional authority; and understanding different theories of change.

As we move into the twenty-first century, state-mandated standards and assessments dominate the conversation about schools. At the center of this conversation is a debate over who should decide what the standards should be and how they should be assessed; what changes in school governance patterns are emerging as a result of these standards; what roles the corporate sector should play in setting standards and in influencing other educational policies; and how the local schools and communities are reacting to change. Throughout the first two chapters, the emphasis is on school administrators bringing balance and reason to the issues at hand as they become involved in the politics of education.

Introduction to Educational Administration

Chapters 3 through 7 introduce readers to educational administration as profession and as a field of study. The purpose of these chapters is to provide readers with perspectives on the emergence of the field and on its professional and intellectual roots. This appraisal is necessarily critical, for, as a relatively young field, educational administration is characterized by progress and promise, by problems and dim prospects. Special attention is given to the cultural perspective in educational administration. Leadership within the cultural perspective and school culture building are discussed, along with the more traditional bureaucratic, human-relations, and political views of school organization and functioning.

These chapters also introduce readers to the substantive aspects of administration. Using a theory-to-practice perspective, emphasis is given to understanding administrative theory and the ways that it can be used to gain insights about administrative practice. Emphasis is also given to the issue of how educational administrators actually spend their time on the tasks they accomplish. This descriptive analysis is then examined in light of prescriptions found in the literature of organizational, administrative, and supervisory leadership. Such scrutiny should help readers determine "the way it is" and contrast this with the best thinking on "the way it should be."

Since the publication of the last edition of this book in 1999, the administrator's role as an instructional leader and as a leader of leaders has moved to the center of the conversation about school leadership, rivaled by an accelerated interest in standards for preparing administrators, monitoring their growth, and assessing their performance. Chapter 4 and Appendix 4.1, for example, provide standards for administrators developed by the National Policy Board for Educational Administration.

Students, Teachers, Principals, and Superintendents

Chapters 8 through 10 examine the roles that students, teachers, principals, and superintendents play in schools today and the interdependence that exists among them. The metaphor is that of an interlocking relationship that exists among all the various actors on the school stage—a relationship typically missed by school improvement experts. The framework for analysis varies from social and cultural to managerial and educational. The importance of teacher quality and commitment are viewed as key.

Particular attention is given to how the roles of principals and superintendents have evolved and changed over the last 150 years and how these roles have influenced the school, its purposes, and its effectiveness. Woven into the discussion is the educational leadership theme and its evolution from that of hero to that of collaborator and leader of change.

Introduction to Governance in Education

Chapters 11 through 14 introduce readers to governance structure and issues in education. These chapters include discussions of policymaking in local school districts, state and federal influences on education, and the broad policymaking structure of schools in the United States. Important changes continue to take place in the governance of education in this country. Over the last decade the state has emerged as the dominant force not only in establishing school policy but also in providing the administrative structures and arrangements for the day-by-day operation of schools. Should this trend continue, the historically dominant local school districts will find themselves with diminished authority. Since the last edition, however, noticeable increases in influence have come from the federal level. The federal government, for example, has become a major player in helping states set standards and requiring states to test their students on a regular basis.

Is the United States moving toward a system of state education with fifty school districts? What are the consequences of such an event should it materialize? Is the next logical step a move from fifty school districts to one? At the same time, there is unprecedented interest in such ideas as site-based management, site councils, and the introduction of marketing concepts to the governing of schools. These developments challenge centralized governing structures. It is difficult to predict which way the winds will blow with respect to changes in the governance of schooling, but clearly the ancient Chinese curse "May you live in interesting times" fits today's educational scene.

Legal and Financial Considerations

Chapters 15 through 17 are concerned with legal and financial considerations in the operation of schools. Supreme Court and federal constitutional standards, as well as state-level legal considerations, are explored, and their influence on public-school administration is assessed. The public values of equity, efficiency, choice, and excellence are revisited within the legal context with regard to schooling and issues of school finance.

A Time of Renewal

Much progress has been made toward understanding the process of schooling and school administration since the first edition of this book was published. An avalanche of research has provided a fairly refined and highly useful image of what a successful school is and how administrators can work to bring about school improvements. Schools are being understood from the cultural perspective, providing new and rich insights to be used in developing promising school policies at the state level and more effective administrative practices at the local level. Heightened interest in viewing schools as learning, caring, and inquiring communities adds still another push to redefine how schools should be organized and led. This edition continues to chronicle not only the difficulties to be faced but also the excitement that is now emerging as educational administration seeks to renew itself as a profession committed to teaching and learning, building better schools, and creating a better society.

New Authors

By now many readers who have used previous editions of this book are wondering about the new line-up of authors. Three of the original authors, Professors Martin Burlingame of Oklahoma State University and Fred Coombs and Paul Thurston of the University of Illinois Urbana-Champaign have retired and decided not to continue with the book. The three contributed seminally to the book's framework—a framework that is maintained in this fifth edition. Their legacy remains and they will be missed. Change has an upside, too. Three new authors have joined the team, and they bring a fresh perspective and new excitement. They are: **Professor Frederick M. Wirt,** who is a nationally acclaimed author and a pioneer in the field of educational policy and governance; **Professor Paul Kelleher,** who not only understands politics and governance, but brings to the book extensive experience as a principal and superintendent; and **Professor Martha M. McCarthy,** an experienced administrator, administrator educator, and an expert in school law. You will learn a little more about the new authors from the Authors page that follows and a lot more as you join them in engaging ideas about topics that provide a foundation for the study and practice of educational administration.

Many people contributed to the preparation of this edition. Most notably was the magic of my assistant, Ruby Dehls. Ruby coordinated the work of the four authors, looked after permissions and other management details, and edited the manuscript with grace and skill. Our thanks.

ABOUT THE AUTHORS

Thomas J. Sergiovanni is Lillian Radford Professor of Education and Administration and Senior Fellow at the Center for Educational Leadership at Trinity University. He received his master's degree from Teachers College, Columbia University, and his Ed.D. from the University of Rochester in educational administration. An active teacher, writer, and editor, he brings to the text his extensive experience as a researcher and in working with numerous school improvement projects. His recent books include *Moral Leadership, Building Community in Schools, Leadership for the Schoolhouse, The Lifeworld of Leadership, The Principalship: A Reflective Practice Perspective* (4th ed.), *Leadership: What's in It for Schools?* and *Supervision: A Redefinition* (7th ed.).

Paul Kelleher is Norine Murchison Professor of Education, Chair of the Department of Education, and Director of the Center for Educational Leadership at Trinity University. He received his A.B. and M.A.T. degrees from Harvard University and his Ed.D. degree from Teachers College, Columbia University. Kelleher has over thirty years of experience as a principal and superintendent. He was principal, for example, of Scarsdale High School and superintendent in Bedford, NY; Westbury, CT; and Laurence, NY. Active in the American Association of School Administrators, the Teachers College Columbia Institute for Superintendents, and the National Society for the Study of Education, Kelleher has written a number of papers and articles on school leadership and educational policy.

Martha M. McCarthy, Chancellor's Professor at Indiana University, specializes in education law and policy. Previously Chair of the Educational Leadership Program, Director of the Indiana Education Policy Center, and Associate Dean of the Faculties at Indiana University, she has also been a public school teacher and central office administrator. She has served as President of the Education Law Association and the University Council for Educational Administration and as Vice-President for Division A of the American Educational Research Association. She has authored or coauthored several books, including *Public School Law: Teachers' and Students' Rights* (5th ed.), and more than 200 articles on students' and teachers' rights, church–state relations, equity issues, school privatization, leadership preparation programs, and education reform efforts.

Frederick M. Wirt is Professor Emeritus in Political Science at the University of Illinois. He has received lifetime achievement awards from both the American Education Research Association and the American Political Science Association. Wirt and Michael Kirst co-authored two editions of *The Political Dynamics of American Education.* He has recently co-authored two articles based on a national sample of principals on their leadership attitudes. Also, his award-winning book, *We Ain't What We Was: Civil Rights and the New South,* traces local changes to the long-run effect of the Civil Rights Acts of the 1960s. A book in progress traces the long-run effects of the GI Bill of Rights on World War II veterans.

1 Public Values and School Policy

The Roots of Conflict

If limited to three words to describe the world of school administration and the nature of managerial work, Rosemary Stewart (1982) would choose *demands, constraints,* and *choices.* She suggests that managerial jobs comprise "an inner core of *demands,* an outer boundary of *constraints,* and an in-between area of *choices*" (p. 14). *Demands* come from the forces and pressures that school administrators cannot ignore—things they must do to avoid sanctions for their schools that ultimately could imperil their jobs. *Constraints* are the factors internal and external to the school that limit what school administrators can do. Sometimes demands and constraints are imposed externally by legal mandates and requirements, budgetary limitations, community pressures, school outcome specifications, and role expectations of important others such as school board members, members of the business community, and parents. Sometimes demands and constraints come from within the school in the form of work rules; expectations of teachers; school organizational arrangements; union contracts; and the norms, mores, unwritten rules, and standard operating procedures that reflect the school's culture.

Choices exist within any demand-and-constraint set. Choices are opportunities for school administrators in similar jobs to do different things or to do the same things in different ways. One of the hallmarks of a successful school administrator is the ability to expand the area of choice by deft handling of demands and constraints. However, there are limits. Further, as the nature of demands and constraints changes, choice options change also. The context and nature of demands and constraints is, therefore, a good starting point in trying to understand what educational administration is and is not, and what school administrators can and cannot do.

In recent years, the configuration of demands and constraints has undergone dramatic changes. Schooling in the United States today is characterized by a new politics of education and a fundamental shift in the basic governance structure for organizing and administering schools. Much of what has happened is only now being sorted out, and the implications for administrative practice in the decades ahead are only beginning to be understood.

Defining the Context

The general pattern for defining the context for schooling in the United States was set politically at this nation's inception. The Constitution of the United States does not mention education, and thus education became a state responsibility. Traditionally, this responsibility has been handed over to local jurisdictions. The Soviet launch of *Sputnik* in 1957 posed the first serious challenge to local control in matters of schooling. The United States appeared to be at risk as the Soviets pulled ahead in the space race. The schools were judged to be at fault, and the proposed solution was for the federal government to protect the public interest by initiating and paying for massive reforms. A major change had begun to take place in how the schools of this nation were to be governed and administered. This federal involvement actually increased the importance of the states. Federal monies and programs, for example, were filtered through the states and monitored by state departments of education. This increased responsibility led to the states having a more powerful role to play in developing policies and making rules that often wound up prescribing what local schools were to do and how to do it.

Some applauded the change, claiming that local control was, at best, a romantic and inefficient vestige of an earlier time. After all, the size and scale of the republic at its inception bears little resemblance to its present state.

> Consider, first, the matter of numbers. It is startling to recall that when the constitution which still guides American society was ratified, there were less than four million persons in the thirteen states of the Union. Of these, 750,000 were Negro slaves outside society. It was a young population—the median age was only sixteen—and at that time fewer than 800,000 males had reached voting age. When George Washington was inaugurated as the first President of the United States, New York City, then the capital of the country, had a population of only 33,000. (Bell, 1973, pp. 69–70)

At that time, the nation was considered to be an agricultural society. Cities were defined as having 2,500 or more people, and only a few cities existed. A highly decentralized school system was ideally suited to the times. Life is much more complex today, and the governance and administration of schools reflects this complexity.

The United States was judged to be at risk again in 1983, only about twenty-five years after the *risk* caused by the launching of the Soviet *Sputnik*. This time, it was the Japanese and the South Koreans who were pulling ahead, warned *A Nation at Risk* (National Commission on Excellence in Education, 1983). New reforms were the answer, as states surged forward again to challenge the authority of local educational agencies. There had been a steady growth of state control in the decade of the seventies, "when states began to get involved in such matters as accountability, school finance reform, categorical programs, school improvement efforts, minimum competency testing, and civil rights regulations" (Kirst, 1989, p. 65). But *A Nation at Risk* was a challenge to state governments to "gather in" their authority in unprecedented ways from local agencies, to initiate reforms on a massive scale.

The language of the report was such that the governors of our states dared not to ignore its message:

> Our once unchallenged preeminence in commerce, industry, science, and technological innovation is being overtaken by competitors throughout the world.... If an unfriendly power had attempted to impose on America the mediocre educational performance that exists today, we might well have viewed it as an act of war. As it stands, we have allowed this to happen to ourselves. We have squandered the gains in student achievement made in the wake of the Sputnik challenge. Moreover, we dismantled essential support systems which help make those gains possible. We have, in effect, been committing an act of unthinking, unilateral educational disarmament. (National Commission on Excellence in Education, 1983, p. 5)

In 1979, for the first time in the history of the nation, state and federal funding of schools exceeded that derived from local sources. *A Nation at Risk* coaxed the states to increase their contribution further. Pocketbooks were opened wide as funded mandates for improvement (such as minimum competence testing, the career ladder for teachers, stipulated curriculum requirements, and providing for school achievement auditing) emerged from our state capitals.

For this *first wave* of reform in the eighties, the favored policy instruments were mandates and inducements. By 1986, the reform reports that appeared began to take on a different flavor. Several of these *second wave* reports were influential: *Tomorrow's Teachers: A Report of the Holmes Group*; the Carnegie Forum on Education and the Economy's report *A Nation Prepared: Teachers for the 21st Century; What Next? More Leverage for Teachers*, a publication of the Education Commission of the States; *What Matters Most: Teaching for America's Future*, a publication of the National Commission on Teaching and America's Future; *Investing in Teaching a Common Agenda* (Koppich, 2001), a publication sponsored by several business organizations; and *Teacher Quality and the Future of Learning in San Antonio*, a publication of the Center for Educational Leadership at Trinity University. These reports addressed bringing about changes in teachers, their work conditions, and their preparation.

The Holmes Group report emphasized increasing the standards for entry into teaching, strengthening the liberal arts foundation of teacher preparation, raising standards of entry into the teacher profession, and strengthening the connections between departments and schools of education and the public schools. The Education Commission of the States report was a plea for reforms to be more responsive to the expertise that exists among teachers. In the foreword, then New Jersey governor and Commission chairman Thomas H. Kean stated:

> The conversation reported in this book sustains my belief that we are on the edge of a second phase of teacher reform, one that builds upon and extends what we did earlier but brings in many new themes. For example, our friends tell us that we should be more careful in what we regulate about teaching. Set firm, clear standards for the results we expect, but let educators have more leeway in deciding how to meet the standards. They say that the kind of people we want in the classroom just won't stay without this kind of professional responsibility. And they warn us that

we must attend to the way schools are organized, and we should avoid state sanctions that add to an already bureaucratic quality in schooling.... They tell us that the profession itself must take up the fight we began for higher professional standards. (Green, 1986, inside cover)

Similarly, the Carnegie Forum's report emphasized the importance of upgrading the preparation of teachers and teaching and of providing teachers more autonomy, on the one hand, and holding them more accountable, on the other. They proposed, for example, creating a National Board for Professional Teaching Standards, upgrading the liberal arts education of teachers, providing incentives for teachers linked to schoolwide performance, and restructuring teacher and administrative roles to give teachers greater access to decision making. Although the emphasis was on teaching, a basic formula was beginning to emerge of tightly connecting the educational establishment to standards and outcomes but loosely connecting them to means. In more recent years the emphasis on teacher learning (Darling-Hammond, 1997) and on standards-driven teaching (*Education Week*, 2001; Resnick & Hall, 1998; Carr & Harris, 2001) has moved closer to the center of the conversation on school reform.

The No Child Left Behind Act

The No Child Left Behind Act of 2001 is the most recent and perhaps the most intrusive effort by the federal government to influence educational policy and practice. This law, a revision of the landmark Elementary and Secondary Education Act first passed in 1965, provides mandates that cut a wide swath across schooling in America. Among the areas affected are state accountability systems, required testing programs, and rules and regulations that mandate standards for teachers that states are required to meet. The law, for example, requires that states test all students in grades 3 through 8 annually. Tests must be standards based and must allow for comparison across schools and school districts. Schools that do not make "adequate progress" for two consecutive years must allow students to transfer to "better schools." Further, by 2005–2006 states must have ensured that all teachers of core academic subjects are "highly qualified" in every subject that they teach. States and districts must also prepare report cards that provide information about teacher qualifications including the number of classes not taught by highly qualified teachers. Schools receiving Title I aid must notify parents when their children are taught by teachers who are not qualified. While few would argue with these requirements regarding teacher quality, not everyone agrees with the mandated testing provisions of the act. Regardless of the intent or the content of the law's provisions, a basic question remains. What is the constitutional status of a law that proscribes in such a broad and detailed way what it is that states should do and how they should do it? At this writing, most Americans seem simply to be shrugging their shoulders and trying to figure out how to implement the law. As we look ahead, however, one should not be surprised if there are legal challenges about the constitutionality of the federal government's new role. After all, this act represents a massive transfer of power from local and state jurisdictions to the federal level.

Policy Instruments

Reforms of the first and second waves can be distinguished by the ways in which policymakers sought to make changes. McDonnell and Elmore (1987) group various instruments for changing school policies into four categories: mandates, inducements, capacity-building strategies, and system-changing strategies (p. 134). *Mandates* are rules and regulations designed to govern directly the choices and actions of educators and schools; *inducements* are the exchange of money, status, and other benefits to educators and schools in return for desired choices and actions; *capacity building* is the use of money, status, and other benefits for the purpose of investing in human resources by building up educators' capacities to choose and act in desired ways; and *system changing* seeks to bring about desired choices and actions by the "reallocation of power and authority among those involved in the process of schooling" (p. 134) (Table 1.1).

Each of the policy instruments is based on different assumptions and has different consequences for the educational system. These assumptions and consequences are summarized in Table 1.1. The first wave of reform emphasized mandates and inducements. For example, mandates require action regardless of whether schools are ready or able to comply. Failure to comply results in penalties. System changing, by contrast, assumes that present structures and operating procedures are simply not able to produce the desired results and must, therefore, be restructured.

As waves push forward and then recede, they create a mixed undercurrent. In recent years for example, it has become apparent that the second wave of reform never replaced the first. Instead, both waves together were applied to schools, creating an undercurrent that provided schools with conflicting and often irreconcilable expectations. The second wave placed more emphasis on capacity building and system changing. The intent of a particular reform proposal and the choice of a favored implementing policy instrument have consequences that determine the mix of demands and constraints facing school administrators and the choices available to them as they act. Intents and instruments represent value statements as do demands and constraints. In this sense, the world of school government and administration represents a struggle over values as administrators seek to find and expand choices.

Part One of this book (Chapters 1 and 2) examines the present context for schooling in the United States at two levels: the underlying basic values of American education that compete for attention and the examples of issues that dominate the agendas of educational policymakers and school administrators. How these issues are resolved and the nature of the balance that is struck between competing values will determine the future of U.S. education for the decades ahead. Among the issues to be considered are the crisis in educational quality, who the schools will serve and who will decide, legislated learning and creeping bureaucracy in the classroom,

TABLE 1.1   Policy Instruments—Assumptions and Consequences

	Assumptions	Consequences
Mandates	Action required regardless of capacity; good in its own right	Coercion required
	Action would not occur with desired frequency or consistency without rule	Create uniformity, reduce variation
		Policy contains information necessary for compliance
		Adversarial relations between initiators, targets
		Minimum standards
Inducements	Valued good would not be produced with desired frequency or consistency in absence of additional money	Capacity exists; money needed to mobilize it
	Individuals, agencies vary in capacity to produce; money elicits performance	As tolerable range of variation narrows, oversight costs increase
		Most likely to work when capacity exists
Capacity-building	Knowledge, skill competence required to produce future value; or	Capacity does not exist, investment needed to mobilize it
	Capacity good in its own right or instrumental to other purposes	Tangible present benefits serve as proxies for future, intangible benefits
System-changing	Existing institutions, existing incentives cannot produce desired results	Institutional factors incite action; provokes defensive response
	Changing distribution of authority changes what is produced	New institutions raise new problems of mandates, inducements, capacities

Source: L. M. McDonnell & R. Elmore, "Getting the Job Done: Alternative Policy Instruments," *Educational Evaluation and Policy Analysis, 9*(2), 1987, p. 141. Copyright 1987 by the American Educational Research Association.

mandated testing of teachers and students, new commitments to improving schools, and equity in the provision of schooling to all Americans. Equality, efficiency, excellence, and choice are identified as four competing values that represent the undercurrent for debates on the issues. The concept of *flow of images* is then examined in the context of schools' attempts to maintain public confidence.

Public Values and School Policy

Even though the values of equity, efficiency, choice, and excellence are deeply embedded in this country's heritage, they exist in a constant state of tension, so that too much emphasis on any one hinders expression of each of the other three. At various times in America's history, one or another of these values has been over-emphasized, with predictable consequences. For example, during the Great Society years of Lyndon Johnson's presidency, the value of equity was targeted for special emphasis. To achieve equity in schooling, the federal government initiated a number of school programs and passed laws that many felt circumscribed the discretion of local educational agencies. These federal initiatives increased the power of the state at the expense of local control. Affirmative-action laws provided school districts with quotas and with specific selection processes to follow, lest they be disqualified from receiving federal funds. Many observers of that scene felt that federal initiatives with respect to teaching programs resulted in a watering down of education that seriously compromised the value of excellence in schooling. Nearly everyone agrees that the overall cost of the Great Society's educational programs seriously endangered the value of efficiency. Inflation and interest rates were high, and excess federal spending was considered the cause. The reforms resulted in increases in the bureaucracy at all levels of school governance.

The first wave of reform of the eighties, some would argue, represented a mirror image of the seventies. In the eighties, the emphasis seemed to be on excellence at the expense of equity, efficiency, and choice. The negative effects of basic skills–oriented uniform standards and standardized testing, rigid "no pass, no play" laws, competency tests for teachers, standardization of details of the curriculum, and one-best-way teaching evaluation systems seemed to be disproportionately felt among minorities. Further, the reforms were costly, with benefits in student achievement and school improvement elusive. The use of mandates and inducements as the prime policy instruments led to the kind of centralization and standardization that provided enough overload in demands and constraints to seriously compromise choices for individual school districts, schools, teachers, and administrators. Local school boards and parents were similarly overwhelmed. The four values and their influence on school policy are considered next.

Equity

Equity means fairness in sharing the resources available for schooling. This educational value corresponds to a general societal value honoring fair play and equal opportunity. Equity does not always mean providing identical resources to each student or school or providing the same access to every educational program. Sometimes identicalness and sameness are considered unfair. In a golf match, for example, some players are given an advantage, a handicap, to offset some advantage in natural or other talent others may have. Admittedly, one often struggles to identify just what constitutes a fair handicap, but the objective is to give each golfer an equal chance to win. Students with special needs or with disadvantaged opportunities for coming to school ready to learn are examples of students who are often given more resources in an attempt to level the learning field for all students.

Often, equity suffers at the hand of excellence. Some policymakers, for example, argue that incentives should be provided to motivate schools to strive for excellence. In states with statewide testing, these policymakers recommend that schools with high test scores be rewarded with increased autonomy or cash bonuses or both. Low-performing schools, by contrast, are typically threatened with loss of autonomy and endure public shame as the school rankings are posted in local newspapers. Low-performing schools do receive extra resources in the form of state help with the development of school improvement plans, but teachers and local school officials sometimes equate this help with attempts to reduce their discretion. Although the distribution of state resources on the basis of merit has appeal to advocates of excellence in schools, equity advocates argue for the distribution of resources based on need.

One way to balance concerns for equity and excellence is by adopting a value-added approach to accountability. This approach provides recognition based on effectiveness gains that are not uniformly benchmarked. Instead, benchmarking is done individually on a school-by-school basis. In effect, instead of schools competing with each other, they compete with their own previous performance levels. This strategy, however, often upsets excellence zealots.

Equity often conflicts with the values of excellence, efficiency, and choice. Adjusting the allocation of resources by formula and enforcing such adjustment through external controls can restrict the freedom of school districts, compromise their basic liberties, and thus pose a threat to local control. As local control is compromised, the argument continues, school districts lack the incentives to strive for excellence. Further, external control typically leads to standardization and uniformity, thus stifling local initiative and reducing the ability of local educational agencies to provide responsive schooling.

Efficiency

Benjamin Franklin's lessons of thrift and getting one's money's worth have traditionally been part of the cultural legacy of the United States. Americans have a historic predisposition for getting their money's worth when it comes to public spending, and the closer this spending is to home, the greater their concern. Our system of local control and local tax support creates a problem as school costs continue to rise. Schools are labor intensive; despite the potential offered by technological advances, technology has not brought about great cost savings. Chrysler can cut costs by using robots. Other production-oriented enterprises fight inflation with advances in technology. Teacher salaries are the greatest costs in any school budget; however, they have risen without measurable increases in productivity, thus raising questions of efficiency in the minds of the public.

This efficiency question is also raised by the apparent increase in the administrative costs of running schools. Former Secretary of Education William J. Bennett notes:

> While total instructional expenditures per pupil went up 64 percent between 1960 and 1980, spending on administration and other noninstructional matters rose 107 percent. The number of non-classroom instructional personnel in our school systems grew by 400 percent between 1960 and 1984. And during those years, money

spent on teacher salaries dropped from over 56 percent to under 41 percent of total elementary and secondary school spending. Too much money has been diverted from the classrooms; a smaller share of the school dollar is now being spent on student classroom instruction than at any time in recent history. It should be the basic goal of the education reform movement to reverse this trend toward administrative bloat and to reduce the scale of the bureaucratic "blob" draining our school resources. (Bennett, 1988, p. 46)

Many policy analysts and educational administrators dispute Bennett's claims. Berliner and Biddle (1995), for example, point out that "across the country, central-office professionals constitute only 1.6 percent of the staffing of public school districts" (p. 79). Eliminating all of the central office professionals in the nation, Berliner and Biddle explain, would enable the reduction of class size by only one student. They note further that in the business world and in the non-school public administration world, the average ratio of employees to administrators is 7.1 to 1.0. In schools, the figure is 14.5 to 1.0. Regardless of who is right in this debate, the image of inefficiency in running our schools remains strong in the minds of the public.

The efficiency value is the undercurrent for the nation's concern for accountability. Accountability is manifested in the form of product testing (students), program budgeting (objectives), and adoption of systems-analysis management designs (emphasizing efficiency in operations). The concern for *fiscal containment* is a political manifestation of the efficiency value. Advocates of fiscal containment seek to limit government spending and promote a balanced budget, advocating across-the-board tax reductions. Sometimes efforts to promote more efficient schools backfire. For example, regulating accountability by standardizing the curriculum and introducing student testing programs and standardized teacher evaluation systems can bring increases in administrative and monitoring staffs that can lead to more bureaucratic *blob* in state education departments and school district central offices. Current research confirms the view that although standardized teaching and testing may be more efficient for achieving basic increases in a student's performance, they are less effective and therefore less efficient for achieving higher level student performance (Newman, Marks, & Gamoran, 1995; Elmore, 1995).

Excessive concern for efficiency compromises the choice value by seriously constraining what local jurisdictions, local communities, and the professional educational establishment are able to do; makes the goal of equity difficult by reducing the amount of resources generally available; and results in a relative decrease in spending, which compromises the value of excellence. Some seek to promote efficiency and excellence by advocating an elitist approach to education. They would spend much more of our resources on the best and brightest students and much less on the rest. This position compromises the values of choice and equity.

Choice

There is a bit of the New England town meeting in all of America, and a strain of Jacksonian democracy permeates our collective personality. Some claim that such images are more myth than reality, perpetuated by a desire to preserve the romantic on the one hand and the necessity to maintain some semblance of control in an age of bureaucracy and impersonality on the other. Whether such images are symbolic or real, schools are particularly significant in maintaining the value of choice, for they represent the last vestige of local control in the tradition of the town meeting and the local tax referendum.

In recent years, local control has been slipping away to state and federal levels. Efficiency in schooling requires that decisions be made at higher and more remote levels of government. This centralization is manifested in regulations prescribing a certain sameness, which often compromises one's right to do what she or he thinks is best for students locally. Even the concept of excellence is thought by many to be defined in a universalistic way. The local standard of excellence, so much a part of this nation's tradition in schooling, is giving ground to one defined by the state and perhaps ultimately by the nation.

Centralists believe that many of the ills of schools resulted from too much choice given to local educational agencies. "They have had their chance, and what is the result?" is the lament often heard. At the other extreme are those who believe that parents and teachers know best and that the best education results from giving these groups the power to decide. Suspicious even of central office control within local school districts, they would advocate school-site management, strong parent councils, and fiscal as well as curricular autonomy for individual schools. Many people of this persuasion choose to leave the public-school system, feeling that these ideals are more easily realized in private schools. Some choose to home-school their children.

Embedded in this controversy are the tensions between those who advocate market choice and those who advocate democratic choice. *Market choice* is decidedly more efficient, requiring neither bureaucratic machinery nor large investments in leadership. The key motivating factor is individual self-interest. *Democratic choice,* by contrast, involves lengthy, complex, and often combative processes of participation as issues are discussed and decisions are made. Advocates of democratic choice believe that some issues in society are too important to be left to the whims of the market. Market choice, they point out, is based on the tendency of individuals to make decisions that maximize self-interest. Democratic choice, by contrast, requires that self-interest be sacrificed for the common good. This theme is explored further in Chapter 2.

Excellence

Of the four values, excellence is the most difficult to define. This difficulty stems in part from the political rhetoric with which the word *excellence* is used by special-interest groups who favor one or another of the other values. Advocates of equity, for example, are quick to define excellence in terms of an educational program's ability to respond to the issues *they* consider important. Similarly, unique definitions of excellence emerge in the rhetoric of advocates of liberty and efficiency. Excellent programs are those locally determined in response to unique local needs, or excellent programs are those that result in higher test scores.

For most, excellence is considered to have something to do with a school's ability to achieve its objectives in a high-quality way. On the one hand, it refers to the school's ability to have students measure up to standards of good work. But as the noted evaluation expert Robert Stake (1985) points out, "Outstanding performance on a trivial task is not excellence" (p. 3). This observation adds still another dimension to the definitional problem. Those who strive for excellence by emphasizing only achievement test scores would not measure up to Stake's standards. He believes that "excellence…means students have keen understanding and the ability to perform well. Excellent performance includes the intellectual powers of recall, reasoning, problem solving, and interpretation" (p. 3).

Newmann, Marks, and Gamoran (1995), for example, view excellence in education as expressions of authentic pedagogy. Their extensive research leads them to define *authentic pedagogy* using three criteria: construction of knowledge, disciplined inquiry, and having value beyond high school. Though many educators agree that this definition is valid, many policymakers disagree. Assessing authentic pedagogy by applying these standards to the work that teachers give students to do, the teaching that takes place in the classroom, and the work that students actually do is both complex and time consuming. As an alternative, these policymakers propose a more efficient definition of excellence, such as high student scores on standardized tests.

Whether excellence conflicts with efficiency, it appears, depends on the definition of excellence that is used. This reality raises the question of which value drives the other. Do advocates of standardized testing, for example, choose this standard for reasons of excellence or for reasons of efficiency? For reasons of excellence or for reasons of tradition? For reasons of excellence or for reasons of simplicity?

Competing Values and Images of Schooling

Though none of the four values alone represents a sufficiently strong banner under which to launch school reform, value pairs seem to have enough credibility and strength for this purpose. Particularly powerful are pairs that combine either excellence or equity with one of the other values. Four such pairs are illustrated in Figure 1.1.

The value of equity combined with efficiency, for example, aptly captures the great push for educational reform that accompanied President Johnson's Great Society programs. The federal government sought both equity and efficiency by funding social programs aimed at leveling the playing field for students and provided a bureaucratic maze of regulations to monitor and evaluate these programs. Skeptics, however, note that although regulations were intended to increase efficiency the actual result was inefficiency and even waste.

The value of equity combined with choice has provided a persistent mindset for schooling highly favored by the educational establishment, taught in the nation's schools of education, and striven for by many liberal groups. The strategy in this case is to empower parents and teachers through site-based management,

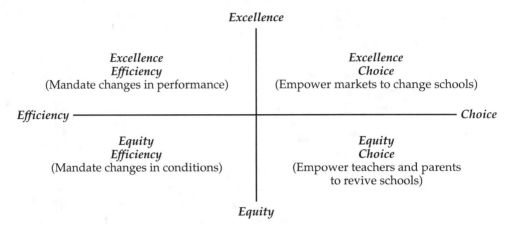

FIGURE 1.1   Competing Values and School Ideals

the building of professional community, and similar means to revive the system. This combination of equity and choice represents the egalitarian ideal that is so much a part of America's cultural legacy.

Excellence combined with efficiency seemed to characterize the thrust of the school-reform movement in the mid-1980s and still persists today. *A Nation at Risk* made the case for this viewpoint that schools must toughen up, students must measure up to tougher standards or leave, more emphasis must be placed on maintaining the nation's competitive edge, and the best and the brightest students must be identified and nurtured. Unlike the situation under the federal centralization of the Johnson years, the states were to set the standards, provide the regulations, and hold the local schools accountable to these standards. Considering each state one at a time, this combination of excellence and efficiency does seem to be more efficient. But when all the states are viewed collectively, this strategy may well be inefficient. The supremacy of the state in matters of school policy resulted in the growth of state education bureaucracies, increases in state educational legislation, and additional costs of doing educational business in the nation's fifty state capitals. Bureaucratic bloat, it appears, may have actually increased with the consolidation of power at the state level.

Excellence combined with choice describes the values of those who subscribe to elitist images but are not willing to give up control over their own destinies. What will be taught, who will be taught, and how schooling will be funded are decisions that they are unwilling to relinquish. The alternative they choose is either to leave the public schools for private schools or to convert their own public schools into the form and shape of private schools. In either case, the value of equity is subordinate, for it interferes with the struggle for excellence.

Many policy experts put all their eggs in the parental and school-choice basket as they seek to reform the schools. Allowing parents to choose schools from among others within the school district or the state introduces market forces that advocates believe will drive out the bad and encourage the good (excellence). For market forces to operate, they point out, schools must provide genuine choices. This kind of diversity requires that school administrators and teachers be given wide discretion in deciding matters of schooling. For this to happen, the schools will have to be deregulated. Further, expensive evaluation systems with costly administrative monitoring will no longer be necessary. Parents will simply vote with their feet by moving their children from schools that are not working to those that are. Deregulation, they maintain, promises to deflate the bureaucratic bloat and create more efficient schooling.

Critics maintain, however, that parents who are more knowledgeable and who can move their students from one school to another easily are the ones who are likely to benefit. Families from middle and upper socioeconomic status (SES) are likely to be overrepresented in this group, with lower SES families underrepresented. This situation, critics maintain, will compromise the value of equity. Proponents counter by suggesting that incentive systems be developed that will encourage schools to recruit lower SES students through information programs and other means. Schools, for example, might be given bonus money for each lower SES student they recruit. Proponents argue, as well, that lower SES families living in inner cities seem to express the most interest in school choice. The support for this movement, in other words, is generally stronger in inner cities than it is in the suburbs.

Life would be simple if educational administrators found a stable and predictable school environment within which to work—if they found a *tabula rasa,* so to speak. Then all they would need to do is to provide the necessary reason and sense of purpose, and all else would follow in harmonious bliss. But the world of school governance and administration is both turbulent and complex. The pulls and tugs of the four dominant values that provide the undercurrent for school policy and administration liken the job of school administration to that of juggler and tightrope walker as values are deftly handled and balanced. Reason and sense of purpose are important too, particularly if they are combined with a certain passion. Educational leaders, for example, are often able to bring about enough balance among key competing values to make things work for teaching and learning because the qualities of reason, balance, purpose, and passion are embodied in their leadership.

A Value-Added Approach to Equity and Excellence

One way to combine both the values of equity and excellence is by taking a value-added approach. This approach does not assume that high-achieving schools and value-added schools are always the same. Let's take the Knightsbridge community school as an example. Knightsbridge is a suburb of a major southern city. According to an advertisement that appeared in a recent edition of the local paper, "Knightsbridge's students attend one of the best high schools in [the state]. Student scores on the [state] accountability tests are equal to or exceed those of students in every district in the area. College statistics are staggering. Ninety-six percent of the high school students plan to attend college. The high school is just one example of the excellent education Knightsbridge's students enjoy. Public grade schools, pre-schools, Montessori schools, church-affiliated schools and day care centers in Knightsbridge also provide outstanding learning environments."

Needless to say, the schools that serve the Knightsbridge community were rated favorably by the state's accountability system. Student attendance rates are high, thanks to parents who insist that they go. Very few students drop out of Knightsbridge's schools, due to parents who insist that they stay. Further, about ninety percent of the families with school-aged children in Knightsbridge have both parents present in the home and virtually all of the families can be considered middle or upper income. These statistics are linked to lower dropout rates, less gang activity, and higher student achievement. Most of the students who enter Knightsbridge's schools speak English fluently; already know their letters and sounds, with many already knowing how to read; come from homes that are filled with books and computers; have community agencies committed to serve their needs; go to summer camp; take lessons in piano, dance, karate, etc.; see doctors regularly, and eat and sleep well. Knightsbridge's students are brought up at home to respond favorably to the competitive environment of the school, to sit quietly, to be studious, and to otherwise respond to the values of the typical school.

If Knightsbridge's scores are linked to these factors rather than to what teachers and principals are doing, then questions have to be raised about how much value its schools are adding to the education of their students. Would students do just as well on the state's indicators if the existing principals and teachers were replaced with new ones? What would happen if large numbers of students were suddenly home-schooled, transferred to private schools, or even transferred to schools that are labeled "low performing" by the state's system? Would they do just as well as before? If they did just as well, then only a small cause and effect relationship would probably exist between what teachers and principals in Knightsbridge are doing and student scores, dropout rates, and attendance statistics. We might even be able to exchange the principals and teachers of Knightsbridge with a random sample of principals and teachers from schools rated in the lower categories of the state's accountability system without seeing much of a change in the accountability indicators. Since only a small cause-and-effect relationship would exist between what the schools are doing and the showing of their students on the state's effectiveness indicators, Knightsbridge's schools might be considered to be high achieving but not value-adding.

Adding Value

Many schools who serve communities similar to Knightsbridge manage to *add value* to the advantages that the students bring. As a result, the performance of their students is not just up to par but extraordinary. These schools are *both* high achieving and value-adding. Unfortunately, in most states the accountability system is not able to differentiate between the "Knightsbridges" that are high achieving but not value-adding and the "Knightsbridges" that are *both* high achieving and value-adding.

Nor are accountability systems able to differentiate between schools with scores lower than Knightsbridge's that manage to add value and those that don't. The scores of such value-adding schools might remain modest on an absolute scale, but would still represent significant gains in student performance. A school that *adds value* in this way is a good school and should be celebrated rather than labeled low performing.

What Does Research Reveal about School Effects?

Variables influencing school achievement may be grouped into three categories, each important but each with different effects: school-level variables, classroom-level variables, and student-level variables. After an exhaustive study of hundreds of school-effectiveness studies from both the United States and abroad, Robert J. Marzano (2000) has made the following conclusions:

- School-level variables account for about 7 percent of the effects on student achievement.
- Classroom-level variables account for about 13 percent of the effects on student achievement.
- Student-level variables account for about 80 percent of the effects on student achievement.
- School-level variables include opportunities to learn, the amount of time spent learning, monitoring student learning, providing reasonable pressure to achieve, parent involvement, school climate, leadership, and cooperation.
- Classroom-level variables include the kind and quality of teaching, curriculum design, and classroom management.
- Student-level variables include home atmosphere, the prior knowledge that students bring to their learning, aptitude, and student interest in what is being taught (p. 85).

A swimming race can be won or lost depending on what happens during the last inch of the final lap. You can't score a touchdown in football without crossing that final yard into the end zone. Even though school variables seem to have powerful effects on student learning, they are not powerful enough to maximize student achievement. Student- and teacher-level effects count too. Indeed, you can't win without them. Still, there are important lessons to be learned from this comparison of variables and their effects. Most of the attention in school improvement focuses on the school and teachers. How do we add student-level effects to this pattern? How high a priority, for example, do we give to student interests as we develop curriculum, set standards, and teach? Are we taking into account students' prior knowledge as we make decisions regarding the subject matter that will be taught and the standards that will be applied, or is a one-size-fits-all the strategy that we use? At the moment, what we teach and how we teach is driven almost exclusively by mandated uniform standards and assessments. Will we be able to maximize student achievement by neglecting student-level effects that account for 80 percent of the variance in student achievement?

Socioeconomic status is often used to summarize many of the variables that comprise student level effects. Marzano (2000) reports that about one-third of the effects of SES on student achievement can be accounted for by *home atmosphere* (p. 69). Yet few schools give much attention to working to improve the home atmosphere of their students.

The Ecology of School Improvement

What are the conditions that are needed for every student to learn to be competent in the basic skills, to master important subject matter, to function in the modern workplace, to accept citizenship responsibilities, and to become a person of character? Educational research tells us that the answer to this question, while difficult to achieve, is easy to understand.

Simply put, the conditions for effective teaching and learning are best when the ecology for learning is in balance. The ecology for learning consists of the family and neighborhood, the community and its institutions, and the schools. All three parts of the ecology for learning contribute to the *development of human capital.* Beginning with birth, each child begins to deposit funds of knowledge into his or her human capital development savings account. These funds of knowledge increase in quantity and kind as the child's interactions increase within the family and the neighborhood, and within the community and its institutions. When children arrive in kindergarten, they bring these human capital savings accounts with them.

The funds of knowledge that children bring to school, however, differ in kind and in quantity. Some children have learned how to "sit quietly and wait their turn." Other children have learned to assert themselves. Some children have learned to respond to the school's competitive environment. Other children have learned to avoid competition. Some children have visited small towns and farms and have learned a great deal about how they work, how they contribute to the economy, and what life in them is like. Other children have never visited a farm or small town, nor have they seen a book or a serious television program about farms and rural life.

Students who bring the *right* funds of knowledge from home and community are better able to accumulate the funds of knowledge that schools offer. For them the ecology for learning is in balance. These students are likely to be high achievers regardless of what the schools do.

The more connected the family is to the community, and the family and community to the school, the more likely the funds of knowledge from these sources are to be properly balanced. Where the ecology for learning is out of balance, the school must help the family and community adjust to the school. And the school must accept its responsibility for adjusting its values to the family and community parts of the learning ecosystem. A good accountability system takes into account ecological factors, thus giving legitimacy to all three categories of variables that affect student achievement: school-level, teacher-level, and student-level.

Three Theories of Leadership

The third and fourth editions of this book pointed out that what appears to be a more balanced view of school reform emerged from studies of high-performing business organizations (Peters & Waterman, 1982) and schools (Sergiovanni, 1991). This view is embodied in a theory of management and organization—high-performance theory—that now guides the practice of educational policy at the state level and is now well entrenched in the literature of educational administration. Despite many shortcomings, this new theory is offered as a progressive alternative to the more traditional pyramid and railroad theories.

The *pyramid theory* assumes that the way to improve schools is to have one person assume responsibility for others by providing directions, supervision, and inspection. But as the number of people to be supervised increases, and as separate work sites develop, management burdens must be delegated to others, and a hierarchical system emerges. Rules and regulations are developed to ensure that all the managers think and act the same way. This managerial structure provides the protocols and guidelines used for planning, organizing, and directing schooling.

The *railroad theory* assumes that the way to improve schools is by standardizing the work processes. Instead of relying on direct supervision and hierarchical authority, a great deal of time is spent anticipating all the questions and problems that are likely to come up. Then answers and solutions are developed that represent tracks people must follow to get from one goal or outcome to another. Once the tracks are laid, all that needs to be done is to train people how to follow them and to set up monitoring systems to be sure that they are followed. When the railroad theory is applied to schools, it creates an instructional delivery system in which specific objectives are identified and tightly aligned to an explicit curriculum and a specific method of teaching. Teachers are supervised and evaluated, and students are tested to ensure that the approved curriculum and teaching scripts are being followed. Critics argue that, as a result, principals and teachers use fewer skills and student work becomes increasingly standardized.

The *high-performance theory* differs from the others by deemphasizing both top-down hierarchies and detailed scripts that tell people what to do. Decentralization is key. Workers are empowered to make their own decisions about how to do things. Schools are advised to take control by connecting people to outcomes rather than rules or work scripts. Borrowing from the practices of efficient business organizations, the high-performance theory assumes that the key to effective leadership is to connect workers tightly to ends, but only loosely to means (Gerstner,

Semerad, Doyle, & Johnston, 1994). When the high-performance theory is applied to schools, the ends are measurable learning outcomes. Though outcomes themselves are standardized, schools are free to decide how to achieve them. Principals and teachers can organize schools and teach in ways that they think will best enable them to meet the standards. The theory emphasizes collecting data to determine how well workers are doing and encouraging them to figure out ways to continuously improve their performance.

In all three theories, schools are perceived as formal organizations, like corporations or transportation systems. At issue for many educators, however, is whether the formal organization metaphor fits the nature of a school's purpose, the work that it does, the relationships needed for serving parents and students, the context of teachers' work, and the nature of effective teaching and learning environments.

Both the pyramid and railroad theories, for example, separate the planning of how work will be done from its actual performance. *Managers* (state or central-office officials) are responsible for the former, and *workers* (principals and teachers) are responsible for the latter. This separation may work in running a chain of fast-food restaurants, but not, so the argument goes, in schools where professional discretion is essential to success.

In high-performance theory, workers are provided with outcomes and other standards and then they decide how to do the work. But because planning what to do is separated from planning how to do it, problems of isolation, fragmentation, and loss of meaning remain. The danger is that when means and ends are separated, professional discretion may be reduced and democratic principles may be compromised. An important question is whether parents, principals, and teachers will feel sufficiently empowered by being involved in decision-making processes that are limited to the issue of *how* but not *what*—in other words, means but not ends.

The School as a Moral Community

An alternative to pyramid, railroad, and high-performance theories is to view the school as a moral community (Sergiovanni, 1991, 1994, 2000; Glickman, 1993; Lieberman, 1988). This theory, advocates argue, has two important advantages over the others: It provides for moral connections among teachers, principals, parents, and students, and it helps all of them to become self-managing. This theory is discussed further in Chapter 5.

All theories of leadership emphasize connecting people to each other and to their work; not all theories emphasize the same kinds of connections, however. The pyramid, railroad, and high-performance theories emphasize contractual connections and assume that people are primarily motivated by self-interest. To get things done, extrinsic or intrinsic rewards have to be traded for compliance, and penalties are threatened for noncompliance. Leadership inevitably takes the form of bartering between the leader and those being led. Moral connections are stronger than extrinsic or intrinsic connections because they come from commitments to shared values and beliefs that teachers, parents, and students accept, and from the obligations they feel toward each other and their work. Moral connections are grounded in cultural norms rather than in psychological needs.

Which of the theories—pyramid, railroad, high-performance, or moral community—will dominate the educational scene is an issue yet to be resolved. The high-performance theory is now clearly in the lead. The struggle over which theory makes sense for the nation's schools provides the undercurrent for the array of more surface issues, which are discussed in Chapter 2.

REFERENCES

Bell, D. (1973). *The coming of post-industrial society.* New York: Basic Books.

Bennett, W. J. (1988). *American education: Making it work.* Washington, DC: U.S. Government Printing Office.

Berliner, D. C., & Biddle, B. J. (1995). *The manufactured crisis: Myths, fraud and the attack on America's public schools.* Reading, MA: Addison-Wesley.

Carnegie Forum on Education and the Economy. (1986). *A nation prepared: Teachers for the 21st century.* New York: Carnegie.

Carr, J. F., & Harris, D. E. (2001). *Succeeding with linking curriculum assessments, and action planning.* Alexandria, VA: ASCD.

Center for Educational Leadership. (2000). Teacher quality and the future of learning in San Antonio. San Antonio: Trinity University.

Darling-Hammond, L. (1997). *The right to learn: A blueprint for creating schools that work.* San Francisco: Jossey-Bass.

Education Week, (2001, January 11). Quality counts 2001—A better balance: Standards, tests, and the tools to succeed. Bethesda, MD: Editorial Projects in Education, *20*(17).

Elmore, R. (1995). Structural reform and educational practice. *Educational Researcher, 24*(9), 23–26.

Gerstner, L. V., Jr., Semerad, R. D., Doyle, D. P., & Johnston, W. V. (1994). *Reinventing education entrepreneurship in America's public schools.* New York: Dutton.

Glickman, C. (1993). *Renewing America's schools: A guide for school-based action.* San Francisco: Jossey-Bass.

Green, J. (Ed.). (1986). *What next? More leverage for teachers.* Denver: Education Commission of the States.

The Holmes Group. (1986). *Tomorrow's teachers: A report of the Holmes Group.* East Lansing, MI: Author.

Kirst, M. W. (1989). Who should control the schools? Reassessing current policies. In T. J. Sergiovanni & J. H. Moore (Eds.), *Schooling for tomorrow. Directing reforms to issues that count.* Boston: Allyn and Bacon.

Koppich, J. E. (2001). *Investing in teaching: A common agenda.* Washington, DC: National Alliance of Business.

Lieberman, A. (Ed.). (1988). *Building a professional culture in schools.* New York: Teacher's College Press.

Marzano, R. J. (2000). *A new era of school reform: Going where the research takes us.* Aurora, CO: Mid-Continent Research for Educational Learning.

McDonnell, L. M., & Elmore, R. F. (1987). Getting the job done: Alternative policy instruments. *Educational Evaluation and Policy Analysis, 9*(2), 133–152.

National Commission on Excellence in Education. (1983). *A nation at risk.* Washington, DC: U.S. Government Printing Office.

National Commission on Teaching and America's Future (1996). *What matters most: Teaching for America's future.* New York: The Commission.

Newmann F., Marks, H., & Gamoran, A. (1995). Authentic pedagogy: Standards that boost student performance. *Issues in Restructuring School* (Report no. 8, Spring). Madison: Center on Organization and Restructuring of Schools, University of Wisconsin.

Peters, T. J., & Waterman, R. H. (1982). *In search of excellence.* New York: Harper & Row.

Resnick, L. B., & Hall, M. W. (1998). Learning organizations for sustainable educational reform. *Daedalus, 127*(4), 89–118.

Sergiovanni, T. J. (1991). *The principalship: A reflective practice perspective* (2nd ed.). Boston: Allyn and Bacon.

Sergiovanni, T. J. (1994). *Building community in schools.* San Francisco: Jossey-Bass.

Sergiovanni, T. J. (2000). *The lifeworld of leadership: Creating culture, community, and personal meaning in our schools.* San Francisco: Jossey-Bass.

Stake, R. (1985). *The essential individualization of excellence and equity.* Unpublished manuscript.

Stewart, R. (1982). The relevance to some studies of managerial work and behavior to leadership research. In J. G. Hunt, U. Sekaran, & C. A. Schriesheim (Eds.), *Leadership beyond establishment views.* Carbondale: Southern Illinois University Press.

2 Issues Shaping School Policy and Administration

Links between school policies and the public values of excellence, equity, efficiency, and choice are deeply embedded in the process and politics of schooling and remain persistent over time, though specific issues for their expression change. During the sixties and early seventies, the push was for more education for more people in an effort to reduce inequality among individuals and groups; improve economic opportunity by raising the nation's supply of intelligence and skill; spread capacity for personal fulfillment by developing talents, skills, and creative energies; improve cultural life in the nation; reduce prejudice and misunderstanding by fostering contact among diverse groups; and improve the quality of civic and political life (Ravitch, 1985, p. 32). This was a national agenda, and the federal government played a major role in prodding local educational agencies to change by providing financial incentives and legal mandates. The values of equity and efficiency loomed large as a basis for educational policymaking.

Educational policymaking in the eighties and nineties, by contrast, was influenced by demands for excellence and efficiency, with state governments assuming direct and highly regulatory responsibility for change. During the decade of the nineties, choice was added to this mix as an important factor in school reform. Many states, for example, began experimenting with charter schools. Also, magnet schools and small schools within schools have enjoyed popularity in many local school districts, a trend still growing during the first decade of the new century. From this context, issues emerge that shape the present and future governance and administration of America's schools. Three are selected for discussion in this chapter to illustrate the interplay between school policy and basic public values: school autonomy and governmental control; legislated learning and bureaucracy in the classroom; and the struggle between democratic and professional authority. As we move into the twenty-first century, standards and assessments dominate the school improvement conversation. Whatever the values being contested they are influenced by the press for standards. The future of schooling will be determined by how standards and related issues are shaped and resolved. Throughout this process, school administrators will need to maintain the confidence of their many constituents and publics. The *flow of images* they communicate to their publics will determine whether such confidence is maintained. This chapter concludes with a discussion of how school administrators manage the flow of images.

School Autonomy and Governmental Control

Is the increased consolidation of power and authority for schooling at the state level a reversible trend? Constitutionally, the states have always had the major share of responsibility for schooling but delegated this responsibility to local juris-dictions. During the seventies and early eighties, much of this authority was re-captured. Increases in the state share of school funding as a result of school finance reform were accompanied by state efforts to extract greater accountability from local schools. Categorical grant programs of various kinds exchanged money for compliance with state and federal agendas. Civil rights regulations also helped in the erosion of local authority by increasing the demands and constraints on local school administrations, thus limiting choices. Kirst (1989) maintains that since 1950, the trend has been toward decreasing the influence of school boards, local superintendents, and local central administration and increasing the influence of federal and state governments, the courts, private business and foundations, and teacher unions. The height of this shift of influence seems to have manifested itself in the reforms of the early 1980s. To the question of why that wave of reform took such a centralized course, Kirst (1989) answers, "Basically, state governments do not believe that local authorities pay sufficient attention to curriculum quality, teacher evaluation, and academic standards" (p. 66). Nelson (1994) puts it this way: "My Minnesota experience teaches me that content standards will not be challenging enough if exclusively designed by school districts or sites. Local con-trol is frequently an excuse for the status quo..." (p. 77).

Standards as an Example

Previously we noted that as we move into the twenty-first century, standards and assessments dominate the conversation about schools. At the center of this con-versation is a debate over which standards should be chosen, which standards should be centralized, which standards should be localized, who should set these standards, how should these standards be assessed, and what the consequences should be for not meeting them. Many consider this attention to standards as being a *third wave* of reform. Spurred on by state governments and encouraged by the business establishment, the focus of this wave is on defining and mandating challenging standards for all students. Once defined, the standards become the substance for an accountability system that uses standardized tests to measure the extent to which standards are reached.

The 1996 National Education Summit of the Nation's Governors and Corpo-rate Leaders, held in Palisades, New York, and hosted by IBM, provides a good benchmark for tracking the standards movement. This summit provided a clear signal that state governments, working together with the business establishment, were going to play key roles in the standards movement and thus key roles in de-veloping educational policies. The theme of the 1996 summit was that America's schools were failing and that decisive action was needed to save them—a theme that can be traced back to the 1983 report *A Nation at Risk* (National Commission on Excellence in Education, 1983). According to the summit:

> Swift action must be taken to address these issues. While we commend those states and school districts that have provided leadership to improve student performance, we urge greater progress, and for others, increased effort. We believe that standards can be effective only if they represent what parents, employers, educators, and community members believe children should learn and be able to do. However, the current rate of change needs to be accelerated, and no process or time line should deter us from the results. (National Education Summit, March 1996, cited in Good, 1996, p. 5)

As of 2003, every state but Iowa had academic standards in one form or another. Every state tests students to find out how well they are doing. Thirty states hold schools accountable by rating the performance of schools and by identifying those that are *low performing*. Although reaction to standards is mixed, the movement is growing in importance as it shapes educational policy from the school house to the state house, bringing to the state even more power at the expense of local school districts.

In a national survey of over 1,000 teachers, reported in "Quality Counts 2001—A Better Balance" (*Education Week,* 2001), *Education Week* researchers found that state standards and their accompanying assessments were affecting both teacher and student behavior in many of America's classrooms. When asked to compare their present situations with their situations three years earlier, the teachers surveyed revealed that:

- Almost eight in ten teachers said the curriculum was "somewhat" or "a lot" more demanding of students.
- More than six in ten said the expectations for what students would learn were "somewhat" or "a lot" higher.
- Nearly seven in ten said teachers in their schools were collaborating more.
- More than six in ten said students were writing more; nearly half reported students were reading more.

Of those who said the curriculum was more demanding, more than six in ten attributed the change to statewide academic standards. (*Education Week,* 2001, p. 8)

Teachers in states that require students to pass exit tests as a graduation requirement reported more changes over the last three years as a result of standards than did teachers in states without these examination. This finding suggests that exit tests are one of many new and powerful levers that states are using to affect what local schools are doing and how they do it.

In the language of the theories of leadership discussed in the last chapter, it seems that the states are becoming increasingly skilled at using the *high-performance theory* to bring about change and are relying less and less on the pyramid and railroad theories. In high-performance theory outcomes, objectives, and standards are set for schools and their progress in achieving these outcomes is measured regularly.

In exchange, schools are supposed to be free to decide for themselves how they will meet the provided outcome requirements. This rosy picture of leadership and organizational theories at work to improve student achievement, however, is darkened by the reality that planning and doing (the ends and means of schooling) are separated, with the state being responsible for the former and locals for the latter. Because the ends typically determine the means, this assignment of responsibility for ends to the state and means to local school districts may well be a mirage. Not everyone agrees with this conclusion as we discuss later in this section. Still, this separation of ends and means raises important pedagogical and democratic questions.

The *Education Week* survey also found that the use of state standardized tests often had a number of unanticipated negative consequences. For example:

- Nearly seven in ten teachers said instruction stresses state tests "far" or "somewhat" too much.
- Sixty-six percent said state tests were forcing them to concentrate too much on what's tested to the detriment of other important topics.
- About 29 percent reported using either state practice tests or commercial test-preparation materials a "great deal" to ready students for state exams, while one-third did not use them at all.
- Nearly half reported spending "a great deal" of time preparing their students in test-taking skills. (*Education Week,* 2001, p. 8)

To help neutralize these unanticipated consequences, the editors at *Education Week* recommend that states develop assessments that more closely and fully reflect their standards and provide students with richer and more varied ways to show that they have met the standards. Most testing experts agree by recommending that states use multiple measures of student performance as part of any accountability system. This is particularly important when the stakes are high (deciding, for example, whether a student graduates or not). A single test, they argue, given at one point in time, cannot provide the information needed to make high-stakes decisions in an authentic, pedagogically sound, and just way. But other factors come to play too as states craft new accountability systems. Standardized tests (particularly those that rely on multiple choice questions and other simple measurement means), for example, do not cost very much, and this is often an important incentive that drives their use.

Many critics of the standards movement (i.e., Meier, 2000; Ohanian, 1999; Kohn, 2000) argue that a one-size-fits-all approach to setting standards, making decisions about curriculum, and assessing what students know ignores the fact that students differ in their levels of development, rates of learning, subject matter interests, and learning styles, creating a system of schools that is not responsive to student needs. Further, critics are concerned about the *de-skilling* factor (McNeil, 1986; Darling-Hammond, 1997). In a tightly aligned system, they argue, teachers do not have the discretion they need to make good decisions about teaching, and teachers run the risk of simplifying their teaching by using fewer skills. Scripted curriculum formats that emerge from uniform standards and aligned assessments, they argue, lead to scripted teaching. Moreover, as states come to dominate curriculum and instructional policymaking, the role of local agencies continues to be reduced, placing local autonomy over the school curriculum and even the pedagogy needed to teach that curriculum at risk (Wise, 1979) and threatening the very existence of local school districts (Cantor, 1980).

Not everyone agrees that centralizing the policymaking and governance functions at the state level reduces the authority of local school districts. After reviewing the research in this area, Spillane (1994) notes that the position of many researchers is that "centralized educational governance and policymaking at one level of the organization...does not result in a concomitant decrease in educational governance and policy-making activities at other levels" (p. 168). He quotes Cohen as follows: "Power and organization have often grown in tandem, rather than growing in one place at the expense of another" (Cohen, 1982, p. 476 as cited in Spillane, 1994, p. 168).

Others avoid the debate about who should be responsible for setting standards in a democratic society, retreating to what is practical. Gandal and Vranek, for example, argue the point this way:

> Five years ago, standards may have been left vague in deference to local control of the curriculum: Let the state set the broad goals, but leave the curriculum to local schools and educators. But that has not turned out to be very practical. As schools and students have begun to be held accountable for results, educators have demanded more specific guidance and teaching tools, and so far demand has outstripped supply. (Gandal & Vranek, 2001, p. 9)

Gandal and Vranek are affiliated with Achieve, an independent and bipartisan organization created by the governors and business leaders to help states develop the *right* policies and programs for standards, assessments, and accountability. One could argue that Achieve and similar organizations are good examples of a new version of the alarm signaled by President Eisenhower: The greatest danger facing America is the growth of power and influence of the "military and industrial complex." But this time the danger comes from the "state government and corporate" complex. Achieve would probably return the fire by stating that their organization, and others like it, are committed to the common school and want to give every youngster the same opportunities to learn, and that sounds more like a learning compact than a state government and corporate complex.

In recent years the state-corporate complex has been relentless in pushing its agenda to reform America's schools by applying a standardized standards and testing formula. The Fourth National Educational Summit was held in October 2001. As was the case with the two previous summits, IBM Chairperson and CEO Louis Gerstner, Jr. and Michigan Governor John Engler chaired the sessions. Using language similar to the 1983 report *A Nation at Risk,* the summit referred to its work as declaring war on the ills of education and promised to intensify its fight to improve low-performing schools. Added to this agenda were making teaching a more attractive profession and improving the way student progress is tracked.

Both Gerstner and Engler agreed that, "This is a national problem. It demands that the entire nation participate in the solution" (cited in Henry, 2001). The summit approved three sets of principles:

- Continuing to *measure results* but collect better data on student performance, which will be measured against clear and rigorous standards.
- *Strengthening accountability* by providing support for the standards alignment and testing strategy. Give schools enough time to align their curriculum with state standards and to train teachers to teach to these standards.
- *Improving teaching* by using "multiple pathways" for talented people to enter teaching. (Henry, 2001, p. 9D; see also *www.achieve.org* for full text)

In her report on the summit, Henry noted that American Federation of Teachers' President Sandra Feldman warned the governors and corporate leaders that a recent union survey of its 275,000 members found *decreasing* support for school improvement initiatives that were based on mandated academic standards. President Feldman noted that "last year, 73 percent of teachers supported standards-based reform but this year the percentage has dropped to 55 percent. The teachers' main complaint is that there are too many tests, with few based on curricula. Also they say test results often are used to punish schools, teachers, or students, rather than to pinpoint problems that need fixing. And, she says, teachers often are forced to teach to the test" (Henry, 2001, p. 9D).

Perhaps one way to deal with differences in points of view is to ask the question, should states alone decide and set standards or should a layered approach to standards be used? In a layered approach, local schools set standards and develop assessments too. Further, these local standards and assessments play a key role, along with those set by the state, in a state's accountability system. Although standardized tests might be appropriate for assessing common standards set by the state, other forms of assessment (the school quality review, for example) might be more appropriate for locally set standards. For details on how a layered system might work and why such a system should be considered see the op-ed article "A Layered System of Standards" that appears as Appendix 2.1.

If you were asked to write an op-ed piece on this topic, what would you say? Keep in mind that most Americans support standardized testing. According to the 33rd Annual Phi Delta Kappa/Gallup Poll (Rose & Gallup, 2001) 53 percent of the respondents favor the use of a single standardized test to determine who gets promoted from grade to grade. Forty-five percent are opposed. Fifty-seven percent favor using a standardized test to determine who should be awarded a high school diploma. Forty-two percent are opposed. Fifty-four percent favor not renewing the contract of principals whose students do not show progress in mastering state standards; 49 percent favor not renewing the contract of teachers in such schools; and 51 percent favor giving parents of students in these schools vouchers to use in other schools. It is hard to know exactly what these data mean in light of the fact that 66 percent of the public who responded to the Phi Delta Kappa/Gallup poll believe that standardized tests should be used to *guide instruction,* while only 30 percent believe that standardized tests should be used to *assess* student learning.

Local Autonomy

Though there appears to be a widespread loss of confidence by states in local authorities, some contradictory trends are apparent. For example, many experts who study school-improvement efforts are convinced that despite the importance of both federal and state efforts, the battle for excellence must be won school by school. This reality requires that not just local school districts but schools within them become sufficiently autonomous for needed and responsive action to take place (Goodlad, 1984; Sizer, 1985). These experts are convinced that though adoption of school-improvement ideas can be mandated, sustained implementation and institutionalization of changes must be school site based. John Goodlad, for example, notes that "for a school to become the key unit for educational change requires a substantially different stance at the district level than now exists" (quoted in Quinby, 1985, p. 17). He maintains that too often school-improvement efforts are conceived at the district level and implemented uniformly by all schools in a district at the same time. As a result of his research, Goodlad concludes that districts should encourage individual schools to develop their own plans based on their own analysis of school problems. School improvement, he maintains, requires district support and sponsorship, but success depends on the extent to which the principal, teachers, students, and parents associated with individual schools participate in thinking about their problems and conceiving of their own school-improvement efforts.

Despite trends toward increased centralization in schooling, an extensive movement toward site-based management (SBM) has developed. One way that site-based management works is for each principal in the school district, representing her or his school community, to propose individual school-improvement plans to the superintendent. Together, the principal and the superintendent develop a school-improvement contract that details planned changes, links plans to specific time lines, and specifies what the superintendent and the central office will do to help the school succeed. When fully implemented, SBM recognizes the importance of the school to effective school improvement and the criticalness of the principal's management and leadership to that school. The principal is responsible for working with teachers, staff, students, and parents to determine the school's objectives and educational program.

Real site-based management is not possible in school districts in which centralized policies and regulations are elaborate and detailed. Responsibilities delegated to the school typically include the development, supervision, and evaluation of an educational program that fits needs determined by the school and its community; the selection, orientation, supervision, and continuing professional development of all staff assigned to the school; the development, supervision, and evaluation of guidance and counseling services, discipline codes, and regulations, including record keeping and reporting of academic progress; the establishment of a parent advisory committee that works closely with the principal and the management team in deciding school policies; and the general management of the buildings and grounds.

Site-based management seems to work best when schools are given a degree of financial independence. Individual schools, for example, receive a lump sum determined by formula but linked to the number of students being served. Once the sum is received, the principal and the management team, perhaps in consultation with a parent advisory group, develop the school's own budget based on the decision makers' perceptions of its problems and needs and the goals and objectives it wishes to pursue. In many respects, the individual school site functions much as does a school district.

How will the future balance be struck between movements toward a stronger state presence in education on one hand and SBM on the other? Both movements have appeal. Part of the American tradition has long held that individuals should be self-governed, subject only to the general mores and rules of society as expressed in legislation and social norms. This basic value is held in common by liberals, conservatives, and moderates (Shirley, 1984). Defining the appropriate balance between individual and school autonomy and government control, however, is not so easily done. With respect to individuals, the Bill of Rights, the Declaration of Independence, and the Constitution define appropriate protections both formally and informally. Shirley (1984) suggests that what may well be needed is a bill of rights for institutions, such as schools, that would provide guidelines for their freedoms and their responsibilities. Among the freedoms that would be guaranteed to institutions by such a bill of rights would be:

- The freedom within general guidelines to define institutional mission, goals, and strategies
- The freedom to manage internal fiscal affairs subject to only two limitations: living within the total dollars appropriated by the state and refraining from transferring funds between operating and capital budgets
- The freedom to determine organizational arrangements and individual workloads and to select and promote personnel

Shirley joins many other observers in suggesting that these three freedoms are now being denied public institutions, such as schools, in many states. What were once general guidelines for helping schools to define their missions are now becoming fairly detailed master plans complete with control devices to ensure that plans are implemented in specific ways. State-mandated standards aligned with standardized tests may be an example.

The institutional bill of rights proposed by Shirley includes the responsibilities that institutions have to the public and to state governments, which appropriately function as the public's watchdog. Among these responsibilities would be reporting the degree to which goals and priorities are being accomplished and the extent to which public funds are managed responsibly.

As a result of his analysis of dozens of commissions and reports examining the quality of schooling in the United States and his examination of the research on effective schools, Harold Howe II (1983), a former U.S. commissioner of education, concludes, "Schools are more likely to change for the better if central office and school board directors allow individual schools to seek their own definitions of excellence.... Individual school initiatives can be strongly encouraged by providing each school with some funds and allowing the staff to decide how this money will be spent" (p. 170).

In the ideal, relationships between levels of government should be guided by the principles of subsidiarity and mutuality (Sergiovanni, 2000).

- The principle of subsidiarity states that every member of every society and every institution in society should be free from excessive intervention, circumscription, or regulation by the state or any other larger institution. This principle places faith and responsibility in local rights and initiatives as guardians of the lifeworlds of schools and societies.
- The principle of mutuality states that interdependence in the form of mutual, beneficial associations characterized by dignity and respect among people, among different institutions, and between different levels of government should characterize relationships. (Sergiovanni, 2000, p. xii)

Suppose you were to share these principles with the administrators in your school district, members of your school board, some teachers, a half dozen parents you meet at a ballgame, and a state legislator or two. How would you imagine that each group would respond? Which groups would be most supportive? At this writing, it appears that the trend toward greater centralization is increasing. As the balance between efficiency and choice and between excellence and equity becomes increasingly upset, it is possible that there will be a strong and widespread movement toward local school autonomy. But, this movement will remain unfulfilled as long as high-performance theory remains the decision-making framework for policymakers. High-performance theory, as noted in Chapter 1, gives schools and their communities autonomy over means but not ends, over process but not substance, and over management concerns but not policy concerns.

Legislated Learning and Bureaucratic Teaching

Wise (1979) has coined the term *legislated learning* to describe what happens when states assume control over the curriculum and begin to provide scripts for local school districts to follow. Legislated learning provides for uniform and tight alignment between student-performance outcomes and the curriculum, between the curriculum and teaching, and between teaching and testing. The beginning and end of this legislated-learning chain are crucial. It is assumed that by specifying in detail what is to be accomplished and then by testing to ensure that objectives are met, greater state control is attained over the school curriculum and how it is taught. In this sense, both the railroad theory and the high-performance theory described in Chapter 1 advocate the practice of legislated learning. The railroad theory specifies both the means to be used and the ends to be accomplished. High-performance theory provides only the ends. But, as suggested previously, standardized ends for everyone wind up creating standardized means by everyone.

As one might expect, the legislation of learning is viewed differently by different interests. Politicians and the public at large generally support the concept (or at least their understanding of the concept). State mandates of this kind promise to raise expectations for learning and to toughen standards, with the result being better schooling. This is an attractive platform in the eyes of the public. Excellence, however, is left undefined. The public responds not to the substance of such mandates but to the rhetoric of excellence within which the substance is embedded. Excellence, like motherhood, is readily subscribed to, whether defined adequately or not.

The impetus for legislated learning is an effort by state legislators to take control of schools away from local jurisdictions in an effort to respond to the general public's dissatisfaction with what it considers to be the lowering of academic standards. Advocates view legislated learning as a means to enhance accountability, a way to stop the downward slide of test scores, and an insurance policy in providing students with the competencies they need for functional participation in society. As Casteen (1984) points out:

> Governments regulate schooling because they see education as an essential public service. Since poor schools and poor teachers threaten the public welfare while good ones enhance it, there must be effective "quality control mechanisms." Historically, it has fallen to the states to provide them. In recent decades, teachers' organizations have frequently called for transfer of quality control from the state to the members of the occupation. "Professionalism" is the banner under which this call is issued. Education is too important to the public welfare for the public, acting through the state, to relinquish responsibility for its quality. (p. 214)

Many experts from within the professional community, by contrast, predict long-range negative consequences of legislated learning on the quality of teaching and learning and on the profession of teaching. As the alignment between outcomes and curriculum, curriculum and teaching, and teaching and testing becomes tighter, they fear that a more rigid educational system will emerge. This system, they argue, is unable to respond to highly idiosyncratic student needs or to society's political, economic, and social changes that define the context of schooling. Further, alignment introduces a high degree of predictability and reliability to the educational system; this influences decision making, makes teaching and schools "teacher and administrative proof," and encourages "pawn" rather than "origin" (DeCharms, 1968) feelings among all those involved.

Wise (1979) maintains that legislated learning unavoidably leads to bureaucratization in the U.S. classroom. In elaborating on this theme, Darling-Hammond (1984) observes,

> Unfortunately the approach to improving education reflected in most of the policy initiatives of the past decade has done little to increase the attractiveness of teach-

ing; it may, in fact, have exacerbated the problem. Based on a factory model of schooling in which teachers are semiskilled low-paid workers, at least two thirds of the states have enacted policies in the nineteen seventies that sought to standardize and regulate teacher behaviors. Elaborate accountability schemes…and other efforts to develop a teacher proof curriculum were imposed in the belief that if teachers do exactly as they are told, students will learn exactly as they are supposed to. Bureaucratic controls on teaching behavior were used as an alternative to upgrading the quality of teachers or of professional decision making. (pp. 13–14)

The amount of discretion that teachers have and how the reduction of discretion affects the quality of their teaching is a worry of many educators who have reservations about the standards movement. Marzano (quoted in Scherer, 2001, p. 17) argues that one way to increase discretion is to have fewer standards. He suggests, for example, that the number of standards be reduced by two-thirds, thus leaving lots of room for teachers to supplement the required curriculum.

Darling-Hammond and Wise (1983) maintain that teachers and other professionals oppose bureaucratic attempts to constrain classroom decisions, not because they are opposed to accountability, but because they believe that standardized teaching prescriptions reduce their ability to teach effectively. The result is not only less effective teaching and learning, these professionals say, but a dissatisfied teaching force as well.

In sum, those who express concern about the legislation of learning fear that teaching will become increasingly bureaucratic and that the occupation will retreat from its present posture as a fledgling profession. Professionals and bureaucrats function quite differently at work. The work of bureaucrats is programmed for them by the system of which they are a part. The work of professionals emerges from an interaction between professional knowledge and individual client needs. A standard definition of a *bureaucrat,* for example, is an official following a rigid, narrow and formal routine. By contrast, a *professional* is assumed to be in command of a body of knowledge that enables him or her to make informed judgments in response to unique situations and individual client needs.

Essential to professionalism is that sufficient freedom exists so that professionals are able to use informed judgments as they practice. Bureaucratic knowledge, on the other hand, is more routine and standardized to enable systematic application by bureaucrats. The emphasis is on standard treatment of standard practical problems. Bureaucrats are expected to respond exactly the same way to specific classes of problems; this way of working is antithetical to the concept of professional work. Further, the argument goes, patterns of teaching practice are actually characterized by instability, complexity, and variety, and thus uniform answers to problems are not likely to be helpful to teachers as they teach. The argument concludes with the observation that as teaching and learning decisions are programmed, the teacher's role changes from that of professional diagnostician and decision maker to bureaucratic follower of directions (Sergiovanni, 1991).

How the issue of legislated learning is played out will influence the new politics of education and will demand attention from policymakers and school administrators alike. Some advocates of legislated learning, for example, recommend that states go even further: "States should consider undertaking an even more active and direct role in education reform. Specifically, from our experience in California, we contend that states should take the lead in defining and controlling educational content.... States should also establish clear expectations for schools in terms of required allocations of time to all subjects at the elementary level and graduation requirements at the high school level" (Murphy, Mesa, & Hallinger, 1984, p. 24).

For the most part, the educational establishment feels more comfortable with John Goodlad's view: "Cosmetic changes can be legislated and mandated; the ways children and youth acquire knowledge and ways of knowing cannot. These depend on the knowledge and creativity of teachers. Better preparation of principals and teachers, along with help and time for designing school programs at the site are necessary ingredients of school improvement" (quoted in Quinby, 1985, p. 16).

The educational establishment would agree as well with Michael Kirst's observation that "centralization may be better for naval units, steel mills and state highway departments," but when it comes to teaching and learning, research shows that effective school reform takes place "when those responsible for each school are given more responsibility rather than less" (*Sunday Express News*, 1984). Research, however, is not the only factor that informs the development of policy. Politicians do not behave in response to evidence or other rational sources as much as they do in response to preferences and beliefs. The development of policy is a subjective process that seeks to maximize certain values, goals, and interests thought to be important, a point often overlooked by school administrations and other members of the educational establishment.

Balancing Democratic and Professional Authority

Wise (1988), a leading spokesperson for increased professional authority in matters of schooling, notes:

> In a profound sense, it doesn't matter who controls education, as long as every young citizen is fully prepared to exercise the rights and duties of citizenship in the democratic, free enterprise tradition of America.... The question of who should control education is a pragmatic...one. Central control is to be deplored not because it represents the shift of power...among the three branches and the three levels of government. Rather central control is to be deplored because with the technology currently available for managing schools, it reduces the responsiveness of schools to their clientele and so reduces the quality of education. (p. 331)

Advocates of increasing professional authority in the control of schools build their case around the premise that quality teaching requires on-the-spot decisions by highly trained teachers—decisions that cannot be preprogrammed or otherwise legislated. The case for professional authority can be summed as follows: "Professionalism assumes that because the members of a particular profession possess a specialized body of knowledge and have been judged competent to practice that profession they should be free to decide how best to serve their individual clients. In other words, accountability should be based on norms and standards collectively defined and enforced by peers" (McDonnell, 1989, p. iv).

Though advocates of professional authority provide compelling arguments for its legitimacy, another form of authority seems equally legitimate—the authority of democratic or popular control. According to McDonnell (1989), "Popular or democratic control requires that schools, as public institutions, be held accountable to the citizenry and its elected representatives. This form of accountability assumes that public officials have the right to impose on schools and those who work there a set of performance standards consistent with the norms and expectations of the larger community" (p. iv). Advocates of democratic authority provide equally compelling arguments that lead to the conclusion that the educational establishment is faced with two legitimate values. Both democratic and professional authority are important in U.S. society and should be reflected in school policies. They are contrasted in Table 2.1.

At the heart of this conflict is whether decisions about how schools should be organized and run, how teachers should be prepared and employed, how

TABLE 2.1   Two Approaches to Governing Public Education

	Popular Control	Professional Control
Practitioners Are Accountable to	Electorate and its representatives	Professional norms, and through them, to clients and the public
Interests Served	Constituents Political parties Organized groups Public interest as defined by political ideology Personal	Client welfare as defined by professional norms and standards Personal
Basis of Authority	Consent of the governed	Expert knowledge and judgment
Implementing Mechanisms	Elections Executive and legislative policymaking Courts Public bureaucracies	Training and licensing Professional associations Teacher involvement in school budgetary, personnel, and curriculum decisions

Source: Lorraine M. McDonnell, *The Dilemma of Teacher Policy.* Joint report issued by The Center for Policy Research in Education and the Center for the Study of the Teaching Profession (Santa Monica: The RAND Corporation, 1989), p. 8.

administrators should function, how teachers and students should be evaluated, and what will be taught should be made by laypersons on the basis of majority preferences either directly through local school councils or indirectly through the electoral process or by professional educators on the basis of their experience and special expertness. Given our system of government, the public enjoys the prerogative to set policy and to evaluate the extent of school compliance with policy. But every professional group enjoys prerogatives of its own as well. In education, these include setting standards, determining the nature of teaching practice, and honoring such values as academic freedom.

If the values of both democratic authority and professional authority are legitimate, how might they be balanced in such a way that the public gets the controls it wants over school quality and the profession gets the discretion it needs to provide that quality? One approach is to tightly connect the schools to a set of professional process and performance outcome standards and then loosely connect them to means for achieving these standards. Professional standards would include requirements for preparing, inducting, and licensing teachers, and performance standards would specify what is expected qualitatively from the schools. In both cases, standards need to be general enough to allow principals, teachers, and schools discretion over their professional lives, but specific enough to provide for direction and accountability.

A second approach is to rely on the market forces that come into play in a choice system of education. The professional establishment, in partnership with parents, would be given considerable autonomy over the nature and functioning of each individual school site. Advocates of this approach maintain that professional autonomy needs to be real if schools are to differ with respect to what they are about and how they seek to accomplish their goals. Subject to market forces, parents will choose to send their children to schools that they consider to be working. Democratic and professional authority, so the reasoning goes, would be achieved through the mechanism of choice as options are developed.

Many policy experts (e.g., Chubb & Moe, 1989) believe that choice is not only the answer to resolving the dilemma of democratic versus professional authority but may be the secret to providing the balance between and among excellence, equity, and efficiency as well. Their reasoning is that school-choice plans offering a variety of teaching and learning options will require substantial deregulation of the existing bureaucracy (efficiency). Market forces inherent in choice will drive out the bad schools and encourage the good (excellence). Undaunted by critics who worry that families that are privileged economically and more knowledgeable about schooling will benefit the most, advocates believe that in the end, all schools will get better (equity).

But some experts doubt whether enough political momentum presently exists to support school choice. Kirst, writing in 1990, pointed out that "vouchers have never been voted on in any state, and federal tuition tax credits were defeated during the Reagan presidency. Consequently, it is hard to see choice as a major reform at this juncture. The period of 1986–1988 appears to be one of digesting the reforms from an earlier era" (p. 28). His comments were speculative at best. In 1990, for example, Wisconsin passed a limited voucher plan allowing about 1,000 Milwaukee public-school students the option of attending a nonsectarian private school at state expense. Voucher advocate John E. Coons (quoted in Snider, 1990, p. 1) called the plan "a very historic day for the poor and for civil rights." He explained, "People who have been pretty much entombed in segregated public schools will have a chance to get their civil rights vindicated in the private sector." Although some disagree, the fact that ten years later this voucher plan seems to be thriving suggests that school choice has more than a foothold in American education. Still, recent polls suggest that the public is less interested in vouchers today than it was in the past. Further, although a number of voucher plans have been discussed in state legislatures they have not been enacted on any wide scale. Charter schools, by contrast, seem to be growing in popularity.

According to a recent report from the Brown Center on Educational Policy on how well American students are learning (Loveless, 2001):

> Charter school legislation has been adopted in thirty-seven states, with nearly 2,000 charters in operation during the 2000–2001 academic year. Publicly-funded vouchers are provided to several thousand poor children in Milwaukee, Cleveland, and the state of Florida. The privately-funded Children's Scholarship Fund annually supplies 40,000 poor urban students with scholarships to attend private schools in dozens of cities. (p. 36)

The report states further that, "Achievement in charter schools has thus far proven difficult to evaluate. Most charters are too new to have generated definitive data. Others serve special populations, such as students at risk or dropouts, skewing results" (Loveless, 2001, p. 36).

On the issue of how successful standards have been in improving student achievement, the Brown Center report cites David Grissmer and his colleagues at RAND (2000) who concluded that Texas and North Carolina both made significant progress on National Assessment of Educational Progress (NAEP) tests in the 1990s. Gains were attributed to the success of the states' accountability systems and backed by rigorous standards. The RAND study pointed out that gains were impressive for minority students. But this same report points out that:

> It is almost impossible to isolate the effects of standards from the effects of other reforms implemented concurrently. If while putting standards into effect states also impose new requirements for teacher training, limit or reduce class sizes, adopt new textbooks, and raise teachers salaries, it could be any, all, or none of these policies that produce changes in test scores. Add the local policies of urban districts to the mix, and determining causality becomes even more difficult. (Loveless, 2001, p. 36)

Linking standards or any other single intervention to gains in student achievement is both messy and complex. In sum, choice may have become a permanent theme on the policy agenda but understood in a more diversified way. Diversity has changed the nature of the debate from "for school choice" or "against school choice" to "for some kinds of choice but against other kinds of choice." Cookson (1994), for example, provides 12 different definitions of *choice* as follows:*

Intradistrict-choice. *A plan that allows students to choose schools within one public school district. Depending on the specific plan, the range of choice may include a few to all schools in a district.*

Interdistrict-choice. *A plan in which students may cross district lines to attend school. Tuition funds from the state follow the student, and transportation costs are usually provided. Unlimited interdistrict choice is equivalent to statewide open enrollment.*

Intrasectional-choice. *A plan that is limited to public schools.*

Intersectional-choice. *A plan that includes both public and private schools.*

Controlled-choice. *A student assignment plan that requires families to choose a school within a community, but choices can be restricted to ensure the racial, gender, and socioeconomic balance of each school. Often, such plans reflect a strategy to comply with court-ordered desegregation.*

Magnet schools. *Public schools that offer specialized programs, often deliberately designed and located so as to attract students to otherwise unpopular areas or schools. Magnet schools are often created to promote racial balance.*

Postsecondary options. *Programs that enable high school students to enroll in college courses at government expense. The courses they take may contribute to high school graduation requirement as well as to their college programs.*

Second-chance programs. *Alternative schools and programs for students who have difficulties in standard public school settings. Most often these students have either dropped out of school, are pregnant or are parents, have been assessed as chemically dependent, or have been expelled from their previous school.*

Charter schools. *Publicly sponsored autonomous schools that are substantially free of direct administrative control by the government but are held accountable for achieving certain levels of student performance (and other specified outcomes).*

Work place training. *Apprenticeship programs to teach students a skilled trade not offered through present vocational training. Costs are divided between the employer and the school district.*

Voucher plans. *Any system of certificate or cash payments by the government that enables public school students to attend schools of their choice, public or private. Vouchers have a fixed value and are redeemed at the time of enrollment.*

Tuition tax credits. *A system of funding choice that allows parents to receive credit against their income tax if their child attends a nonpublic school. Such a system is, by definition, intersectional. (pp. 14–16)*

Different Theories of Change

Why do people who share the same goals and who have the same information wind up on different sides when issues of how to improve schools are debated? One explanation is they bring to the debate different theories of human nature. Theories of human nature are at the center of the decisions we make about educational policies and about the management systems we use to implement them. Theories of human nature define human action and codify human behavior. They determine how we treat others and others treat us, and they determine what is just and good and what is unjust and evil (e.g., see Sergiovanni, 1997).

Hobbes believed that human nature has both a *virtuous* side rooted in moral conceptions of goodness and a *selfish* side rooted in psychological egoism. The virtuous side includes our *capacity* to embody such ideals as altruism, moral bearing, self-sacrifice, and cooperation aimed at the enhancement at what we believe to be the common good. The selfish side recognizes our *propensity* to satisfy our physical and psychological needs, to compete to win, and to accumulate wealth aimed at enhancing our own pleasure. Hobbes (1950) believed that humankind's selfish side is a natural condition. The virtuous side, by contrast, must be learned.

In the ideal, the two sides of human nature exist in reasonable balance. Despite this complexity, most policymakers operate from more simple theories of human nature, believing that people are inclined toward good or inclined toward evil. The first inclination represents the unconstrained view of human nature and the second inclination represents the constrained view (Sowell, 1987).

Change agents who hold the *unconstrained* view believe that teachers, for example, can be trusted to act morally, and therefore must be provided with the freedom to optimize their moral propensity to do what is right. They have both the capacity and the need to sacrifice their self-interests for valued causes and for conceptions of the common good that they value. As professionals, they are willing to accept responsibility for their own practice, and they commit themselves to the learning needs of their students above other concerns. When teachers do not respond to this ideal, it is thought not to be because of their human nature but because of factors that they do not control.

Within the *constrained* view, it is believed that teachers will act selfishly if given the chance. Their primary concern is to maximize their self-interests. Thus, constraints in the form of incentives and penalties must be provided to force them to do the right thing. Advocates of this view believe that the moral limitations of human nature must be accepted, but can be manipulated in favor of the common good by the proper use of checks and balances such as rewards and punishments (Smith, 1937). Teachers may have the capacity to do the right thing, they reason, but this capacity is motivated only if constraints are provided.

Constrained Change Strategies

Both constrained and unconstrained views of human nature influence the strategies that policymakers use to improve schools. Those with constrained views rely on bureaucratic leadership and on market strategies. *Leadership* in this discussion is defined as relying on the leaders' interpersonal styles and motivational skills to *motivate* change by trading psychological gratification and other forms of need fulfillment for compliance with proposed changes. Those with unconstrained views rely on professional, cultural, and democratic strategies. Both bureaucratic and leadership strategies offer teachers and schools trades of rewards and punishments, incentives and disincentives, for their compliance with change directions. In the first instance, these trades are managed by rules, mandates, and direct supervision. In the second instance, these trades are managed by the styles and interpersonal skills of leaders as they motivate and inspire change. Market forces also rely on trades. But these trades do not require intensive administration or intensive leadership. Instead, they rely on rational choice theory linked to the propensity of people to function as individuals who seek to maximize their gains and cut their losses in an open marketplace. The *invisible hand* of the market is depended on to motivate change.

Rational Choice Theory

Bureaucratic, leadership, and market change strategies rely on versions of rational choice theory to motivate change. The origins of rational choice theory are found in the fields of economics, evolutionary biology, and behavioral psychology. From economics comes the image of the person as one who is always in pursuit of self-interest and who is never satisfied with what has been accumulated. He or she operates alone, meaning that the drive to maximize gains and cut losses is pursued without regard for the welfare of others (Simon, 1950; Samuelson, 1947).

Darwin's (1985) theories of natural selection expanded the emphasis on competition that plays a major role in market change force strategies. Competition, he argued, weeds out the weak players, thus making the pool of survivors and new replacements for the weak stronger over time. Self-interest motivates competitive play. Darwin's theory provides the script for many school-choice proposals that are based solely on free-market principles.

Behavioral psychology contributed the law of effect (Skinner, 1953) to the market change force equation. According to the law of effect, human behavior is controlled by past consequences. Thus, having received a reward or punishment in the past, the individual is conditioned to repeat the behavior again and again to get the reward and to avoid the punishment in the future.

One particular variation of rational choice theory is agency theory (Moe, 1984). *Agency theory* assumes that the interests of managers and workers are not the same. Workers are interested in the best deal for the least effort. Managers are interested in the best performance at the least cost. Managers are dependent on workers who have more information about how to do the job. Given the choice, workers will take advantage of this situation. Thus, managers must use checks and balances as well as rewards and punishments to control and motivate workers (Bimber, 1993). Agency theory fits school change by substituting change agent for manager and teacher for worker, or the state for manager and the school site for worker.

Unconstrained Change Strategies

Professional, cultural, and democratic change strategies embody the unconstrained view of human nature. Professional strategies, for example, rely on professional training, standards of practice, and norms for behavior that, once internalized, are believed to compel change. Change behavior, advocates of this view argue, is motivated by professional virtues that function as substitutes for bureaucratic, personal, and market change forces (Sergiovanni, 1994). One professional virtue is a commitment to practicing in an exemplary way by staying abreast of new developments, researching one's own practice, trying out new approaches, and otherwise accepting responsibility for one's own development. Another professional virtue is to accept responsibility not only for one's own individual practice but for the practice of teaching itself that exists in the school. Embodiment of this virtue transforms teaching from a collection of individual teaching practices to a single and shared practice of teaching. As teachers come to share the same practice, the argument continues, a third virtue comes into play: *colleagueship*, defined as teachers being connected together by morally held webs of obligations and commitments. Taken together, advocates believe, the professional virtues enable the development of communities of practice.

Change agents who rely on cultural change strategies believe that schools can become covenantal learning communities with norms that compel changes among teachers and students that result in better teaching and learning. Cultural change strategies rely on community norms, values, and ideals that, when internalized, speak to everyone in a moral voice. Teachers, students, and other members of this community, it is argued, will then be motivated by felt obligations that emerge from the shared values and norms that define the school as a covenantal community (e.g., see Etzioni, 1988; Sergiovanni, 1994).

Democratic change strategies rely on commitment to democratic social contracts that function as the source for values to guide school decision making and as the source for patterns of obligations and duties that compel change. Advocates of this strategy seek to transform teachers and students into *citizens* committed to civic virtue. *Civic virtue* is defined as the willingness to sacrifice one's self-interest for the common good.

Not only do professional, cultural, and democratic change strategies embody the unconstrained view, they share the purpose of building community in schools as a means to leverage deep changes. When used together, the three change strategies seek to transform schools from organizations or markets to professional, learning, and democratic communities.

The six strategies for bringing about change in schools, along with their characteristics and likely consequences, are summarized in Table 2.2. Note that when bureaucratic, leadership, and market strategies are used, schools are likely to change just enough to avoid penalties, get rewards, or win in the marketplace. But once the prospects for penalties, rewards, or winning are removed, changes are likely to disappear. Professional, cultural, and democratic forces, by contrast, compel change from within and are thus likely to be more enduring.

TABLE 2.2   Change Strategies, Characteristics, and Consequences

Change Strategies	Change Practices	Theories of Human Nature	Change Consequences
Bureaucratic	1. Rely on rules, mandates, and requirements to provide direct supervision, standardized work processes, and/or standardized outcomes to prescribe change	*Constrained*: The visible hand of rational choice theory linked to penalties is necessary to motivate change	School changes just enough to avoid sanctions. Change stops when sanctions are removed
Leadership	2. Rely on personality, leadership style, and interpersonal skills of change agents to motivate change	*Constrained*: The visible hand of rational choice theory linked to psychological rewards is necessary to motivate change	School changes just enough to receive gratification of needs. Change stops when rewards are not available
Market	3. Rely on competition, incentives, and individual choice to motivate change	*Constrained*: The invisible hand of rational choice theory linked to individual self-interest is necessary to motivate change	School changes just enough to win in the marketplace. Winning becomes less important after repeated losses
Professional	4. Rely on standards of expertise, codes of conduct, collegiality, felt obligations, and other professional norms to build professional community	*Unconstrained*: The visible hand of professional socialization provides standards of practice and norms that compel change	School internalizes norms of competence and virtue that compel change
Cultural	5. Rely on shared values, goals, and ideas about pedagogy, relationships, and politics to build covenantal community	*Unconstrained*: The invisible hand of community norms, values, and ideas speak in a moral voice to compel change	School internalizes community norms that compel change
Democratic	6. Rely on democratic social contracts and shared commitments to the common good to build democratic community	*Unconstrained*: The invisible hand of democratic traditions and internalized norms compel change	School internalizes democratic norms that compel change

Source: Adapted from Thomas J. Sergiovanni, "Organization, Market and Community as Strategies for Change: What Works Best for Deep Changes in Schools?" In Andy Hargreaves and Ann Lieberman (Eds.), *International Handbook of Educational Change* (Vol. 5) (Boston: Kluwer Academic Publishers, 1997).

Educational administration as both a discipline and a practice is in a constant state of evolution. During the twentieth century, both pyramid and railroad theories first dominated and were then challenged by high-performance theory. Despite this new vision's progressive features, all three of the theories share the constrained view of human nature. The theory of school as a moral community embodies the unconstrained view. During the nineties, advocates of schools as learning communities have been successful in establishing a beachhead assault on the three theories based on the constrained view. It is too early to tell, however, whether the new movement will be successful.

Maintaining Public Confidence

It should be clear from this discussion that easy solutions to fundamental value differences are not likely to be forthcoming and that whatever answers do emerge will not result from simplistic and rational conceptions of decision making. The destiny of schools is and will continue to be in the hands of various interests, each seeking advantage over others. Though state and local educational agencies, professionals in schools, politicians, and laypersons all appeal to the same rhetoric (excellence in schooling, improving teaching and learning, and so on), the real world of schooling is a creation of how this rhetoric is interpreted by interests and how these meanings are exchanged as a highly political process unfolds. Simply put, what is best for pupils, teachers, and schools is perceived differently by different groups.

Throughout the process, school administrators must maintain an adequate degree of public confidence at the local level in order for schools to function reasonably well. Without such confidence, the necessary material, political, and moral support will not be forthcoming. Carol and Cunningham (1984) define *confidence* as "belief in, faith in, understanding of, willingness to support, pride in, loyalty to and willingness to defend a school or school system" (p. 111).

This definition is significant in the sense that it speaks to confidence in a particular school rather than in the institution of schooling. The annual Gallup survey of public opinion with respect to schooling, for example, typically reveals that the public differentiates between schooling in general and schools with which they are familiar. In the 2001 Phi Delta Kappa/Gallup Poll, for example, 51 percent of the respondents gave their local schools grades of A or B. When asked to grade the nation's schools as a whole, however, only 23 percent gave them As or Bs. Roughly half of the respondents gave them Cs. This difference in how schooling, in general, and known schools are viewed suggests that public support can be maintained by local school officials.

Using the Phi Delta Kappa/Gallup Poll data and interpretations of this data as reported by *Education Week,* Figure 2.1 tracks public support for schools at three-year intervals since 1974. An upswing in opinion begins in 1983. Thirty-one percent of the respondents gave their local schools an A or B in 1983 as compared with 51 percent in 2001. How do you account for the increase in support over the last eighteen years? Would a poll of your community reveal similar data?

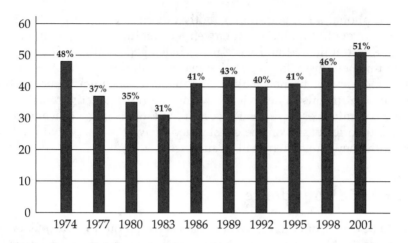

FIGURE 2.1   Public Support for Local Schools, 1974 through 2001

Sources: The 33rd Annual Phi Delta Kappa/Gallup Poll of the "Public's Attitude toward the Public Schools", 2001, *www.pdkintl.org/kappan/k0109gal.htm#5a;* Catherine Gewertz, "Public Support for Local Schools Reaches All-Time High, Poll Finds" *Education Week,* September 5, 2001, p. 18; and George H. Gallup, "The 21st Annual Gallup Poll of the Public's Attitude toward the Public Schools," *Phi Delta Kappan,* 1989, p. 198.

The Public Education Network and *Education Week* (2001) asked over 1,000 registered voters a variety of questions about schools and reported their findings in "Action for All: The Public's Responsibility for Public Education." One question in particular bears on the topic of building confidence and support for schools at the local level. Respondents were read a list of people and organizations typically found in communities. They were then asked to tell how much they trusted each one to give good information about how they could help the local schools. The response choices were trust a great deal, trust a lot, somewhat, a little, or not at all. The response tallies, given in percentages, are shown in Table 2.3.

Teachers and principals, parents and the PTA are viewed as being the most credible sources of information and help by respondents. By contrast, business leaders and elected officials did not fare very well. Sixty-nine percent and 73 percent of the respondents said they trusted business leaders and elected officials only a little or not at all. This finding will surely delight those who worry about the growth and influence of the state government–corporate complex discussed earlier. What explanation would you give for this poor showing by business leaders and elected officials? If this survey were conducted in your community, would the results be similar?

Impressions are important. Not only do they help to earn support for the schools but they increase legitimacy. The school is seen as a valued community asset and the decisions its administrators make are viewed as authoritative and credible. As public perception improves, schools are allowed more discretion by

TABLE 2.3 **Who Americans Trust**

Person or Organization	A Great Deal or a Lot	A Little or Not at All
Teachers	59%	39%
Parents	57%	41%
The PTA	56%	41%
School principals	51%	47%
School superintendent	47%	50%
The school board	46%	51%
Community organizations	44%	53%
Neighbors	41%	58%
Students	41%	57%
Local newspapers	32%	65%
Business leaders	26%	69%
Elected officials	25%	73%

Source: From data summarized in Public Education Network/*Education Week*, April 2001, "Action for All: The Public's Responsibility for Public Education," p. 34. *www.publiceducation.org/download/actionforall.pdf.*

the state. Further, funding from state and local sources is easier to get. But impressions need to be managed properly.

Laswell (1971) uses the term *flow of images* to refer to the aggregate of perceptions an organization communicates to the public that results in the forming of an impression. This impression is shaped over time as the public experiences a "multitude of small, individual experiences acquired personally through direct contact with schools or with children, learned through the media, heard from one's neighbors, or gained perhaps from an acquaintance who works in the school" (Carol & Cunningham, 1984, p. 114). The problem is complicated by the reality that schools serve many publics and that contradictory flows of images must often be communicated.

Managing Public Confidence

The management of public confidence requires deft handling of the flow of images communicated to various constituencies. Since the needs, requirements, and interests of constituencies differ, image flows must differ and thus often contradict each other. Contradictory flows are possible because of the loose structuring or coupling that characterizes schooling. For example, despite efforts of states to create a tight alignment between school goals and objectives and curriculum, between curriculum and teaching, and between teaching and testing to ensure control over the process, this alignment is difficult to accomplish within the actual process of schooling. As Cusick (1983) points out, the reality is that in most schools, each classroom operates independently of all others, as if it were a separate school.

If Cusick is right, then public confidence can be managed by paying close attention to the flow of images that counts the most—images closest to home. And this seems to characterize what school administrators actually do. They typically express a healthy concern for public debates regarding schooling in the nation and participate in those debates. But they are far more concerned about the flow of images communicated in their own schoolyards.

Carol and Cunningham (1984) surveyed parents in an attempt to identify those perceived school characteristics that led to increased public confidence. Not surprisingly, they found that dedicated and competent teachers headed the list, tied for top rank with special instructional and extracurricular programs. These investigators comment, "Of equal importance was the availability of 'special programs.'

TABLE 2.4   Ranking of Responses Leading to Confidence at a School Building Level

Rank	Reasons	No. of Responses
1.5	Dedicated, competent teachers	75
1.5	Special instructional and extracurricular programs	75
3.5	Administrator(s) effectiveness	61
3.5	Buildings and grounds	61
5.	Student-centered, "caring" atmosphere	51
6.	Positive attitudes of students/staff	40
7.	Student discipline	38
8.	Curriculum	36
9.	Student achievement	30
10.	Parent participation	28
11.	Communication with parents	22
12.	Public image	22
13.5	High standards, goals, expectations	15
13.5	Board/superintendent relations, policies, decisions	15
15.	Administrator/staff community service	13
16.	Courteous office staff	12
17.	Linkages with other institutions, sectors	11
18.	Successful graduates	10
19.33	Student awards, honors	9
19.33	Testing, guidance, and counseling programs	9
19.33	Community involvement with school	9
22.	Adequate funding	5
23.	Students' dress	4
24.5	Equity	3
24.5	Community education	3

Source: L. N. Carol & L. L. Cunningham, "Views of Public Confidence in Education," *Issues in Education,* 2(2), 118, 1984. Copyright 1984 by the American Educational Research Association. Reprinted by permission of the publisher.

Such programs might address the needs of handicapped youngsters, those with learning disabilities, or those in need of specialists, they might provide excellent music classes, field trips or travel. Together with other extracurricular programs (particularly sports programs) the inclusion of 'special programs' contributed significantly to confidence in the school" (Carol & Cunningham, 1984, p. 115).

Next in the rankings were perceptions that the school was effectively administered and pride in the buildings and grounds. Respondents commented on the importance of administrators being leaders of teams of teachers and on their capacity to be problem solvers on behalf of parents and students. When the school was perceived as having a caring, student-centered atmosphere and as having positive attitudes toward students and staff, public confidence was enhanced. These two qualities enjoyed fifth and sixth rank. Student discipline, curriculum, and achievement ranked seventh, eighth, and ninth, respectively, among the twenty-five items identified. The ranks are summarized in Table 2.4.

The findings from this study provide an indication of why school administrators often spend more time projecting images of confidence and effectiveness, pride, and climate than they spend on curriculum, student achievement, and other characteristics included in Table 2.4. The findings suggest further that despite the public debates and intense policy deliberations that characterize the national agenda, school administrators focus primarily on the affairs of schooling in their own backyards.

Is this the case in your school district? Given today's emphasis on student achievement, would these findings still hold up? How much time, for example, do the administrators in your school or in other district schools spend in instructional leadership that is directed specifically to student achievement? How would today's parents rank the reasons listed in Table 2.4? Try finding out by asking some parents in your community to rank the reasons with respect to their importance in winning public confidence.

APPENDIX 2.1

A Layered System of Standards

An Op-Ed* by Thomas J. Sergiovanni

No movement in recent history has greater potential for improving teaching and learning than the push for rigorous and authentic standards linked to quality assessments. But even too much of a good thing can be harmful.

When state-mandated standards and high-stakes tests are part of a larger system of accountability that includes local standards and local assessments, they are more likely to be helpful in holding schools accountable and in helping schools get better. Used alone, mandated standards and tests provide a dangerously narrow approach to accountability.

In today's standards world, local control has not so much been abandoned as redefined. Most citizens in your community and mine are as committed to this value as ever. But the language state officials use in pushing the standards movement changes the meaning of local control. Governors, for example, routinely tout their standards-based reforms as examples of high expectations with local control involving shifts in power from Washington, DC, to their respective state capitals. But rarely does this brand of local control make its way to the town square.

One important way to restore some sense of balance to all of this and especially to restore the original meaning of local control, without neglecting legitimate state interests, is to add the voices of school superintendents and other locals to all levels of this debate. And the place to start is in each local community in every state. Here are my suggestions for talking points that may help superintendents and other locals as they begin the conversations we need.

- The ends determine the means.

Many states have come to view local control as giving school districts and their communities more control over the means of education but less control over the ends. States set the standards that schools are to meet and then tell schools they are free to use virtually any means to achieve these standards.

But because standards and assessments pretty much determine the curriculum, how time is spent, how financial and other resources are deployed, how teachers teach, who gets promoted, and even how a good school is defined, the ends of schooling wind up determining the means. This reality leaves schools

*This Op-Ed is an abridged version of "Standards and the Lifeworld of Leadership," *The School Administrator*, Vol. 8, No. 57, September 2000, pp. 6–12.

with precious little real discretion over the policy process as it affects teaching, learning, and assessments.

George Madaus, a testing expert from Boston College, identifies five principles that emerge from practice as a result of the ends-determining-the-means problem:

- If important decisions such as who gets promoted, how schools are rated, and which teachers are rewarded and punished are related to test results, teachers will teach to the test, thus narrowing the curriculum by omitting other, often more important, outcomes.
- When high-stakes tests operate, past examinations come to define the curriculum, placing curriculum development as a field of study and practice and educators as curriculum developers at risk.
- Teachers pay particular attention to the types of questions (short answer, multiple choice, essay, and so on) on high-stakes tests and adjust their teaching accordingly. (Madaus tells the story of school reformer Deborah Meier testifying before a minimum competency hearing that reading instruction in many New York City schools resembles the practice of taking reading tests. She pointed out that when synonyms and antonyms were dropped from the tests, teachers immediately dropped the material that stressed them.)
- When tests are the only determiner of future education choices or future life choices, society tends to treat test results as the goal of schooling, rather than as an indicator of achievement.
- Mandated standards and high-stakes tests transfer control over the curriculum, teaching and learning to the agency or group that controls the examination. In today's environment, control over what is taught, how it is taught, and what is learned is being increasingly transferred from parents, teachers, and local citizens in the schoolhouse to legislators and other elites in the statehouse.

Standards as Values

Standards can be intimidating. Many ordinary citizens come to think of a learning standard or a school standard as something similar to the gold standard—a scientific and objective measure of something valuable that ordinary people had better not challenge. Thus, parents and other citizens rarely ask what a standards-based, state-assigned school rating such as A, B, C, D, or F means. They just assume that whatever is being measured should be measured and whatever the ratings are they must be scientific ones. But standards are neither objective nor scientific. Some standards are good and some are bad. Some standards are measured properly and some are not. In some cases, the rating schemes designed to measure standards are set too high. And in other cases, the rating schemes are set too low.

Superintendents and principals have a responsibility to keep the standards record straight on objectivity. Setting standards is a process best served by broad-based, reasoned consideration and deliberate action, neither of which is possible when parents and other citizens are moon-struck by images of standards as infallible and unchallengeable. Our message must be: Standards are set by people who make human decisions about what they believe or think is appropriate or is not appropriate.

Not surprisingly these people often differ. One group, for example, might prefer some standards, accept others, and reject still others, whereas another group in the same room dealing with the same standards might prefer, accept, or reject different ones. We have little to gain by viewing the setting of standards across the curriculum as a zero-sum game where some people win and others lose. By not considering standards and standardization as the same thing, our eyes are opened to other possibilities.

Many citizens and government officials assume that standard setting may be values based in some areas but is certainly objective in the hard sciences such as mathematics or science or the basic skill areas such as reading. After all, 2 + 2 = 4; H_2O is water; and cat is spelled C-A-T. But the evidence indicates otherwise.

In California, the setting of science standards by a state-appointed committee turned out to be a nightmare. The committee splintered into two groups: One group favored an inquiry approach and the other group favored a content-acquisition approach. The first group pushed for standards that would help students think like scientists, experience science first hand, learn general scientific principles, and be able to solve scientific problems. The second group pushed for standards that were more graded and content oriented. In the end the committee members reached a compromise. The California State Board of Education refused to accept the compromise package, deciding instead to approve the second group's version of science standards.

What about the skill areas such as reading? By law, the state of Texas requires that most of the words in 1st grade reading textbooks be phonics based or decodable. In the past, the Texas Education Agency has interpreted *most* to mean 51 percent of the words. More recently, the Texas State Board of Education, which oversees the agency, ordered the agency to raise the percentage of decodable words to 80 percent. Different percentages of decodable words mean different reading standards will be set. Though one could argue evidence justifies increasing the percentage of words to 80 percent, ample evidence points to the other direction as well. The issue of phonics is about more than what research says—it's about values.

Imagine passing laws and other regulations that require physicians to prescribe aspirin (e.g., Bayer) over acetaminophen (Tylenol) at least 80 percent of the time. It just wouldn't happen, and it shouldn't happen in education either. Yet even in the basic skills areas, such as reading, different ideologies lead to different conclusions.

Standards setting in the real world resembles a game of winning and losing, rather than a process of scientific inquiry into a discipline in search of some sort of truth. Simply put, standards are subjective reflections of those who set them. Different people set different standards. Thus, the process is as much political as it is anything else. If you want standards that you like, make sure the people who set the standards are people with whom you agree.

Subjectivity should not scare us. Politics in a democracy should play an important role in setting standards. But the schooling of one's children and other life-world concerns are so important that hardball win or lose approaches to deciding which standards to choose should be avoided. It should not be a matter of all or none. When 60 percent of the people prefer one set of standards and 40 percent another, instead of forcing everyone to accept the standards of the majority, we should consider legitimizing two different sets of standards.

One way that more people can win is by having different standards. With different standards some would be common for all but most would be diverse. Some would be decided centrally, but most would be decided locally. One thing must be certain: All of the standards must be rigorous and authentic, challenging and meaningful.

The issue here is not standards versus no standards, nor is it quality standards versus weak standards. The issue, plain and simple, is that standards need not be standardized to be rigorous and authentic, challenging and meaningful. Indeed our present system of standards and assessments may get average marks for rigor and for challenge, but it gets low marks for authenticity and for meaning. We need a plan that gets high marks in all four areas.

Layered Standards

I believe we can create a responsive system of rigorous accountability that includes testing and other assessments and public disclosure of results if we are willing to adopt a layered approach to standards and a shared approach to accountability with a strong local component.

Moving in this direction will require that schools make known what their purposes are, make promises to the public as to what they hope to accomplish, engage in rigorous inquiry to ensure that promises are kept, and invite public scrutiny of their intents, actions, and results.

Before describing what a layered system of standards and assessments might look like, let's summarize with some assertions:

- States should participate in setting standards for schools.
- School boards, parents, teachers, and even students at the local school should participate in setting standards.
- When standards and assessments are set by the state alone, standardization is likely to emerge, with schools becoming more and more similar as a result.
- When school boards, parents, teachers, and students at the local level participate in the setting of standards and in determining assessments, schools become standardized in some areas but diverse in most others.
- Letting parents choose the schools their children will attend only has meaning when students, parents, and teachers are provided with real options from which to choose.

- The state should assume responsibility for developing standards and assessments for all schools in the areas of reading, writing, mathematics, and perhaps civics.
- Citizens, parents, teachers, and students at the local level should share in the responsibility for developing standards and assessments in all other areas of the curriculum.
- Because school districts and schools within them differ, it should be expected that many standards will differ as one moves from district to district and from school to school within the same district.
- The state has a responsibility to provide both technical assistance and professional development for helping schools set standards and develop assessments.
- The state has a responsibility to provide a centralized standards bank from which local authorities might draw as needed.
- Students should participate by setting standards for themselves and by assessing their own performance.
- Student assessments should count along with state, school district, and local school assessments in evaluating a school.
- The state should provide constructive oversight by ensuring that the standards set locally and the assessments developed locally are defensible and trustworthy. Developing standards for standards and standards for assessments would help.
- No single set of standards and no single assessment system should dominate another.

Five Prongs

In developing a system of layered standards, I propose that there be standards in five areas:

- Uniform standards for all schools in basic reading, writing, and mathematics (and possibly civics) would be set by the state.
- Varied standards in key curriculum areas such as history, advanced mathematics, English, art, music, and social science would be set primarily by local communities.
- Varied standards in social and emotional learning areas including character development would be set jointly by the state and local communities.
- School standards in noncurriculum areas such as teacher development, use of resources, and sense of community would be set jointly by the state and local communities.
- Teacher standards in such areas as professionalism, collegiality, and professional growth would be set primarily by the state.

Although standardized tests would dominate in assessing uniform standards in basic reading, mathematics, and writing, they would play a much less important role for the varied standards in key curriculum areas, a negligible role for assessing the varied standards in social and emotional areas, and no role in assessing school standards and teacher standards. In these areas the dominant assessment vehicle would be a whole-school quality review process.

This process would involve both an internal self-study conducted by the school and its community and an external study conducted by an external visitation team from a neighboring community (the whole-school quality review team) that would engage in an intensive examination of each school. Members of the team would include educators, parents, representatives of the corporate and civic community, and perhaps a representative from the state education department. Visits might take place every four years.

What kinds of data would be examined? In the social and emotional areas, performance exhibitions, portfolios, and perhaps a service requirement would make sense. For school standards in noncurriculum areas, the state should develop an indicator system that the whole-school quality review team would have to consider along with local self-study data.

A similar approach might work for teachers' standards if no independent teachers' standards board exists in the state. The state would be responsible for assessing standards in basic reading, mathematics, and writing. Its findings would have to be considered by the whole-school quality review team as it brings together information from a variety of sources to reach conclusions about the school.

The whole-school quality review team would be the major player in all other assessments. This team would develop one report that provides an in-depth study of the school and a summary rating that takes into account all layers of standards and their assessments. No one source of data would be used alone in reaching a summative evaluation.

Localism and Disclosure

Although local in origin, the school quality review process would have to be opened wide to the public. Beginning with a self-study that inventories the promises a given school is making to its local community, its students, its teachers, and to itself, the school then would detail how it expects to keep those promises and the evidence it is providing for having kept those promises.

External reviews would be grounded in the school's promises and school improvement plans, in some minimum requirements set by the state, as well as widely accepted standards for teaching and learning, teacher development, and school effectiveness.

The review team would have to take into account student results on state-mandated tests in the basic skills of mathematics, reading, writing, and perhaps civics in its write-up. The write-up should be distributed widely at the local level, to the state, maybe even summarized and published in the local newspaper, and made available in its entirety on the Internet.

This sort of public disclosure has its disadvantages as well as advantages. But I believe a good accountability system is based on trust. A system that is locally oriented must be viewed as trustworthy by local citizens, the state, and other legitimate interests. One way to earn trust is through public disclosure. Thus, my vote, at the moment, would be for full and wide disclosure of the report.

School visitations are not a new idea. Most, however, bring externally developed, detailed frameworks in the form of standards that schools must provide evidence they are meeting. If the school quality review process evolves in this direction, then it probably will not work.

A system is needed that is local in origin and anchored in some overarching conceptualization, but that allows the majority of standards to be generated by the local community. Further, although it is likely to be a challenge, emphasis needs to be placed on the real thing rather than on the accumulation of paperwork. Thus, visiting teams would spend a good deal of their time interviewing students, teachers, parents, and others; shadowing students; examining student work; visiting classrooms; and paying particular attention to the sorts of standards for quality intellectual work suggested, for example, by Fred Newmann and his colleagues at the University of Wisconsin.

Larry Cuban, a Stanford University professor and former superintendent, has argued that successful schools come in many different shapes and styles. Some are traditional, some are progressive, and others are somewhere in the middle. But regardless of their form, successful schools share three characteristics: parents, teachers, and students are satisfied with them; they are successful in achieving their own goals and objectives; and their graduates exhibit democratic values, attitudes, and behaviors.

This unique focus and the support that parents, teachers, and students give it are key. To use the language of this article, successful schools have character. Local passions, local beliefs, local participation, and local support are key to their effectiveness. We are not likely to get very far in cultivating these virtues of localism unless we rethink our present course in developing standards and assessments. This reassessment, I believe, is key to the future of school leadership and school success.

REFERENCES

Bimber, B. (1993). *School decentralization lessons from the study of bureaucracy.* Institute of Education and Training. Santa Monica, CA: Rand Corporation.

Cantor, L. (1980). The growing role of states in American education. *Comparative Education, 16*(1), 24–31.

Carol, L. N., & Cunningham, L. L. (1984). Views of public confidence in education. *Issues in Education, 11*(2), 110–126.

Casteen, J. T. (1984). The state's responsibility for teacher quality. In C. E. Finn, Jr., D. Ravitch, & R. T. Fancher (Eds.), *Against mediocrity. The hu-*manities in America's high schools. New York: Holmes and Meier.

Chubb, J. E., & Moe, T. M. (1989). A report to the people of Connecticut. *Educational Choice.* Norwalk, CT: The Yankee Institute.

Cohen, D. (1982). Policy and organization: The impact of state and federal educational policy in school governance. *Harvard Educational Review, 54*(3), 474–499.

Cookson, P. W. (1994). *School choice: The struggle for the soul of American education.* New Haven, CT: Yale University Press.

Cusick, P. A. (1983). *The egalitarian ideal and the American high school.* New York: Longman.

Darling-Hammond, L. (1984). *Beyond the commission reports: The coming crisis in teaching.* Santa Monica, CA: Rand Corporation.

Darling-Hammond, L., & Wise, A. E. (1983). Teaching standards or standardized teaching? *Educational Leadership, 41*(2), 66–69.

Darling-Hammond, L. (1997). *The right to learn: A blueprint for creating schools that work.* San Francisco: Jossey-Bass.

Darwin, C. (1985). *The origin of species by means of natural selection.* Harmondsworth, NY: Penguin.

DeCharms, R. (1968). *Personal causation: The internal affective determinants of behavior.* New York: Academic Press.

Education Week (2001, January 11). Quality counts 2001—A better balance: Standards, tests, and the tools to succeed. Bethesda, MD: Editorial Projects in Education, *20*(17).

Etzioni, A. (1988). *The moral dimension: A new economics.* New York: The Free Press.

Gandal, M., & Vranek, J. (2001). Standards: Here today, here tomorrow. *Educational Leadership, 59*(1), 7–13.

Good, T. (1996). Educational researchers comment on the education summit and other policy proclamations from 1983–1996. *Educational Researcher, 25*(8), 4–6. See also *http://www.Summit96.ibm.com.*

Goodlad, J. I. (1984). *A place called school.* New York: McGraw-Hill.

Grissmer, D. W., Flanagan, A., Kawata, J., & Williamson, S. (2000). *Improving student achievement: What state NAEP test scores tell us.* Santa Monica, CA: Rand Corporation.

Henry, T. (2001, October 11). Governors stand on principles: Education summit vows to help low-performing public schools. *USA Today,* 9D.

Hobbes, T. (1950). *Leviation.* New York: E. P. Dutton.

Howe, H., II. (1983). Education moves to center-stage: An overview of recent studies. *Phi Delta Kappan, 65*(3), 167–172.

Kirst, M. (1989). Who should control the schools? Reassessing current policies. In T. J. Sergiovanni & J. H. Moore (Eds.), *Schooling for tomorrow: Directing reforms to issues that count.* Boston: Allyn and Bacon.

Kirst, M. (1990). The crash of the first wave recent reform in the U.S.: Looking forward and backward. In S. Bacharach (Ed.), *Education reform: Making sense of it all.* Boston: Allyn and Bacon.

Kohn, A. (2000). *The case against standardized testing: Raising the scores, ruining the schools.* Portsmouth, NH: Heinemann.

Laswell, H. D. (1971). *A pre-view of policy sciences.* New York: American Elsevier.

Loveless, T. (2001). *The 2001 Brown Center report on American education: How well are American students learning?* Washington, DC: The Brookings Institution.

McDonnell, L. M. (1989). *The dilemma of teacher policy.* Center for the Study of the Teaching Profession. Santa Monica, CA: Rand Corporation.

McNeil, L. (1986). *Contradictions of control: School structure and school knowledge.* New York: Routledge.

Meier, D. (2000). *Will standards save public education?* Boston: Beacon Press.

Moe, T. (1984). The new economics of organizations. *American Journal of Political Science, 28*(4), 739–777.

Murphy, J., Mesa, R. P., & Hallinger, P. (1984). A stronger state role in school reform. *Educational Leadership, 42*(2), 20–26.

National Commission on Excellence in Education. (1983). *A nation at risk.* Washington, DC: U.S. Government Printing Office.

Nelson, K. (1994). Commentary on national and state education policy developments: A state legislator's perspective. In R. F. Elmore & S. H. Fuhrman (Eds.), *The governance of curriculum 1994 yearbook of the Association for Supervision and Curriculum Development.* Alexandria, VA: ASCD.

Ohanian, S. (1999). *One size fits few: The folly of educational standards.* Portsmouth, NH: Heinemann.

Public Education Network and *Education Week* (2001, April). Action for all: The public's responsibility for public education. http://www.publiceducation.org/download/actionforall.pdf.

Quinby, N. (1985). Improving the place called school: A conversation with John Goodland. *Educational Leadership, 42*(6), 16–19.

Ravitch, D. (1985). The *schools we deserve.* New York: Basic Books.

Rose, L. C., & Gallup, A. M. (2001). The 33rd annual Phi Delta Kappa/Gallup poll of the public's attitude toward the public schools. http://www.pdkintl.org/kappan/k0109gal.htm.

Samuelson, P. (1947). *Foundations of economic analysis.* Cambridge, MA: Harvard University Press.

Sergiovanni, T. J. (1991). *The principalship: A reflective practice perspective* (2nd ed.). Boston: Allyn and Bacon.

Sergiovanni, T. J. (1994). *Building community in schools.* San Francisco: Jossey-Bass.

Sergiovanni, T. J. (1997). Organization, market and community as strategies for change: What works best for deep change in schools? In A. Hargreaves & A. Lieberman (Eds.), *International*

Handbook of Educational Change (Vol. 5). Boston: Kluwer Academic.

Sergiovanni, T. J. (2000). *The lifeworld of leadership: Creating culture, community, and personal meaning in our schools.* San Francisco: Jossey-Bass.

Scherer, M. (2001). How and why standards can improve student achievement: A conversation with Robert J. Marzano. *Educational Leadership 59*(1).

Shirley, R. C. (1984). Institutional autonomy and government control. *Educational Forum, 48*(2), 217–222.

Simon, H. A. (1950). *Administrative behavior: A study of decision-making processes in administration organization.* New York: Macmillan.

Sizer, T. R. (1985). Common sense. *Educational Leadership, 42*(6), 21–22.

Skinner, B. F. (1953). *Science and human behavior.* New York: Macmillan.

Smith, A. (1937). *An inquiry into the nature and causes of the wealth of nations.* New York: Modern Library.

Snider, W. (1990, March 28). Voucher system for 1000 pupils adopted in Wisconsin. *Education Week, 9*(27), 1, 14.

Sowell, T. (1987). *A conflict of visions.* New York: Morrow.

Spillane, J. P. (1994). How districts mediate between state policy and teachers' practice. In R. Elmore & S. Fuhrman (Eds.), *The governance of curriculum 1994 yearbook of the Association for Supervision and Curriculum Development.* Alexandria, VA: ASCD.

Sunday Express News (San Antonio). (1984). Interview with Michael Kirst, December 16.

Wise, A. E. (1979). *Legislated learning: The bureaucratization of the American classroom.* Berkeley: University of California Press.

Wise, A. E. (1988). Legislated learning revisited. *Phi Delta Kappan, 69*(5), 329–332.

3 Educational Administration

An Overview

Who are school administrators? What are their responsibilities? How do they obtain and exercise authority? How can their authority be checked? Are they leaders or managers? Are they really necessary? Can schools function successfully without them? Parents and teachers often ask such questions, as do members of the general public. Occasionally, the questions are asked skeptically. Administrators are not always portrayed in a favorable light. But few will deny that ours is a complex society with difficult problems that are hard to solve by relying solely on informal administrative arrangements.

In his classic treatment of the art of administration, for example, Tead (1951) invites readers to journey with him on a mythical voyage designed to illustrate the complexity of organization and administration in U.S. society.

> Fly over New York City imaginatively in an airplane, and remove the roofs from successive buildings in your mind's eye. What do you see? You see people, tens of thousands of them, at work. You see top executives in quiet offices thinking, planning, conferring, issuing orders which affect people in distant localities where their companies have plants. You see boards of directors hearing reports and adopting policies which may mean more or less employment in Akron, Detroit, Pittsburgh. You see department store heads in conference with merchandise managers. You see office managers in insurance companies, banks, investment houses, wholesaling firms, facilitating the labors of many. You see huge hospitals in which doctors, nurses, and auxiliary staffs are working to restore health. You see universities, colleges, and schools in which administrators and teachers are providing education. You see governmental bureaus—Federal, state and municipal—in all of which some phase of the public welfare is being served.
>
> Everywhere there are people managing and there are people being managed. This is taking place in organizations, large or small, and for all kinds of purposes. (p. 1)

The governance and administration of education provide a good example of the nature and importance of administrative activity in our society. The educational establishment ranks among the largest of public and private enterprises.

More than 3 million teachers and roughly 53 million students in thousands of public and private schools throughout the nation function daily (U.S. Department of Education, 2000). Fifty state departments of education, several departments of federal government, as well as dozens of private and semiprivate organizations assume responsibility for the analysis and development of broad policy to guide this vast enterprise. Thousands of school boards and tens of thousands of administrators function in the development and administration of policies that govern the day-by-day operation of schools.

The United States is committed to universal education through the high school and in some communities through the junior college. Much progress has been made toward this goal but much more needs to be done. Past accomplishments and future success have relied on and will continue to rely on the quality of educational leadership and governance available to local schools: Educational administration at all levels, from superintendent to department chairperson, assume key roles in the process of building quality education. No one would deny the importance of enacting sound education policy at the state and federal levels, but sound policy in itself is not the answer to school problems and issues. One cannot legislate or mandate superior teaching and learning or other aspects of quality education. These result from the efforts of competent and committed professionals who work with youngsters day after day, the commitment and support a school enjoys from its community, and organizational and other logistical support provided to the school—characteristics that are the domains of educational leadership and administration.

Policy and Policy in Use

Some experts argue that too much emphasis is given to the educational policy-development process and not enough to the articulation of policy into administrative designs and structures and the embodiment of policy into school practice. Others take the opposite position. Both positions assume that policy and administration are separate. The classical literature in administration and public policy, for example, makes a fairly clear distinction between the policy-development process (establishing mission statements, guidelines, general regulations, and mandates) and the articulation of policies into administrative rules and professional practices. The first modern distinction between policy and administration appears in Frank J. Goodnow's book *Politics and Administration*, published in 1900.

Earlier distinctions were made by Woodrow Wilson (1887) in "The Study of Administration": "Public administration is detailed and systematic execution of public law. Every particular application of general law is an act of administration.... The broad plans of governmental action are not administrative...administration lies outside the proper sphere of politics. Administrative questions are not political questions" (p. 97). Approximately one hundred years earlier, Alexander Hamilton had written in *The Federalist*: "The Administration of Government, in its largest sense, comprehends all the operations of the body politic...but in its most usual, and perhaps its most precise significance, *it is limited to executive details,* and falls peculiarly within the province of the executive department" (italics added) (Rossiter, 1961, p. 435). In his later writings, Goodnow (1905) would emphasize again that "politics has to do with policies and expressions of the state will. Administration has to do with execution of these policies" (p. 15).

Traditionally, the policy process was presumed to be the arena for deciding our future by providing the decision-making parameters and structures designed to shape the implementing decisions of administrators and other professionals. Policymakers create policy, and professionals articulate policy in practice. Policymakers decide, and professionals do. This time-honored distinction may serve as a source of legitimacy and rationality. Separating the two may be ideal, but in practice it is more myth than reality.

In 1945, Nobel laureate Herbert A. Simon commented on the distinction between policy and administration as follows: "Yet, neither in Goodnow's study nor in any of the innumerable distinctions that have followed it have any clear-cut criteria or marks of identification been suggested that would enable one to recognize a 'policy question' on site, or to distinguish it from an 'administrative question'" (p. 54). And in 1949, Paul H. Appleby, then dean of the Maxwell School of Public Administration at Syracuse University, commented, "Congress and legislators [state education departments and school boards] make policy for the future, but have no monopoly on that function.... Administrators are continually laying down rules for the future and administrators are continually determining what the law is, what it means in terms of action, what the rights of parties are with respect both to transactions in process and transactions in prospect. Administrators make thousands of such decisions to one made by the courts.... Administrators also...formulate recommendations for legislation, and this is a part of the function of policy-making" (pp. 6–7). He noted further, "Executives do not sit at different desks, treating policy as one and administration as the other...they more often deal with whole problems than they deal with them as exclusively problems of policy or problems of administration" (p. 19).

A more realistic view of the policy process in practice makes a distinction between policy as stated and policy in use. *Policy in use* refers to policy that is created as guidelines are interpreted, mandated characteristics are weighed, differential priorities are assigned, action theories are applied, and ideas come to life in the form of implementing decisions and professional practice. Policy in use is the policy that is felt by students and teachers as schooling takes place. It results from the interpretation of policy statements. For these reasons, in the real world the line between policy and administrative practice is blurred.

The role of research in developing policy and in creating policy in use is important. But research rarely informs the development of stated policy. Typically, politicians don't behave as a result of objective research findings. They act on behalf of preferences and beliefs. The *stating of policy* is a subjective process that seeks to maximize certain values and aspirations thought to be important. Because these values are often not shared in identical ways by various groups, decisions are made as special interests seek to maximize gains according to their held beliefs. Though research plays an important role in the political process of policy-making, the findings of research are rarely considered to be privileged by policy-makers. Administrators often lament this situation. "Research shows that small schools and multiage classrooms make sense. Why doesn't the school board pay attention to this research?" they might reason and ask. But administrators, too, are inclined to make decisions more on the basis of values and perspectives than research findings. Perhaps the answer is that research findings should not substitute for decisions that policymakers or administrators make. Instead, research findings should inform those decisions. It is in this way that stated policy becomes sensible and reasonable practice.

Administration Defined

Administration is generally defined as a process of working with and through others to accomplish school goals effectively and efficiently. There is a performance quality to most definitions of administration, and since resources are limited and decisions must be made as to how best to allocate these resources, efficiency becomes an additional quality.

A distinction is often made between administration and leadership. The school principal's job, for example, is to coordinate, direct, and support the work of others by defining objectives, evaluating performance, providing organizational resources, building a supportive psychological climate, running interference with parents, planning, scheduling, bookkeeping, resolving teacher conflicts, handling student problems, placating the central office, and otherwise helping to make things go. Many experts would consider these administrative, rather than leadership, activities. Administration, according to this view, refers to the normal behaviors associated with one's job. To Hemphill (1958), Lipham (1964), Kotter (1990), and Zaleznik (1977), the differences between the two can be seen in the behavior of leaders who initiate new structures, procedures, and goals. Leadership, they would suggest, emphasizes newness and change.

Zaleznick (1977), for example, describes leaders as follows:

They are active instead of reactive, shaping ideas instead of responding to them. Leaders adopt a personal and active attitude toward goals. The influence a leader exerts in altering moods, evoking images and expectations, and in establishing specific desires and objectives determines the direction a business takes. The net result of this influence is to change the way people think about what is desirable, possible, and necessary. (p. 1)

Though this distinction between administration and leadership has become widely accepted in the literature and has a number of advantages, on balance, negative consequences seem to dominate. Administration comes to be seen as a less essential, lower status activity, whereas leadership is viewed as superior. Further, the glamour of the leadership concept results in its receiving far more attention in the literature than may be warranted. As a result, administration is viewed as a routine, mundane and perhaps mechanical concept as writers glamorize leadership. This distinction leads to a literature that is often out of kilter with reality. This literature encourages unreasonable expectations for change for administrators; causes feelings of inferiority, anxiety, and guilt among them; and provides the public with unrealistic images of what administrators can actually do. Though administrators are important, for example, the fate of schools depends on teachers and others sharing the responsibility for leadership. In a sense, leadership is a form of social capital. The more this capital is shared, the more new leadership is created.

In our comments below we assume that leadership and administration are so interrelated that, practically speaking, both should be considered necessary and important variations in administrative style. The choice is not either leadership or administration, but a better balance between the two and a more realistic view of the possibilities for each. Important also are issues of education and the significance of educational leadership that focuses directly on problems and issues of curriculum, teaching, learning, and assessment. We argue that leadership qualities, missions, and roles in *education* should be examined as a set of concepts somewhat similar to but largely distinct from leadership and administration in general.

Taking the position that we should not overplay distinctions between management and leadership recognizes the value of both. We should note, however, that the two should not be balanced in the sense that each is assigned 50 percent. One should be at the center of our attention and work, and the other should be at the periphery. Unfortunately, it is management, not leadership, that dominates today's educational scene. Larry Cuban (1988), for example, argues:

> that schools as they are presently organized press teachers, principals, and superintendents toward managing rather than leading, toward maintaining what is rather than moving to what can be. The structures of schooling and the incentives buried within them produce a managerial imperative. The images, roles, and practices dominant in teaching, principaling, and superintending, shaped largely by the ways that public schools have been designed over the last century and a half, shrink the margin for the practice of leadership further. (p. xxi)

For leadership to emerge at the center and to flourish in schools, teachers and principals need to be able to have more choices than is now the case. Cuban explains, "From choice comes autonomy. Autonomy is the necessary condition for leadership to arise. Without choice, there is no autonomy. Without autonomy, there is no leadership" (p. xx).

In business and other settings, the terms *management* and *management behavior* are used to refer to administration and sometimes to both administration and leadership. As many of the references in this book suggest, much of the management literature is appropriate to educational administration (see, for example, Sergiovanni, 1990). In many respects, educational administration is a first cousin to public administration and carries with it some of the same traditions. In that field, the term *administration* is preferred over *management* because of the acknowledged intermingling of administration with policy. Administration is a "broad term involving policy-making as well as execution.... 'Management' involves the same intermingling of policy-making and execution but it is here assigned arbitrarily to a lower level and used to signify executive action with least policymaking significance" (Appleby, 1949, pp. 24–25). To many, the separation from policy makes management a form of script-following rather than script-writing. Script-following emphasizes doing things right rather than doing right things. This emphasis compromises the school administrator's governance and stewardship responsibilities (Selznick, 1957; Sergiovanni, 1990). The following sections review critical responsibilities of administrators, generally accepted administrative processes, and necessary administrative skills in an attempt to provide a basic overview, definition, statement of purpose, and conception of educational administration. Later, more specific attention is given to the educational administrator's responsibilities for providing educational leadership to his or her school community.

Critical Responsibilities of Administrators

To survive, all schools must be concerned with achieving their goals, maintaining themselves internally, being adaptive, and responding to their culture. These are the critical responsibilities that must be successfully assumed by principals, superintendents, and other administrators for their schools to function well. Argyris (1964) and Parsons (1951, 1960) view these as organizational core activities. The four are outlined below:

- Goals—goal attainment
- Norms—cultural patterns
- Morale/coordination—internal integration
- Change—external adaptation

To Parsons (1951, 1960), the four activities define the survival and growth requirements of social systems such as groups, organizations, communities, and societies. The core activities represent organizational imperatives because the neglect of any one can threaten the survival of the school. School administrators must experience certain levels of success in handling these critical responsibilities that define their roles.

Maintaining Cultural Patterns

Maintaining the school's cultural pattern is concerned with protecting and nurturing school and community traditions and cultural norms. School administrators and school-board members must be sensitive to the salient motivational and cultural patterns that exist in the community over time. These patterns are an important part of both the school's official and hidden curricula. School traditions emerge, images are fabricated and nurtured, and accepted ways of operating become established as a system of written and unwritten norms that provide a given school or school community with a distinct personality. Graduation ceremonies, football games, holiday programs, newsletters, and public-relations programs are some of the more visible ways of fabricating and maintaining cultural-pattern images, as are student-conduct codes, policy handbooks, and other public attempts to control the behavior of students. Often, the symbols of cultural patterns are more important than actual conditions. Some schools are known for their athletic prowess, others foster an elite academy image, and still others are thought of as well-rounded traditional schools where the ideal student is viewed as having a B average and being a cheerleader or an athlete, taking an active role on the yearbook, being prom king or queen, and later attending the local state university. Some of the most critical times for school administrators occur when cultural-pattern demands are in transition, often as a result of population shifts, desegregation mandates, or other abruptions in the normative character of the school community. Many experts believe that making changes that count in schools requires altering existing cultural patterns (Fullan, 1999).

Cultural patterns are expressed in the formal written and unwritten rules or codes that provide teachers, students, administrators, and others with expectations, norms, assumptions, and beliefs. They define the acceptable way of school and community life and give meaning to this life.

Attaining Goals

Goal attainment suggests administrative and school-board responsibilities that are direct and well understood—defining objectives and mobilizing resources to attain them. Because of its visibility, goal attainment becomes the public agenda for recruiting and evaluating administrators and board members, though in reality, judgments of ineffectiveness result most frequently from deficiencies in other responsibility areas, such as maintaining the school's cultural pattern.

Peshkin's (1977) account of the hiring of a new school superintendent in "Mansfield" illustrates the public acknowledgment of goal attainment criteria by a school board. But the board's real concern is maintaining the school/community's cultural pattern. And this concern is reflected in their making the hiring decision. Consider, for example, the following excerpts from school-board discussions in Mansfield following interviews of several candidates:

> Should we talk about Hagedorn to see why we don't want him?
>
> Yes, let's get the feeling of the board on him. I believe we have better men. Not quality-wise, though. He could handle the job and the P.R. (Public Relations). I don't think he's the type we're looking for.
>
> I hate to say it, but his physical appearance is against him. You need to call a spade a spade.
>
> He's not stable like some of the others.
>
> I'm afraid he'd be the brunt of behind-the-back jokes.
>
> He's carrying far too much weight. That's a strain on the heart.

He was tired. A man that size gets physically tired. We shouldn't kid our-selves. Image is very important. That size is against him.

The next one is Dargan.

I was impressed, but I feel he is too big for our town and school. His ideas are for the city, for bigger schools. We're not ready for all that.

I felt he would probably be anxious to start a lot of things I don't know if we're ready for. He's definitely for a nongraded system. He said he'd start slow, but he wanted it pretty bad. Knocking down walls scares you just a bit.

I was impressed, but then we had more fellows in. We learned more about this nongraded idea. He would be a pusher, I'm sure.

He had too many ideas to start off with. You need to see what a school has before jumping in.

I thought he might be a little slow with discipline problems.

I saw dollar signs clicking around in my head when he talked. He may be too intelligent for this community. He may talk over the heads of the community.

Another thing. He was emphatic about four weeks vacation.

Salary-wise he asked for the most.

Well, this Dargan, he said he wanted to come to a small community. I think he may want to bring too many ideas from the city with him. He may be more than we want.

What did you like about Morgan? These next three are a hard pick.

He gave a nice impression here, I believe, of getting along with the public and the kids. This impressed me more than anything.

To me he talked generalities.

He had a tremendous speaking voice. He's young.

His voice got very nasal at the end when he got relaxed.

He wouldn't stay.

I believe he'd be a forceful individual.

Take this other man, Rogers. I had a feeling about him. He said, "If you hired me and I accepted it." I don't think he's too anxious for the job.

I can see why he was offered a job selling real estate. He's got the voice. He'd have your name on the line. I'm inclined to believe he'd talk himself out of most sit-uations. Getting down to brass tacks, he spoke in generalities. He admitted he didn't know too much about new things in education. We need more specific answers.

More or less, this leaves us with Vitano.

He's the man to put on top.

I'd hate to pick any of the top three over the others.

Both Vitano and Rogers said that they have no hours. They work by the job. Vitano worked his way through college.

He was on ground floor as far as salary goes.

And he's country. (pp. 187–188)*

Though the board had established public selection criteria around the theme of goal attainment, its actual criteria revolved around the cultural-pattern theme. Dargan, for example, was considered by the board to be overqualified and too cos-mopolitan, though his goal-attainment qualifications were acknowledged. Hage-

*Source: A. Peshkin, "Whom Shall the Schools Serve? Some Dilemmas of Local Control in a Rural School District," *Curriculum Inquiry, 6*(3), 186–188. Copyright 1977. Reprinted by permission.

dorn, despite goal-attainment qualifications, just did not "look right" to the board. He did not fit their image of a good superintendent. Morgan and Rogers are rejected for similar reasons. As Peshkin (1977) notes, "Perhaps it should have been self-evident that no one could be chosen Superintendent of Schools in Mansfield who did not appear 'country,' the board's short-hand term to describe a person who would be suitable for their rural dominated, traditionally oriented school" (p. 188). Vitano was the candidate who best fit Mansfield's cultural pattern.

Adapting to External Environment

A third area of critical responsibility for school administrators reflects the need for schools and communities to adapt to their external environments. Communities change and schools change with them. The advance of technology and the evolution of political processes place enormous pressures on schools. Coping with environmental demands for change as a result of large increases or declines in enrollment, for example, requires substantial changes in finance formulas, personnel policies, organizational structures, facility usages, district boundary lines, teacher-association—board contracts, and educational-program designs. The challenge for school administrators and boards is to adapt externally in a fashion that preserves some sense of internal identity, continuity, and balance. A growing literature deals with adaptation problems of schools from the perspectives of politics and public policy, the sociology and politics of innovation, and the social psychology of change (see, for example, Hargreaves and Lieberman, 1998).

Maintaining Internal Integration

Maintaining internal maintenance requires the coordination and unification of units, departments, and schools into a coherent entity. Psychologically, internal maintenance refers to the building of a sense of identity and loyalty to the school among teachers and students and providing them with a sense of satisfaction and well-being in return. Some theorists have defined administrative effectiveness around the internal-maintenance theme by suggesting that effectiveness is the integration of individual and organizational needs; indeed, this social-systems theme dominated the literature of educational administration during the 1950s and 1960s (e.g., Getzels, Lipham, & Campbell, 1968). More recently, studies of successful schools reveal the presence of a strong culture that bonds teachers to a common purpose and provides them with increased opportunities for finding meaning in work (see, for example, Sergiovanni, 1984, 2001). These schools are highly successful in tending to cultural patterns and the maintenance of internal integration.

Balancing Core Areas

Different schools and school districts can be expected to emphasize different patterns of core activities in response to their unique situational characteristics, but all four areas must be provided for to some degree by all schools and school districts. Following Parsons, Bales, and Shils (1953) and Deutsch (1963), Mills (1967) suggests that core-activity patterns under conditions of survival are different from those under conditions of growth. The *survival pattern* will look something like the following:*

1. Adaptation—*when external resources are cut off, the group must be able to find new ones; when current techniques become obsolete or ineffective, it must invent new ones.*
2. Goal attainment—*when blocks appear before the goal, it must be able to circumvent them; when members become confused or frustrated or distracted, it must be able to reorient them and remobilize their resources.*
3. Integration—*when one part of the group threatens to destroy other parts, the group must be able to check, protect, and coordinate them; it must bridge differences between the strong and the weak, the competent and the inept, the active and the passive, and so on; it must create concepts or symbols of itself as a collective unit that unites its sub-parts.*
4. Pattern-maintenance—*in the face of contrary pressures, the group must be able to sustain its standard procedures, reinforce members' feelings and affective relations, enforce its rules, confirm its beliefs and affirm its values; and it must, for example, be able to "remember" its customs from one meeting to the next.* (Mills, 1967, p. 17)

By contrast, the *growth pattern* will resemble the following:*

1. Adaptation
   a. *"An increase in openness—that is, an increase in the range, diversity, and effectiveness of [a group's] channels of intake of information from the outside world"* (Deutsch, 1963, p. 140)
   b. *Capacity to extend the scope of the group's contacts and obligations beyond current boundaries*
   c. *Capacity to alter the group's customs, rules, techniques, and so on, to accommodate new information and new contacts*
2. Goal attainment
   a. *Capacity to hold goal-seeking effort in abeyance while alternative goals are being considered*
   b. *Capacity to shift to, or add, new goals*
3. Integration
   a. *Capacity to differentiate into sub-parts while maintaining collective unity*
   b. *Capacity to export resources without becoming impoverished and to send emissaries without losing their loyalty*
4. Pattern-maintenance and extension
   a. *Capacity to receive new members and to transmit to them the group's culture and capabilities*
   b. *Capacity to formulate in permanent form the group's experience and learning and to convey them to other groups and to posterity* (Mills, 1967, p. 21)

*Both patterns are from Theodore M. Mills, *The Sociology of Small Groups.* © 1967, pp. 17, 21. Reprinted by permission of Prentice Hall, Inc. Englewood Cliffs, New Jersey.

The problem becomes more complex with the realization that too much emphasis in one area can often jeopardize the other areas. For example, an overemphasis on internal maintenance may actually jeopardize goal attainment, and an overemphasis on external adaptation can often upset the maintenance of cultural patterns. In the first instance, consider a school that agrees to a policy of teacher supervision and evaluation that emphasizes the development of good human relations and high morale among the teachers (internal maintenance) at the expense of providing teachers with sufficient responsibility, evaluative feedback, and other performance results (goal attainment). Adopting the inverse strategy is also problematic. Imagine a school with what it considers to be "effective" supervision and evaluation of teachers that destroys their morale. In the second instance, consider a school that responds to its perception of societal needs by implementing an educational program characterized by individualized instruction and an abundance of student alternatives (external adaption) but in so doing projects an image of permissiveness and anarchy to a community with a more traditional conception of schooling (maintaining community cultural patterns). Here, adapting to the perceived needs of society in general is at odds with the prevailing value system of the local community.

As even a brief study of educational administration will reveal, progress is slow and incremental. Administrative activity takes place within time constraints. Typically, administrators are not able to wait until everything is perfect before making or implementing decisions. Compromises are more the rule. Satisfactory solutions that are agreeable under current circumstances are accepted in favor of better or ideal solutions that are not possible at the moment. Each of the four organizational imperatives, therefore, are better seen as having qualities of elasticity that enable stretching and contracting. By capitalizing on this elastic quality, administrators seek to balance one critical responsibility area against another without forcing one or neglecting another to the point where survival of the school is endangered.

Evaluating Administrators

The four critical responsibility areas provide the basis for the evaluation of school administrators. Superintendents are evaluated by their school boards and communities based on perceptions of their performance in all four areas, though goal attainment is likely to be the public standard and other areas more implicitly considered. Superintendents evaluate principals similarly (Peterson, 1984). Principals, in turn, use the same general pattern to evaluate teachers (Cusick, 1983).

Principals, as an example, are presumed to be evaluated primarily on the basis of goal-attainment criteria. Much attention is given to educational goals and objectives they are expected to pursue and to evaluation designs attendant to the quality of teaching and learning and to student learning outcomes. The intent is to link what principals do to various dimensions of successful student learning and other goal-attainment indicators. Peterson (1984), however, finds that principals generally perceive goal attainment to be secondary to criteria that emerge from cultural patterns, maintaining internal integration, and the external environment.

He notes, for example, that half of the 120 elementary principals studied believed that the central office relied heavily on the community and impressions of parents as sources of evaluation information (p. 592). Indeed, "public reaction, parents are happy, no complaints, and public relations" accounted for 207 of the items mentioned. By contrast, "student performance and progress: test scores, academic performance" and "instructional programs: innovation, good programs, instructional leadership" accounted for only 9 percent and 8 percent, respectively (Peterson, 1984, p. 593). The full array of evaluation criteria as perceived by principals is shown in Table 3.1. The fourth column in Table 3.1 indicates which of the critical responsibility areas are most associated with each criterion. The table suggests that, despite the rhetoric, goal attainment alone is too simplistic an indicator of what constitutes the typical school administrator's agenda.

Dimensions and Measures of School Effectiveness

The criteria used to evaluate administrators and the four critical responsibility areas to which they must attend suggests that despite simplistic definitions of school effectiveness that focus on student outcomes, many dimensions actually exist. Schools, for example, must not only attain teaching and learning goals but must do so efficiently and in a manner that keeps faculty morale high, order in the school, and peace in the community. In light of this reality, school measurement and evaluation experts and organizational sociologists who specialize in studying effectiveness in organizations concentrate on many dimensions as they conduct their studies and make their calculations (Goodman & Associates, 1977). Most experts agree that school effectiveness is multidimensional. Table 3.2 illustrates some of the criteria and measurements that are often used in determining how effective a school is. Note that only seven of the twenty-four measures are classified as goal attainment (GA).

Critical Administrative Processes

Administration has been broadly defined as the process of working with and through others to accomplish organizational goals and to successfully assume the other three critical responsibilities effectively and efficiently. Administration can also be defined as a process of functions. *Planning, organizing, leading,* and *controlling* are the four functions that have traditionally been most often mentioned by theorists (e.g., Gulick & Urwick, 1937; Koontz & O'Donnell, 1972; Sears, 1950).

Planning involves setting goals and objectives for the school and district and developing blueprints and strategies for their implementation. *Organizing* involves bringing together human, financial, and physical resources in the most effective way to accomplish goals. *Leading* has to do with guiding and supervising

TABLE 3.1 Criteria Perceived to Be Important When Central Office Evaluates Principals

Criteria	Number of Times Category Mentioned by Respondents ($N = 360$)	Percentage of Respondents Listing Item ($N = 112$)	Percentage of All Items Mentioned	Critical Responsibility Areas
1. Public reaction: parents are happy, no complaints, public relations	72	64	30	CP, EA
2. Teacher reaction: good morale, no grievances, teacher-principal relations	54	48	15	II
3. Principal and teacher compliance to district rules and procedures; includes meeting attendance and paperwork	44	39	12	CP, II
4. Not making waves: smooth running, few problems taken to central office, keeping superintendent informed, not raising difficult questions	37	33	10	CP, EA, II
5. Student performance and progress: test scores, academic performance	31	28	9	GA
6. The instructional program: innovation, good programs, instructional leadership	29	26	8	GA
7. Overall school operation: includes atmosphere and climate	21	19	6	II
8. Relations with students, student compliance, and discipline	14	12	4	CP
9. Good working relations with central office	7	6	2	CP, EA
10. Miscellaneous 1: includes plant management, leadership style, peer relations	25	22	7	
11. Miscellaneous 2: all single items	26	23	7	
Critical responsibility areas:	Cultural patterns (CP) External adaptation (EA) Maintaining internal integration (II) Goal attainment (GA)			

Source: Adapted from "Mechanisms of Administrative Control Over Managers in Educational Organizations" by K. D. Peterson, 1984, published in *Administrative Science Quarterly, 9*(4), p. 593 by permission of *Administrative Science Quarterly.* Copyright © 1984 by Cornell University.

Note: The critical responsibility areas are added to Peterson's table.

TABLE 3.2   Dimensions and Measures of School Effectiveness

Dimensions	Measures	Critical Responsibility Areas
1. *Productivity*	The extent to which students, teachers, groups, and schools accomplish outcomes or services intended. Productivity contains many dimensions but is usually measured by examining student test scores.	GA
2. *Efficiency*	The ratio of individual and school performance to the costs involved for that performance. Costs are calculated not only in terms of time and dollars but in objectives or outcomes neglected so that other objectives or outcomes might be emphasized or accomplished. Small schools, for example, may be a little more expensive to operate but they can still be more cost-effective than larger schools if students learn significantly more. It is the amount of learning that schools get for a given cost, not the number of students served, that counts the most.	II
3. *Quality*	The level and quality of accomplishments, outcomes, performance, and services of individuals and the school. Some educational experts, for example, believe that exhibitions of student performance are higher quality indicators of student performance than just test scores.	GA
4. *Growth*	Improvements in quality of offerings, responsiveness and innovativeness, talent, and general competence, when a school's present status is compared with its own past state. Growth in learning occurs, for example, when schools are able to add value to what students already know.	GA
5. *Absenteeism*	The number of times not present and frequency of nonattendance by teachers, students, and other school workers.	II
6. *Turnover*	The number of voluntary transfers and terminations on the part of students, faculty, and other workers.	II
7. *Teacher job satisfaction*	The extent to which teachers are pleased with the various job outcomes they are receiving.	II
8. *Student satisfaction*	The extent to which students are pleased with the learning and caring they are receiving and with the overall school experience.	II
9. *Motivation*	The willingness and drive strength of teachers, students, and other school workers as they engage in the work of the school at a high level and with little supervision.	II

TABLE 3.2 **Continued**

Dimensions	Measures	Critical Responsibility Areas
10. *Morale*	The general good feeling that teachers, parents, students, and others have for the school, its traditions, and its goals and the extent to which they are happy to be a part of the school.	CP
11. *Cohesion*	The extent to which students and teachers like one another, work well together, communicate fully and openly, coordinate their efforts and approximate a community of relationships.	CP
12. *Flexibility-adaptation*	The ability of the school to change its procedures and ways of operating in response to community and other environmental changes.	EA
13. *Planning and goal setting*	The degree to which the members plan future steps and engage in goal-setting behavior.	GA
14. *Goal consensus*	The extent to which community members, parents, and students agree that the same goals exist for the school.	CP
15. *Internalization of organizational goals*	The acceptance of the school's goals and belief by parents, teachers, and students that the school's goals are right and proper.	CP
16. *Leadership-management skills*	The overall level of ability of principals, supervisors, and other leaders as they perform school-centered tasks.	GA
17. *Information management and communications*	The completeness, efficiency of dissemination, and accuracy of information considered critical to the school's effectiveness by all interested parties, including teachers, parents, and the community at large.	II
18. *Readiness*	The probability that the school could successfully perform some specified task or accomplish some specified goal if asked to do so.	EA
19. *Utilization of the environment*	The extent to which the school interacts successfully with its community and with other arenas of its environment and acquires the necessary support and resources to function effectively.	EA
20. *Evaluation by external entities*	Favorable assessments of the school by individuals, organizations, and groups in the community and in the general environment within which it interacts.	EA
21. *Stability*	The ability of the school to maintain certain structures, functions, and resources over time and particularly during periods of stress.	CP

(continued)

TABLE 3.2   Continued

Dimensions	Measures	Critical Responsibility Areas
22. *Shared influence*	The degree to which individuals in the school participate in making decisions that affect them directly.	II
23. *Training and development emphasis*	The amount of effort and resources that the school devotes to developing the talents of teachers and other school workers.	GA
24. *Achievement emphasis*	The extent to which the school places a high value on achieving existing and new goals.	GA
Critical responsibility areas:	Cultural patterns (CP) External adaptation (EA) Internal integration (II) Goal attainment (GA)	

Source: Adapted from J. P. Campbell et al., *The Measurement of Organizational Effectiveness: A Review of Relevant Research and Opinion.* Final Report, Navy Personnel Research and Development Center Contract N00022-73-C-0023. (Minneapolis: Personnel Decisions, 1974), pp. 38–133.

subordinates. Plans of organizations are implemented by people, and people need to be motivated, expectations need to be defined, and communication channels need to be maintained. *Controlling* refers to the administrator's evaluation functions and includes reviewing, regulating, and controlling performance, providing feedback, and otherwise tending to standards of goal attainment and internal-maintenance responsibilities of administration, with some attention to external adaptation. Maintaining the school's cultural-pattern responsibilities is typically neglected by those who write about administrative processes. These functions are generic and thus apply to administrative work in a variety of settings. When applied to the school, the four functions are ideally directed to defining and enhancing teaching and learning.

Critical Administrative Skills

Still another way in which administration can be examined is by identifying competencies and skill areas necessary for carrying out the processes of administration. Katz (1955) has identified three basic skills on which, he feels, successful administration rests—technical, human, and conceptual.

Technical skill assumes an understanding of and proficiency in the methods, processes, procedures, and techniques of teaching and learning, curriculum and assessment. Noninstructional technical skills include knowledge in finance, accounting, scheduling, purchasing, construction, and maintenance. Instructional technical skills are more important to administrative and supervisory roles "lower" in the school hierarchy. Typically the department chairperson or grade-level supervisor, needs far greater command of technical skills relating to teaching and learning in a particular field than does the principal. The business manager needs a more technical command of accounting procedures and computer uses than does the superintendent.

Human skill refers to the school administrator's ability to work effectively and efficiently with others on a one-to-one basis and in group settings. This skill requires considerable self-understanding and acceptance as well as appreciation, empathy, and consideration for others. Its knowledge base includes an understanding of and facility for leadership, adult motivation, attitudinal development, group dynamics, human needs, morale, conflict management, and the development of human resources. Human skills seem equally important to administrative and supervisory roles throughout the school hierarchy. Regardless of position, all administrators work through others; that is, they use human skills to achieve goals.

Conceptual skill includes the school administrator's ability to view the school, the district, and the educational program as a whole. This skill includes the effective mapping of interdependence for each of the components of the school as an organization, the educational program as an instructional system, and the functioning of the human organization. The development of conceptual skill relies heavily on a balanced emphasis of administrative theory, knowledge of organizational and human behavior, educational philosophy, and knowledge about teaching and learning. Conceptual skills are considered more important to roles further up the organizational hierarchy. The superintendent, for example, may not know much about the technical aspects of teaching youngsters with learning disabilities to read but must know how this piece of the puzzle fits and interacts with other aspects of operating the school district.

Figure 3.1 summarizes the dimensions of educational administration. The four critical responsibility areas are listed on the left margin, and the four critical processes on the bottom margin. Together, they form a sixteen-cell, two-dimensional grid for mapping administrative activity. The shaded area, which marks the intersection of maintaining cultural patterns with the controlling functions, might be illustrated by an administrator who is surveying community attitudes toward a particular school policy or program. The grid becomes three dimensional when the three critical administrative skills are added. In surveying community attitudes, for example, the administrator needs to know the technical rudiments of survey conducting and reporting. Human skills will be needed in obtaining public participation in the project and in resolving disputes that might be evident in the survey. Conceptually, the administrator needs to understand the implications of the intended and unintended consequences of the survey on educational program planning, the school's public relations program, and other factors. Additional insights into the role and function of educational administrators—which highlight needed competencies, specific tasks, and descriptions of how administrators actually spend their time—are provided in later chapters.

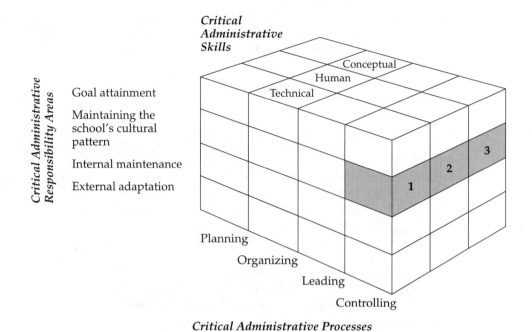

FIGURE 3.1   **Mapping Educational Administration**

Educational Administration as Educational Leadership

Before proceeding further, the important topic of educational leadership and its relationship to administration will be considered. It will become increasingly clear that administrative responsibilities are vast and encompass a variety of roles and an array of problems and issues—many of which seem not to be clearly or directly related to education.

Increasingly, for example, educational administrators are portrayed as managers. School boards and community publics demand sound fiscal management and expect the school to be run in a businesslike fashion. Indeed, such topics as cost-effectiveness, accountability, fiscal integrity, efficiency, wage administration, and personnel policy capture increasingly large shares of the headlines in education. Rivaling the manager image of education administration is that of politician. On the local scene, for example, communities are more diverse, expectations and demands for resources are more ambiguous and vocal, power and authority are more diffuse, and public participation in the affairs of the schools is more intense. At a broader level, the strengthened role of state education departments—through mandated legislation, the federal government, and the courts—and the shifts in school-funding patterns that afford greater responsibility to federal and state levels are further reinforcers of the politician image for educational administration. Educational leadership often gets squeezed out by the urgency and complexity of other problems of schooling.

Managerial, Political, and Educational Roles

Though many decry the emergence of managerial and political roles in educational administration, the inescapable realities of modern educational administration require that administrators understand and articulate these roles. But to borrow a metaphor from management, the *bottom line* for educational administrators remains *educational leadership.* Management roles, therefore, though critically important, are not central. Indeed, they exist only to support and complement the educational leadership roles needed to enhance student learning.

By the same token, political roles are supplements to and supporters of educational governance roles. Both leadership and governance have qualities beyond what presently is; they suggest a vision of what is desirable and good and a determination to marshal organizational energy in this direction. Leaders and statespersons, however, cannot neglect managerial and political roles. Still, good management and good politics are not in themselves sufficient.

Perhaps the point can best be made by focusing in detail on the educational leadership aspects of educational administration and contrasting these with good management. Levitt (1976), for example, describes management as follows:

> Management consists of the rational assessment of a situation and the systematic selection of goals and purposes (what is to be done?); the systematic development of strategies to achieve these goals; the marshalling of the required resources; the rational design, organization, direction, and control of the activities required to attain the selected purposes; and, finally, the motivating and rewarding of people to do the work. (p. 73)

The administrator as manager, according to this view, is concerned with such questions as, What should be accomplished? and How are best results achieved? Certainly these are important considerations in the effective operation of schools and school districts. But as Zaleznik (1977) points out, "It takes neither genius nor heroism to be a manager, but rather persistence, tough-mindedness, hard work, intelligence, analytical ability and, perhaps most important, tolerance and good will" (p. 68).

Educational leadership, by contrast, is a more expansive concept that includes concern for the worth of objectives and their impact on school and society. The administrator as manager suggests a utilitarian quality (What are the best means to achieve given ends?); educational leadership suggests a normative quality (How adequate are the ends themselves?). Beyond concern for the value of objectives and the overall mission of the school, leadership evokes a quality of living and attractiveness that moves individuals and organizations beyond the ordinary in their zeal, commitment, and work habits. As Zaleznik (1977) suggests, leaders

> are active instead of reactive, shaping ideas instead of responding to them. Leaders adopt a personal and active attitude toward goals. The influence a leader exerts in altering moods, evoking images and expectations, and in establishing specific desires and objectives determines the direction.... The net result of this influence is to change the way people think about what is desirable, possible, and necessary. (p. 71)

Earlier we suggested that little is gained and much is lost by disparaging management and being grandiose about leadership. In seeking a balance between the two, Starratt (1990) suggests that it might be helpful to view the educational administrator as being an actor with two parts to play. Each of the parts, educational leader and manager, comes with its own and very different script. When following the managerial script, the administrator is concerned with instrumental and process matters articulated in accordance with the values of bureaucracy:

> (a) Students and teachers should be treated uniformly; (b) policies and rules are applied uniformly for all specific instances; (c) because of scarce resources, the school must get the most for every dollar by concentrating on efficiency; (d) the school-wide results are what counts (improving test scores, lowering overall truancy and vandalism, achieving overall budgetary balance); (e) in order to assess overall results, there is a need for maintaining extensive records and information banks and reports; (f) loyalty to the school, rather than to individuals or groups is important; (g) one's sense of authority derives from the wider governing body, and is based on the organization's charter and by-laws. (p. 47)

When following the educational leader script, by contrast, the administrator is concerned with matters of purpose and substance, with struggling to identify the right thing to do, with creating the designs and pathways that help schools work to improve student learning and to accomplish other learning goals. The administrator strives to bring to the forefront the kind of rationality that is based on what makes sense educationally and what is morally right. It makes sense, for example, to treat teachers and students differently, to provide teachers with discretion so that they are able to make informed decisions in light of the situations that they face, and so on. As with the actor, sometimes the professional administrator is able to bring the scripts into harmony. At other times, they tug at each other and often the wrong one becomes dominant.

Qualitative Aspects of Leadership

Having established that educational leadership requires good management but that good management is not sufficient, the nature of leadership will now be examined more closely. Starratt (1977), for example, suggests that, in addition to management skill, the leader brings to her or his work extra qualities of vision, intensity, and creativity. Leaders are concerned with a vision of what is possible and desirable for them and others to achieve and a vision of the significance of what they are presently doing. The leader engages in organizational activities with great energy and brings to the job an intensity of desire, commitment, and enthusiasm that sets him or her apart from others. The leader brings to the organization and its work a certain freshness of thought, a commitment to new ideas, and a belief in creativity change. Concentrating on the qualities of vision, intensity, and creativity, Starratt (1977) believes that leaders can be distinguished from others as follows:

1. Leaders work beneath the surface of events and activities, seeking a deeper meaning and deeper value. They are able to identify the roots of meaning in the ebb and flow of daily life in schools and, as a result, to provide students, teachers, and community members with a sense of importance, vision, and purpose above the seemingly ordinary and mundane.
2. Leaders bring to the school a sense of drama in human life that permits one to surface above the dulling routine which often characterizes day-by-day activity. They see the significance of what a group is doing and could be doing. They have a feel for the more dramatic possibilities inherent in most situations and are able to urge people to go beyond the routine, to break out of the mold into something more lively and vibrant.
3. Leaders are able to communicate their sense of vision by words and examples. They use language and symbols which are easily understood but which also communicate a sense of excitement, originality, and freshness.
4. Leaders provide opportunities for others to experience their vision and sense of purpose so that others come to share in their ownership.
5. Leaders are able to transform their vision, intensity, and creativity from idiosyncratic or personal meanings into goals, structures, and processes for the school. Ideas become programs, visions become goals, and senses of commitment from others become operating structures. Indeed the leader translates qualities of leadership into characteristics of the school as an organization. (p. 5)

Bennis (1984) finds that compelling vision is the key ingredient of leadership among heads of highly successful organizations he studied. *Vision* refers to the capacity to create and communicate a view of the desired state of affairs that induces commitment among those working in the organization. Vision becomes the substance of what is communicated as symbolic aspects of leadership are emphasized. Lieberman and Miller (1984) refer to this as the power of "moral authority." The school administrator makes symbolic statements by his or her actions, statements, and deeds. In describing this power from case-study notes involving a student discrimination incident, they state:

> Principals can maintain neutrality and let things progress as they always have; even that is a moral statement. Or they may take an active stance, threatening the assumptions of staff members and moving the school in more progressive or more regressive directions. Principals condone or condemn certain behaviors and attitudes; they model moral precepts as they go about their job. When the administrators at

Albion took the side of minority students in the lunchroom radio incident, they gave a clear message to faculty that discrimination by race was not to be tolerated. A powerful message was transmitted. Had there been administrative apathy, an equally powerful point would have been made. (p. 76)

Principals and other school administrators are cast into powerful symbolic roles whether they intend it or not and whether they like it or not. Taking no action, in certain circumstances, can be as powerful a symbolic statement as taking any action.

Bennis (1984, p. 64) and Bennis and Nanus (1985, p. 17) view leadership as a form of power that represents one's capacity to translate intention into reality and sustain it. This is the idea of transformative leadership described in Burns's seminal *Leadership* (1978). This is also what Follett (1941) had in mind when she wrote, "The most successful leader of all is one who sees another picture not yet actualized. He sees the things which belong in his present picture, but which are not yet there.... Above all, he should make his co-workers see that it is not *his* purpose which is to be achieved, but a common purpose, born of the desires and activities of the group" (pp. 143–144).

Studies of leadership in highly successful and effective schools provides support for the importance of vision and other qualitative aspects of leadership. The work of Edmonds (1979) and of Brookover and Lezotte (1979) reveals that effective schools are characterized by high agreement among staff regarding goals and purposes and a clear sense of mission. Similarly, studies by Bossert and colleagues (1982) and Greenfield (1982) reveal that goal orientation and the articulation and modeling of school purposes by principals are important characteristics. The research of Blumberg and Greenfield (1980) reveals that effective principals show active and direct behaviors at building and articulating a vision of what the school is. Lipsitz (1984), in her case studies of successful middle schools, observes:

The schools made powerful statements both in word and in practice, about their purposes. There is little disagreement within them and little discrepancy between what they say they are doing and what they are actually doing. As a result everyone can articulate what the school stands for....

Each of the four schools has or had a principal with a driving vision who imbues decisions and practices with meaning, placing powerful emphasis on why things are done as well as how. Decisions are not made just because they are practical but for reasons of principle. (pp. 172, 174)

In sum, leaders are able to grasp the deeper meaning and value of seemingly common events, translate these into a dramatic sense of purpose and vision, convincingly communicate both meaning and purpose to others, obtain their commitment and sense of partnership, and articulate these qualities into organizational goals, structures, and programs (Sergiovanni, 1990). Managerial skills remain important, for once programs are identified, they need to be effectively and efficiently articulated.

It is clear that defining leadership is a little more complex than one might at first think. There are many meanings to leadership. Some of them are summarized in Table 3.3. It is no easy task to identify a single view of leadership that beats all other views all the time. Probably each of the meanings for leadership has roles to play. As you review the meanings, distribute twenty points across the five to indicate the extent to which you think each is important. Which of the five best captures the leadership approach of your principal? Share your point distribution with others and get their reaction.

The Substance of Leadership in Education

Some qualities of leadership are universal to all types of organizations. Hospital, business, military, governmental, and educational administrator-leaders, for example, bring to their respective organizations common qualities of vision, intensity, and creativity. The substantive aspects of leadership, on the other hand, have to do with the unique and central context of the work of a particular organization. Educational program, curriculum and instruction, teaching and learning, and supervision and evaluation are the central concerns of schools, and these comprise the substance of educational leadership.

One problem with recent trends toward pressuring educational administrators to assume more managerial and political roles is that these have become central, displacing educational roles. Goodlad (1978) describes this problem as follows:

> Recent years have been harrowing ones for school administrators. We have yielded to the pressures and temptations of becoming experts in fiscal and personnel management, public relations, collective bargaining, and the political process. Few of us are trained or experienced in any of these, even though we must take responsi-

---

TABLE 3.3 **Meanings for Leadership**

- Leadership means influencing parents, teachers, and students to follow the leader's vision (see, for example, Bennis & Nanus [1985] on visionary leadership).
- Leadership means influencing parents, teachers, and students to identify, understand, and find solutions to the problems that they face (see, for example, Heifetz [1994] on learning and problem-solving leadership).
- Leadership means not only pursuing useful goals that meet the needs of parents, teachers, and students, but goals that elevate them to a higher moral level (see, for example, Burns [1978] on transformational leadership).
- Leadership means enhancing purpose, meaning, and significance that parents, teachers, and students experience by serving shared ideas and ideals (see, for example, Sergiovanni [1992] on moral leadership).
- Leadership means being practical by selecting means to achieve purposes that take into account the loosely connected, messy, and generally nonlinear characteristics of schools (see, for example, Cohen and March [1974] on educational organizations as organized anarchies).

Source: Sergiovanni, T. J. (2001). Leadership: *What's in it for schools?* London: Routledge Falmer, p. 76. ©TJS.

bility for them.... It is now time to put the right things at the center again. And the right things have to do with assuring comprehensive, quality educational programs in each and every school under our jurisdiction. (p. 322)

Continuing, Goodlad (1978) feels that serious steps need to be taken to reverse this trend.

One step is to check our present perspectives regarding what is central to our work. If, in so doing, we conclude that collective bargaining, balancing the budget, and informing the public are central, something has gone amiss. These are the conditions surrounding, complicating and, perhaps, endangering our jobs. We ignore them at our peril; we would be well advised to attend special institutes or workshops so as to be thoroughly updated on the issues and our role in dealing with them. But to put these matters at the center, often for understandable reasons of survival and expediency, is to commit a fundamental error which, ultimately, will have a negative impact on both education and one's own career. Our work, for which we will be held accountable, is to maintain, justify, and articulate sound, comprehensive programs of instruction for children and youth. (p. 326)

Certainly Goodlad's arguments are persuasive, but keeping matters of educational program central to one's roles is not easy. A first step is to make a commitment to educational leadership, viewing managerial and political roles as important to educational leadership but not as ends in themselves.

What can one expect from making a commitment to educational leadership? Some evidence exists that such a commitment is at the heart of noticeable differences between effective and ineffective educational administrators. In a study of effective and ineffective elementary school principals conducted by Goldhammer and associates (1971), principals of effective schools had the following characteristics in common:

1. Most did not intend to become principals. Most indicated that they had intended to teach, but were encouraged to become principals by their superiors.
2. Most expressed a sincere faith in children. Children were not criticized for failing to learn or for having behavioral difficulties. The principals felt that these were problems that the school was established to correct; thus the administrators emphasized their responsibilities toward the solution of children's problems.
3. They had an ability to work effectively with people and to secure their cooperation. They were proud of their teachers and accepted them as professionally dedicated and competent people. They inspired confidence and developed enthusiasm. The principals used group processes effectively; listened well to parents, teachers, and pupils; and appeared to have intuitive skill and empathy for their associates.
4. They were aggressive in securing recognition of the needs of their schools. They frequently were critical of the restraints imposed by the central office and of the inadequate resources. They found it difficult to live within the constraints of the bureaucracy; they frequently violated the chain of command, seeking relief of their problems from whatever sources that were potentially useful.

5. They were enthusiastic as principals and accepted their responsibilities as a mission rather than as a job. They recognized their role in current social problems. The ambiguities that surrounded them and their work were of less significance than the goals they felt were important to achieve. As a result, they found it possible to live with the ambiguities of their position.
6. They were committed to education and could distinguish between long-term and short-term educational goals. Consequently, they had established philosophies of the role of education and their relationship within it.
7. They were adaptable. If they discovered something was not working, they could make the necessary shifts and embark with some security on new paths.
8. They were able strategists. They could identify their objectives and plan means to achieve them. They expressed concern for the identification of the most appropriate procedures through which change could be secured. (p. 233)

These characteristics suggest that effective principals were certainly concerned with good management and politics, but clearly, educational leadership was their paramount concern. This observation is supported by numerous studies of effective and successful schools. A fundamental assumption underlying this book is that managerial and political roles, no matter how important, must be judged on the basis of how they serve educational-leadership aspirations of administration. Indeed, this is the yardstick by which one assesses the usefulness and appropriateness of further administrative study in such areas of law, finance, facilities, politics, organizational behavior, and other topics.

The good news is that during the last decade educational administration has taken a sharp turn toward emphasizing educational leadership and specifically the improvement of student achievement as measured by tests and other means. This turn will be chronicled in the next chapter as we examine the development of educational administration and its status as a profession.

REFERENCES

Appleby, P. H. (1949). *Policy and administration.* Tuscaloosa: University of Alabama Press.

Argyris, C. (1964). *Integrating the individual and the organization.* New York: John Wiley.

Bennis, W. (1984). Transformative power and leadership. In T. J. Sergiovanni & J. E. Corbally (Eds.), *Leadership and organizational culture* (pp. 64–71). Urbana: University of Illinois Press.

Bennis, W., & Nanus, B. (1985). *Leaders: The strategies for taking charge.* New York: Harper & Row.

Blumberg, A., & Greenfield, W. (1980). *The effective principal. Perspective on school leadership.* Boston: Allyn and Bacon.

Bossert, S. T., Dwyer, D., Rowan, B., & Lee, G. (1982). The instructional management role of the principal. *Educational Administration Quarterly, 3*(18), 34–64.

Brookover, W. B., & Lezotte, L. W. (1979). *Changes in school characteristics coincident with changes in school achievement.* East Lansing, MI: Institute for Research on Teaching, Michigan State University.

Burns, J. M. (1978). *Leadership.* New York: Harper & Row.

Cohen, M. D., & March, J. G. (1974). *Leadership and ambiguity: The American college president.* New York: McGraw-Hill.

Cuban, L. (1988). *The managerial imperative and the practice of leadership in schools.* Albany: SUNY Press.

Cusick, P. A. (1983). *The egalitarian ideal and the American high school.* New York: Longman.

Deutsch, K. W. (1963). *The nerves of government.* New York: The Free Press of Glencoe.

Edmonds, R. (1979). Some schools work and more can. *Social Policy, 9*(2), 28–32.

Follett, M. P. (1941). *Dynamic administration.* New York: Harper & Row.

Fullan, M. (1999). *Change forces: The sequel.* London: Falmer Press.

Getzels, J. W., Lipham, J., & Campbell, R. (1968). *Educational administration: A social process.* New York: Harper & Row.

Goldhammer, K., Becker, G., Withycombe, R., Doget, F., Miller, E., Morgan, C., DeLoretto, L., & Aldridge, B. (1971). *Elementary school principals and their schools.* Eugene, OR: University of Oregon, Center for the Advanced Study of Educational Administration.

Goodlad, J. I. (1978). Educational leadership: Toward the third era. *Educational Leadership, 35*(4), 319–323.

Goodman, P. S., & Associates. (1977). *New perspectives on organizational effectiveness.* San Francisco: Jossey-Bass.

Goodnow, F. J. (1900). *Politics and administration.* New York: Macmillan.

Goodnow, F. J. (1905). *The principles of administrative law in the United States.* New York: G. P. Putnam.

Greenfield, W. (1982). *A synopsis of research on school principals.* Washington, DC: National Institute of Education.

Gulick, L., & Urwick, L. (Eds.). (1937). *Papers on the science of administration.* New York: Institute for Public Administration.

Hargreaves, A., & Lieberman, A. (Eds.) (1998). *International Handbook of Educational Change.* Vol. 5. Boston: Kluwer Academic.

Heifetz, R. A. (1994). *Leadership without easy answers.* Cambridge, MA: Harvard University Press.

Hemphill, J. K. (1958). Administration as problem-solving. In A. Halpin (Ed.), *Administrative theory in education.* Chicago: Midwest Administration Center, University of Chicago.

Katz, R. L. (1955). Skills of an effective administrator. *Harvard Business Review, 33*(1), 33–42.

Koontz, H., & O'Donnell, C. (1972). *Principles of management* (5th ed.). New York: McGraw-Hill.

Kotter, J. P. (1990). *A force for change: How leadership differs from management.* New York: Free Press.

Levitt, T. (1976, Summer). Management and the post industrial society. *The Public Interest.*

Lieberman, A., & Miller, L. (1984). *Teachers, their world and their work.* Arlington, VA: Association for Supervision and Curriculum Development.

Lipham, J. (1964). Leadership and administration. In National Society for the Study of Education yearbook, *Behavioral science and educational administration* (pp. 119–141). Chicago: University of Chicago Press.

Lipsitz, J. (1984). *Successful schools for young adolescents.* New Brunswick, NJ: Transaction Books.

Mills, T. M. (1967). The *sociology of small groups.* Englewood Cliffs, NJ: Prentice-Hall.

Parsons, T. (1951). *Toward a general theory of social action.* Cambridge, MA: Harvard University.

Parsons, T. (1960). *Structure and process in modern society.* Glencoe, IL: The Free Press.

Parsons, T., Bales, R. F., & Shils, E. A. (1953). *Working papers in the theory of action.* New York: The Free Press of Glencoe.

Peshkin, A. (1977). Whom shall the schools serve? Some dilemmas of local control in a rural school district. *Curriculum Inquiry, 6*(3), 181–204.

Peterson, K. D. (1984). Mechanisms of administrative control over managers in educational organizations. *Administration Science Quarterly, 29*(4), 573–597.

Rossiter, C. (Ed.). (1961). *The federalist papers: Alexander Hamilton, James Madison, and John Jay.* New York: New American Library.

Sears, J. B. (1950). *The nature of administrative process.* New York: McGraw-Hill.

Selznick, P. (1957). *Leadership in administration: A sociological interpretation.* Berkeley: University of California Press.

Sergiovanni, T. J. (1984). Leadership and excellence in schooling. *Educational Leadership, 45*(5), 4–13.

Sergiovanni, T. J. (1990). *Value-added leadership: How to get extraordinary performance in schools.* San Diego: Harcourt Brace Jovanovich.

Sergiovanni, T. J. (1992). *Moral leadership: Getting to the heart of school improvement.* San Francisco: Jossey-Bass.

Sergiovanni, T. J. (2001). *Leadership: What's in it for schools?* London: Routledge-Falmer.

Simon, H. A. (1945). *Administrative behavior: A study of decision making processes in administrative organizations.* New York: The Free Press.

Starratt, R. J. (1977, June). *Apostolic leadership.* San Jose, CA: Jesuit Commission on Research and Development Workshop.

Starratt, R. J. (1990). *The drama of schooling, the schooling of drama.* Bristol, PA: Falmer Press.

Tead, O. (1951). *The art of administration.* New York: McGraw-Hill.

U.S. Department of Education, National Center for Education Statistics, unpublished projections and estimates. August 2000.

Wilson, W. (1887). The study of administration. *Political Science Quarterly,* 2.

Zaleznik, A. (1977). Managers and leaders: Are they different? *Harvard Business Review, 55*(3).

4 Educational Administration as an Emerging Profession

The virtues of creating a strong and admired profession of school administration are spoken widely and loudly by both the academic and professional administration communities. Suggestions otherwise are considered heresy. As a result, no serious conversation exists within educational administration that addresses the unanticipated negative consequences. One reason for this silence is that the present leadership of our schools has the most to gain by pushing for increased professionalism. Thus, this leadership is likely to resist considering other possibilities, and is more likely to gloss over unanticipated problems associated with professionalism. Professors of educational administration, for example, have a vested interest in what has been taught and written over the years. Practicing administrators, too, have vested interests themed to power and job security that might be threatened if professionalism was slowed down or if its direction changed.

Professionalism in educational administration is an issue worth discussing critically (Sergiovanni, 1991). Nearly everyone agrees, for example, that some special preparation is needed for school administrators, but the question of how much is not as easily resolved. For example, will increases in professional preparation and standards for admission and training further divide teachers and administrators? Is too much specialized professional preparation a threat to democratic authority? What is the long-term effect on teacher professionalism as the professionalization of educational administration increases? Could it be, for example, that increased professionalization of administrative roles is a form of hidden hierarchy that further subordinates teacher roles? If more and better study in educational administration is desirable, what specifically should be studied? Does a common knowledge base exist? If so, whose interests does it serve?

The Importance of Instructional Leadership

In recent years more and more emphasis has been given to principals behaving as instructional leaders as the defining hallmark of their role. But if principals are strong instructional leaders, what roles do teachers play? Would we be better off investing in building the capacity of teachers to be strong instructional leaders and viewing principals as *leaders of leaders*?

Some evidence suggests that this is indeed the case. For example, examine Table 3.1 again. Consider only the first nine criteria that principals perceive to be important when central office evaluates them. Sort each of the criteria into one of three categories:

- Instructional leadership: the extent to which principals focus directly on teaching and learning, the importance of increasing student achievement, curriculum and assessment, and the development of improved instructional programs
- School leadership: the extent to which principals provide the climate, opportunity, capacity-building resources, and support for teachers, parents, and students to function at their best both academically and socially
- Manager: the extent to which principals emphasize the establishment and following of procedures, directions, and rules to avoid problems or otherwise upset the stability and smooth running of the school

It is likely that you placed criteria 1, 2, 7, 8, and 9 in the school leadership category; 5 and 6 in the instructional leadership category; and 3 and 4 in the manager category. If this is the case, then school leadership criteria were mentioned 168 times, accounting for a total of 57 percent of all the criteria provided. Instructional leadership criteria, by contrast, were mentioned sixty times, accounting for 17 percent, and manager eighty-one times for 22 percent. Both instructional leadership and school leadership have to do with improving student achievement, but in different ways. Instructional leadership addresses teaching and learning in a direct way, and school leadership addresses teaching and learning in an indirect way. This information suggests that the indirect leadership that principals provide in support of teaching and learning dominates their roles.

A series of authoritative papers published by Hallinger and Heck (1996a, 1996b, 1999) provides solid support for the importance of the principals' indirect leadership in improving student achievement. Their conclusion is that the behavior of principals does not provide a measurable direct effect on school effectiveness or on student achievement, but does provide a measurable indirect effect. It will be interesting to examine how this emphasis on direct versus indirect leadership plays itself out as educational administration strives to become a profession anchored more to teaching and learning than had been the case before.

Perhaps what is more important than the direct versus indirect question is what the content and focus of principal leadership is. A 2001 survey of high school principals and how they spend their time found that although the rhetoric is right, gaps exist between what principals want to do and ought to do and what they wind up doing. According to the National Association of Secondary School Principals (NASSP) report:

> Although high school principals are hard working, highly committed, and dedicated to the business of teaching and learning, they report spending much of their

time and energy carrying out functions that have little to do with student learning, effective teaching, or creating a climate conducive to both of these. The role of the principal, as presently structured, is reported by the survey respondents to be that of a manager mostly engaged in urgent activities. Principals need help extinguishing the "fires" that flare up continuously throughout the 13-hour days principals regularly work. (NASSP, 2001, p. 31)

In the report the NASSP combines indirect and direct leadership by defining instructional leadership as follows:

Being an instructional leader requires the purposeful and intentional action of principals spending significant time doing those things that are important, but often not urgent: planning, team building, teacher development, and relationship building. For principals to decrease their time as managers and increase their time in instructional leadership, the following must be available: relevant preparation and preservice and inservice professional development; organizational structures and personnel to assist with school management tasks; and resources to support staff professional development. Leadership will vary from school to school, depending upon the experience, the skills, and the will of the principal as well as the support available in the community. But the focus of the leader of every high school must be student learning and instruction. (NASSP, 2001, p. 31)

Despite the difficulties, it is clear that when principals work to provide the conditions and means for teacher learning, student achievement increases (Darling-Hammond, 1997). When principals emphasize the building of effective learning and caring communities for teachers within the school, teacher learning improves and student achievement benefits as a result (Sergiovanni, 1994). When principals work to provide a safe, respectful, and caring environment for students, student achievement improves (Sebring et al., 1995, 1996). School culture counts, and every effort that principals give to building strong and effective cultures is an investment in student learning.

Resnick (2001/2002) believes that given what we know about effective teaching and learning, principals must know and engage in matters of instruction to a greater extent and with greater depth than is now the case. She suggests the following as examples of things that principals who are instructional leaders might do regularly:

- Lead faculty in analyzing classroom-by-classroom test data, disaggregated by socioeconomic status, race, ethnicity and language group.
- Lead a grade-level group of teachers in analyzing examples of student work from their classes with reference to *benchmark* work that meets state or district standards.
- Lead a faculty committee in aligning textbook or other teaching materials to standards.
- Visit classrooms daily to observe teaching—after developing with teachers descriptions of criteria of good teaching.

- Build professional development plans with individual teachers, based on classroom observations, student data, and characteristics of the adopted instructional program.
- Plan details of professional development activities with content coaches and mentors who are available to work with teachers in the school. (Resnick, 2001/2002, p. 2)

For those who argue that principals are not now prepared for this kind of practice, Resnick responds by stating it is reasonable to expect principals to learn these and other instructional leadership competencies. As we shall discuss later, enough people agree with this position that it is reflected in the new standards for principal practice established by the National Policy Board for Educational Administration. Before putting these issues squarely on the table for discussion, it will be helpful to back up and examine the events that have led to today's situation.

Background

Educational administration has a short history. Only since World War II has it shown signs of establishing itself as a fully organized and distinct profession. Though much groundwork was done during the early decades of the twentieth century in building a *science* of education and administration, the years 1946 and 1947 are considered critical. During this period, the American Association of School Administrators (AASA) received a report from its planning committee urging a long-range commitment to the professionalization of educational administrators. This committee recommended that AASA work to improve preparation programs in administration at colleges and universities, to encourage school boards to develop more adequate standards for the selection of superintendents, and to become more active as an organization in the general professional affairs of education. The 1947 annual AASA conference was characterized by initial planning for the formation of the National Conference of Professors of Educational Administration. Its members, professors, and others involved in the preparation of administrators at colleges and universities, met that summer in Endicott, New York, and produced a landmark report titled *Educational Leaders: Their Functions and Preparation.*

Three years later, the emerging profession of educational administration received an important boost—the development of the Cooperative Program in Education Administration (CPEA). Founded as a result of a Kellogg Foundation grant and of planning by the AASA, the National Association of Rural Superintendents, and the Council of Chief State School Officers, CPEA resulted in the establishment, by 1951, of regional centers at eight American universities (University of Oregon, Stanford University, University of Texas, University of Chicago, Ohio State University, George Peabody College for Teachers, Columbia University, and Harvard University). An account of CPEA activities can be found in Moore (1947). The purposes of these centers were:

1. to improve preparation programs for preservice training of potential administrators and in-service training of administrators already in the field.

2. to develop greater sensitivity to large social problems through an interdisciplinary approach involving most of the social sciences.
3. to disseminate research findings to practicing administrators.
4. to discover new knowledge about education and about administration.
5. to develop a continuing pattern of cooperation and communication among various universities and colleges within a region and between these institutions and other organizations and agencies working in the field of educational administration. (Kellogg Foundation, 1961, p. 13)

A significant outgrowth of CPEA activity was the establishment in 1956 of the University Council for Educational Administration (UCEA). The initial membership nucleus consisted of thirty-three major universities with doctoral-level preparation programs in educational administration. The purposes of UCEA were to improve the preservice and in-service education of school administrators, stimulate and conduct research, encourage innovation through development projects, and disseminate materials growing out of research and development activities. Originally located at Teachers College, Columbia University, UCEA moved its headquarters staff to Ohio State University in 1959, to Arizona State University in 1984, to Pennsylvania State University in 1992, and to the University of Missouri in 1996, where it remains today with a membership of seventy universities.

The UCEA had a significant effect on building an identity among professors of educational administration and on improving their training. Further accomplishments included beginning the task of developing a knowledge base in the social and management sciences for preparing administrators. The UCEA has also served as a public forum on behalf of the academic community in influencing federal and state policy decisions relating to educational administration. Other landmark developments during this formative period were the publication in 1964, by the National Society for the Study of Education, of a yearbook devoted to the relationship of the behavioral sciences to educational administration (Griffiths, 1964) and the establishment of the Center for the Advanced Study of Educational Administration in 1964 at the University of Oregon. In recent years, the UCEA has been a leader in working for equity in educational administration, particularly with respect to women. During the 1980s, the organization took the lead in pushing for reform in the preparation of educational administration and in standards for admission and reestablished itself as a leader in developing the knowledge base of the profession through a series of annual conferences begun in 1987. This latter theme, as discussed later in this chapter, remains prominent today.

In 1968, the AASA established the National Academy for School Executives. Modeled after similar advanced in-service arms of other professions, the academy offered intensive workshops, seminars, and other activities designed to keep superintendents in touch with current developments and issues and up to date in current concepts and skills. Activities of the academy were highly regarded, as evidenced by wide attendance, expanding programs, and the awarding of academic credits by several universities to administrators who participated in academic programs.

During the 1970s and 1980s, preparation programs for school administrators were under increased scrutiny by licensing agents of state departments of education and by universities. This was a period of restlessness within the profession and of dissatisfaction by policymakers and others on the outside. Calls for reform were common. Some policy experts doubted whether the school administration establishment has either the will or the ability to initiate needed changes. Peterson and Finn (1985), for example, stated:

> It may be that piecemeal reform is simply inadequate to the task of overhauling the training, licensure, and professional standards of school administrators. It may also be that the profession lacks the fortitude or the perspective for a thoroughgoing, self-induced overhaul. Perhaps governors, business leaders, and blue ribbon commissions will need to bring school administration under the kind of intense scrutiny that they have applied to school teaching. Maybe one state needs to burst from the pack with a radically different model of training, licensure, selection, evaluation, and recruitment into this field. Perhaps the universities need a modern day Flexner to map their route through a systematic—and system wide—reformulation of the precepts and practices of administrator training. (p. 62)

During the sixties and seventies, university preparation programs for school administrators emphasized the curious blend of administrative and organizational theory on the one hand and management technicalities on the other. This resulted in a curriculum that in some ways was more academic than professional, as it mimicked the basic social science disciplines, and in other ways resembled vocational curriculum with emphasis on the nuts and bolts of buildings, bonds, and budgets. Far less emphasis was given to schooling as an institution, to its philosophical, social, and historical basis, and to the knowledge and skills needed for administrators to function as leaders able to enhance teaching and learning. As Peterson and Finn (1985) pointed out:

> The required courses in such programs—closely tracking those spelled out in state certification requirements—commonly emphasized building management rather than instructional leadership, paying far closer attention to such subjects as school law and school finance (sometimes even to such minutiae as "facilities and transportation" or "scheduling") than to understanding what makes good teaching, what constitutes an outstanding history textbook, or how to determine whether a youngster is learning up to the level of his ability. (p. 62)

These analysts refer to a study by James Guthrie and associates (Peterson & Finn, 1985) that concluded, after examination of programs approved by the California State Education Department, that they "give great attention to human relations and public relations courses and skills" (p. 50). Recognizing that these techniques may be worth pursuing, the Guthrie study concludes that "the knowledge and skills needed to become an effective educational leader and school manager are generally not those provided" (Peterson & Finn, 1985, p. 50).

In 1978, Lawrence A. Cremin, then president of Teachers College, Columbia University, urged that the preparation and dissertation for professional educators not mimic that required for the Ph.D. in traditional academic areas. Among his many recommendations was that professional studies include a well-organized and closely supervised clinical or apprentice experience and that the dissertation be much more professional in its focus and orientation.

The problem of piecemeal part-time study at the doctoral level has been addressed by a few smaller *established* universities and by a handful of *innovative* universities. In 1974, for example, Jesuit-run Seattle University developed a doctoral program in educational leadership that featured identifiable cohorts who studied together on the university campus over a period of three years by engaging in intensive weekend and summer sessions. Nova Southeastern University of Fort Lauderdale, Florida, introduced its now famous external doctoral program that featured identifiable groups, or *clusters,* of students who studied together in intensive sessions for fixed periods (weekends and summers). Nova awarded more than 1,300 doctorates between 1972 and 1979 (*Kappan* editors, 1979, p. 565). Nova has continued this productivity pace over the years and today is a leader in the number of educational administration doctorates awarded and in the number of students of color enrolled.

In many respects, these programs resembled the pattern of study provided for experienced executives seeking MBA degrees in business schools throughout the country. The University of Chicago, Northwestern University, and other prestigious schools feature executive programs that do not require traditional full-time study, and this pattern has become accepted throughout the business schools of the country. A quick check of the ads placed by business schools in the *Economist* from all over the world reveals that part-time executive MBA programs are pervasive internationally.

New on the scene is the emergence of for-profit universities, with the best known being the University of Phoenix. Offering educational administration degrees throughout the country that are focused on the problems of practice, Phoenix relies on part-time faculty who are recruited from the schools in the areas in which programs are offered. Phoenix uses state-of-the-art technology, with heavy reliance on personal computers. If Phoenix's success in offering MBA and other business degree programs is repeated in educational administration, we can expect to see new preparation models emerge from the more established universities.

Though considered odd, and even criticized a few years ago, the part-time intensive study designs for school administrators of innovators such as Seattle University and Nova Southeastern University are now being used by such established institutions as Teachers College, Columbia University, Texas A & M University, Seton Hall University, and the University of Illinois at Urbana-Champaign. Further, preparation programs are becoming more clinically focused—emphasizing the everyday problems of schools and school leadership as opposed to extensive academic study in the various social science disciplines. Greater emphasis is also given to ethical issues and to developing a critical stance consistent with democratic norms and traditions. This is true not only for the universities experimenting with new time frames for study but for others as well (e.g., Miami University, Oxford Ohio).

In discussions of school administration programs, most of the emphasis is given to study at the doctoral level. This is curious because the vast majority of students who become certified to practice as school principals, assistant principals, and other school-based supervisors study at the master's level. Further, they typically study part time. With this reality in mind, many universities in the 1980s and 1990s broke new ground in strengthening their programs by requiring cohort study within a fixed and compact time frame and by offering programs that focused on the problems of school practice (e.g., Stanford University and Trinity University).

Over the last decade the cohort study design has been widely adopted for both master's and doctoral study, but master's-level programs designed to prepare principals remain woefully neglected. Doctoral-level programs, by contrast, are better financed, and courses at this level are more likely to be taught by full-time and usually tenured faculty. Until recently most state systems of higher education allowed only a few *flagship* universities to offer doctorates. Now the dominant pattern across much of the country is for regional state universities to offer the doctorate as well. This popularization of doctoral study has resulted in even more resources being shifted away from master's study that prepared principals for certification and licensure and toward doctoral study. Most doctoral students are already administrators, with many being successful principals. Under these circumstances one must ask the question: Does doctoral study offer programs that are similar to what successful principals and others already know through their experience as practitioners and through their previous certification study at the master's level? If the answer is yes, then why bother with doctoral study? If the answer is no, what value does doctoral study add to a principal's practice?

Stirrings of change can also be heard from professional organizations such as the AASA and academic organizations such as the UCEA. In 1983, the AASA issued *Guidelines for the Preparation of School Administration,* which called for school administration training to encompass seven critical knowledge and skill areas: "School climate and how to improve it, critical theory and how to apply it, the curriculum and how to construct it, 'instructional management systems' and how to run them, staff members and how to evaluate them, school resources and how to allocate them, educational research and how to utilize it" (Peterson & Finn, 1985, p. 55). In 1985, the executive committee of UCEA passed a resolution to establish the National Committee on Excellence in Educational Administration, charged with studying and making recommendations concerning the preparation of school administrators for the future (discussed in the next section).

AASA, with approximately 14,600 members, remains the most influential professional organization for administrators. Superintendents dominate this organization. Though principals and other administrators are not excluded, they typically identify with more specialized professional groups such as the NASSP, the National Association of Elementary School Principals (NAESP), the Association of School Business Officials, and similar organizations for supervisors, personnel administrators, and others.

Unlike teachers, who are bound together in the over 2-million-member National Education Association or the smaller but influential American Federation of Teachers, educational administrators lack a strong national voice and strong rallying organization. Changes can be expected in this situation as administrators feel the need to maintain a strong, unified, professional interest in the face of increased concentration of power over education at the state and federal levels, and of increased influence of teachers on school boards at the local level. This is now occurring in many states, with the development of all-inclusive administrative organizations (e.g., the Association of California School Administrators and the Colorado Association of School Executives). In recent years, the Association for Supervision and Curriculum Development (ASCD) has grown to an organization of approximately 165,000 members by appealing to all to join together around a common interest—improved teaching and learning and better schooling. Perhaps their success is a harbinger of further efforts to unite not only administration but all educational professionals in a common cause.

During the 1990s, the UCEA increased its efforts to become a community of scholars committed to building up the knowledge base of educational administration and to be a potent voice in the reform of the profession. The organization has been in the forefront of women's rights, has commissioned a number of policy studies on the future of educational administration, and has rededicated itself to scholarly inquiry focusing much more on the problems of schooling, thus correcting its historically unbalanced emphasis on the social science disciplines. In a 2001 statement UCEA listed "1) Promoting, sponsoring and disseminating research on the essential problems of practice; 2) Improving the preparation and professional development of school leaders and professors; and 3) Influencing policy and practice through establishing and fostering collaborative networks" (UCEA, 2001, p. 3) as its goals. At this writing it appears that UCEA is making progress in achieving its goals. Educational administration's standing as a discipline and as a field of practice has never been stronger. This progress is evident by two recent yearbooks published by the National Society for the Study of Education: Volume 101 edited by Joseph Murphy (2002) and entitled *The Educational Leadership Challenge: Redefining Leadership for the 21st Century,* and Volume 102 edited by William L. Boyd (2003) and entitled *American Educational Governance on Trial: Change and Challenges.* These books provide new benchmarks for charting the future development of the field.

Recent Pressures to Reform

Since the publication of *A Nation at Risk* in 1983 (National Commission on Excellence in Education), dozens of reports from blue-ribbon committees have appeared, seeking to reform teaching and schooling. The reports of the Carnegie task force on teaching as a profession (Carnegie Forum, 1986) and of a group of about 100 leading research-oriented universities that make up the Holmes Group were particularly influential. They recommended radically restructuring the way that teachers are prepared and licensed. Instead of relying on mandates and inducements as policy instruments to bring about change, Carnegie and Holmes based their recommendations on building up the capacities of teachers to function more effectively on the one hand and on changing the structure of the profession itself on the other (McDonnell & Elmore, 1987). The Carnegie task force worked to establish a national board for professional standards that would "board certify" teachers. Board certification is strictly voluntary. The board issued a report, *Toward High and Rigorous Standards for the Teaching Profession,* which sketched out its initial policies and perspectives in 1989. The Holmes Group agenda included requiring five years of university study to qualify as a teacher (Holmes Group, 1986). During the first four years, the prospective teacher would study in the liberal arts; the fifth year would include intensive clinically focused study in a Professional Development School (Holmes Group, 1990). The Holmes plan loosely follows the general pattern now in place for medical doctors.

In both cases, the reforms were successful in strengthening the general and professional education of teachers. Better preparation, the reformers reasoned, would increase the teacher's professional standing in society. As this standing increased, states, school boards, and the general public would grant more autonomy to teachers. The emphasis would shift from regulating what teachers do to what results schools are getting. The reformers were confident that increased and better preparation combined with on-the-job autonomy would result in better teaching and learning.

For the most part, the reforms of the early and mid-1980s were silent on the preparation of educational administrators. Teachers got all the attention. Moves to increase the professionalization of teaching have the potential to threaten the standing of the educational administration establishment. The creation of a national board for teachers, for example, raised more than a few anxious eyebrows. Not to be outdone, in 1986, the UCEA created the National Commission on Excellence in Educational Administration. The commission was funded by a number of foundations, including Danforth, Ford, and MacArthur, and included among its twenty-seven commissioners then Arkansas governor Bill Clinton, Atlanta superintendent Alonzo Crim, California State University system chancellor W. Anne Reynolds, and Michigan State education dean Judy Lanier. Albert Shanker, the president of the American Federation of Teachers, was also a member. Of the twenty-seven commissioners, twelve represented the academic educational administrator community, three were school superintendents, four represented professional associations for school administrators, and among the eight others, only Shanker represented teachers. The commission was chaired by Daniel E. Griffiths, a highly respected professor of educational administration and former dean of education at New York University.

The commission issued a sixty-page report, *Leaders for Tomorrow's Schools,* in March 1987. The report called for sweeping changes in the recruitment, preparation, regulation, and evaluation of school administrators. According to Griffiths (*UCEA Review,* 1987):

> This commission was asked to examine the quality of educational leadership in this country and I must say that our research reveals troubling aspects through the field including: lack of definition of good educational leadership; lack of leadership recruitment programs in the schools; lack of collaboration between school districts

and universities; the discouraging lack of minorities and women in the field; lack of professional development for school administrators; lack of quality candidates for preparation programs; lack of preparation programs relevant to the job demands of school administrators; lack of sequence, modern content, and clinical experiences in preparing administrators; lack of licensure systems which promote excellence; and lack of a national sense of cooperation in preparing school leaders. (p. 1)

The eight major recommendations of the commission were:

1. Educational leadership should be redefined.
2. A national policy board on educational administration should be established.
3. Administrative preparation programs should be modeled on those in professional schools.
4. At least 300 universities and colleges should cease preparing educational administrators.
5. Programs for recruitment and placement of ethnic minorities and women should be initiated by universities, school boards, state and federal governments, and business and industry.
6. The public schools should become full partners in the preparation of school administrators.
7. Professional development activities should be an integral component of the careers of professors and practicing administrators.
8. Licensure programs should be substantially reformed. (*UCEA Review*, 1987, p. 1)

The report was greeted with enthusiasm by the educational administration establishment though murmurs of dissent could also be heard. Commissioners Shanker and Lanier refused to endorse the report, claiming it did not go far enough in recommending the restructuring of the roles of school administrators and teachers and of how schools should be organized and operated.

Some academics were concerned that the report merely repackaged traditional conceptions of administrators in a way that repositioned the educational administration establishment to ensure its survival in the light of new pressures. Gibboney's (1987) views reflect some of these reservations:

How can it [the report] speak seriously about reform when it resurrects and builds on the same trivial courses in management and administration that have been taught for several decades?… The commission…reveals its management obsession—for example in the concern for "skills." The word "skills" abounds in the report, while the word "idea" as an energizing force in leadership is barely apparent. The commission urges districts to set up "assessment centers" that would identify and improve the skills of potential school principals and practicing administrators. Why not, I wonder, have idea-assessment centers as well?… It is no accident that such questions do not arise in reform talk cast in the image of good management, because managerial skills, by their very nature, cannot deal with issues of educational substance. (p. 28)

Gibboney believes that the report emphasizes managerial processes and skills in the preparation of school administrators at the expense of educational purposes and substance.

As a result of the commission's recommendations, in 1988, the UCEA took the lead in establishing the National Policy Board for Educational Administration (NPBEA). David Clark, another well-known professor of educational administration and former education dean at Indiana University, was its first executive director. Member organizations included the American Association of Colleges of Teacher Education, the AASA, the ASCD, the Council of Chief State School Officers, the NASSP, the National Conference of Professors of Educational Administration, the National School Boards Association, and the UCEA. The Danforth Foundation joined the sponsoring organizations in providing funding.

In 1989, the NPBEA issued a report titled *Improving the Preparation of School Administrators: Agenda for Reform* that detailed existing shortcomings in the preparation of school administrators and provided a bold blueprint for change. *Agenda for Reform* recommended that preparation programs follow a professional studies model rather than one that either mimics the academic disciplines or resembles a series of ad hoc and disconnected staff-development workshops.

A number of commission recommendations sparked considerable controversy. Requiring a core educational administration faculty of at least five persons, eliminating study at the master's-degree level completely, requiring that the doctorate in educational administration be a prerequisite for national certification, and requiring state licensing for line administrators, for example, would very likely result in the closing of several hundred administrative preparation programs. Small liberal arts colleges and universities would be particularly affected, as would many state university colleges. In all, the report was not viewed as being practical enough to accommodate to the realities that face educational administration students as they study and to the political realities of turf competition among colleges and universities.

In November 1989, the NPBEA incorporated as an independent organization. Scott D. Thompson, former executive director of the NASSP, became the new executive secretary in January 1990, replacing Clark. The board issued a new report, *The Preparation of School Administrators: A Statement of Purpose,* in March 1990. Though reiterating the knowledge base recommendations that appeared in the first report, this report softened its recommendations for full-time study, for eliminating the master's degree, and for a required critical mass of educational administration faculty. It provided for two levels of certification as follows: "An entry level certificate would require a master's degree in teaching or a content field, plus 30 semester hours in school leadership including clinical experiences, followed by an assessment of competence. The advanced level would require a doctorate which includes one academic year of full-time study and successful field experiences beyond the entry level certification requirements, followed by an assessment of competence" (NPBEA, 1990).

Since the appearance of the 1990 report, the UCEA, the NPBEA, and the various school administrator professional associations have been working together to change the emphasis in preparation programs for school administrators away from generic management concerns and away from a direct leadership by giving more emphasis to teaching and learning concerns and by advancing the view that school administrators should be leaders of leaders. Both changes reflect the progress that is being made in the professionalization of teaching.

The educational administration profession continues to research, examine, and debate the two issues that will shape its future—how best to prepare school administrators and what is the knowledge base for the discipline of educational administration. The issues are joined as various groups within the educational administration community look more and more to the development of standards and the use of standards to evaluate the performance of principals, superintendents, and other administrators and to evaluate the effectiveness of administrative preparation and certification programs. These are the topics that are discussed here.

Over the forty-five years of its existence, the UCEA has been giving leadership to professionalizing efforts by bringing people together to study the issues and to make recommendations. In August 2001, for example, the UCEA, in cooperation with the NPBEA, established a National Commission for the Advancement of Educational Leadership Preparation to identify issues impacting the preparation of school leaders, to examine successful programs, to define what universities must do to ensure quality programs, to recommend policy changes, and to create action plans for the future (UCEA, 2001). Commissioners include Paul Houston, Gerald Tirozzi, Vincent Ferrandino, and Gene Carter representing the AASA, NASSP, NAESP, and ASCD respectively; Art Wise, president of National Council for the Accreditation of Teacher Education (NCATE); Tom Houlihan, the executive director of the Council of Chief State School Officers (CCSSO); Joseph Schneider, executive secretary of the NPBEA; and an assortment of educational administration professors and practitioners. It is too early to tell just what the outcome of this commission's work will be, but expectations are high. The quality of the commissioners and the determination of both the academic and professional wings of educational administration to push a reform agenda that refocuses school leadership on teaching and learning raises hope among many observers for a major breakthrough.

The Dark Side of Professionalism

Professionalism can also have downsides that negatively impact study. For this reason the quest for professionalism should be pursued with our lights on and beams high. Americans, for example, tend to feel that the professionalization of anything makes it better. Beneath the glamour and material benefits associated with educational administration's achieving status as a recognized profession, however, are a number of possible unanticipated negative consequences for schools and communities. (This section closely follows Sergiovanni [1991].)

To succeed, emergent professions need to develop a definition, role, and function distinctly different from those of other occupations working in the same area, particularly those with *lower* organizational status. To do otherwise may endanger their claim to distinctiveness and special importance. Professionals, after all, are presumed to be experts in something that others are not. It is this expertness that gives them authority over others. Educational administrators as "experts are presumed to deliver their services to the limits of their competence, to respect the confidences granted them by their clients [teachers, parents, students], and not to misuse for their own benefit the special powers given them within the boundaries of their relationship. In return, clients are expected to accept the professional's authority in specific areas of expertise, to submit to the professional's ministrations.... In short, clients are expected to behave as though they accept and respect the professional's autonomy as an expert" (Fischer, 1990, p. 358). One could argue, however, that being an expert requires having a monopoly over specialized knowledge and skill.

If having a knowledge and skill monopoly is key, then for educational administrators to enjoy full status, their knowledge and skill monopoly needs to be different from that of teachers. Expertness as an educator may not do, because it is common to both teachers and administrators. In the past, educational administration has relied on management themes as it sought to build a distinctive knowledge monopoly. And, because administrators are hierarchically superior to teachers, one unanticipated consequence has been that managerial expertise became hierarchically superior to educational expertness. Such an arrangement has never been acceptable in medicine, law, or other more established professions and should not be acceptable in education.

One alternative to managerial expertness is to build the educational administrator's knowledge monopoly around interpersonal themes and leadership abilities. Intensive study would be required in organizational behavior, human relations, and similar topics. The purpose would be to beef up the administrator's psychological authority instead of or in combination with the bureaucratic authority. Doing so, however, may place process over substance, thus reinforcing the *managerial mystique* that seems now to be entrenched in the cultures of both corporate and schooling America. Zaleznik (1989) points out that "the managerial mystique is only tenuously tied to reality. As it evolved in practice, the mystique required managers to dedicate themselves to process, structures, roles, and indirect forms of communication and to ignore ideas, people, emotions, and direct talk" (p. 2).

To Haller and Strike (1986), building the educational administrator's expertness around interpersonal themes in an effort to bolster psychological authority raises serious ethical questions.

> We find this an inadequate view of the administrative role.... Its first deficiency is that it makes administrative success depend on characteristics that tend to be both intangible and unalterable. One person's dynamic leader is another's tyrant. What one person sees as a democratic style, another will see as the generation of time-wasting committee work...our basic concern with this view, however, is that it makes the administrative role one of form, not content. Being a successful administrator depends not on the adequacy of one's view, not on the educational policies that one adopts and how reasonable they are, and not on how successful one is in communicating these reasons to others. Success depends on personality and style, or on carefully chosen ways for inducing others to contribute to the organization. It is not what one wants to do and why that is important; it is who one is and how one does things that counts. We find such a view offensive. It is incompatible with

the values of autonomy, reason and democracy, which we see as among the central commitments of our society and our educational system. Of course educational administrators must be leaders, but let them lead by reason and persuasion, not by forces of personality. (p. 326)

Walton (1969) provides three scenarios for building the knowledge base of educational administration: (1) a common profession of administrators and teachers with shared educational expertness as the authority, (2) a profession built on generic management skills, and (3) a policy-politics–based profession. In his words:*

> 1. The first of these arises from the assumption that the administrative function cannot be abstracted from the other functions of the educational organization. From this assumption it follows that the educational administrator must be a teacher, a scholar, or an educator. While he has administrative duties and responsibilities, these are so closely related to the purposes and processes of education that they cannot be understood or performed adequately apart from the intrinsic educational activities of the organization. As an educator, the educational administrator is not and cannot be restricted to purely administrative tasks, but he engages in the same professional activities as the teacher, the counselor, the scholar, and the researcher. He is primarily a specialist in education, or in some academic discipline, rather than in administration per se; and he is on part, or full-time, assignment to attend to the administrative aspects of his profession, which involve primary considerations of education. (p. 41)
>
> 2. The second…centers around the regard for administration as a function that can be abstracted from the other functions of an organization and the belief that its nature is essentially the same in all organizations. This type…would provide…for an administrative class, specialists in administration rather than in education, who conceivably would be interchangeable from one type of institution to another. (p. 42)
>
> 3. A third…Education, along with other institutions in society, has become tremendously complex, heterogeneous, unwieldy and competitive. This state of affairs has given rise to the need for administrators who conceive the various components in relationship to one another and, also, can ensure the survival of educational organizations. So important is this function for the prevention of chaos and disintegration that the person who knows how to run an educational enterprise should also have, and, as a matter of fact, will have, a great deal to say about the purposes for which it is run. The specialist may provide the administrator with facts and technical information, but decisions about the purposes of education and the methods required to accomplish these purposes should be left to the administrator, whose mind can encompass the complex and far-reaching effects of such decisions. (pp. 42–43)

The second scenario resembles the model now in place in hospitals. In general, a professional management team runs the hospital as a complex organization and a separate professional medical team runs the hospital as a healing organization. Though both hierarchies coexist, when push comes to shove, the latter hierarchy is

---

*John Walton, *Administration and policymaking in education* (rev. ed.) (Baltimore: Johns Hopkins University Press, 1969), pp. 41, 42, 43. Reprinted by permission.

the more powerful. Further, those associated with the medical hierarchy enjoy higher average salaries and greater prestige than their management counterparts. Opting for scenario 2 in education would require that the present educational hierarchy be radically restructured. Schools, for example, might have a principal teacher at the education helm and a building administrator at the management helm. This pattern is often found in the United Kingdom where both a head teacher and a bursar run the school together.

The third scenario has the potential to compromise the value of democratic authority in running our schools. It would bring to the administrative role the kind of policy clout that is now heavily shared with local school boards, state legislators, state departments of education, and other stateholders. Neither education nor management would comprise the "core technology" of profession of educational administration, but politics and policy instead.

To the authors, scenario 1 deserves consideration as the metaphor of choice for an emerging profession of educational administration. But scenario 1 suggests that we may need to rethink the present direction in building the profession of educational administration. For this scenario to work, a more modest view of administrative training and certification may be needed—one that does not compete with teaching but complements it. Educational administration would simply be an extension of teaching. Educational expertise in this scenario would be shared with teachers. Shared expertise is key, for the knowledge of teachers always rivals the educational knowledge of administrators.

Some specialized knowledge of management and organization and some skill in organizational matters would be added to this shared educational expertness. But the question is, How much? Too much expertness in management may compromise shared educational expertise. Further, though highly specialized management expertise may be appropriate for large corporations and other vast bureaucracies, the typical school is comparatively small.

The Changing Focus

More recent studies of the effectiveness of formal training in educational administration raise important questions about the present and future direction of preparation programs. Zheng (1996), for example, found that an inverse relationship exists. The more preparation in educational administration the 12,000 administrators in his sample had, the less effective they were perceived to be by their teachers. In his words:

> Most states require principals to have a degree in Educational Administration in order to qualify for a principal license. Nevertheless, statistical evidence from this study fails to provide support to the logic of this requirement. While having a degree in Educational Administration makes no difference for private school principals in terms of their perceived effectiveness of instructional leadership, it decreases the rating of principals in public schools. Public school principals who have a degree in Education Administration are rated 0.101 points ($p < 0.001$) lower than other principals when other factors are being held constant. (p. 19)

Related to the question of formal preparation in educational administration is the value of administrative experience. Zheng (1996) found that principals with more experience were actually perceived as being less effective: "The longer a principal stays in school administrative positions, the more negatively he/she is perceived by teachers" (p. 20).

After reviewing the literature on administrative preparation and effectiveness Brent (1998) noted that "In sum, our analyses suggest that graduate training in educational administration has no significant positive influence on school effectiveness (unnumbered). He continues, "…we are arguing that, on average, effective schools are more likely to have a competent principal, and that if graduate training in school administration improves competence, then the principals of those schools should, on average, be more highly trained than principals of less effective schools. This is not what we found" (unnumbered). Brent cautions that there may be many reasons for these ratings. The authors of this book believe that the *culprit* may not be the amount of administrative preparation itself but the context and content of administrative preparation programs.

In short, these findings may raise the question of whether what is now being studied as one prepares to be a principal is actually helpful or harmful. Further is the question of whether there is something inherent about the ways in which schools are presently organized and run that, over time, encourages principals to behave in ways that they are perceived as being less effective by their teachers.

Despite this and other studies that point to negative effects of preparation in educational administration, some bright spots may be on the horizon. Since the mid-1980s, the trend has been for school administrators, particularly school principals, to emphasize instructional leadership tasks and to view themselves once again as principal–teachers. Indeed, in many schools, it is becoming fashionable for administrators to teach (albeit part time) once again. The emphasis today on building school cultures, enhancing collegiality and empowerment, and renewing a commitment to shared decision making suggests that the two professions may be coming back together again. Indeed, one optimistic forecast is that the two professions of educational administration and teaching will be brought together as one common profession bonded by a shared commitment to teaching and learning on the one hand but allowing for differentiated roles on the other. Efforts to redefine the *core technologies* of both professions gives this forecast a chance. For example, the NAESP document *Proficiencies for Principals: Kindergarten through Eighth Grade*, first issued in 1986, identified four principles that are remarkably similar to those required of expert teachers:*

> Summing up, among the numerous characteristics and skills and proficiencies that mark the effective K–8 principal, four areas are basic:
> Child growth and development: The principal must bring to the position expert knowledge in the field of child growth and development, preferably fortified by extensive practical experience in teaching children, and must be capable of

---

*National Association of Elementary School Principals, *Proficiencies for Principals: Kindergarten through Eighth Grade* (Alexandria, VA: Author, 1986), pp. 3–4. Reprinted by permission.

guiding the staff toward assuring the curriculum is relevant and appropriately challenging.

Teaching and learning processes: The principal must similarly be soundly grounded in the teaching and learning processes, in both contemporary and traditional patterns of instruction and in validated instructional techniques and strategies.

General knowledge: The principal must bring to the position a basic liberal arts foundation productive of a firm grasp of basic curriculum content and an understanding of the relationship between the body of knowledge and the elementary/middle school curriculum.

School climate: The principal must be a caring person who knows how to create a school climate or "culture" that is based on mutual trust and respect, is productive of high morale, and places strong emphasis on children's social and academic development. (NAESP, 1986, pp. 3–4)

Professional Standards for Superintendents, published by AASA in 1993, and the 1996 NASSP report *Breaking Ranks: Changing an American Institution* make similar overtures to a new kind of leadership that would be more suitable for an increasingly professionalized teaching force. *Breaking Ranks,* for example, stands out for its emphasis on teaching and learning and on the conditions that enhance both as the central focus of the principalship. Arguing that "high school is, above all else, a learning community and each school must commit itself to expecting demonstrated academic achievement for every student in accord with standards that can stand up to national scrutiny" (p. 2), the report recommends that "every student have a personal adult advocate; the Carnegie Unit be replaced or redefined; student anonymity be banished; teachers meet no more than 90 students per day; every student have a Personal Plan of Progress; imaginative flexible scheduling be the order of the day; every principal and teacher have a Personal Learning Plan" (p. vi).

Signs of change are evident not only from the various educational administration professional associations but also many state departments of education. In a dramatic departure from its usual managerial perspective on school administrators as bureaucratic functionaries, for example, the Texas Education Agency adopted a new set of proficiencies for school administrators in 1994. The new proficiencies call for administrators who will guide "the learning community and the development of a vision that reflects students' needs for academic achievement and success in life and makes that vision tangible for others through positive action. The administrator encourages the collaborative planning, implementation, assessment, and ongoing modification of strategies to achieve this mission. While continually striving to expand the base of support for the learning community, the administrator also creatively allocates resources such as money, time, facilities, technology, and volunteers. In addition, the administrator uses innovative governance structures and methods to further the mission of the learning community" (Texas Education Agency, 1994, p. 11). Other proficiencies include establishing a climate of mutual trust, facilitating a sound curriculum and effective teaching and learning, communicating the learning community's vision, demonstrating a commitment to learning for all students and staff, and promoting equity and diversity within a common framework that bonds people together.

Since the establishment of the NPBEA in 1988, significant steps have been made in developing new standards for the preparation of educational administrators. Working closely with the UCEA, the American Association for Colleges of Teacher Education, the National Council of Professors of Educational Administration (NCPEA), the ASCD, the AASA, the NAESP, and the NASSP, the policy board developed a set of curriculum guidelines that included eleven knowledge and skill areas grouped into five broad categories: strategic leadership, instructional leadership, organizational leadership, political and community leadership, and the internship. The guidelines provide standards that specify the leadership skills needed for school administrators "to generate a culture for effective teaching and learning in restructured schools where teachers are viewed as professionals" (NCATE, 1995). The curriculum guidelines were approved by NCATE in 1995 and comprised the standards that universities were required to follow as they sought to have their school administration preparation programs accredited by the association.

The 1995 NCATE standards were noteworthy for the emphasis they gave to teaching and learning, to building inclusive learning communities, and to providing leadership within an emerging culture of teacher professionalism. This emphasis is in contrast to the more generic view of leadership themed to organizational and management issues of a more decontextualized variety that has characterized school administration preparation programs in the past. Arthur Wise, president of NCATE, described the standards as follows: "For the first time we have a set of standards which begin to envision a role for administrators consistent with the emerging conception of the new professional teacher.... The new vision is one in which the teacher is an independent professional who bases instructional decisions on knowledge of research and the wisdom of practice rather than a semi-skilled professional who must be told what to do" (NCATE, 1995).

The New Standards for Leadership

Beginning in 2003, new NCATE standards are being used to assess the preparation programs of universities seeking accreditation. Although covering most of the same content territory found in the standards previously used, the new standards differ by being *performance based.* Not only must universities show that they are addressing the right content, they must provide compelling evidence that their students are able to perform in each of the standards areas at a required level of competence.

The new standards appear as Appendix 4.1. Note that although the performance standards for principals and central office administrators are the same, they are expected to be mastered at a higher level by central office administrators. This feature raises several important questions: Should we assume that those higher up in the hierarchy should know more about teaching and learning and other standards than those lower? Does this matching of competence through hierarchy apply as well to teachers? Although it is safe to assume that principals should know more about some of these standards areas, should we assume that principals should know more than teachers do about teaching and learning? The answer may well be yes; but if it is, then the profession will have to require massive doses of ongoing professional development for principals to keep up with teachers as they give attention to a broad array of standards areas.

Another question is does the job of principal require all of the same competencies as do the jobs of superintendent and central office administration? Should a curriculum specialist, the director of research, and an assistant superintendent for professional development be required to display the same competencies as principals although at a higher level? If the answer is no, then perhaps developing and using two or more *different* sets of standards might make more sense than a single generic list presumed to apply to all administrative roles.

Earlier, it was suggested that present efforts to professionalize educational administration may need to be rethought and indeed redirected. As things now stand, increased professionalization in the form of lengthier study, elongated certification requirements, certifying boards, and more advanced degrees may well create a *core technology* for educational administration that is heavily weighted toward management themes.

The solution proposed by the authors is to build a more limited and hierarchically flatter professional administration, one based on shared educational expertness with teachers and limited specialized knowledge in management and organization. The NAESP, NASSP, and NPBEA seem to be moving in this direction by joining with NCATE in developing standards for educational administration that acknowledge the emergence of a new kind of leadership that is more suitable for a professionalized teaching force and that places teaching and learning at the center of the principal's job. The recent rush, however, to standards-based preparation, accreditation, and evaluation of school administrators may not be helpful if it leads to the narrowing of choices and to the development of rigid boundaries for practice. Too often, for example, this approach leads to a single template or one-size-fits-all approach, a one best way kind of thinking. This thinking is more at home with yesterday's vision of educational administration preparation and practice than it is today's vision.

New Standards for Advanced Programs in Education Leadership

Prepared by the NPBEA for the Educational Leadership Constituent Council

Standard 1.0

Candidates who complete the program are educational leaders who have the knowledge and ability to promote the success of all students by facilitating the development, articulation, implementation, and stewardship of a school or district vision of learning supported by the school community.

Elements	Meets Standards for School Building Leadership
1.1 Develop a Vision	(a) Candidates develop a vision of learning for a school that promotes the success of all students. (b) Candidates base this vision on relevant knowledge and theories, including but not limited to an understanding of learning goals in a pluralistic society, the diversity of learners and learners' needs, schools as interactive social and cultural systems, and social and organizational change.
1.2 Articulate a Vision	(a) Candidates demonstrate the ability to articulate the components of this vision for a school and the leadership processes necessary to implement and support the vision. (b) Candidates demonstrate the ability to use data-based research strategies and strategic planning processes that focus on student learning to inform the development of a vision, drawing on relevant information sources such as student assessment results, students and family demographic data, and an analysis of community needs. (c) Candidates demonstrate the ability to communicate the vision to staff, parents, students, and community members through the use of symbols, ceremonies, stories, and other activities.

Source: National Policy Board for Educational Administration on behalf of the Educational Leadership Constituent Council, reprinted by permission. The standards presented here are those for school building level administrators only.

1.3 Implement a Vision	(a) Candidates can formulate the initiatives necessary to motivate staff, students, and families to achieve the school's vision. (b) Candidates develop plans and processes for implementing the vision (e.g., articulating the vision and related goals, encouraging challenging standards, facilitating collegiality and teamwork, structuring significant work, ensuring appropriate use of student assessments, providing autonomy, supporting innovation, delegating responsibility, developing leadership in others, and securing needed resources).
1.4 Steward a Vision	(a) Candidates demonstrate an understanding of the role effective communication skills play in building a shared commitment to the vision. (b) Candidates design or adopt a system for using data-based research strategies to regularly monitor, evaluate, and revise the vision. (c) Candidates assume stewardship of the vision through various methods.
1.5 Promote Community Involvement in the Vision	(a) Candidates demonstrate the ability to involve community members in the realization of the vision and in related school improvement efforts. (b) Candidates acquire and demonstrate the skills needed to communicate effectively with all stakeholders about implementation of the vision.

Standard 2.0

Candidates who complete the program are educational leaders who have the knowledge and ability to promote the success of all students by promoting a positive school culture, providing an effective instructional program, applying best practice to student learning, and designing comprehensive professional growth plans for staff.

Elements	Meets Standards for School Building Leadership
2.1 Promote Positive School Culture	(a) Candidates assess school culture using multiple methods and implement context-appropriate strategies that capitalize on the diversity (e.g., population, language, disability, gender, race, socioeconomic) of the school community to improve school programs and culture.
2.2 Provide Effective Instructional Program	(a) Candidates demonstrate the ability to facilitate activities that apply principles of effective instruction to improve instructional practices and curricular materials. (b) Candidates demonstrate the ability to make recommendations regarding the design, implementation, and evaluation of a curriculum that fully accommodates learners' diverse needs.

	(c) Candidates demonstrate the ability to use and promote technology and information systems to enrich curriculum and instruction, to monitor instructional practices, and provide staff the assistance needed for improvement.
2.3 Apply Best Practice to Student Learning	(a) Candidates demonstrate the ability to assist school personnel in understanding and applying best practices for student learning. (b) Candidates apply human development theory, proven learning and motivational theories, and concern for diversity to the learning process. (c) Candidates demonstrate an understanding of how to use appropriate research strategies to profile student performance in a school and analyze possible differences among subgroups of students to promote an environment for improved student achievement.
2.4 Design Comprehensive Professional Growth Plans	(a) Candidates design and demonstrate an ability to implement well-planned context-appropriate professional development programs based on reflective practice and research on student learning consistent with the school vision and goals. (b) Candidates demonstrate the ability to use observations, collaborative reflection, and adult learning strategies to form comprehensive professional growth plans with teachers and other school personnel. (c) Candidates develop and implement personal professional growth plans that reflect a commitment to life-long learning.

Standard 3.0

Candidates who complete the program are educational leaders who have the knowledge and ability to promote the success of all students by managing the organization, operations, and resources in a way that promotes a safe, efficient, and effective learning environment.

Elements	Meets Standards for School Building Leadership
3.1 Manage the Organization	(a) Candidates demonstrate the ability to optimize the learning environment for all students by applying appropriate models and principles of organizational development and management, including research and data drive decision-making with attention to indicators of equity, effectiveness, and efficiency. (b) Candidates develop a plan of action for focusing on effective organization and management of fiscal, human, and material resources, giving priority to student learning, safety, curriculum, and instruction. (c) Candidates demonstrate an ability to manage time effectively and deploy financial and human resources in ways that promote student achievement.

3.2 Manage Operations	(a) Candidates demonstrate the ability to involve staff in conducting operations and setting priorities using appropriate and effective needs assessment, research-based data, and group process skills to build consensus, communicate, and resolve conflicts in order to align resources with the organizational vision. (b) Candidates develop communications plans for staff that includes opportunities for staff to develop their family and community collaboration skills. (c) Candidates demonstrate an understanding of how to apply legal principles to promote educational equity and provide safe, effective, and efficient facilities.
3.3 Manage Resources	(a) Candidates use problem-solving skills and knowledge of strategic, long-range, and operational planning (including applications of technology) in the effective, legal, and equitable use of fiscal, human, and material resource allocation and alignment that focuses on teaching and learning. (b) Candidates creatively seek new resources to facilitate learning. (c) Candidates apply and assess current technologies for school management, business procedures, and scheduling.

Standard 4.0

Candidates who complete the program are educational leaders who have the knowledge and ability to promote the success of all students by collaborating with families and other community members, responding to diverse community interests and needs, and mobilizing community resources.

Elements	Meets Standards for School Building Leadership
4.1 Collaborate with Families and Other Community Members	(a) Candidates demonstrate an ability to bring together the resources of family members and the community to positively affect student learning. (b) Candidates demonstrate an ability to involve families in the education of their children based on the belief that families have the best interests of their children in mind. (c) Candidates demonstrate the ability to use public information and research-based knowledge of issues and trends to collaborate with families and community members. (d) Candidates apply an understanding of community relations models, marketing strategies and processes, data-based decision-making, and communications theory to craft frameworks for school, family, business, community, government, and higher education partnerships.

4.2
Respond to
Community Interests
and Needs

(e) Candidates develop various methods of outreach aimed at business, religious, political, and service organizations.
(f) Candidates demonstrate the ability to involve families and other stakeholders in school decision-making processes, reflecting an understanding that schools are an integral part of the larger community.
(g) Candidates demonstrate the ability to collaborate with community agencies to integrate health, social, and other services.
(h) Candidates develop a plan for a comprehensive program of community relations and effective relationships with the media.
(a) Candidates demonstrate active involvement within the community, including interactions with individuals and groups with conflicting perspectives.
(b) Candidates demonstrate the ability to use appropriate assessment strategies and research methods to understand and accommodate diverse school and community conditions and dynamics.
(c) Candidates provide leadership to programs serving students with special and exceptional needs.
(d) Candidates demonstrate the ability to capitalize on the diversity (cultural, ethnic, racial, economic, and special interest groups) of the school community to improve school programs and meet the diverse needs of all students.

4.3
Mobilize Community
Resources

(a) Candidates demonstrate an understanding of and ability to use community resources, including youth services, to support student achievement, solve school problems, and achieve school goals.
(b) Candidates demonstrate how to use school resources and social service agencies to serve the community.
(c) Candidates demonstrate an understanding of ways to use public resources and funds appropriately and effectively to encourage communities to provide new resources to address emerging student problems.

Standard 5.0

Candidates who complete the program are educational leaders who have the knowledge and ability to promote the success of all students by acting with integrity, fairly, and in an ethical manner.

Elements	Meets Standards for School Building Leadership
5.1 Acts with Integrity	Candidates demonstrate a respect for the rights of others with regard to confidentiality and dignity and engage in honest interactions.

| 5.2 Acts Fairly | Candidates demonstrate the ability to combine impartiality, sensitivity to student diversity, and ethical considerations in their interactions with others. |
| 5.3 Acts Ethically | Candidates make and explain decisions based on ethical and legal principles. |

Standard 6.0

Candidates who complete the program are educational leaders who have the knowledge and ability to promote the success of all students by understanding, responding to, and influencing the larger political, social, economic, legal, and cultural context.

Elements	Meets Standards for School Building Leadership
6.1 Understand the Larger Context	(a) Candidates act as informed consumers of educational theory and concepts appropriate to school context and can demonstrate the ability to apply appropriate research methods to a school context. (b) Candidates demonstrate the ability to explain how the legal and political systems and institutional framework of schools have shaped a school and community, as well as the opportunities available to children and families in a particular school. (c) Candidates demonstrate the ability to analyze the complex causes of poverty and other disadvantages and their effects on families, communities, children, and learning. (d) Candidates demonstrate an understanding of the policies, laws, and regulations enacted by local, state, and federal authorities that affect schools, especially those that might improve educational and social opportunities. (e) Candidates demonstrate the ability to describe the economic factors shaping a local community and the effects economic factors have on local schools. (f) Candidates demonstrate the ability to analyze and describe the cultural diversity in a school community. (g) Candidates can describe community norms and values and how they relate to the role of the school in promoting social justice. (h) Candidates demonstrate the ability to explain various theories of change and conflict resolution and the appropriate application of those models to specific communities.
6.2 Respond to the Larger Context	(a) Candidates demonstrate the ability to communicate with members of a school community concerning trends, issues, and potential changes in the environment in which the school operates, including maintenance of an ongoing dialogue with representatives of diverse community groups.

6.3 Influence the Larger Context	(a) Candidates demonstrate the ability to engage students, parents, and other members of the community in advocating for adoption of improved policies and laws. (b) Candidates apply their understanding of the larger political, social, economic, legal, and cultural context to develop activities and policies that benefit students and their families. (c) Candidates advocate for policies and programs that promote equitable learning opportunities and success for all students, regardless of socioeconomic background, ethnicity, gender, disability, or other individual characteristics.

Standard 7.0

Internship: The internship provides significant opportunities for candidates to synthesize and apply the knowledge and practice and develop the skills identified in Standards 1 through 6 through substantial, sustained, standards-based work in real settings, planned and guided cooperatively by the institution and school district personnel for graduate credit.

Elements	Meets Standards for School Building Leadership
7.1 Substantial	(a) Candidates demonstrate the ability to accept genuine responsibility for leading, facilitating, and making decisions typical of those made by educational leaders. (b) Each candidate should have a minimum of six months (or equivalent, see footnote) of full-time internship experience.
7.2 Sustained	(a) Candidates participate in planned intern activities during the entire course of the program, including an extended period of time near the conclusion of the program to allow for candidate application of knowledge and skills on a full-time basis.
7.3 Standards-Based	(a) Candidates apply skills and knowledge articulated in these standards as well as state and local standards for educational leaders. (b) Experiences are designed to accommodate candidates' individual needs.
7.4 Real Settings	(a) Candidates' experiences occur in multiple settings that allow for the demonstration of a wide range of relevant knowledge and skills. (b) Candidates' experiences include work with appropriate community organizations such as social service groups and local businesses.
7.5 Planned and Guided Cooperatively	(a) Candidates' experiences are planned cooperatively by the individual, the site supervisor, and institution personnel to provide inclusion of appropriate opportunities to apply skills, knowledge, and research contained in the standards. These three individuals work together to meet candidate and program needs.

| | (b) Mentors are provided training to guide the candidate during the intern experience. |
| 7.6
Credit | (a) Candidates earn graduate credit for their intern experience. |

Note: Length equivalency: The six-month internship experience need not be consecutive and may include experiences of different lengths. However, all internships must include an extended, capstone experience to maximize the candidate's opportunities to practice and refine their skills and knowledge. This culminating experience may be two noncontiguous internships of three months each, a four-month internship and two field practicums of one month each, or another equivalent combination. Full-time experience is defined as the number of hours per week required by a full-time student, receiving federal financial assistance (generally nine to twelve hours per week).

REFERENCES

American Association of School Administrators. (1993). *Professional standards for superintendents.* Arlington, VA: Author.

Boyd, W. L. (Ed.). (2003). *American educational governance on trial: Change and challenge.* The 102nd Yearbook of the National Society for the Study of Education. Chicago: The University of Chicago Press.

Brent, B. (1998). Should graduate training in educational administration be required for principal certification? Existing evidence suggests the answer is no. *Teaching in Educational Administration, 5*(2).

Carnegie Forum on Education and the Economy. (1986). *A nation prepared: Teachers for the 21st century* (Report of the Task Force on Teaching as a Profession.) New York: Author.

Darling-Hammond, L. (1997). *The right to learn: A blueprint for creating schools that work.* San Francisco: Jossey-Bass.

Fischer, F. (1990). *Technocracy and the politics of expertise.* Newbury Park, CA: Sage.

Gibboney, R. A. (1987, April 15). Education of administrators: "An American Tragedy." *Education Week,* p. 28.

Griffiths, D. (Ed.). (1964). *Behavioral science educational administration.* 63rd yearbook. Chicago: National Society for the Study of Education.

Haller, E. J., & Strike, K. A. (1986). *An introduction to educational administration: Social, legal and ethical perspectives.* New York: Longman.

Hallinger, P., & Heck, R. (1996a). Reassessing the principal's role in school effectiveness: A review of empirical research 1980–1995. *Educational Administration Quarterly, 32*(1), 5–44.

Hallinger, P., & Heck, R. (1996b). The principal's role in school effectiveness: A review of methodological issues, 1980–1995. In K. Leithwood et al. (Eds.), *The international handbook of research in educational administration.* New York: Kluwer.

Hallinger, P., & Heck, R. (1999). Can leadership enhance school effectiveness? In T. Bush, L. Bell, R. Bolan, R. Glatter, and P. Ribbens (Eds.), *Educational management: Redefining theory, policy and practice.* London: Paul Chapman.

The Holmes Group. (1986). *Tomorrow's teachers.* East Lansing, MI: Author.

The Holmes Group. (1990). *Tomorrow's schools.* East Lansing, MI: Author.

Kappan editors. (1979). In defense of the external Ed.D. *Phi Delta Kappan, 60*(8), 31–32.

Kellogg Foundation. (1961). *Toward improved school administration: A decade of professional effort to heighten administrative understanding and skills.* Battle Creek, MI: Author.

McDonnell, L. M., & Elmore, R. F. (1987). Getting the job done: Alternative policy instruments. *Educational Evaluation and Policy Analysis, 9*(2), 133–152.

Moore, H., Jr. (1947). *Studies in school administration.* Washington, DC: American Association of School Administrators.

Murphy, J. (Ed.) (2002). *The educational leadership challenge: Redefining leadership for the 21st century.* The 101st Yearbook of the National Society for the Study of Education. Chicago: The University of Chicago Press.

National Association of Elementary School Principals. (1986). *Proficiencies for principals.* Alexandria, VA: Author.

National Association of Secondary School Principals. (1996). *Breaking ranks: Changing an American institution.* Reston, VA: Author.

National Association of Secondary School Principals. (2001). *Priorities and barriers in high school leadership: A survey of principals.* Reston, VA: The Association. *http://www.principals.org/pdf/HSSurvey.pdf*

National Board for Professional Teaching Standards. (1989). *Toward high and rigorous standards for the teaching profession.* Detroit, MI: The Board.

National Commission on Excellence in Education. (1983). *A nation at risk.* Washington, DC: U.S. Government Printing Office.

National Conference of Professors of Educational Administration. (1948, August–September). *Educational leaders—Their function and workplace.* A Report of the Second Work Conference, Madison, WI.

National Council for Accreditation of Teacher Education. (1995). NCATE unveils new education administration standards. *NCATE NEWS,* October 2.

National Policy Board for Educational Administration. (1989). *Improving the preparation of school administrators: An agenda for reform.* Charlottesville, VA: Author.

National Policy Board for Educational Administration. (1990). *The preparation of school administrators. A statement of purpose.* Fairfax. VA: Author.

Peterson, K. D., & Finn, C. E. (1985, Spring). Principals, superintendents, and the administrator's art. *The Public Interest,* (79), 127–131.

Resnick, L. (2001/2002). Learning Leadership on the Job. *Wallace-Readers Digest Funds Leaders Count Report.* Fall/Winter, *1*(2).

Sebring, P. B., Bryk, A. S., Easton, J. Q., Luppescu, S., Thum, Y. M., Lopez, W., & Smith, B. (1995). *Charting reform: Chicago teachers take stock.* Chicago: Consortium on Chicago School Research.

Sebring, P. B., Bryk, A. S., Roderick, M., Camburn, E., Luppescu, S., Thum, Y. M., Smith, B., & Kahne, J. (1996). *Charting reform in Chicago: The students speak.* Chicago: Consortium on Chicago School Research.

Sergiovanni, T. J. (1991). The dark side of professionalism in educational administration. *Phi Delta Kappan, 72*(7), 521–526.

Sergiovanni, T. J. (1994). *Building community in schools.* San Francisco: Jossey-Bass.

Texas Education Agency. (1994). *Learner-context school for Texas: A vision of Texas educators.* Austin, TX: Author.

University Council for Educational Administration. (1987, Spring). National Commission report released. *UCEA Review, 28*(3),1–2.

University Council for Educational Administration (2001). UCEA Establishes National Commission for the Advancement of Educational Leadership Preparation available. *http://www.ucea.org/current%20I%20&%20A/ucea_establishes_national_commis.htm*

Walton, J. (1969). *Administration and policymaking in education* (rev. ed.). Baltimore: Johns Hopkins University Press.

Zaleznik, A. (1989). *The managerial mystique: Restoring leadership in business.* New York: Harper & Row.

Zheng, H. P. Y. (1996). *School context, principal characteristics and instructional leadership effectiveness: A statistical analysis.* Paper presented at the annual meeting of the American Educational Research Association, New York City, April 8–12.

5 The Development of Thought in Educational Administration

A general overview of educational administration was provided in Chapters 3 and 4. This overview included definitions of *administration;* a consideration of the critical responsibility areas, processes, and tasks associated with administration; and an analysis of educational administration as a field of professional practice. Special attention was given to the importance of educational leadership roles. Chapter 5 is concerned with the intellectual heritage of educational administration. Administrators and other professionals practice their art from certain perspectives or accepted ways of operating, which are directly related to the development of thought in their respective fields over time. For this reason, professional practice in any field can be better understood by examining its intellectual heritage.

Models of Administrative Practice

In the professions, paradigms expressed as models of practice determine standards, operating procedures, and other characteristics of practice. Models of practice are systematic approximations of reality that come complete with a convincing internal logic—a set of assumptions, postulates, data, and inferences about some phenomena. Sometimes models are formal and explicit, but often models are implicit—and, indeed, are articulated unknowingly by administrators. Models determine what problems are critical for a profession and provide the practitioner with a theoretical framework for understanding and dealing with problems. Models underlying the administration of special education, for example, have a tendency to emphasize remediation of difficulties rather than prevention. Thus, special education administrators are more likely to be concerned with the critical problem of learning disabilities in urban youth than with poor nutrition of pregnant women in urban areas, though the second seems causally related to the first.

Models also suggest which actions or routines are more valid than others and suggest certain standards of proof for determining effectiveness of these methods. An administrator who operates from a human-relations model, for example, might consider interpersonal relationships as the critical administrative priority in a school. This administrator would employ specific techniques, such as participating in decision making, to improve these relationships and would judge his or her effectiveness by positive changes in morale of the staff. An administrator who operates from an accountability model might consider increased performance as the critical concern in this same school. This administrator would employ specific techniques such as management by objectives and teaching by objectives to improve performance and would judge her or his effectiveness by the number of management objectives achieved or gains in student test scores. The behavior and orientation of each administrator is governed by the model from which he or she is working.

Changes in professional practice are a result of shifts in the models that characterize thinking in the field. In discussing this point, Kuhn (1962) argues that science does not change as a result of piecemeal accumulation of knowledge but by "conceptual revolutions," which result in critical shifts in the intellectual thinking for a particular field—changes in its prevailing models. This chapter examines the development of thought in modern administration, seeking to identify the major models and paradigms that undergird the profession and the shifts that help explain changes in professional practice.

Setting the Stage: Managers of Virtue

It is popular to think of eras as if they have fixed beginnings and endings that coincide with the beginning of the next era. The development of thought in educational administration is more realistically observed as being additive. For example, the moral tone that guided the reformers who sought to create the common school during the period from 1820 to 1880 is alive and well in recent efforts to construct school cultures around themes of shared values and visions; the one-best-way efficiency prescriptions of scientific management during the period from 1890 to 1930 are alive and well in recent efforts to increase school productivity by introducing linear planning, tight alignment of curriculum, teaching and evaluation strategies, and monitoring systems that ensure such strategies are implemented properly. The concern for the social needs of people during the period from 1930 to 1945 and higher order needs during the time from 1950 to 1980 are alive and well in the present emphasis on building interpersonally competent school climates, on empowering teachers, and on using quality circles and shared decision making.

Today's administrators are giving increased attention to building school cultures and relying on cultural norms as ways to get teachers and students to be better connected to the school and its work. These practices are justified by the literature on nonlinear decision making, loose structure, and nonrational organizational functioning that gained prominence during the politics and decision making eras from 1960 to 1975. Knowledge development in educational administration tends to accumulate, with different views representing competing claims on policymakers and school administrators. Some views gain prominence and fade; other views then become prominent only to fade themselves. But none seems to go entirely away.

This analysis of the development of thought begins at about 1900, for it was in the twentieth century that educational administration began its trek toward becoming a distinct management profession connected to but still separate from and hierarchically superior to teaching. During the period from 1820 to 1890, a different kind of quest took place—the establishment of the common school in America. The common school was intended to build a nation by socializing, indeed homogenizing, the young to reflect the values of being an American. In Tyack and Hansot's (1982) words:

> The central challenge for common school crusaders of the mid-nineteenth century was to mobilize the people in support of public education and to construct an educational system. They worked with an overwhelmingly rural nation. State departments of education were small and weak, and the federal government exerted little influence over public schools. Schooling was largely unbureaucratized and unprofessionalized.... Largely Protestant in religion and Anglo-Saxon in ethnic background, they shared a common religious and political conception of the role of public education in shaping a Christian nation.... The school promoters tended to see themselves linked by a common moral earnestness and civic activism. (p. 5)

The emphasis was quite different from 1890 to the 1950s. According to Tyack and Hansot (1982), this was a period that witnessed a changing of the guard from school administrators as part-time "educational evangelists" who crusaded for the common school to a new breed of professional managers—"administrative progressives." This new breed sought to reshape the school through the use of business efficiency and scientific expertness. Like the crusaders before them, the new breed viewed its trust as sacred—the need to save the schools from uninformed lay participation and willy-nilly politics by separating education from politics. The means to this goal was to create a profession of educational administration based on scientific knowledge. The administrative progressives believed that this scientific knowledge would be respected by laypersons and politicians, thus affording the school administrator greater autonomy in running the affairs of schooling.

As Tyack and Hansot (1982) explain, education leaders of this era

> were social engineers who sought to bring about a smoothly meshing corporate society.... Their task was not to create but to redesign the public-school system, not to arouse public participation in education but to constrain it, not to campaign for a common denominator of education so much as to differentiate it according to the needs of a complex society *(as they interpreted these needs).* Most of these leaders made education a lifelong career and were pioneers in its professionalization. They wished the state to take an active role in transforming education. (p. 6)

They note further:

> The members of the "educational trust" (as the administrative progressives were sometimes called) embraced the new managerial models developed in business...

they sought legitimacy through expertise rather than through deference to character or through broad public participation in policymaking…they shaped their preferred policies into a standard template of reform which they applied to state after state, district after district, in their school surveys and legislative proposals. They successfully changed the structures of decision-making and sought to turn political issues into matters for administrative decisions, confident that schools could rise "above politics." (p. 7)

The common school crusaders of the nineteenth century saw themselves as constituting an "aristocracy of character." By contrast, in the twentieth century, school leaders regarded themselves as professional experts certified by specialized training. They banded together "into exclusively professional associations like the American Association of School Administrators (AASA), sponsoring and being sponsored by fellow experts, elaborating legal and bureaucratic rules, and turning to science and business as sources of authority for an emergent profession" (Tyack & Hansot, 1982, p. 6). This quest for professionalism continued throughout the twentieth century, reaching a crescendo in recent years with the establishment of the National Policy Board for Educational Administration (NPBEA) and the linking of its efforts with the powerful National Council for the Accreditation of Teacher Education (NCATE). The underlying theme for determining the nature of this profession changes as various models of educational administration wax and wane.

Earlier common school crusaders such as Horace Mann and Henry Barnard sought to create the common school by enlisting the support of politicians, school people, and lay citizens alike. During this era, schools were considered to be political enterprises governed by democratic authority. Grass roots participation became the norm. As a result, powerful school boards emerged that often assumed responsibility for hiring and firing teachers and administrators, approving curriculum, and performing other tasks now thought to be the province of professions. Superintendents and other school administrators had to contend with and compete with this political power. In the end, it was the will of the people that prevailed, not the school person, and the administrative progressives felt that this situation needed to be corrected by professionalizing educational administration.

Some of the leaders of the movement to professionalize educational administration during this period were Ellwood P. Cubberly, Stanford University; George Strayer, Teachers College, Columbia University; Edward C. Elliott, University of Wisconsin; Frank Spaulding, Yale University; and Franklin Bobbitt, University of Chicago. Teachers College, Columbia University, and Stanford University were particularly influential, preparing the lion's share of professors and superintendents who spread the gospel of efficiency and scientific management and who became charter members of the new profession of educational administration.

The Cubberly story, as told by Tyack and Hansot (1982, pp. 122–128) was particularly revealing. When Cubberly, a physical scientist by training, with no background in elementary and secondary education, was appointed superintendent of schools in San Diego in 1896, he found a school board mired in politics and heavily involved in making decisions that he thought should be the province of the superintendent. He became convinced that school boards should not be political and that school districts should be run by experts—professional administrators who knew their business. This view is still widely shared today by policymakers, school administrators, and citizens. When appointed to the education faculty at Stanford University in 1888, Cubberly welcomed the opportunity to prepare that kind of school administrator. He introduced and taught such courses as "School Administration, School Problems, School Organization, School Statistics, Secondary School, History of Education, Relationship of Ignorance and Crime to Education" (Sears & Henderson, cited in Tyack & Hansot, 1982, p. 124).

Cubberly and other professors of the time relied on the limited literature that existed in educational administration, on their own experiences as school administrators, and, for the most part, on the burgeoning literature in business administration—most notably the works of Frederick Taylor on scientific management and later of other management experts such as Fayol, Gulick, and Urwick. Cubberly, for example, advocated scientific management and bureaucratic conceptions of hierarchy. To him, the superintendent was *the* person to whom and from whom authority, directions, and even inspiration should flow. He was not an advocate of teacher participation in defining school policies, and he felt that schools should give up the idea that all persons were equal (Tyack & Hansot, 1982, p. 128).

Another influential person during this period was George Strayer, a well-known professor at Teachers College, Columbia University, and an expert on uniform statistical accounting, school finance formulas, and standardized school building designs. He was prominent in the school survey movement that developed a comprehensive standardized template of how schools should be efficiently organized, staffed, and operated and then measured the extent to which schools and school districts measured up to this one-best-way standard. To Strayer (1914), the survey was designed to provide a record of the "organization, administration, supervision, cost, physical equipment, courses of study, teaching staff, methods of teaching, student body, and results as measured by the achievement of those who are being trained or have been trained therein" (p. 302). Surveys were very popular because their findings provided superintendents with a source of professional authority in the form of *research* to override the democratic authority of board members or the professional authority of teachers who might have alternate visions of what the school should be. After all, what counts more—teacher opinions and board preferences or expert knowledge backed by survey research?

Strayer believed that much of the progress of urban schools during the time from 1905 to 1930 could be attributed to the application of scientific management and to the professional training of school administrators. By progress, he had in mind such advances as:

Development of clear line and staff organization;

Reorganization of traditional uniform elementary and secondary schools into differentiated institutions, including junior high schools, that treated individuals and groups according to abilities and needs;

Creation of special classes for the "backward, delinquent, physically handicapped and the like," vocational tracks, and instruction in subjects like health and physical education;

Professionalization of the occupation of teaching and administration by upgrading standards of education, certification, tenure, specialization of function, and supervision;

Standardization of methods of "public accounting" and enforcement of attendance;

Introduction of "sound business administration" in budgeting, planning and maintenance, and finance. (Strayer, 1930, pp. 376–378, cited in Tyack & Hansot, 1982, p. 153)

Cubberly, Strayer, and other administrative progressives were, in many respects, a small part of a larger movement that sought to professionalize business management, bureaucratize the country's institutions, and transform the United States into a corporate state. For these reasons, one cannot understand the development of thought in educational administration without giving attention to the development of management thought in general. The analysis that follows gives attention to both. It sketches the main strands of thought that have evolved in management in general and how these ideas have affected the ways in which schools have been and are organized, managed, and led.

Major Strands of Thought in Administration

To simplify matters, recent intellectual development in administration will be grouped into four major strands of thought, each of which suggests a fairly distinct model for viewing administration. These models are concerned with *efficiency*, the *person, politics* and *culture.*

The efficiency period began in the early 1900s and remained popular until about 1930. Models of organization and administration that emphasized concern for people were dominant from about 1930 to the mid-1960s and remain popular today in the literature of school administration and among practitioners.

Political views span a period from the end of World War II to the present. These views are considered by many to dominate present thinking in educational administration. Models characterized by a concern for efficiency and a concern for the person have not been replaced completely. Both have advocates from within the academic community and from among practicing professionals. Indeed, much of what the models offer remains appropriate and can be incorporated into political and decision-making views. In spite of their present popularity, political and decision-making views, too, will be replaced by others as part of the natural progression of knowledge expansion in the field. An emergent view in educational administration reflects a high concern for culture in its analysis of organizational structure, work design, and organizational behavior. Culture, as is the case with efficiency, person, and politics, is a metaphor used to help one think about organizational life in a specific way.

Academic advocates of one or another model are often ideological and dogmatic about what good practice is in educational administration. Ideas from competing models are viewed negatively. Most experienced administrators, by contrast, assume a more moderate and tolerant posture by looking for the good in all views. They adopt a reflective practice posture within which knowledge from theory and research is not used directly to prescribe practice but indirectly to inform one's intuition and judgment as decisions are made in practice (see, e.g., Schon, 1983; Sergiovanni, 1987). They use knowledge gleaned from available models of administration conceptually rather than instrumentally (Kennedy, 1984). Ideally, models should be used to help school administrators think about professional problems and thus augment subsequent decisions, and not to tell them what to do or blind them to other models. Unfortunately, models of administration sometimes become *mindscapes* for administrators, and when this is the case, their thinking and behavior are programmed in a specific fashion and they become blind to or suspicious of other views. Thus, as the major strands of thought are overviewed here, keep in mind that each has features appropriate to certain aspects of professional practice but not to others. Further, when used exclusively, *none of the views is sufficiently comprehensive or true to be helpful.* The efficiency model, for example, can be helpful in establishing high school scheduling routines or in developing a series of attendance or purchasing-management policies. Applying insights from the same model to problems of teacher motivation, supervision, and evaluation, however, is likely to result in bureaucratic teaching, rigid learning, and subsequently serious staff morale problems. As the strands of thought and inferred models are discussed and compared, keep in mind the costs and benefits of using each in professional practice. This analysis should help one in using the models as alternative possibilities, each appropriate to different aspects of practice. This is the essence of reflective practice in any profession.

An important disclaimer to this discussion is that the overview presented is not exhaustive. The intent is only to provide highlights of the models and to accent the differences among them.

Concern for Efficiency

In many respects, schools today are organized and operated according to certain established principles of good management. A division of labor exists whereby instructional and coordinative tasks are allocated to specific roles. Roles are defined by job descriptions that are clearly linked to some overall conception of what the school is to accomplish. Certain guides, such as span of control and student/teacher ratio, have been accepted to help decide the number of teachers needed and how they should be assigned. Tasks are subdivided and specialists are hired for some functions. Roles are ordered according to rank, with some enjoying more authority and privilege than others. The development of rank helps to ensure that those who are lower in the hierarchy will function in manners consistent with job expectations and goals. Day-to-day decisions are routinized and controlled by establishing and monitoring a system of policies and rules. These, in turn, ensure more reliable behavior on behalf of goals. Proper communication channels are established and objective mechanisms are developed for handling disputes, allocating resources, and evaluating personnel.

Scientific Management and the Efficiency Model.   Much of what is taken for granted as good management today can be traced to an era of development in administration referred to as *scientific management.* Frederick Winslow Taylor is credited as the founding father of the scientific-management movement. His impact on organization and management in education is now a matter of record (Callahan, 1962) and is reviewed only briefly.

In his *Principles of Scientific Management,* published in 1911, Taylor offered four principles that were the foundation for his science of work and organization. The first was to replace intuitive methods of doing the work of the organization with a *scientific method* based on observation and analysis to obtain the best cost-benefit ratio. He felt that for every task, a *one best way* should be determined. The second principle was to *select the best person* for the job scientifically and train this person thoroughly in the tasks and procedures to be followed. The third principle was to "heartily cooperate with the men" to ensure, through *monitoring,* close supervision, and incentive systems, that the work is being done according to established standards and procedures. The fourth principle was to *divide* the work of managers and workers so that managers assume responsibility for planning and preparing work and for supervising. Taylor believed that what workers did needed to be tightly connected to management through systems of monitoring that emphasized data collection on the one hand and close firsthand supervision on the other. Taylor's ideas quickly found their way into the study and practice of educational administration. Franklin Bobbitt, an educator of the period and an advocate of scientific management, stated:

> In any organization, the directive and supervisory members must clearly define the ends toward which the organization strives. They must coordinate the labors of all so as to attain those ends. They must find the best methods of work, and they must enforce the use of these methods on the part of the workers. They must determine the qualifications necessary for the workers and see that each rises to the standard qualifications, if it is possible; and when impossible, see that he is separated from the organization. This requires direct or indirect responsibility for the preliminary training of workers before service and for keeping them up to standard qualifications during service. Directors and supervisors must keep the workers supplied with detailed instructions as to the work to be done, the standards to be reached, the methods to be employed, and the materials and appliances to be used. They must place incentives before the worker in order to stimulate desirable effort. Whatever the nature or purpose of the organization, if it is an effective one, these are always the directive and supervisory tasks. (Bobbitt, 1913)

Taylor's theories of management and organization became the means to create a science of education and educational administration themed to efficiency principles—a science that Cubberly believed represented a new professional model for administrators. In Cubberly's words (cited in Callahan, 1962),

> The recent attempts to survey and measure school systems and to determine the efficiency of instruction along scientific lines have alike served to develop a scientific method for attacking administrative problems which promises to compel us soon to rewrite the whole history of our school administration in terms of these new units and scales of measuring educational progress and determining educational efficiency. All of these developments point unmistakably in the direction of the evolution of a profession of school administration as distinct from the work of teaching on one hand and politics on the other. (p. 217)

For the next three decades, basic concepts and strategies of the efficiency model were applied to the broader question of administration and organizational design by many European and American writers. French theorist Henri Fayol (1949) offered a universal list of good management principles that became very popular. These included division of work, authority, and responsibility; discipline; unit of command; and unity of direction. Gulick and Urwick (1937) offered the principles of unity of command, span of control, and matching of people to the organizational structure. They were advocates of division of work, not only by purpose, but by process, person, and place. Scientific management did not offer a theory of administration and organization as such, but a set of principles and simple injunctions for administrators to follow. Efficiency was to be maximized by defining objectives and outputs clearly, by specializing tasks through division of labor, and—once the *best way* is identified—by introducing a system of controls to ensure uniformity and reliability in workers' tasks and to ensure standardization of product.

The following principles of management offered by Fayol (1949, pp. 20–40) are examples of the efficiency literature of administration in the management of schools—all of which are still used today in various degrees:

1. *Division of work* based on task specialization should be practiced. Jobs should be broken down into small parts and grouped in a fashion that permits individuals to work on only a limited number.
2. *Authority* should be clearly delineated so that responsibilities of each worker are known and their relationships to other workers, up, across, or down the hierarchical chain, are clear.
3. *Discipline* should be established in the sense that superiors (i.e., administrators and teachers) have a right to expect deference and obedience from subordinates.
4. *Unity of command* should be practiced as a mechanism for clearly delineating authority relationships. Fayol believed that an employee should receive direction from and, in return, be accountable to only one superior. (One of the arguments often cited in opposition to team-teaching plans is that the traditional authority structure of the teacher and students becomes confused and students are not sure to whom they *belong*.)

5. *Unity of direction,* whereby each objective should be accompanied by a specific plan for achievement of a specific group of people who would be accountable for achieving that objective.
6. *Subordination of individual interest* in favor of those of the organization and of the work group should be encouraged.
7. *Remuneration* should be fair but routinized so that unreasonable overpayments are avoided. The standard salary schedule, for example, is considered better than merit pay.
8. *Centralization* of decision making should be practiced to permit proper coordination, with judicious decentralization accompanied by proper controls when needed.
9. *Scalar chain,* as a mechanism for defining the line of command flow of communication from the highest to lowest rank, should be practiced.
10. Material and social *order* should be the rule to ensure that everything and everyone is in the proper place.
11. *Equity* should be practiced, in the sense that justice should govern administrative action.
12. *Stability* of tenure of personnel is desirable and should be sought.
13. *Initiative* should be encouraged at all levels of the organization.
14. *Esprit,* in the form of harmony and unity of workers, should be encouraged.

Some would argue that the first ten of Fayol's principles contradict the last four. Equity, stability, initiative, and esprit are likely to suffer in the absence of more flexibility in management and organization and a greater distribution of authority within the organization.

Efficiency principles persevere today as strong considerations in curriculum development, in selecting educational materials, in developing instructional systems, and in other aspects of educational administration. Scientific-management thinking has weathered ups and downs for three-quarters of a century and today enjoys a resurgence. Fueled by demands for accountability and political conservatism in society, and by advancements in management techniques (such as operation research, systems analysis, and computer systems), earlier scientific management has emerged into a new, more sophisticated form.

In education, this neoscientific or modern scientific management offers such efficiency ideas as performance contracting, behavioral objectives, state and national assessment, cost-benefit analysis, management by objectives, strategic planning, and management information system, each prescribed to maximize educational reliability and productivity at decreased cost.

The school-reform movement that began in the early 1980s emphasized mandates and incentives as policy instruments (McDonnell & Elmore, 1987). This movement reflected a high concern for efficiency in management and embodied many of the principles of scientific management. The tight alignment of measurable goals with curriculum, curriculum with specific teaching formats, teaching with systems of close supervision and evaluation, and everything with testing is an example. Typically, quality control within this reform movement was viewed as a management problem solvable by designing external control mechanisms such as standardized evaluation systems and testing programs. In most states, the school-reform movement was biased toward identifying the one best way to provide schooling.

Even recent reform efforts embody scientific-management characteristics. Schools are provided with the power to decide the means of education but not the ends. They remain accountable to uniform standards decided at the state and federal levels. The provided standards wind up determining the means anyway. With this unofficial but real scripting, scientific management endures.

In neoscientific management, however, traditional scientific-management control mechanisms such as face-to-face supervision are replaced by more impersonal, technical, or rational control mechanisms. Even when face-to-face supervision cannot be avoided, the control mechanism is so impersonal and so programmed that the faces do not count. This is the case with measurement-oriented and teacher assessment systems that script what evaluators must consider and provide the rules that govern this consideration. The evaluation systems themselves function as *decision makers* and call the shots with a minimum of help from people. In a sense, they are both teacher-proof and evaluator-proof. Neoscientific management systems assume that if visible standards of performance, objectives, or competencies can be identified and measured, then the work of teachers and that of students can be better controlled by holding them accountable to these standards, thus ensuring greater reliability, effectiveness, and efficiency in performance.

The issue of motivating workers is handled similarly. In scientific management, it is assumed that people are primarily motivated by economic and other extrinsic incentives and that they will do that which brings them the greatest extrinsic gain. Workers can be controlled by manipulating these incentives. Applications of scientific-management thinking are perhaps most easily recognized in the organization and instruction of many classrooms. Decisions with respect to class objectives, assignments, activities, and supervision of students are made unilaterally by teachers. Students are evaluated against class objectives, and grades are the primary incentive offered to students. If the curriculum is programmed in sufficient detail, teachers play a minor role in this process—that of following and giving directions—and are themselves supervised and evaluated according to scientific-management principles by administrators. Evaluating teachers by using student test scores or by relying on heavily prescribed and standardized evaluation systems are examples.

In 1916, Cubberly used the metaphors of factory and production to describe schools:

> Every manufacturing establishment that turns out a standard product or a series of products of any kind maintains a force of efficiency experts to study methods of procedure and to measure and test the output of its works. Such men ultimately bring the manufacturing establishment large returns, by introducing improvements in processes and procedure, and in training the workmen to produce larger and better output. Our schools are, in a sense, factories in which the raw products (children) are

to be shaped and fashioned into products to meet the various demands of life. The specifications for manufacturing come from the demands of twentieth-century civilization, and it is the business of the school to build its pupils according to the specifications laid down. This demands good tools, specialized machinery, continuous measurement of production to see if it is according to specifications, the elimination of waste in manufacture, and a large variety in the output. (p. 388)

At this writing, factory and production metaphors are still very common in discussions of schooling. Educators still frequently conceive of students as raw material, the teacher as worker, the principal as supervisor, the curriculum as a processing script, and teaching as the processing itself as students are converted from raw materials to finished products that meet predetermined specifications. Neoscientific thinking in schools remains strong.

Bureaucratic Theories and the Efficiency Model. Bureaucratic thinking refined the norms of rationality and certainty that were characteristic of scientific management. It was assumed that all aspects of the organization—from its objectives, technical requirements, and work flow, to the details of its organizational structure—could be defined and organized into a permanent grand design. All that remained was to find people who could be programmed into this design. According to Weber (1946),

> The fully developed bureaucratic mechanism compares with other organizations exactly as does the machine with the non-mechanical modes of production...precision, speed, unambiguity, continuity, discretion, unity...these are raised to the optimum point in a strictly bureaucratic administration.... The individual bureaucrat cannot squirm out of the apparatus in which he is harnessed.... In a great majority of cases, he is only a single cog in an ever moving mechanism which prescribes to him an eventually fixed route of march. (pp. 34–37)

Bureaucracy shares with scientific management the assumptions that people are primarily motivated by economic (or other extrinsic) concerns and work to maximize their economic gain. Economic gain is under control of the organization, however, and the person is to be engineered and controlled by this organization. The individual rationality of scientific management is replaced by organizational rationality as defined by standard operating procedures, formal organization charts, job descriptions, policy manuals, and other organizational routines. This impersonal quality of organizational rationality suggests the metaphor *mechanistic* when one speaks of bureaucratic theories.

Bureaucracy remains a part of the image of most educational organizations, and its advocates work diligently to incorporate its principles of order and certainty. Though the relatively harsh conception of humankind typically associated with this efficiency model may not fully characterize the relationships that generally exist between administrators and teachers, this conception remains ubiquitous as applied to students. Indeed, as one might well predict from bureaucratic thought, the lower a person is in the organizational hierarchy, the more she or he will be seen as fitting the underlying assumptions of human characteristics of the efficiency model.

Bureaucracy in schools endures because of the assurances of order, rationality, accountability, and stability it provides to the public. School administrators are often among its most avid fans. Clear lines of authority and specialization of functions provide a convincing justification for professional management on the one hand and proliferate managerial roles on the other (Parkinson, 1958).

Morgan (1986) sums up the strengths and limitations in practice of the concern-for-efficiency view as follows:

> The strengths can be stated very simply. For mechanistic approaches to organization work well only under conditions where machines work well:
>
> (a) when there is a straightforward task to perform;
> (b) when the environment is stable enough to ensure that the products produced will be appropriate ones;
> (c) when one wishes to produce exactly the same product time and again;
> (d) when precision is at a premium; and
> (e) when the "human machine" parts are compliant and behave as they have been designed to do. (p. 34)
>
> However, despite these successes, mechanistic approaches to organization often have severe limitations. In particular they:
>
> (a) can create organizational forms that have great difficulty in adapting to changing circumstances;
> (b) can result in mindless and unquestioning bureaucracies;
> (c) can have unanticipated and undesirable consequences as the interests of those working in the organization take precedence over the goals the organization was designed to achieve; and
> (d) can have dehumanizing effects upon employees, especially those at the lower levels of the organizational hierarchy. (p. 35)

Concern for the Person

By the 1930s, an effective counterforce on behalf of the human side of enterprise began to emerge. This force was later to evolve into a distinct pattern of thought about administration that is labeled the *person model*. Person views are divided into two phases, human relations and human resources, with the latter being a progressive development of the former. The word *organic* is often used to describe the human-resources version of the person model. The analogy is that of a biological organism capable of feeling and growing but also capable of ill health if not properly nurtured. Maintenance and nurturance of the human organization are important concerns of administrators who operate within the person model. The building blocks to organizational health are individuals and their needs and groups of individuals. According to this view, an ideal school is one characterized by highly motivated individuals who are committed to school objectives from which they derive intrinsic satisfaction. These individuals are linked together into highly effective work groups. The work groups are characterized by commitment to common school objectives, by group loyalty, and by mutual support.

Whereas scientific management and bureaucracy emphasize *task* specialization, the human-resources version of the person model emphasizes *person* specialization. Task specialization requires the careful sectioning, dividing, and assigning of work by those in authority. Person specialization permits individuals to function as experts who enjoy discretionary prerogatives and who are influenced more by client needs and their own expert abilities than by carefully delineated duties and tasks.

As early as 1909, Chicago school superintendent Ella Flag Young noted:

> There has been a tendency toward factory-evolution and factory-management, and the teachers, like the children who stand at machines, are told just what to do. The teachers, instead of being the great moving force, educating and developing the powers of the human mind in such a way that they shall contribute to the power and efficiency of this democracy, tend to become mere workers at the treadmill, but they are doing all through this country that which shows that it is difficult to crush the human mind and the love of freedom in the hearts and lives of people who are qualified to teach school. As a result they are organizing federations to get together and discuss those questions which are vital in the life of the children and in the life of the teachers—you cannot separate the life of the children and the life of the teacher if you know what you are about. (cited in Tyack & Hansot, 1982, p. 181)

Young was the first woman to become superintendent of a big-city school district and the first woman to become president of the National Education Association. She was a vocal critic of scientific management, a pioneer in advocating democratic planning among teachers and democratic administration for the schools, and a strong voice for women's rights in both teaching and school administration.

Social philosopher Mary Parker Follett was also among the first whose views in opposition to a strictly mechanistic view of organization and administration were heard. Writing in the 1920s, she called for the integratation of the views of scientific management and efficiency principles of organizational design and functioning with insights from individual psychology and the psychology of work groups. Professional administration, in her view, was to be built on a foundation of science on the one hand and the motive of service on the other (Metcalf & Urwick, 1940). To this end, Follet continued, administration should be built on a trinity of values: artful practice, scientific understanding, and ethical considerations. This "trinity of values" seems remarkably contemporary as one reads today's literature on school leadership. Should any of the three values be unduly emphasized, then the other two are likely to be neglected. In her book *Creative Experience,* Follett (1924) turned her attention to the dynamic nature of administration and the importance of human relationships and a harmonious group climate to this nature.

Follet's and Young's ideas were quite advanced for the time and provided the philosophical base for administrative and organizational theorizing that emphasized concern for the person, particularly as it evolved into the human-resources view.

Human Relations.   The benchmark most frequently mentioned as the beginning of the human-relations movement in administration is the work of the research team that operated from 1922 to 1932 at the Cicero, Illinois, Hawthorne plant of the Western Electric Company. This research team, headed by Elton Mayo and Fritz Roethlisberger, sought to determine the relationship between physical factors such as level of lighting at the workplace, rest periods, and length of the workday on increased performance of workers (Roethlisberger & Dickson, 1939). They found that regardless of whether physical conditions such as lighting, rest periods, and length of the workday were positively or negatively varied, production continued to increase. The researchers finally concluded that changes in physical job conditions did not result in increased production; rather, such increases seemed to result in changed social conditions of the worker. Changes in worker motivation and satisfaction were most often credited with increased production. These, in turn, seemed related to more democratic patterns of supervision used by the researchers and others during the experiments. Relative to existing conditions, workers received unprecedented attention from researchers, were able to socialize easily with other workers, and had some say in deciding working conditions. These conditions, in turn, seemed to have resulted in higher motivation and commitment levels, greater effort at work, and higher production records for people involved in the Hawthorne experiment.

Mayo's (1945) work is of particular importance to the development of this movement. His extensive interview studies at Western Electric revealed that workers subjected to more efficiency-oriented management suffered from alienation and loss of identity. As a result of his work, Mayo offered a set of assumptions to characterize people, which were quite different from those of efficiency management. He suggested that people are primarily motivated by social needs and obtain their basic satisfactions from relationships with others. He maintained that management had robbed work of meaning, and therefore meaning must be provided in the social relationships on the job. On the basis of his interviews, Mayo also concluded that people are more responsive to the social forces of their peer group than to extrinsic incentives and management controls. Finally, Mayo maintained that a person's identity and loyalty to management and organization depended on his or her ability to provide for self-social (interaction and acceptance) needs.

Leadership principles that took into account the social group, satisfaction of workers' social needs, and psychological manipulation of workers through counseling were examples of management to be gleaned from the historic Hawthorne studies.

Human-relations thought is often criticized for overemphasizing human social needs at the expense of needs for accomplishment and responsibility. A person's social needs were often considered separate from other concerns more directly related to the tasks of the organization. It was assumed that as long as a worker was happy and comfortable, he or she would show little interest in the policy decision affecting his or her work.

Human Resources.   Human relations began to mature with the work of Kurt Lewin (1951) as he sought to link human behavior more closely with such environmental factors as role expectations and organizational climate. His social-systems view of people in organizations provided a more complete picture of reality. The writings of Abraham Maslow, Douglas McGregor, Chris Argyris, Warren Bennis, and Rensis Likert became the new tenets as human-relations thought matured. These theorists had academic credentials in social psychology or in the new interdisciplinary field at the time—organizational psychology.* Some authors referred to this maturity of human relations as *human resources,* to suggest the change of emphasis from social needs of individuals at work to needs expressed as a desire for more intrinsic satisfaction from increased organizational responsibility and from achievement of organizational goals (Miles, 1965; Sergiovanni & Starratt, 1979).

Human-resources theorists agreed with earlier human-relations writers that applications of the efficiency model typically resulted in loss of meaning in work. But this loss was not attributed to neglect of a person's social needs as much as to his or her inability to use talents fully. Certainly, social needs were important, but a person's capacity for growth and challenge were the needs that received the greatest attention from human-resources theorists.

The famous analysis and comparison of Theories X and Y by Douglas McGregor (1960) is a good representation of human-resources thinking. McGregor believed that Theory X and Theory Y managers behaved differently, because they had internalized two very different theories of management. Theory X comprised assumptions and propositions generally associated with efficiency views of administration. Theory Y, on the other hand, had a higher regard for the value and potential of the person. The assumptions and propositons of Theories X and Y follow.†

Theory X

1. The average human being has an inherent dislike of work and will avoid it if he can.
2. Because of this human characteristic of dislike of work, most people must be coerced, controlled, directed, threatened with punishment to get them to put forth adequate effort toward the achievement of organizational objectives.
3. The average human being prefers to be directed, wishes to avoid responsibility, has relatively little ambition, wants security above all.

Theory Y

1. *The expenditure of physical and mental effort in work is as natural as play or rest.* The average human being does not inherently dislike work. Depending upon controllable conditions, work may be a source of satisfaction (and will be voluntarily performed) or a source of punishment (and will be avoided if possible).
2. *External control and the threat of punishment are not the only means for bringing about effort toward organizational objectives. Man will exercise self-direction and self-control in the service of objectives to which he is committed.*

---

*See, for example, McGregor (1960) and Rensis Likert, *The Human Organization* (New York: McGraw-Hill, 1967). For examples of books in educational administration identified with this era, see Jacob Getzels, James Lipham, and Roald Campbell, *Administration as a Social Process* (New York: Harper & Row, 1968); and Thomas Sergiovanni and Fred D. Carver, *The New Social Executive: A Theory of Administration* (New York: Dodd Mead, 1973).

†From *The Human Side of Enterprise* by D. McGregor, pp. 33–34, 47–48. Copyright © 1960 McGraw-Hill. Used with permission of McGraw-Hill Book Company.

3. *Commitment to objectives is a function of the rewards associated with their achievement.* The most significant of such rewards, e.g., the satisfaction of ego and self-actualization needs, can be direct products of effort directed toward organizational objectives.

4. *The average human being learns, under proper conditions, not only to accept but to seek responsibility.* Avoidance of responsibility, lack of ambition, and emphasis on security are generally consequences of experience, not inherent human characteristics.

5. *The capacity to exercise a relatively high degree of imagination, ingenuity, and creativity in the solution of organizational problems is widely, not narrowly, distributed in the population.*

6. *Under the conditions of modern industrial life, the intellectual potentialities of the average human being are only partially utilized.* (McGregor, 1960, pp. 33–34, 47–48)

The nature of interaction between personality and organization became another key focus of study (Argyris, 1957; Getzels & Guba, 1957). Human-relations theorists viewed personality and organization as being hopelessly in conflict and sided with personality. Efficiency theorists shared this view of conflict, but its advocates sided with organization. Human resources recognized personality and organization conflict but did view it as inherent. According to this view, the two were to be integrated, with workers receiving maximum satisfaction and enrichment from achievement at work and, in turn, work reaching new levels of effectiveness because of worker commitment to organizational goals.

Human resources urged that shared decision making, joint planning, common goals, increased responsibility, and more autonomy be the sorts of power-equalization strategies developed by educational administrators. Motivation was to be intrinsic because jobs were to be interesting and challenging. Job enrichment was advocated as a means to build into the jobs of students and teachers increased opportunities for experiencing achievement, recognition, advancement, opportunities for growth, and increased competence. Human-resources theories reflected not only an interest in people at work but also a new regard for their potential. Teachers, for example, were to be considered as professionals, well able to respond to these progressive, optimizing ideas. In education, such organizational concepts as team teaching, family grouping, open space, school within a school, open corridor, integrated day, and multiunits are often based on human-resources concepts. In Table 5.1, assumptions basic to human-relations views and human-resources views are summarized and compared.

Person views of administration, particularly human-resources views, place a great deal of emphasis on autonomy, inner direction, and the desire for maximum self-development at work. As long as these conditions hold for teachers at one level and for students at another, then the optimizing characteristics of these views are likely to work. But the desire for universal self-actualization and the centrality of the work setting in one's life are debatable. In speaking of this issue, Dubin (1959) notes:

Work, for probably a majority of workers, and even extending into the ranks of management, may represent an institutional setting that is not the central life interest of

TABLE 5.1 Comparing Human-Relations and Human-Resources Views

Human-Relations Model	Human-Resources Model
Attitudes toward People	
1. People in our culture, leaders among them, share a common set of needs—to belong, to be liked, to be respected.	1. In addition to sharing common needs for belonging and respect, most people in our culture, teachers among them, desire to contribute effectively and creatively to the accomplishment of worthwhile objectives.
2. Teachers desire individual recognition, but, more importantly, they want to *feel* useful to the school and to their own work group.	2. The majority of teachers are capable of exercising far more initiative, responsibility, and creativity than their present jobs or work circumstances require or allow.
3. They tend to cooperate willingly and comply with school goals if these important needs are fulfilled.	3. These capabilities represent untapped resources, which are presently being wasted.
Kind and Amount of Participation	
1. The administrator's basic task is to make each teacher believe that he or she is a useful and important part of the team.	1. The administrator's basic task is to create an environment in which subordinates can contribute their full range of talents to the accomplishment of school goals. She or he works to uncover the creative resources of subordinates.
2. The administrator is willing to explain her or his decisions and to discuss subordinates' objections to the plans. On routine matters, he or she encourages subordinates in planning and in decision making.	2. The administrator allows and encourages teachers to participate in important as well as routine decisions. In fact, the more important a decision is to the school, the greater the administrator's efforts to tap faculty resources.
3. Within narrow limits, the faculty or individual teachers who make up the faculty should be allowed to exercise self-direction and self-control in carrying out plans.	3. Administrators work continually to expand the areas over which teachers exercise self-direction and self-control as they develop and demonstrate greater insight and ability.
Expectations	
1. Sharing information with teachers and involving them in school decision making will help satisfy their basic needs for belonging and for individual recognition.	1. The overall quality of decision making and performance will improve as administrators and teachers make use of the full range of experience, insight, and creative ability that exist in their schools.
2. Satisfying these needs will improve faculty morale and will reduce resistance to formal authority.	2. Teachers will exercise responsible self-direction and self-control in the accomplishment of worthwhile objectives that they understand and have helped establish.
3. High faculty morale and reduced resistance to formal authority may lead to improved school performance. It will at least reduce friction and make the administrator's job easier.	3. Faculty satisfaction will increase as a by-product of improved performance and the opportunity to contribute creatively to this improvement.

Source: R. E. Miles, "Human Relations or Human Resources?" *Harvard Business Review,* 43(4), 1965, p. 151. Copyright 1965 by the *Harvard Business Review.* Adapted by permission.

the participants. The consequence of this is that while participating in work, a general attitude of apathy and indifference prevails.... Thus, the industrial worker does not feel imposed upon by the tyranny of organizations, company, or union. (p. 161)

Strauss (1963) cautions:

1. Although many individuals find relatively little satisfaction in their work, this may not be as much of a deprivation as the hypothesis would suggest, since many of these same individuals center their lives off the job and find most of their satisfactions in the community and the home. With these individuals, power-equalization may not liberate much energy.
2. Individuals are not motivated solely to obtain autonomy, self-actualization, and so forth. With various degrees of emphasis, individuals also want security and to know what is expected of them. Power-equalization may certainly stir up a good deal of anxiety among those who are not prepared for it, and at least some individuals may be reluctant to assume the responsibility that it throws upon them.
3. Power-equalization techniques are not too meaningful when management needs no more than an "adequate" level of production, as is often the case when work is highly programmed. Under such circumstances the costs entailed by modification in job design and supervisory techniques may be greater than the gains obtained from increased motivation to work. (p. 48)

A further criticism of person views, which applies as well to efficiency theories, is their internal-to-the-organization emphasis. By focusing almost exclusively on individual and group issues, the larger social, political, and legal contexts of educational administration are underemphasized and often ignored. This issue is explored further in the discussion of the political and the cultural models of administration that appear next.

Concern for Politics

Political thinking represents a recent and important development in the literature of educational administration. In many respects, this view of organization and administration represents a major change in thinking—a significant paradigm shift. Four critical emphases distinguish political views from those that emphasize efficiency of the person.

1. Whereas each of the other views was primarily concerned with forces, events, and activities internal to the school as an organization, the political view is concerned with the dynamic interplay of the organization with forces in its external environment.

The school, for example, is viewed as an open rather than a closed system and therefore as an integral part of its larger environment, rather than as a bounded entity isolated from its environment. As an organization, the school receives inputs, processes them, and returns outputs to its environment. Because inputs are typically diverse (e.g., youngsters differ in ability) and output demands are generally contradictory (e.g., the school is expected to maintain tight control over youngsters but at the same time teach them self-responsibility and initiative), there is constant interplay between school and environment. The nature of this interplay is political, as issues are resolved, bargains struck, and agreements reached. Internally, the school is comprised of interdependent subunits and groups, each with interests that compete with those of others. Each of these subunits is affected as others are affected, and together they comprise an array of mini-open systems subject to the same laws of political behavior that characterize the school's larger organizational—environmental interplay.

2. Whereas the emphasis in other views is on the administration of policy decisions, the emphasis in the political view is on policy development.

Political views do not consider goals as givens to be administered. Goals are considered to be highly unstable and constantly changing. Therefore, understanding the process of bargaining in the development of goal consensus and understanding the sensitivity of such agreements to external forces are considered important. Further, the notion that educational administrators typically have little control over these forces, and at best play a brokerage role in the development of goal consensus, is central. For these reasons, analysis of goal development and building coalitional strategies for gathering and holding together sufficient support for goals are far more central to political thinking than is mere implementation.

3. Whereas the other views seek to suppress, program, gloss over, or resolve conflict, conflict is considered as both natural and necessary in political views.

Conflict resolution is an important concern to theorists and practitioners who work from the person model; indeed, to them, conflict is considered pathological. Since finding and using the one best way are characteristics of both rational and mechanistic models, advocates of efficiency also regard conflict as a deviation to be corrected. Contrast these images of conflict with those of Baldridge (1971):

> Conflict is natural, and is to be expected in a dynamic organization. Conflict is not abnormal, nor is it necessarily a symptom of a breakdown in the organization's community.

> The organization is fragmented into many power blocks and interest-groups, and it is natural that they will try to influence policy so that their values and goals are given primary consideration.

> In all organizations small groups of political elites govern most of the major decisions. However, this does not mean that one elite group governs everything; the decisions may be divided up, with different elite groups controlling different decisions.

> Formal authority, as prescribed by the bureaucratic system, is severely limited by the political pressure and bargaining tactics that groups can exert against authorities.

> Decisions are not simply bureaucratic orders, but are instead negotiated compromises among competing groups. Officials are not free simply to order decisions; instead they have to jockey between interest groups, hoping to build viable compromises among powerful blocks.
>
> External interest groups have a great deal of influence over the organization, and internal groups do not have the power to make policies in a vacuum. (p. 14)

The emphasis in political views is on policy formulation. This emphasis, in turn, requires debate over appropriate goals, values, and strategies. Conflict is considered a natural outgrowth of the process and indeed is seen by advocates of this model as a sign of organizational health, rather than organizational pathology.

4. Whereas each of the other models assumes norms of rationality in decision making, political theories are not based on such norms.

This characteristic is related to each of the other three that distinguish political views from person and efficiency models. Because it is assumed that goals are not given but negotiated, and because the interplay within the organization and between the organization and its environment is viewed as based on bargaining, the rational pattern of establishing clear goals—and subsequently programming individual and organizational behavior to maximize these goals—is held suspect by advocates of political and decision-making views. With respect to the organic model, the rational pattern of building a core of common values and commitments among workers is also suspect. In the political view, a *satisficing* image of humankind and organization is offered as a substitute for the more traditional rational images. School administrators, for example, do not seek optional solutions to the problem they face but seek solutions that will satisfy a variety of demands. Thus, they are more likely to select not the best reading program for children, but the one that is easier for teachers to implement and costs less.

Rational and Nonrational Perspectives.   Political views began to receive attention from administrators in the late 1950s as scholars from political science and the decision sciences systematically began to study the problem of organization and administration. As with each of the other models, this group first gained strong acceptance among those interested in business organizations and business administration and later became the dominant strand of thought in educational administration. Herbert Simon's now classic work *Administrative Behavior: A Study of Decision-Making Processes in Administrative Organization,* first published in 1945, is considered by many as the forerunner of this movement. In Simon's (1945) view, the limits of rationality

> have been seen to derive from the inability of the human mind to bring to bear upon a single decision all the aspects of value, knowledge, and behavior that would be relevant. The pattern of human choice is often more nearly a stimulus-response pattern than a choice among alternatives. Human rationality operates,

then, within the limits of a psychological environment. This environment imposes on the individual as "givens" a selection of factors upon which he must base his decisions. However, the stimuli of decision can themselves be controlled so as to serve broader ends, and a sequence of individual decisions can be integrated into a well-conceived plan. (pp. 108–109)

Later, in a classic critique of the efficiency models of organization, Herbert Simon and James G. March discussed not only the cognitive and affective limits of individual rationality but also the limits of rationality implicit in the detailed organizational designs characteristic of bureaucratic theories (March & Simon, 1958).

In collaboration with Richard M. Cyert, March laid down the basic tenets of the decision-making view of organizational functioning (Cyert & March, 1963). Organizations, within this view, are composed of various groups and departments holding diverse interests. Decision making is constrained by the inability of people to account for and use all the available information that under optimal conditions would produce a maximum decision; by the need to maintain internal coordination and control and to keep the peace among competing groups; and by a highly uncertain and unstable external environment. Given these conditions, organizations are best viewed as *messy* arenas for shifting multiple-goal coalitions rather than tidy and rational pyramids made up of tightly connected and properly placed building blocks. The job of the administrator is to make sense of this messy situation in an effort to find some basis and enough support for reasonable and supported action to occur.

Conflict is inevitably part of the process of decision making under these conditions. Conflict occurs even in situations in which a general consensus exists regarding the organization's overall, albeit vague, goals—for when it comes to articulating goals into operational objectives requiring action, consensus typically disappears. Administrators reckon with conflict by emphasizing *local rationality*. When this occurs, attention is given to a problem as defined by a specific interest without concern for other interests. Thus, as Cusick (1983) points out, the problem of maintaining order in high school classrooms and keeping the peace between teachers and students is addressed separately from the problem of academic achievement. His research reveals that principals put pressure on teachers to get along with students and keep them in class, even if it means sacrificing academic goals. He notes, for example, "It was more important to keep them in school, in class, and in order than it was to teach them something and see that they learned it" (Cusick, 1983, p. 39). Standards of rationality are kept simple and focused on the immediate problem at hand. As the problem changes, so does the standard of rationality, and this enables the "quasi-resolution" of conflict (Cyert & March, 1963).

This quasi-resolution is also achieved by adopting *acceptable-level decision rules*. If all goals are to be achieved fully, then conflict among them is heightened. But when one is willing to settle for an acceptable level of achievement, it is possible to pursue several conflicting goals in a satisfactory way. *Sequential attention to goals* is also used to quasi-resolve conflict. Rather than be committed fully to one goal or another (academic achievement or student satisfaction), or to integrating the two goals so that they become one, the school attends first to one, as if it were the only goal, and then to another, as if *it* were the only goal.

In the 1970s, March and his colleagues turned their attention to the analysis of educational organizations. Characterizing educational organizations as "organized anarchies," they identified three distinct, important, and troublesome features of such organizations, which seem to justify the anarchy label.

First, their goals are problematic. It is difficult to specify a consistent set of goals. Instead, goals seem to shift over time; they seem to vary from one part of the school to another; they seem to be stated in terms that are hard to translate into action. There is conflict over goals, and the conflict is not resolved easily. Although it is sometimes possible to impute goals to the organization by observing behavior, such imputations appear often to be unstable or to define goals that are not acceptable to all participants in the organization. The decision process seems to reflect more a series of actions by which goals are discovered than a process by which they are acted upon. Speeches on goals express platitudes that are not useful administratively.

Second, their technologies are unclear. Although we know how to create an educational institution, to staff it, and to specify an educational program for it, we do not know much about the process by which it works. It does work, at least in some senses. Students seem to change. Moreover, we can duplicate our results. If we recreate the procedures in a new school, they will often have approximately the same outcomes. But we have remarkably little capability for designed change in the system. We do not, in general, know what will happen if we make changes; we do not, in general, know how to adapt the standard system to non-standard students or situations. New occasions require a new set of trial-and-error procedures, either in the school or in an experimental laboratory.

Third, participation in the organization is fluid. Participants come and go. Students, teachers, and administrators move in and out. There is even more turnover in other participants or potential participants. Parents, individually and collectively, are erratic in their involvement; community leaders sometimes ignore the schools, sometimes devote considerable time to them; governmental agencies are active, then passive. All of the potential actors in the organization have other concerns that compete with the school for their attention. Thus, whether they participate in the school depends as much on the changing characteristics of their alternatives as it does on the characteristics of the educational organization involved. (Cohen, March, & Olsen, 1972)

This description of schools challenges conceptions implicit in the more traditional theories of administration and organization. March (1962) suggests that organizations should be viewed as political coalitions and administrators as political brokers. As a political coalition, the form, shape, and structure of a school as well as its goals and missions are negotiated. He further notes that within the organization, individuals frequently join together into subcoalitions. Coalition members in schools would include teachers, chairpersons, supervisors, administrators, janitors, students, the school board, the PTA, the teacher's union, the central office, volunteers, interest groups, regulatory agencies, and municipal departments.

Planning and Decision Making as Examples.   The concern for politics as it applies to making decisions within organizations suggests that organizational life is not as rational as one might like and that administrative behavior is limited by human characteristics of administrators as persons and by political, financial, and other constraints that define the administrator's work context. In accord with this view, Cohen, March, and Olsen (1972) liken decision making in an organization to a garbage can. Various school problems and solutions are deposited in this can, though typically solutions are only loosely connected to the problem. Given the garbage-can metaphor, March and his associates suggest that a better image of planning and decision making is one assuming that *solutions exist that must be matched to problems.* It is often presumed, for example, that a group of teachers who adopt a teaching program, such as mainstreaming instruction in the arts with the traditional academic program (a solution), do so in response to a problem—such as neglect of the arts in the curriculum. But what may really be the case is that *the problem is invented* to accommodate a *solution* based on the preferences, training, and beliefs of the teacher.

In his important essay "The Science of Muddling Through," Charles Lindblom (1959) makes an important distinction between rational-linear planning and deciding described in theory and the more realistic and practical planning found in administrative practice. Administrators and policymakers, Lindblom maintained, practice disjointed incrementalism by making decisions based on small, incremental successive and limited comparisons of fairly familiar alternatives found close to home. Instead of rationality routing out all the available possibilities, solution search is highly limited. Frequently, the solutions favored do not match the problem at all, and thus the problem is changed to fit the solution. Information is often revised and reinterpreted, solutions are redesigned, and goals are changed in fashions that make each of these components compatible with the other.

Disjointed incrementalism scales problems down to manageable size, limits the amount of information collected, restricts choices, and shortens horizons because all these make the process of decision making more manageable and practical. The net result is a science of decision making that features muddling through. Lindblom's "science of muddling through" fits well with Simon's (1945) assertion that administrators do not search for the best needle in the haystack but accept the first one found that will do the job and with Cohen, March, and Olsen's (1972) metaphor of the garbage can to characterize decision making.

Much remains to be learned about the constructive use of conflict in organizations and about the bargaining role of the school administrator. Recognizing first that conflict can have constructive consequences for schools is in itself an important contribution of the political and decision-making view of schools. Indeed, viewing the school as a political system adds a rich dimension to understanding how schools actually operate. But as enhancing as these glimpses of reality are, serious caveats are in order. Political views and their application to decision making in organizations are largely descriptive, not prescriptive. They attempt to describe and understand what is actually occurring rather than what should be occurring, and these are important undertakings.

School administrators should not assume, however, that because events are as they are, the name of the game is only to learn the rules and play by them. *The rules themselves are at issue and must be evaluated for how well they fit to the unique values of the school as a particular kind of organization.* In educational enterprises, means and ends are often indistinguishable. Teachers and students alike learn as much from how one organizes and behaves in schools as they do from the official educational program. Management and organization are part of the school's hidden curriculum, and they teach important lessons to students.

Concern for Culture

In recent years, interest in the cultural perspective has mushroomed. Concepts such as school culture, changing the culture of the school, and cultural leadership are now routinely discussed at conferences, in workshops, and in journal articles and books.

Anthropologists speak of culture as webs of meaning organized in terms of symbols and other representations (Geertz, 1973). Symbols are key in understanding cultural meaning. Smircich (1985), for example, suggests that understanding organizational culture requires that one focus on symbols, not culture. "Culture does not exist separately from people in interaction. People hold culture in their heads, but we cannot really know what is in their heads. All we can see or know are representations or symbols" (p. 67). Louis (1980) characterizes a group's culture as follows: "A set of understandings or *meanings shared* by a group of people. The meanings are largely *tacit* among members, are clearly *relevant* to the particular group, and are *distinctive* to the group. Meanings are *passed on* to new group members" (p. 16). Hofstede (1980, p. 13) describes culture as the collective programming of the mind that distinguishes the members of one group from another.

Underlying the cultural perspective is the concern for community and the importance of shared meanings and shared values. The concept of *center* is often considered to be key. Organizational and societal centers represent the locus of values, sentiments, and beliefs that provide the cultural cement for holding together human groups (Shils, 1961, p. 119).

Leadership within the Cultural Perspective.   Many studies of successful schools (Lipsitz, 1984; Deal, 1987; Sergiovanni, 1994; Hill, Foster, & Gendler, 1990) suggest that they have central zones composed of values and beliefs that take on sacred characteristics. Indeed, it might be useful to think of them as having an official *religion* that gives meaning and guides appropriate actions. As repositories of values, these central zones are sources of identity for teachers and students from which their school lives become meaningful. The focus of leadership within the cultural perspective, then, is on developing and nurturing these central-zone patterns so that they provide a normative basis for action within the schools.

Leadership activities associated with the cultural view include articulating school purposes and mission; socializing new members to the school; telling stories and maintaining or reinforcing myths, traditions, and beliefs; explaining "the way things operate around here"; developing and displaying a system of symbols; and rewarding those who reflect the school's culture. Such leadership, according to this view, is designed to bond together students, teachers, and others to the work of the school as believers. The school and its purposes become revered, and in some respects they resemble an ideological system dedicated to a sacred mission. It is believed that as persons become members of this strong and binding culture, they are provided with opportunities for enjoying a special sense of personal importance and significance. Their work and their lives take on a new importance, one characterized by richer meanings, an expanded sense of identity, and a feeling of belonging to something special—all of which are considered to be highly motivating conditions (Peters & Waterman, 1982).

School culture includes values, symbols, beliefs, and shared meanings of parents, students, teachers, and others conceived as a group or community. Culture governs what is of worth for this group and how members should think, feel, and behave. The substance of culture includes a school's customs and traditions; historical accounts and unstated understandings; habits, norms, and expectations; and common meanings and shared assumptions. The more understood, accepted, and cohesive the culture of the school, the better able it is to move in concert toward ideals it holds and objectives it wishes to pursue. It is in this sense, the argument goes, that culture serves as a compass setting to steer people in a common direction, furnishes a set of norms that define what people should accomplish and how, and provides a source of meaning and significance for teachers, students, administrators, and others as they work.

Once shaped and established in the school, this strong culture acts as a powerful socializer of thought and programmer of behavior. But the shaping and establishment of culture does not just happen. It is instead a negotiated product of the shared sentiments of school participants. Often, competing views and competing ideologies exist in schools, and deciding which ones will count requires some struggling. Administrators are in an advantageous position to strongly influence the outcome of this struggle. They are, for example, in control of the communications system of the school and thus can decide what information to share with whom. Further, they control the allocation of resources and are able to reward desirable and sanction undesirable behavior. Bates (1981) further elaborates the principal's influence in shaping school culture: "The culture of a school is therefore the product of conflict and negotiation over definitions of situations. The administrative influence on school language, metaphor, myths and rituals is a major factor in the determination of a culture which is reproduced and the consciousness of teachers and pupils" (p. 43).

Building School Culture.   Culture building requires that school leaders give attention to the informal, subtle, and symbolic aspects of school life. It is presumed that teachers, parents, and students need answers to such questions as: What is this school about? What is important here? What do we believe in? Why do we function the way we do? How are we unique? How do I fit into the scheme of things? Answers to questions of this sort provide an orderliness to one's school life that is derived from the sense of purpose and enriched meaning. As Greenfield (1973) states, "What many people seem to want from schools is that schools reflect the values that are central and meaningful in their lives. If this view is correct, schools are cultural artifacts that people struggle to shape in their own image. Only in such forms do they have faith in them; only in such forms can they participate comfortably in them" (p. 570). Greenfield (1984) believes that "the task of leadership is to create the moral order that binds [leaders] and the people around them" (p. 159).

Leadership in culture building is not a new idea but one solidly embedded in the literature of leadership and well known to successful school leaders. In 1957, for example, Selznick wrote:

> The art of the creative leader is the art of institution building, the reworking of human and technological materials to fashion an organism that embodies new and enduring values.... To institutionalize is to *infuse with value* beyond the technical requirements of the task at hand.... Whenever individuals become attached to an organization or a way of doing things as persons rather than technicians, the result is a prizing of the device for its own sake. From the standpoint of the committed person, the organization is changed from an expendable tool to a valued source of personal satisfaction.... The institutional leader, then, is primarily an expert in the promotion and protection of values. (p. 28)

Within the cultural perspective, successful leaders emphasize leadership by purpose. Vaill (1984) defines *purposing* as "that continuous stream of actions by an organization's formal leadership which has the effect of inducing clarity, consensus, and commitment regarding the organization's basic purposes" (p. 91). Bennis (1984) defines *purposing* as "a compelling vision of a desired state of affairs... which clarifies the current situation and induces commitment to the future" (p. 66). Purposing, according to these researchers, derives its power from the needs of persons at work to have some sense of what is important, some signal of what is of value.

The focus of cultural leadership shares with efficiency, person, and political leadership a highly instrumental bias. In all cases, the emphasis is on how administrators can gain more control over the achievement of school goals and objectives and obtain greater compliance from teachers to ensure that their efforts are sufficiently motivated and coordinated to that end. On behalf of this effort, school administrators within the cultural perspective give less attention to managerial controls, interpersonal psychology, and political negotiating and more attention to understanding, using, and, if necessary, reconstructing school artifacts, perspectives, values, and assumptions. These constitute four levels of organizational culture (Dyer, 1982). The four levels are described by Lundberg (1985) as follows:

1. *Artifacts:* These are the tangible aspects of culture shared by members of an organization and include language, stories, myths, rituals, ceremonies, and visible products which are considered to have symbolic value.
2. *Perspectives:* These are the socially shared rules and norms which provide solutions to common problems encountered by organizational members and guide-

lines which allow members to define and interpret the situations they face and which prescribe the bounds of acceptable behavior.

3. *Values:* These provide the evaluational basis that organizational members use for judging situations, acts, objects and people. Values represent important goals, ideals, standards, as well as taboos of an organization and are often embodied in statements of the organization's philosophy or mission.

4. *Assumptions:* These constitute the tacit beliefs that members hold about themselves and others which govern their relationships and define for them the nature of their connection to the organization of which they are a part. Unlike perspectives and values assumptions are typically not stated and indeed may even be unconscious. (p. 171)

Can school administrators actually reconstruct the artifacts, perspectives, values, and assumptions of their schools in a fashion that builds the necessary sense of community, shared meaning, and indeed sacred culture to enable highly successful school functioning? Some educational researchers such as Lipsitz (1984), Greenfield (1985), and Firestone and Wilson (1985) provide some evidence that suggests they can. Leading researchers in the area of corporate cultures, such as Ouchi (1981), Pascale and Athos (1981), Peters and Waterman (1982), Deal and Kennedy (1982), and Bennis and Nanus (1985), also seem to support this view. But many experts feel that cultural leadership does not create new sacred cultures but rather shapes and legitimizes the culture that emerges within the organization. They would assert that the *lead first* view of cultural leadership attributes too much homogeneity to organizations and views them as having a monolithic and dominant culture. A more accurate view, by their way of thinking, would portray organizations in terms of heterogeneity and lack of consensus and as being composed of overlapping and nested subcultures (Martin, Sitkin, & Boehm, 1985, p. 102). According to this view, "Creating a culture is like surfing. You cannot make a wave. All you can do is wait and watch for the right wave, then ride it for all it's worth" (Martin, Sitkin, & Boehm, 1985, p. 105). Which of these views best describes reality has yet to be resolved.

A nagging question accompanying the cultural view is: *Should* administrators actually reconstruct the artifacts, perspectives, values, and assumptions of their schools in an effort to create strong cultures? Some theorists would argue, if building strong cultures results in administrators increasing their control over the thinking and behavior of teachers and students, then the cultural perspective results in little more than a further refinement of the art and science of manipulation (Bates, 1984). A similar charge of manipulation is leveled by critics at person and efficiency views. For example, is being concerned about work needs of teachers in an effort to *motivate* them little more than a form of manipulation (Foster, 1984)? The question critics raise is whether *any* form of social engineering is appropriate. The issue, however, may be less whether school administrators should seek to influence than whether ethical guidelines can be established to guide such influence (Sergiovanni, 1980).

During the 1990s, work on the cultural perspective in educational administration took on a new twist. Instead of emphasizing school culture as a manifestation of cultural characteristics in general, the focus changed to understanding schools as a distinct form of social organization that could be understood as a community. According to Sergiovanni (1994), communities are collections of people who are connected together because they share common commitments, ideas, and values. He suggests that schools can be understood as:

1. Learning communities where not only students but all members of the school community are committed to thinking, growing, and inquiring and where learning is an attitude as well as an activity, a way of life as well as a process
2. Collegial communities where members are connected to each other for mutual benefit and to pursue common goals by a sense of felt interdependence and mutual obligation
3. Caring communities where members, motivated by altruistic love, make a total commitment to each other and where the characteristics that define their relationships are moral in character
4. Inclusive communities where economic, religious, cultural, ethnic, family, and other differences are brought together into a mutually respective whole
5. Inquiring communities where principals and teachers commit themselves to a spirit of collective inquiry as they reflect on their practice and search for solutions to the problems they face

Three characteristics are central to gauging the extent to which a school measures up to being a community: the extent to which members share common interpersonal bonds; the extent to which members share an identity with a common place (such as my class, my space, my school); and the extent to which members share a commitment to values, norms, and beliefs. In strong school communities, members share in a community of relationships, a community of place, and a community of mind. Advocates of community argue that as connections in a school strengthen, webs of obligations are created that have moral overtones. The school begins to speak to members in a moral voice, which compels compliance with community purposes and norms (e.g., see Etzioni, 1993).

Educational Administration as an Applied Science

March (1974) has accurately referred to educational administration as being "managerially parasitic," speaking to its tendency to borrow heavily from the insights, theories, and practices associated with the organization and administration of business enterprises. Superior funding and greater demand have brought business organization to the attention of scholars, and most of the literature on organization and administration has been developed with this type of organization in mind. This section discusses some of the differences between management in educational and other public organizations and that in business organizations. These differences suggest that great care must be taken in adapting management practices from other sectors for use in schools.

It is easily recognized that, at one level of analysis, management is management. Although public and private organizations share many features, the differences are significant. The well-known management professor Wallace Sayre has stated that "business and government administration are alike in all unimportant respects" (quoted in Bower, 1977, p. 140). Joseph Bower (1977) of the Harvard Business School notes that "American business is an inappropriate analogy for discussing and evaluating public management. In the public sector, *purpose, organization* and *people* do not have the same meaning and significance that they have in business" (p. 140).

Following are some important differences between schools, as one kind of public organization, and private organizations:

1. Power over money, organization, and personnel rests in the hands of the legislature, school legal code, and local school board rather than in the hands of management.
2. Measures of progress toward goals are difficult to devise. What are the school measures of good citizenship, intellectual enrichment, problem-solving ability, independent thinking, a desire to learn, economic sufficiency, and effective family living, for example? These are contrasted with the readily understood and quantifiable economic objectives of private organizations. One result of this measurement problem is to select goals for schools that are easily quantifiable. This strategy is reminiscent of the person who searched under the lamppost for keys lost a block away.
3. Public accounting to which the school is subjected is designed to *control* current expenditures, as contrasted with business accounting, which tends to support future planning, research, and development.
4. Tenure laws and civil-service laws tend to protect educational workers from the control of administrators and supervisors.
5. School purposes and organizational processes designed to achieve these purposes are influenced indirectly by administrators through individuals and groups (a political process), rather than directly by administrators (a management process).
6. Goals and objectives are often unclear and contradictory. The latent custodial functions of schools, for example, contradict the goal-achievement functions.
7. No market exists to determine effectiveness. Expensive special education programs, for example, are maintained for moral, political, and legal reasons, though if they were subjected to a market economy, general consumer interest would not likely be sufficient to sustain them. By comparison, product lines of firms are thinned out by a market economy.
8. Resources are distributed on the basis of formula and other approximations of *equity* rather than on *merit*. Allocating greater resources to so-called high-producing schools, for example, has historically not been considered appropriate.

9. Administrators work with an array of people whose careers are outside of management control.
10. A tight coupling exists between means and ends, or products and processes. Schooling is a human activity with human ends.
11. Many objectives are pursued with scarce resources, as contrasted with the firm, which allocates more resources to fewer—indeed, more focused—objectives.

Perhaps the most critical difference between the school and most other organizations is the human intensity that characterizes its work. Schools are human organizations in the sense that their products are human and their processes require the socializing of humans. Further, unlike most organizations that rely on machinery and technology, schools are labor intensive. More than 70 percent of the money spent for education, for example, goes to the educational labor force—mostly to the roughly 2 million teachers.

This human intensity in educational organizations makes critically important the role of values in schooling, as Broudy (1965) notes:

> The educator, however, deals with nothing but values—human beings who are clusters and constellations of value potentials. Nothing human is really alien to the educational enterprise and there is, therefore, something incongruous about educational administrators evading fundamental value conflicts.... The public will never quite permit the educational administrator the moral latitude that it affords some of its servants. For to statesmen and soldiers men entrust their lives and fortunes, but to the schools they entrust their precarious hold on humanity itself. (p. 52)

For these reasons, many experts find it useful to view educational administration as a distinct applied science. This applied science relies heavily on concepts, insights, and practices from the various disciplines and from the study of organization and administration in general but evaluates these ideas for goodness to fit to the unique value structure of educational organizations. In this process, some ideas are rejected and others accepted. An applied science is concerned with means as well as ends and focuses on quality of process as well as on quality of goal achievement. *Educational administration is also an ethical science concerned with good or better processes, good or better means, and good or better ends, and, as such, is thoroughly immersed in values, preferences, idea, aspirations, and hopes.*

A Reflective-Practice Perspective

Despite the usefulness of the concept of applied science and the importance of ethical considerations, many theorists feel that such a view still does not capture the nature of professional practice. Applied science, they argue, portrays a highly instrumental view of knowledge (Kennedy, 1984) that assumes that professional practice involves the fairly mechanical process of pigeonholing problems and then searching a series of perfected practice treatments for the right ones to apply (Mintzberg, 1979). Schon (1983) says that patterns of professional practice are actually characterized by a great deal of uncertainty, instability, complexity, and variety. Value conflicts and uniquenesses are accepted aspects of educational administration. These characteristics are, according to Schon (1983, p. 14), central to the world of professional practice in all the major professions, including medicine, engineering, management, and education. Schon concludes that "professional knowledge is mismatched to the changing characteristics of the situation of practice" (p. 14). In support of this view, Ralph Tyler maintains that researchers do not have a full understanding of the nature of professional practice in education. He states:

> Researchers and many academics also misunderstand educational practice. The practice of every profession evolves informally, and professional procedures are not generally derived from systematic design based on research findings. Professional practice has largely developed through trial and error and intuitive efforts. Practitioners, over the years, discover procedures that appear to work and others that fail. The professional practice of teaching, as well as that of law, medicine and theology, is largely a product of the experience of practitioners, particularly those who are more creative, inventive, and observant than the average. (cited in Hosford, 1984, p. 9)

Science, according to Tyler, "explains phenomena, it does not produce practices" (cited in Hosford, 1984, p. 10).

Professionals rely heavily on informed intuition as they create knowledge in use. Intuition is informed by theoretical knowledge on the one hand and by interacting with the context of practice on the other. When administrators use informed intuition, they are engaging in reflective practice.

Applied science within educational administration seeks to establish a body of *artificial* professional intelligence. Scientific knowledge would be the key aspect of such intelligence. School administrators would only have to diagnose problems they face and draw from this intelligence standard treatments to apply. These treatments would be screened to ensure that they meet certain ethical requirements.

By contrast, reflective practice seeks to establish augmented professional intelligence. Here, educational administrators would be key aspects of this intelligence, for it would not stand apart as an abstract body of theoretical knowledge. Augmented professional intelligence serves to inform the intuitions of principals as they practice. As this practice unfolds, practical knowledge is created in use as unique treatments are developed, applied, refined, and shared. Instead of using scientific knowledge instrumentally, as is the case in applied science, this knowledge is used conceptually to inform the administrator's judgment as she or he makes a decision.

The concept of reflective practice is relatively new, and much more thinking needs to be given to its development and use in educational administration.

Educational Administration as a Moral Craft

Blumberg (1989) uses the metaphor *craft* to present a view of the nature of administrative work that can provide the long missing bridge between what is known in the minds and experiences of successful administrators and the practice situations they face. To some, the word *craft* communicates an endeavor that is low level and even pedestrian. Blumberg has in mind, however, the accomplished and prized work of artisans that stands out from the work of amateur hobbyists. This distinction between amateurism and artisanship strengthens the use of the craft metaphor, for though school administrators do not hold the monopoly on exercising management and leadership, their practice should be qualitatively superior to that of others who share these roles.

Blumberg explores the craft metaphor by describing how the mind, heart, and hand of the artisan "potter" working in tandem with the "clay" are brought together to produce something useful. Similarly, the craft of school administration "is the exercise in individual fashion of practical wisdom toward the end of making things in a school or school system 'look like one wants them to look'" (Blumberg, 1989, p. 46). Recognizing that there are certain skills involved in any craft, Blumberg focuses on the know-how that goes beyond just being able to employ these skills. It is this know-how that differentiates the artisan from the more pedestrian amateur—the prized craft product from the run of the mill.

Artisanship is associated with dedication, experience, personal knowledge of the material and mastery of detail, sense of harmony, integration, intimate understanding, and wisdom (Mintzberg, 1987). Artisans, according to Blumberg (1989), develop a special kind of know-how that is characterized as having a refined nose for things, a sense of what constitutes an acceptable result in any particular problematic situation, an understanding of the nature of the materials with which they work, a mastery of the basic technology undergirding the craft, the skill to employ this technology in an efficacious manner, and, most important, knowing what to do and when to do it. School administrators make pragmatic and moral decisions and are able to diagnose and interpret the meaning of what is occurring as they work in any situation.

In sum, reflective school administrators practice as artisans by bringing together deep knowledge of relevant techniques and competent application of tried and true "rules of thumb" with a "nose" for their practice and a penchant for reflecting on this practice as they create something of practical utility. In this effort, craft knowledge represents one source of information and insight that is equal to and sometimes superior to theoretical knowledge; together, craft and theoretical knowledge make up one's theories of practice. These theories are not designed to *tell* the school administrator but rather to *inform* her or his professional practice. The hallmark of the artisan is the ability to reflect on practice.

Administering schools, as Blumberg suggests, is no ordinary craft, however. It is instead a moral craft, a fate shared with teaching (Tom, 1984) and supervision (Sergiovanni & Starratt, 1993). The reasons for the prominence of the imperative in the work of school administration are as follows (summarized from Sergiovanni, 1995, pp. 309–311):

1. The job of the school administrator is to transform the school from an organization composed of technical functions in pursuit of objective outcomes into an institution. Organizations are little more than technical instruments for achieving objectives. As technical instruments, they celebrate the value of effectiveness and efficiency by being more concerned with "doing things right" than "doing right things." Institutions, on the other hand, are effective and efficient and more. They are responsive, adaptive enterprises that exist not only to get a particular job done but as entities in and of themselves. As Selznick (1957) points out, organizations become institutions when they transcend the technical requirements needed for the task at hand. In his words, "Institutionalization is a process. It is something that happens to an organization over time, reflecting the organization's own distinctive history, people who have been in it, groups it embodies and the vested interests they have created, and the way it has adapted to its environment" (Selznick, 1957, p. 16). He continues, "Organizations become institutions when they are *infused with value,* that is, prized not as tools alone but as sources of direct personal gratification and vehicles of group integrity. This infusion produces a distinct identity for the organization. Where institutionalization is well advanced, distinctive outlooks, habits, and other commitments are unified, coloring all aspects of organizational life and lending it a *social integration* that goes well beyond formal coordination and command" (Selznick, 1957, p. 40). Selznick's conception of institution is similar to the familiar conception of school as a *learning community.* To become either, the school must move beyond concerns for goals and roles to the task of building purposes into its structure and embodying these purposes in everything it does. When this happens, school members are transformed from neutral participants to committed followers. The embodiment of purpose and the development of followership are inescapably moral.

2. The job of the school is to transform its students not only by providing them with knowledge and skills but by building character and instilling virtue. As Cuban (1988) points out, both technical and moral images are present in teaching and administering. "The technical image contains values that prize accumulated knowledge, efficiency, orderliness, productivity, and social usefulness; the moral image, while not disregarding such values, prizes values directed at molding character, shaping attitudes, and producing a virtuous and thoughtful person" (p. xvii). Technical and moral images of administration cannot be separated in practice. Every technical decision has moral implications. Emphasizing orderliness, for example, might comprise a lesson in diligence for students and might be a reminder to teachers that professional goals cannot be pursued to the extent that bureaucratic values are compromised.

3. Whether concern is for virtue or efficiency, some standard has to be adopted. What is efficient in this circumstance? How will virtue be determined? Determining criteria for effective teaching, deciding on what is a good discipline policy, or coming to grips with promotion criteria standards, for example, all require value judgments. Answers to questions of how and what cannot be resolved objectively as if they were factual assertions but must be treated as normative assertions. Normative assertions are true only because we decide that they are. "We must decide what ought to be the case. We cannot *discover* what ought to be the case by investigating what is the case" (Taylor, 1961, p. 248). Normative assertions are moral statements.

4. Despite commitments to empowerment and shared decision making, relationships between school administrators and others who work in schools are inherently unequal. Though often downplayed and regardless of whether they want it or not, school administrators typically have more power than teachers, students, parents, and others. This power is derived, in part, legally from their hierarchical position, but for the most part is *de facto* by virtue of the greater access to information and people that their position affords them. This access allows them to decide what information will be shared with others, what information will be withheld, and frequently what information will be forgotten. Often teachers and others in the school rely on school administrators to serve as the "coordinating mechanism" that links together what they are doing with what others are doing. In teaching, where much of the work is invisible, the coordinating function is a powerful one. Further, much of the information that principals accumulate is confidential. Information is a source of power and the accumulation of power has moral consequences. Moreover, whenever there is an unequal distribution of power between two people, the relationship becomes a moral one. Whether intended to or not, leadership involves an offer to control. The follower accepts this offer on the assumption that control will not be exploited. The test of moral leadership under these conditions is whether the competence, well-being, and independence of the follower is enhanced as a result of accepting control and whether the school benefits.

5. The context for administration is surprisingly loose, chaotic, and ambiguous. Thus, despite demands and constraints that circumscribe the school administrator's world, *de facto* discretion is built into the job and this discretion has moral implications.

A key point in understanding the moral imperative in school administration is understanding the difference between normative rationality and technical rationality. Normative rationality is based on what we believe and consider to be good. Technical rationality, by contrast, is based on what is effective and efficient. Happily the two are not mutually exclusive. School administrators want both what is good and what is effective for their schools. But when the two are in conflict, the moral choice is to prize the former over the latter. Normative rationality provides the basis for moral leadership. Instead of just relying on bureaucratic authority to compel compliance or psychological authority to manipulate compliance, the practice of leadership is based on ideas, purposes, and values.

A nagging question in coming to grips with administration as a moral craft deals with the place of scientific authority in the form of expertness established by educational research. Isn't it enough that research says we ought to do this or that? Of course research is important and the insights gleaned from this kind of knowledge are often invaluable to administrators. But this knowledge cannot represent a source of authority for action that replaces moral authority. As Smith and Blase (1987) explain:

> A leader in moral terms is one who fully realizes the...serious limitations on our ability to make accurate predictions and master the instructional process. Moreover, such a leader must encourage others to fully realize these limitations. Based on this

awareness, a moral leader refuses to allow discussions of major pedagogical issues to be dominated by what the research supposedly demonstrates.... To do so would be to perpetuate the fiction that we have the kind of knowledge that we do not in fact possess. Rather, disagreements over how and what to teach must be played out in terms of reasoned discourse. The generalizations of educational inquiry can of course be part of these reasons, but they are not epistemologically privileged—they must share the stage with personal experience, a recounting of the experience of others, with philosophical and sociological considerations, and so on. (p. 39)

This chapter has focused on the intellectual heritage of educational administration. Administrators practice their art from certain perspectives or sets of biases related to the development of thought in educational administration. Efficiency, person, political, and cultural models were used to illustrate and summarize the major strands of thought affecting administrative practice. Though the models exist as objective accumulations of concepts, the ideological and value differences among them add richness and controversy to the field.

Particular attention was given to political and decision making and to cultural theories, for these represent the most recent conceptions of educational administration. Educational administration was then viewed as an applied science with values and other characteristics unique to the school, as a standard by which concepts from the science of administration and those tried and true from the real world of practice are evaluated for appropriateness. This analysis includes a contrast of differences between administration of public and private organizations. The concept of reflective practice was discussed as a possible alternative to applied science. Reflective practice, it was argued, comprises the basis for understanding school administration as a moral craft—a view remarkably similar to that espoused by Mary Parker Follett in the 1920s. Follett proposed that administration be built on a trinity of values that include artful practice, scientific understanding, and ethical consideration (Metcalf & Urwick, 1940; Follett, 1924).

REFERENCES

Argyris, C. (1957). *Personality and organization.* New York: Harper & Row.

Baldridge, J. V. (1971). *The analysis of organizational change: A human relations strategy versus a political systems strategy* (R&D memo 75). Stanford: Stanford Center for R&D in Teaching, Stanford University.

Bates, R. (1981). Management and the culture of the school. In R. Bates & Course Team (Eds.), *Management of resources in schools. Study Guide I.* Victoria: Deakin University.

Bates, R. (1984). Toward a critical practice of educational administration. In T. J. Sergiovanai & J. E. Corbally (Eds.), *Leadership and organizational culture* (pp. 260–274). Urbana: University of Illinois Press.

Bennis, W. (1984). Transformation power and leadership. In T. J. Sergiovanni & J. E. Corbally (Eds.), *Leadership and organizational culture* (pp. 64–71). Urbana: University of Illinois Press.

Bennis, W., & Nanus, B. (1985). *Leaders.* New York: Harper & Row.

Blumberg, A. (1989). *School administration as craft.* Boston: Allyn and Bacon.

Bobbitt, F. (1913). The supervision of city schools: Some general principles of management applied to the problems of city school systems. *Twelfth Yearbook of the National Society for the Study of Education.* Bloomington, IL: NSSE.

Bower, J. (1977, March–April). Effective public management: It isn't the same as effective business management. *Harvard Business Review,* 131–140.

Broudy, H. S. (1965). Conflict in values. In R. Ohm & W. Monohan (Eds.), *Educational administration: Philosophy in action* (pp. 42–54). Norman: University of Oklahoma, College of Education.

Callahan R. E. (1962). *Education and the cult of efficiency: A study of the social forces that have shaped the administration of the public schools.* Chicago: University of Chicago Press.

Cohen, D. M., March, J. G., & Olsen, J. P. (1972). A garbage can model of organizational choice. *Administrative Science Quarterly, 17*(1).

Cuban, L. (1988). *The managerial imperative in the practice of leadership in schools.* Albany: State University of New York Press.

Cubberly, E. P. (1916). *Public administration.* Boston: Houghton Mifflin.

Cusick, P. A. (1983). *The egalitarian ideal and the American high school.* New York: Longman.

Cyert, R. M., & March, J. G. (1963). *A behavioral theory of the firm.* Englewood Cliffs, NJ: Prentice-Hall.

Deal, T. (1987). The culture of school. In L. T. Scheive & M. B. Schoenheit (Eds.), *Leadership examining the elusive.* 1987 Yearbook of the Association for Supervision and Curriculum Development. Alexandria, VA: ASCD.

Deal, T. E., & Kennedy, A. (1982). *Corporate cultures.* Reading, MA: Addison-Wesley.

Dubin, R. (1959). Industrial research and the discipline of sociology. *Proceedings of the 11th Annual Meeting, Industrial Relations Research Association,* Madison, WI (p. 161). (As quoted in Strauss, G. [1963]. Some notes on power equalization. In H. J. Leavitt [Ed.], *The social science of organization* (p. 48). Englewood Cliffs, NJ: Prentice-Hall.)

Dyer, W. G., Jr. (1982). *Patterns and assumptions: The keys to understanding organizational culture.* Office of Naval Research, Technical Report TR-ONR-7. Washington, DC: U.S. Government Printing Office.

Etzioni, A. (1993). *The spirit of community rights, responsibilities, and the communitarian agenda.* New York: Crown.

Fayol, H. (1949). *General and industrial management* (C. Storrs, Trans.). London: Pitman.

Firestone, W. A., & Wilson., B. L. (1985). Using bureaucratic and cultural linkages to improve instruction: The principal's contribution. *Educational Administrator Quarterly, 21*(2), 7–30.

Follett, M. P. (1924). *Creative experience.* New York: Longmans, Green.

Foster, W. P. (1984). Toward a critical theory of educational administration. In T. J. Sergiovanni & J. E. Corbally (Eds.), *Leadership and organizational culture* (pp. 240–259). Urbana: University of Illinois Press.

Geertz, C. (1973). *The interpretation of cultures.* New York: Basic Books.

Getzels, J. W., & Guba, E. (1957, Winter). Social behavior and administrative process. *The School Review,* pp. 413–441.

Greenfield, T. B. (1973). Organizations as social inventions: Rethinking assumptions about change. *Journal of Applied Behavioral Science, 9*(5), 551–574.

Greenfield, T. B. (1984). Leaders and schools: Willfulness and non-natural order in organization. In T. J. Sergiovanni & J. E. Corbally (Eds.), *Leadership and organizational culture* (pp. 142–169). Urbana: University of Illinois Press.

Greenfield, W. (1985). *Instructional leadership: Muddles, puzzles and promises.* The Doyne M. Smith Lecture, University of Georgia, Athens, June 29.

Gulick, L., & Urwick, L. (Eds.). (1937). *Papers on the science of administration.* New York: Institute of Public Administration.

Hill, P. T., Foster, G. E., & Gendler, T. (1990). *High schools with character.* Santa Monica, CA: Rand.

Hofstede, G. (1980). *Cultural consequences.* Beverly Hills: Sage.

Hosford, P. (Ed.). (1984). *Using what we know about teaching.* 1984 Yearbook of the Association for Supervision and Curriculum Development. Alexandria, VA: ASCD.

Kennedy, M. (1984). How evidence alters understanding and decisions. *Educational Evaluation and Policy Analysis 6*(3), 207–226.

Kuhn, T. (1962). *The structure of scientific revolution.* Chicago: University of Chicago Press.

Lewin, K. (1951). *Field theory in social science.* New York: Harper & Row.

Lindblom, C. E. (1959). The science of muddling through. *Public Administration Review, 19,* 79–88.

Lipsitz, J. (1984). *Successful schools for young adolescents.* New Brunswick, NJ: Transaction.

Louis, M. R. (1980). Organizations as culture-bearing milieux. In L. R. Pondy et al. (Eds.), *Organizational symbolism* (pp. 157–166). Greenwich, CT: JAI Press.

Lundberg, C. C. (1985). On the feasibility of cultural intervention in organizations. In P. Frost et al. (Eds.), *Organizational culture* (pp. 169–185). Beverly Hills: Sage.

March, J. G. (1962). The business firm as a political coalition. *Journal of Politics, 24.*

March, J. G. (1974). Analytical skills and the university training of educational administrators. *Journal of Educational Administration, 12*(1), 43.

March, J., & Simon, H. (1958). *Organizations.* New York: John Wiley.

Martin, J., Sitkin, S. B., & Boehm, M. (1985). Founders and the elusiveness of a cultural legacy. In P. Frost et al. (Eds.), *Organizational culture* (pp. 99–124). Beverly Hills: Sage.

Mayo, E. (1945). *The social problems of an industrial civilization.* Boston: Harvard Graduate School of Business.

McDonnell, L. M., & Elmore, R. F. (1987). Getting the job done: Alternative policy instruments. *Educational Evaluation and Policy Analysis, 2,* 133–152.

McGregor, D. (1960). *The human side of enterprise.* New York: McGraw-Hill.

Metcalf, H. C., & Urwick, L. (Eds.). (1940). *Dynamic administration: The collected papers of Mary Parker Follett.* New York: Harper.

Miles, R. E. (1965). Human relations or human resources? *Harvard Business Review 43*(4), 148–163.

Mintzberg, H. (1979). *The structuring of organizations.* Englewood Cliffs, NJ: Prentice-Hall.

Mintzberg, H. (1987, July–August). Crafting strategy. *Harvard Business Review, 66–75.*

Morgan, G. (1986). *Images of organization.* Beverly Hills: Sage.

Ouchi, W. (1981). *Theory Z.* Reading, MA: Addison-Wesley.

Parkinson, C. N. (1958). *Parkinson's laws and other studies of administration.* London: Murray.

Pascale, R. T., & Athos, A. G. (1981). *The art of Japanese management.* New York: Simon & Schuster.

Peters, T. J., & Waterman, R. H., Jr. (1982). *In search of excellence.* New York: Harper & Row.

Roethlisberger, F., & Dickson, W. (1939). *Management and the worker.* Cambridge, MA: Harvard University Press.

Schon, D. A. (1983). *The reflective practitioner: How professionals think in action.* New York: Basic Books.

Selznick, P. (1957). *Leadership in administration: A sociological interpretation.* New York: Harper & Row. (California paperback edition, 1984. Berkeley: University of California Press.)

Sergiovanni, T. J. (1980). A social humanities view of educational policy and administration. *Educational Administration Quarterly, 16*(1), 1–20.

Sergiovanni, T. J. (1987). *The principalship: A reflective practice perspective.* Boston: Allyn and Bacon.

Sergiovanni, T. (1994). *Building community in schools.* San Francisco: Jossey-Bass.

Sergiovanni, T. J. (1995). *The principalship: A reflective practice perspective* (3rd ed.). Boston: Allyn and Bacon.

Sergiovanni, T. J., & Starratt, R. J. (1979). *Supervision: Human perspectives* (2nd ed.). New York: McGraw-Hill.

Sergiovanni, T. J. & Starrat, R. J. (1993). *Supervision: A redefinition* (5th ed.). New York: McGraw-Hill.

Shils, E. (1961). Centre and periphery. In *The logic of personal knowledge: Essays presented to Michael Polanyi* (pp. 117–131). London: Rutledge and Kegan Paul.

Simon, H. A. (1945). *Administrative behavior.* New York: Macmillan.

Smircich, L. (1985). Is the concept of culture a paradigm for understanding organizations and ourselves? In P. Frost et al. (Eds.), *Organizational culture* (pp. 55–72). Beverly Hills: Sage.

Smith, J. K., & Blase, J. (1987). *Educational leadership as a moral concept.* Washington, DC: American Educational Research Association.

Strauss, G. (1963). Some notes on power equalization. In H. J. Leavitt (Ed.), *The social science of organization* (p. 48). Englewood Cliffs, NJ: Prentice-Hall.

Strayer, G. (1914). Report of the Committee on Tests and Standards of Efficiency in Schools and School Systems. In *Addresses and proceedings of the National Education Association.* Washington, DC: Bureau of Education.

Strayer, G. (1930). Progress in city school administration during the past twenty-five years. *School and Society, 30,* 375–378.

Taylor, F. W. (1911). *Principles of scientific management.* New York: Harper & Row.

Taylor, P. W. (1961). *Normative discourse.* Englewood Cliffs, NJ: Prentice-Hall.

Tom, A. (1984). *Teaching as a moral craft.* New York: Longman.

Tyack, D., & Hansot, E. (1982). *Managers of virtue: Public school leadership in America, 1820–1980.* New York: Basic Books.

Vaill, P. B. (1984). The purposing of high performing systems. In T. J. Sergiovanni & J. E. Corbally (Eds.), *Leadership and organizational culture* (pp. 85–104). Urbana: University of Illinois Press.

Weber, M. (1946). Bureaucracy. In M. Weber, *Essays in sociology.* H. H. Gerth & C. W. Mills (Eds. and Trans.). London: Oxford University Press. (Reprinted in Litterer, J. [1969]. *Organizations: Structure and behavior.* New York: John Wiley.)

6 Administrative Work, Roles, and Tasks

What are administrative jobs in schools really like? What roles and tasks actually make up the school administrator's job responsibilities? What are the key responsibility areas to which administrators must attend? What administrative processes are used in executing these responsibilities? What administrative skills are key as these processes unfold? Answers to these questions can help to map various dimensions of the nature of administrative work in education. In this chapter, the focus is on the actual context and nature of administrative work as well as the roles and tasks school administrators actually engage in. The *real world* mapping is a characteristic of the work-activity school discussed next.

The Work-Activity School

Lists of competencies and tasks that administrators are supposed to have and do are typically compiled by studying what administrators, particularly successful ones, do, and on the weight of expert judgment and deductions gleaned from theory. This is a deductive approach. Conclusions are inferred from general principles. The principles themselves are based on assumptions or premises. The work flow of deductive research is as follows: Start with assumptions or premises; theorize; extract propositions; state and test hypotheses; analyze results; draw conclusions; reevaluate premises; and redefine theory, thus repeating the process. The work-activity school, by contrast, relies on inductive research. Here, the actual activities of administrators are studied systematically. Diary methods that record actual work of managers and actual distribution of how their time is used, activity sampling whereby through actual observation the researcher records activities of administrators at random intervals, and structured observation whereby administrators are observed over extended periods of time are the techniques typically employed. In work-activity research, conclusions are drawn and theoretical statements are inferred when they can be supported by empirical evidence.

Work-activity research strives to develop an accurate description of the characteristics and content of administrative work. The descriptions help provide such job-characteristics information as where administrators work, how long they work, what means they use to communicate, how they handle and send mail, and what work patterns exist day to day and week to week. The descriptions also help provide such job-role information as what administrators actually do, what activities do they carry out, and why. Often these roles are in sharp contrast to what experts say and what standards hold for the roles administrators should fulfill.

The Nature of Managerial Work: Mintzberg

A *role* can be defined as a set of integrated behaviors associated with an identifiable position. Following the thinking of the work-activity school, determining administrative roles requires that one have an accurate picture of how administrators spend their time for the patterns of behavior they use. In short, what an administrator actually does determines his or her real administrative roles. Missing in role analysis is the actual substance of the job behaviors displayed. Two principals, for example, assume the roles of *resource allocation* and *figurehead* (see Table 6.1 for details). One principal consistently plays these roles as part of his efforts to motivate and direct the attention of teachers, students, and their parents to teaching and learning themes. The other principal plays the *same* roles as she tries to build a cohesive school culture around competitive sports themes. What counts for her are varsity triumphs that bring students and teachers together into a community of fans. Thus, although both principals assume the same roles, the role contexts and substance themes of their behavior have different consequences for their schools.

In Mintzberg's (1973) extensive structural-observation study of five executives (one a school superintendent), he sought to describe the content of administrative work. Work-content descriptions were then used to infer a number of critical administrative roles that, Mintzberg suggests, characterize the nature of managerial work.

Mintzberg identified ten administrative roles, which could be grouped into three major categories: (1) *interpersonal,* containing figurehead, leader, and liaison roles; (2) *informational,* containing monitor, disseminator, and spokesperson roles; and (3) *decisional,* containing entrepreneur, disturbance-handler, resource-allocator, and negotiator roles. These roles are depicted in Table 6.1 and are examined and discussed within the context of educational administration.

Interpersonal Roles

Interpersonal roles require that the school administrator be involved either directly or indirectly in the activities of others. This set of roles takes a great deal of time. Though demanding, many role activities included here seem only remotely connected to the central job of administering a school. Some of the roles are symbolic, as in the case of *figurehead.* Others are more directly involved in the work of the school, as in the case of *leader.* Still others are more political in nature, as in the case of *liaison.* But all are critically important to an administrator's success and to the welfare of the school. All are highly visible roles that lend themselves to easy

TABLE 6.1   A Summary of Administrative Roles and Activities

Role	Description	Identifiable Activities from Study of Chief Executives
Interpersonal		
Figurehead	Symbolic head; obliged to perform a number of routine duties of a legal or social nature	Ceremony, status requests, solicitations
Leader	Responsible for the motivation, capacity building, and activation of others (students, teachers, and parents); responsible for staffing, training, and associated duties	Virtually all managerial activities involving others
Liaison	Maintains self-developed network of outside contacts and informers who provide favors and information	Acknowledgments of mail; external board work; other activities involving outsiders
Informational		
Monitor	Seeks and receives wide variety of special information (much of it current) to develop thorough understanding of organization and environment; emerges as nerve center of internal and external information of the organization	Handling all mail and contacts categorized as concerned primarily with receiving information (e.g., periodical news, observational tours)
Disseminator	Transmits information received from outsiders or from others to members of the organization; some information factual, some involving interpretation and integration of diverse value positions of organizational influencers	Forwarding mail into organization for informational purposes, verbal contacts involving information flow to others (e.g., review sessions, instant communication flows)
Spokesperson	Transmits information to outsiders on organization's plans, policies, actions, results, etc.; serves as expert on matters of education and schooling	Board meetings; handling mail and contacts involving transmission of information to outsiders
Decisional		
Entrepreneur	Searches organization and its environment for opportunities and initiates "improvement projects" to bring about change; supervises design of certain projects as well	Strategy and review sessions involving initiation or design of improvement projects
Disturbance handler	Responsible for corrective action when organization faces important, unexpected disturbances	Strategy and review sessions involving disturbances and crises
Resource allocator	Responsible for the allocation of organizational resources of all kinds—in effect the making or approval of all significant organizational decisions	Scheduling; requests for authorization; any activity involving budgeting and the programming of subordinates' work
Negotiator	Responsible for representing the organization at major negotiations	Negotiation

Source: The Nature of Managerial Work (pp. 92–93) by Henry Mintzberg. Copyright © 1973 by Henry Mintzberg. Reprinted by permission of Pearson Education, Inc.

evaluation by students, teachers, parents, other administrators, board members, and various segments of the community.

The most basic and simple administrative role is that of the *figurehead*. This role requires that administrators, because of their formal authority and high status, perform a number of duties, most of which on the surface seem to have little direct connection with the information-processing and decision making work of the school. But they are important, as any educational administrator will attest.

Consider the hours that high school principals spend at such activities as basketball games, pep rallies, proms, school plays, picnics, honor-society ceremonies, and other events of this sort. Add to this the chores of greeting visitors, leading school tours, attending school/community meetings, hosting social events, and such requirements as being available to parents and other community members whose requests and complaints seem never satisfied unless attended to by the *top* person. Consider also such responsibilities as the signing of documents, letters, and reports prepared by others on the staff that require the principal's general imprimatur as head of the school, and one begins to sense the flavor of the figurehead role. Though superficiality often characterizes the figurehead role, it is carried out with a tone of sincerity befitting the status and dignity the administrator brings to an event. The superintendent receives a call of complaint from a parent about a teacher attentively and sympathetically, only to privately refer the complaint to the principal. The superintendent reads a series of warm and personal statements of commendation for several students at an awards assembly for parents, having only just met the students and reading from a script prepared by the guidance counselor.

Before recent interest in the cultural perspective in educational administration, the figurehead role received only slight attention in the literature of administration. It is now considered to be much more important. Still, the *leader* role has received the most attention. As leader, the administrator sets the tone or climate of the school. The focus of this role is on the interpersonal relationships between the leader and those being led. The administrator, for example, uses her or his formal authority to achieve better integration between the needs of teachers and the goals of the school. The administrator does this through such leadership role activities as directing, guiding, developing, motivating, evaluating, correcting, and rewarding subordinates. This role is also manifested in such administrative tasks as recruiting, selecting, training, promoting, and dismissing subordinates.

Unlike the leader role, which focuses on vertical relationships between the administrator and others, the *liaison* role focuses on horizontal relationships. Like the figurehead role, this role has not received the attention it should in the literature of school administration. The liaison role involves the web of relationships that the educational administrator maintains with groups and individuals outside the school. As Homans (1950, p. 186) has pointed out, the higher a person's social rank in a group or organization, the more frequently he or she interacts with persons outside the group or organization. Thus, the liaison role is likely to be more visible in the administrative activities of the superintendent of schools than in those of the department chairperson or grade-level supervisor.

The network of contacts that are the fruits of liaison activities is cultivated by joining important community organizations, engaging in social activities, and attending conferences. Keeping in touch with important others, building bridges with influential groups, making contact with the right people, and keeping the channels open to all who can have an impact on the school are the benefits sought by the administrator. This external linkage system can be both a source of information and a source of political support.

Informational Roles

Mintzberg (1973) suggests that in exercising informational roles, the administrator can be viewed metaphorically as a nerve center that receives information of various types from an array of sources; processes this information by rejecting, altering, or approving; and disseminates this information to others in the organization. The nerve-center metaphor suggests the central position administrators occupy in receiving and moving information. This influential and advantageous vantage point at the organizational nerve center results from the administrator's unique access to external information (e.g., liaison role) and her or his access to internal information derived from formal authority (e.g., leader role). Three informational roles are identified by Mintzberg to characterize administrative activity associated with this nerve-center position: the *monitor* role, through which the administrator becomes informed about the school and its environment, and the *disseminator* and *spokesperson* roles, through which the administrator transmits information to others inside and outside the organization.

As *monitor,* the administrator seeks information from others and at the same time is bombarded by information from others that helps in understanding what is going on within the school and the school's environment. Information received by the administrators Mintzberg studied fell into five categories:

1. Information about the progress of *internal operations* and events gleaned from reports, meetings, informal conversations, and observational tours of his or her organization.
2. Information about *external events* concerning parents and other community groups; other schools; political, civic, and governmental agencies; and new developments in education.
3. Information derived from the *analysis of reports* on various issues. Reports come from a variety of solicited and unsolicited sources. Some are internal reports; others are policy memoranda from the state department of education or the federal government; still others arrive in the mail from state universities, professional associations, and seemingly endless other sources.
4. Information gleaned from conferences, formal and informal meetings, and other sources that helps the administrator to better understand significant *ideas and trends* from the environment that touches his or her organization.
5. Information brought to the administrator in the form of, or as a result of, *pressures* and demands from a variety of sources.

Much of the information obtained and processed in the monitoring role is simply transferred into the organization or passed on to others outside the organization.

In the *disseminator* role, the administrator passes into the organization both factual (what is) and value (what ought to be) information. Exactly what information to pass, in what detail, to whom, and how often can pose significant problems for the administrator. Because most of the information he or she has is stored in memory, it generally requires oral dissemination, which can be a time-consuming process. Therefore, in the interest of conserving time, not all of the relevant information gets passed down to subordinates, and this, in turn, affects the nature and quality of the administrator's work.

To ensure that subordinates better meet their standards, the administrator can increase the amount and kind of information disseminated, but at the risk of role overload. As Mintzberg characterizes this dilemma, "Hence the manager is damned by his own information system either to a life of overwork or to one of frustration. In the first case, he does too many tasks himself or spends too much time disseminating verbal information; in the second case, he must watch as delegated tasks are performed inadequately, according to his standards, by the uninformed" (1973, p. 75). Though normative views of administration emphasize the maximum flow of information and require that the administrator settle for nothing less than top performance, evidence from the real world suggests that, of necessity, not all the available information is disseminated and administrators do settle for less than best.

In the *spokesperson* role, the administrator transmits information out to the school's environment. The administrator is expected, for example, to speak on behalf of the organization, to lobby for the organization, to serve as a public relations figure, and to represent the organization as an expert. Two groups need to be kept informed: the organization's set of key influencers, as defined by legitimate authority, and the array of publics who by virtue of the political process exert influence on the school. With regard to the first group, for example, department chairpersons are obliged to keep principals informed of department activities, and similarly, school superintendents are obliged to keep school boards informed. The second group to whom the spokesperson role is addressed is vast but typically includes parents, business groups, teacher organizations, state department representatives, suppliers, newspaper reporters, and potential employers of graduating students.

In executing the spokesperson role, the administrator is required to have accurate and up-to-the-minute information about the organization and its environment. Further, the information needs to be disseminated in a dignified and credible manner. The administrator must therefore be an expert on the affairs of the organization and be able to activate this expertise in a commanding and convincing manner. The information roles are summarized and illustrated in Figure 6.1.

Decisional Roles

The third set of administrative activities identified by Mintzberg involves the making of significant decisions. Decisional roles are typically considered to be at

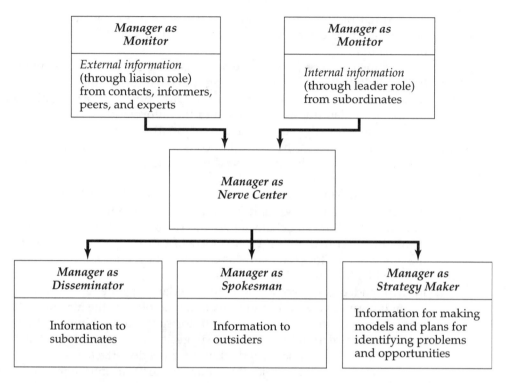

FIGURE 6.1   The Manager as Information-Processing System

Source: The Nature of Managerial Work by Henry Mintzberg. Copyright ©1973 by Henry Mintzberg. Reprinted by permission of Pearson Education, Inc.

the heart of administrative work and to be a natural outlet of the administrator's formal authority and strong access to information. Formal authority and access to information are important sources of power that legitimize the administrator's decision-making prerogatives. On occasions in which the former can be successfully challenged, the latter is sufficiently strong to assure these prerogatives. Though the prescriptive literature speaks often of the value of shared or participatory decision making, Mintzberg was impressed with the extent to which the executives he studied were in command of the decision-making process. He notes that they were substantially involved in all significant decisions made by their organizations. He further suggests that, contrary to prescriptive views, which prescribe rational and goal-maximizing decision making, the administrators he studied tended to "satisfice" (Simon, 1957, p. 204). They were inclined to accept courses of action that were "good enough" rather than best. Indeed, decision making might better be viewed as a "science of muddling through" rather than a rational science (Lindblom, 1959).

Mintzberg identified four decisional roles: *entrepreneur, disturbance handler, resource allocator,* and *negotiator*. In the *entrepreneur* role, the administrator initiates and designs programs intended to improve the organization. To this effect, she or he is constantly scanning the organization, being alert to problems. Once problems are identified, a program is begun that may directly involve the administrator further or, more typically, require delegating to others. As this program is implemented, the administrator is constantly called on to authorize and approve activities of subordinates. The administrator maintains supervisory control and retains responsibility for all design decisions associated with the program.

As an entrepreneur, the administrator initiates action of his or her own will but, as a disturbance handler, is forced into situations—some of which may well be beyond her or his control. A teacher strike, cafeteria fight, student insurrection, or false fire alarm might be examples of disturbance crises to which the administrator must respond. But many other instances are less dramatic and require more long-range attention. Handling competition among elementary schools or high school departments for scarce resources, deciding which school will be closed, settling on a reduction-in-force policy, constantly reassigning students in an effort to meet desegregation commitments, and dealing with personality clashes among staff members might be examples.

The *disturbance-handler* role often receives more notice than other administrative roles because of the suddenness with which disturbances tend to emerge, the presumption of high stakes at risk by those involved, emotional overtones, and the general urgency felt to get things resolved. Therefore, though activities associated with other roles may be more important, they take a backseat as the administrator is pressed into the disturbance-handler role.

In any organization, resources such as time, money, materials, equipment, and human talent must be allocated. When an administrator is involved in making decisions about significant organizational resources, he or she is behaving as a *resource allocator.* This role was evidenced in the Mintzberg study in three essential ways—scheduling time, programming work, and authorizing decisions by others. As the administrator schedules time, she or he communicates to others what is important and what is not. Issues of low priority, for example, do not command much of the administrator's time. By programming work, the administrator controls and schedules the time of others. In effect, he or she decides what will be done, by whom, and under what conditions, ensuring that high-priority issues are attended to. Human resources are allocated toward ends considered important. By authorizing action, the administrator maintains control over significant decisions made by subordinates, again ensuring that time and energy are used in a manner considered appropriate. Budget control is, of course, still another facet of the resource-allocating role of administrators. There is no doubt that the administrator is aware of the power implicit in controlling the allocation of organizational resources. Further, she or he shows little hesitation in exercising this power.

The administrator as *negotiator* is the final decisional role identified by Mintzberg. In exercising this role, the administrator represents the group or organization as it negotiates with other units within the organization (one department with another, one school with another), negotiates with identifiable subgroups associated with the organization (the teachers' union), and negotiates with outside agencies (accrediting teams, park district, mayor's office). This role is difficult to delegate because other partners to the negotiation often refuse to settle for substitutes, typically demanding to negotiate with the chief administrator.

Variations in Administrators' Work

The literature in administration suggests that role activities are more similar than different across administrative jobs in different kinds of organizations and across administrative jobs within the same organization. Each of the ten roles discussed are likely to be present to some degree in virtually all administrative positions. Differences, therefore, would be in emphasis rather than in kind. Though all the roles can be identified in the activities of both elementary and secondary school principals, for example, different combinations of roles will likely be emphasized for each.

Hierarchical level within an organization also seems to influence the combinations of role emphasis one observes. Chairpersons, principals, and superintendents engage in each of the roles but emphasize some more than others, depending on level. The leader role might be dominant for chairpersons; resource allocator for principals; and spokesperson for the superintendent of a given district. Size of school, complexity of educational programs, expectations of teachers and community, and the personal idiosyncrasies of individual administrators can also be expected to influence the emphasis given to activities of each role.

Mintzberg noted in his study that the activities and work conditions of the school superintendent he studied differed somewhat from those of noneducational administrators (1973, pp. 262–264). The superintendent's work, for example, was characterized by greater formality and more scheduled meetings. The meetings often took place in the evening. The superintendent met more frequently than did others with the school board and, particularly, with the parents. He also experienced more formal authority requests and relied more on analysis in the form of written reports. The greater flow of information to and from government agencies was another important difference noted.

What about men and women school administrators? Are there different patterns of roles for each? Probably yes with respect to the content emphasized within roles, but probably no for the actual roles that Mintzberg identified. Although the roles remain the same for both men and women, the ways they are understood, valued, and practiced differ. And these differences seem to serve women well as they manage and lead in schools.

In her book *The Female Advantage* Helgesen (1990) argues that because of their socialization, women have an advantage in their role as leaders in schools. Noting that Mintzberg studied only men, Curry (2000) compares Helgesen's findings with those of Mintzberg in Table 6.2.

Eight Styles

Further research is needed to map out the specific role descriptions that typify various educational administrative jobs and settings. We are able, in a general sense,

TABLE 6.2   Comparing Men and Women

Mintzberg's Findings about Men	Helgesen's Findings about Women
1. They work at an unrelenting pace, with no breaks in activities during the day	1. They work at a steady pace, but with small breaks scheduled in throughout the day
2. Their days are characterized by interruptions, discontinuity, and fragmentation	2. They do not view unscheduled tasks and encounters as interruptions
3. They spare little time for activities not directly related to their work	3. They make time for activities not directly related to their work
4. They exhibit a preference for live action encounters	4. They prefer live action encounters but schedule time to attend to mail
5. They maintain a complex network of relationships with people outside their organizations	5. They maintain a complex network of relationships with people outside their organizations
6. Immersed in the day-to-day need to keep the company going, they lack time for reflection	6. They focus on the ecology of leadership
7. They identify themselves with their jobs	7. They see their own identities as complex and multifaceted
8. They have difficulty sharing information	8. They schedule time for sharing information

Source: Helgesen, S. (1990) *The Female Advantage: Women's Ways of Leadership,* New York: Doubleday Currency, pp. 10–14 and 19–28 summarized by Barbara Curry. Reprinted by permission of the publisher from Curry, B., *Women in Power,* (New York: Teachers College Press, © 2000 by Teachers College, Columbia University. All rights reserved.), pp. 15–16.

however, to speak of clusters of role emphasis and of the administrative styles they represent. Mintzberg (1973, p. 127) suggests eight such styles, each of which emphasizes a certain combination of key roles. These are summarized here:*

Administrative Style	*Key Roles*
Contact person	Liaison, figurehead
Political administrator	Spokesperson, negotiator
Entrepreneur	Entrepreneur, negotiator
Insider	Resource-allocator, leader
Real-time administrator	Disturbance handler
Team administrator	Leader
Expert administrator	Monitor, spokesperson
New administrator	Liaison, monitor

- ■ The *contact person administrator,* for example, spends a great deal of time outside the organization. The liaison and figurehead roles dominate. Activities that characterize this style are doing favors for others, winning favors in

The Nature of Managerial Work (p. 127) by Henry Mintzberg, 1973, New York: Harper & Row. Copyright © 1973 by Henry Mintzberg. Adapted by permission of Pearson Education, Inc.

return, building a friendship network of support, giving speeches, and attending a variety of functions. The emphasis is on public relations, and the intent is to build favorable linkages with individuals and groups outside the organization who are in a position to influence the organization.

- The *political administrator* also spends a great deal of time and energy with outside groups and individuals but not for superficial, polite, or ceremonial reasons. This type of administrator, often caught in a complex web of controversy, enters the outside arena with the intent to reconcile conflicting forces acting on the school.
- The *entrepreneur administrator* seeks opportunities for change and for introducing programs within the school. Entrepreneur and negotiator roles characterize this style.
- The *insider administrator* is primarily concerned with the operation and maintenance of smoothly running schools. Working primarily from resource-allocator and leader roles, she or he concentrates on overseeing school operations, nurturing and developing internal programs, and supervising the staff. Sometimes the insider is a lieutenant, responsible for running the school or district, letting the superintendent or principal tend to outside affairs or increasingly, letting the superintendent or principal focus on issues of teaching and learning.
- The *real-time administrator* is an insider of a different sort. She or he is primarily interested in internal maintenance and focuses on day-to-day problems. The real-time administrator is constantly busy with "putting out fires" and seems to have a "finger in every pie." Disturbance handler is the dominant role. In schools where discipline is a serious problem, school security is tenuous, or other constant crises exist, the administrator may be forced into this style.
- The *team administrator* is also oriented to the inside, but her or his interest is in building a highly effective, cohesive work group characterized by high morale and mutual support among teachers. By comparison, other roles are overshadowed by the attention that team administrators give to the leader role.
- The *expert administrator* is one who, in addition to assuming administrative responsibility, continues to participate in the specialized work of the school. Special education and art supervisors, teaching principals, department chairpersons and principals who are committed to and skilled in providing instructional leadership are examples. Key roles here are monitor and spokesperson.
- The *new administrator* typically lacks a network of contacts and does not have sufficient information to get the job done well. She or he often compensates by emphasizing liaison and monitor roles. As network building is accomplished and information becomes increasingly available, the *new* administrator is less new and is ready to assume other roles.

The Seven Basic Competencies

Time is a scarce resource in the sense that any future allocation of time is diminished by the amount allocated to present activities. Further, because the number of activities that can be simultaneously tended to is limited, time spent on one activity results in neglect of others. But time distribution is a social-psychological concept as well as one in economics. Symbolically, how an administrator uses time is a form of administrative attention with meaning to others in the school. It is assumed that an administrator gives attention to the events and activities he or she values. Spending a great deal of time on interpersonal relationships, developing educational program objectives, building student identity with the school and its programs, or some other area, communicates to teachers and students that this sort of activity is of worth to the administrator and the school. As others learn the value of this activity to the administrator, they are also likely to give it attention. Administrative attention, then, can be considered a form of modeling for others who work in the school. Through administrative attention, the principal contributes to setting the tone or climate of the school and communicates to others the goals and activities that should enjoy high priority.

When administrators assume one or another combination of managerial roles, little is revealed about leadership or effectiveness. Paying attention to the roles alone is a little like paying attention to the notes that appear on a sheet of music and not the music itself. Depending on how they are played, the same notes can lead to different music. Accomplished musicians know that great music is found between the notes. Similarly, although the same administrative roles may be played by different administrators, how they are played and the intents they communicate lead to different results. Administrators are more likely to play the game of leadership effectively as they master seven basic competencies: the management of attention, the management of meaning, the management of trust, the management of self, the management of paradox, the management of effectiveness, and the management of commitment. The seven basic competencies are summarized below:*

- *The management of attention* is the ability to focus others on values, ideas, goals, and purposes that bring people together and that provide a rationale, a source of authority for what goes on in the school. Leaders manage attention by what they say, what they reward, how they spend time, the behaviors they emphasize, and the reasons they give for decisions they make.
- *The management of meaning* is the ability to connect teachers, parents, and students to the school in such a way that they find their lives useful, sensible, and valued. Even the seemingly mundane routines of schools are valued and are connected to the larger purposes and meanings that define who people are, why they are in the school, why the school needs them, and why their participation with the school is worthwhile.
- *The management of trust* is the ability to be viewed as credible, legitimate, and honest. It is not enough to make decisions; leaders have to explain them and show how the decisions are linked to the heart and soul of the school as well.

*The seven basic competencies are drawn from T. J. Sergiovanni, *Leadership: What's in it for schools?* London: Routledge/Falmer, 2001, pp. 51–54. ©TJS.

- *The management of self* is the ability of leaders to know who they are, what they believe, and why they do the things they do. When a leader's behavior can be defended in such a way that others at least understand and respect the leader, then self-knowledge has been achieved.
- *The management of paradox* is the ability to bring together ideas that seem to be at odds with each other. When leaders emphasize rigorous standards without imposing standardization or without compromising local discretion; when leaders respond to adolescent needs for independence while providing disciplined safe havens that they need in schools; and when leaders bring everyone together in a common quest united by shared values while honoring diversity and promoting innovation they are practicing three examples of managing paradox. The management of paradox is easier when leaders look to ideas as a source of authority for what they do and when leaders know the difference between power over and power to achieve something. They distribute power widely with the understanding that its purpose is to achieve goals rather than to control others.
- *The management of effectiveness* is the ability to focus on the development of capacity in a school that allows it to improve performance over time. When effectiveness is managed well schools get results and more. Success involves learning and cultivating relationships, building the capacity of teachers, figuring out better pathways to success, and providing the support that teachers need to come together as communities of practice. The management of effectiveness, in the language of economics, focuses on increasing human capital by paying attention to developing intellectual capital and social capital in the school as well.
- *The management of commitment* provides the framework for leadership practice as the other six competencies are implemented. This competency involves moving leadership away from bureaucratic and personal factors toward cognitive factors—toward ideas. Idea-based practice, as has been discussed elsewhere, calls on members of the school community to accept responsibility for what happens in the school.

This discussion of managerial roles and leadership competencies, along with a discussion of administrative processes, critical responsibility areas, administrative skills, and the importance of substance in leadership that appear in Chapter 3, provides an overview of the complexity that one is likely to find as she or he undertakes administrative work.

Mintzberg (1973) believes that one way in which administrators can make sense out of this complexity is through the process of self-reflection. In his words *"The manager's effectiveness is significantly influenced by his insights into his own work. His performance depends on how well he understands and responds to the pressures and dilemmas of the job. Thus managers who can be introspective about their work are likely to be effective at their jobs"* (p. 59). In this spirit, Exhibit 6.1 provides a series of self-study questions that Mintzberg believes can help administrators sort

Exhibit 6.1   Self-Study Questions for Administrators

1. Where do I get information and how? Can I make greater use of my contacts to get information? Can other people do some of my scanning for me? In what areas is my knowledge weakest, and how can I get others to provide me with the information I need? Do I have powerful enough mental models of those things within the organization and in its environment that I must understand? How can I develop more effective models?

2. What information do I disseminate in my organization? How important is it that my subordinates get my information? Do I keep too much information to myself because dissemination of it is time consuming or inconvenient? How can I get more information to others so they can make better decisions?

3. Do I balance information collecting with action taking? Do I tend to act prematurely before enough information is in? Or do I wait so long for "all" the information that opportunities pass me by and I become a bottleneck in my organization?

4. What rate of change am I asking my organization to tolerate? Is this change balanced so that our operations are neither excessively static nor overly disrupted? Have we sufficiently analyzed the impact of this change on the future of our organization?

5. Am I sufficiently well informed to pass judgment on the proposals made by my subordinates? Is it possible to leave final authorization for some of them with subordinates? Do we have problems of coordination because subordinates in fact now make too many of these decisions independently?

6. What is my vision of direction for this organization? Are these "plans" primarily in my own mind in loose form? Should they be made explicit in order to better guide the decisions of others in the organization? Or do I need flexibility to change them at will?

7. Are we experiencing too many disturbances in this organization? Would they be fewer if we slowed down the rate of change? Do disturbances reflect a delayed reaction to problems? Do we experience infrequent disturbance because we are stagnant? How do I deal with disturbances? Can we anticipate some and develop contingency plans for them?

8. What kind of a leader am I? How do subordinates react to my managerial style? How well do I understand their work? Am I sufficiently sensitive to their reactions to my actions? Do I find an appropriate balance between encouragement and pressure? Do I stifle their initiative?

9. What kind of external relationships do I maintain and how? Are there certain types of people that I should get to know better? Do I spend too much of my time maintaining these relationships?

10. Is there any system to my scheduling, or am I just reacting to the pressures of the moment? Do I find the appropriate mix of activities, or do I tend to concentrate on one particular function or one type of problem just because I find it interesting? Am I more efficient with particular kinds of work at special times of the day or week and does my schedule reflect this? Can someone else (in addition to my secretary) take responsibility for much of my scheduling and do it more systematically?

11. Do I overwork? What effect does my workload have on my efficiency? Should I force myself to take breaks or to reduce the pace of my activity?

(continued)

EXHIBIT 6.1   Continued

12. Am I too superficial in what I do? Can I really shift moods as quickly and frequently as my work patterns require? Should I attempt to decrease the amount of fragmentation and interruption in my work?

13. Do I orient myself too much toward current, tangible activities? Am I a slave to the action and excitement of my work, so that I am no longer able to concentrate on issues? Do key problems receive the attention they deserve? Should I spend more time reading and probing deeply into certain issues? Could I be more reflective?

14. Do I use the different media appropriately? Do I know how to make the most of written communication? Do I rely excessively on face-to-face communication, thereby putting all but a few of my subordinates at an informational disadvantage? Do I schedule enough of my meetings on a regular basis? Do I spend enough time touring my organization to observe activity firsthand? Am I too detached from the heart of our activities, seeing things only in an abstract way?

15. How do I blend my rights and duties? Do my obligations consume all my time? How can I free myself sufficiently from obligations to ensure that I am taking this organization where I want it to go? How can I turn my obligations to my advantage?

Source: The Nature of Managerial Work by Henry Mintzberg. Copyright © 1973 by Henry Mintzberg. Reprinted by permission of Pearson Education, Inc.

out the environment that characterizes their work and can provide them with more solid footing for initiating reasonable administrative action.

The intent of this chapter is to provide readers with a glimpse of the real world and work of administration. Relying on the work of Mintzberg, ten administrative roles characteristic of most administrative jobs were identified. The roles were grouped into three major categories: interpersonal, informational, and decisional. It was observed that despite the presence of the roles in most jobs, differences could be found based on the emphases each of the roles received. Eight administrative styles were identified, each resulting from a distinct combination of role emphasis. The focus of this chapter is on the *real* rather than the *ideal* and the *is* rather than the *ought*. This descriptive emphasis, where administrators have to satisfy constraints, is in contrast to the more common prescriptive view of administration, where it is assumed that administrators behave to maximize objectives. Though the balance in the literature is clearly in favor of prescriptive views and the need is great to enrich the descriptive literature, a caveat is in order. Administrators cannot be seduced by the descriptive literature into acceptance of affairs as they are, and thus behave accordingly. This position would gravely distort the concept of leadership. But neither can administrators ignore the realities of their world. To do so would result in a naive and less effective leadership practice. What is needed is a better balance and integration of both views, and this need suggests a likely future for research-and-development efforts in educational administration.

REFERENCES

Curry, B. (2000). *Women in power: Pathways to leadership in education.* New York: Teachers College Press.

Helgesen, S. (1990). *The female advantage: Women' ways of leadership.* New York: Doubleday/Currency.

Homans, G. C. (1950). *The human group.* New York: Harcourt Brace Jovanovich.

Lindblom, C. E. (1959). The science of muddling through. *Public Administrator Review, 19*(2), 79–88.

Mintzberg, H. (1973). *The nature of managerial work.* New York: Harper & Row.

Simon, H. A. (1957). *Models of man.* New York: John Wiley.

7 Women in Administration

Despite significant gains in recent years teaching remains heavily staffed by women and administration remains heavily staffed by men. Traditionally, educational administration has emerged as a male profession concerned with male themes of bureaucracy, control, and power. Campbell and Lam (1993), for example, point out that "there is no other profession or field in the United States which has an equivalent history of numerical domination by women coupled with a continuing legacy of exclusion of women from key decision-making roles" (p. 205).

Women in the Superintendency

The status of women in the superintendency, for example, during the 1969–1970 school year was bleak. Fully 98.7 percent of the superintendents who participated in an American Association of School Administrators (AASA) study were men. No women were represented among the 137 superintendents of school districts with student enrollments above 25,000, and only 20 percent of the remaining 1,266 superintendent participants were women. In a 1975 statistical report issued by the U.S. Department of Health, Education and Welfare, only 65 of the 13,037 superintendents in the country were identified as women (p. 173). In 1988, a report issued by the National Center for Educational Information pointed out that women comprised 65 percent of the teaching force but accounted for only 4 percent of the school superintendents, 10 percent of the secondary school principals, and 30 percent of the elementary school principals (Feistritzer et al., 1988). Shakeshaft (1987) reported that the 1972 figures were 1 percent, 1.4 percent and 19.6 percent, respectively. When compared with the 1972 and 1988 data, the more recent figures suggest some improvements. Using data provided by the American Association of University Women, Campbell and Lam (1993) note that approximately 5 percent of superintendents are women, the majority employed in suburban districts, and that a large number of school board members are women. Bell and Chase (1993) put the figure at 5.6 percent, and a 1992 AASA survey (Glass, 1992) reports that 6.6 percent of all superintendents nationwide are women. In a 1996 publication, Gupton and Slick estimated that women accounted for between 6 and 11 percent of high school principals. Glass, Björk, and Brunner's 2000 estimate was 13.2

percent. That works out to roughly 1,964 female superintendents and 12,919 male superintendents (Skrla, 1999). Using 1997 data from the National Center for Educational Statistics, Skrla (cited in Young & McLeod, 2000) concluded that male teachers have a one in forty-three chance of becoming a school superintendent. Female teachers have only a 1 in 825 chance.

Shakeshaft (1987) explains that the problem is androcentrism—"the practice of viewing the world and shaping reality from a male perspective. It is the elevation of the masculine to the level of the universal and the ideal and honoring of men and the male principle above women and female" (p. 94). She continues, "In an androcentric world, hierarchy of status exists. Men and women must do different things; women and what women do are less valued than are men and what men do [and thus teaching is less valued than administration]...discrimination on the basis of sex is necessary for the existence of an androcentric (male-defined) world to exist.... Thus it is this ideology...that explains why men, and not women, occupy the formal leadership positions in school and society" (p. 95).

In recent years, and on a comparative basis, women have made significant gains in educational administration. Some women with a foot in the door are strong advocates of increased professionalization of educational administration *as traditionally defined*, feeling that their own roles will be enhanced as they embody traditional management values and leadership styles. The authors of this book have doubts. There is little reason to believe that androcentricity will be reduced in a highly professionalized educational administration simply because of increases in the number of women. The problem is that the process of professionalization itself—themed to bureaucratic, organizational, and managerial values—may be androcentric. For androcentricity to be reduced, the substance of educational administration will need to shift to teaching and learning and to caring (see, e.g., Noddings, 1992; Beck, 1994; Marshall, Patterson, Rogers, & Steele, 1996). Also, *community* will need to replace *organization* as the metaphor for the school (Sergiovanni, 1994). But this is time for optimism. As today's teaching and learning themes continue their march to the center of school administrative work, the doors will be open to more women.

Women and the School Principalship

Approximately every ten years, the National Association of Elementary School Principals (NAESP) and the National Association of Secondary School Principals conduct studies of the status of the principalship (see, e.g., Pharis & Zakariya, 1979; McCleary & Thomson, 1979; Pellicer et al., 1988). From these studies, a portrait of principalship characteristics can be charted over time. In 1928, for example, 55 percent of the elementary school principals surveyed by NAESP were women. This figure decreased to 41 percent in 1948, 38 percent in 1958, 22 percent in 1968, and 18 percent in 1978. The 1988 NAESP study (Doud, 1989) shows a slight increase by estimating the percentage of women in the principalship to be 20 percent. It appears from these figures that women are a vanishing breed among principals of elementary schools. This assertion is also supported by age statistics. In 1968, for example, 71 percent of the male principals were under fifty years of age, and their median age was forty-three. During this same year, 77 percent of the female principals were fifty years of age or older, and their median age was fifty-six. These figures are particularly interesting in light of the fact that during this period only 15.4 percent of the teachers in public elementary schools were men. In a 1976 study of Illinois administrators, Carver found that though there were 102 women elementary principals age fifty-six or older, fewer than 100 women teachers with administrative certificates were available from the prime age group (under age thirty-six) to replace these women principals upon retirement.

The 1978 NAESP study of the principalship (Pharis & Zakariya, 1979) revealed some improvements in age balance among the sexes. About 35 percent of the men principals were over age 50, as compared with approximately 50 percent of the women principals. The median ages for men and women principals reported in the 1988 NAESP study (Doud, 1989) were 47 and 50, respectively. Nonetheless, one can still conclude that in the late 80s, women were fewer in number, the number was declining, and the few women in this role were, on the average, older than their male counterparts.

But there is good news. The 1998 NAESP survey of elementary school principals (Doud & Keller, 1998) reveals a dramatic gender shift in the 1990s. The 1988 NAESP study reported 20 percent of the principals were women. The 1998 study put the figure at 42 percent. This shift is even more dramatic among principals with five years or less experience; 65 percent are women. However, minorities—African Americans, Native Americans, Latinos, and Asian/Pacific Islanders—continue to be underrepresented, which is troubling in light of the diversity of the nation's student population (NAESP, 1998).

Statistics for the secondary school principal have been even less encouraging. Accounting for 10 percent of the principalship force in 1965, women accounted for only 7 percent in 1977. In 1981, the typical junior high or middle school principal could be described as a white male between the ages of 45 and 54. Only 6 percent of this group were women. According to a 1993–1994 survey conducted by the National Center for Educational Statistics (1995), the typical school principal could be described as a white male between 45 and 48 years old. Roughly 80,000 principals were included in this survey—52,000 men and 27,000 women. The male principals averaged about twenty years of experience in education with ten of those years being in the principalship. Female principals averaged about eighteen years of experience, with five of those years being in the principalship.

A 2001 NASSP survey revealed that from 1965–1988 the percentage of women in the high school principalship remained fairly constant (from 10 percent in 1965 to 7 percent in 1978 and 12 percent in 1988). The 2000 figure was 20 percent. One in five high school principals was a woman. Women were more inclined to lead smaller schools, but the differences in an absolute sense are not great. About 40 percent of the men are principals in schools with less than 600 students as compared with 34.4 percent of the women. Women principals were more likely than men to lead schools with 2,000 or more students (13.8 percent for women and 8.8 percent for men). Because women are underrepresented in the high school principalship, accounting for only 20 percent, they are overrepresented as principals of small schools.

This pattern continues for elementary schools. Approximately one-third of the women elementary school principals, for example, head schools with enrollments of 100 or fewer students. More than half of all female principals can be found in schools with enrollments of less than 400. To the extent that size of school can be considered as an indicator of prestige, one can conclude that the least prestigious principalships are more likely to be filled by women.

When asked why they chose the principalship, 20 percent of the principals who participated in the 1968 national study indicated that they preferred administration and supervision over classroom teaching, 17 percent indicated that they needed a larger income, 30 percent considered the principalship to be especially important, and 30 percent had been encouraged to take the principalship by the superintendent's office. Some 56 percent of the female supervisory principals (as opposed to 16 percent of the men) took the principalship because they were encouraged to do so by the superintendent's office. Studies of the principalship find that the most highly effective principals are very much oriented to teaching and learning rather than to an administrative *career* in an executive sense.

Opportunities for women who aspire to the principalship seem to be greater in larger cities. The National Council of Administrative Women in Education (1973) reports that in the largest cities of the United States, women occupy about 30 percent of the principalships. In 2001 the AASA commissioned a study of fifteen highly successful urban superintendents that would profile how they sought to raise student achievement in their school districts (Stricherz, 2001). As of this writing the association has named eleven of the fifteen. Among the eleven were four women (Carol Johnson of Minneapolis; Barbara Byrd-Bennet of Cleveland; Beverly Hall of Atlanta; and Diana Lam of Providence). This pattern suggests that women have achieved a respectable measure of equity—at least in the urban principalship and superintendency.

It is not likely that the underrepresentation of women in the ranks of educational administration can be attributed to lack of supply. According to a New York State Education Department report issued in 1988, women accounted for 4 percent of New York state's superintendents, 13 percent of its high school principals, and 28 percent of its elementary principals during the 1987–1988 year. But during the 1984–1987 period, women in New York state earned half of the doctoral degrees awarded in educational administration, earned over half of the master's degrees, and accounted for half of all of the administrative certificates issued. The 2001 NASSP study revealed that women high school principals are more likely than men to hold a doctoral degree (18 percent compared with 13 percent). It appears that the number of women certified each year well exceeds the number employed, leading some experts to conclude that the supply of qualified women is plentiful but they are not being hired in equitable numbers (Sadker, Sadker, & Klein, 1991).

Women's Presence in Successful Schools

More than sex equity is at stake as one examines these figures. The evidence suggests that, though in the minority, women principals are *overrepresented* in schools considered to be highly effective. This assertion is based, in part, on an examination of articles describing successful schools that have appeared in *Educational Leadership* and other journals in the last dozen years, on the case study literature of successful principals (see, e.g., Dwyer et al., 1985; Lipsitz, 1984; Sergiovanni, 1994), and on the burgeoning literature that contrasts the leadership effectiveness of male and female principals. Reasons for the success of women can be traced, in part, to their greater commitment to the values of teaching and learning as opposed to the values of bureaucratic management and control and to a more democratic and value-oriented leadership style that serves school rather than organizational purposes. On the first count, Meskin (1979) explains:

> The woman principal begins her working years strongly committed to the occupation of teaching. Her eye is rarely on career advancement, and she concentrates instead on knowing the ins and outs of her profession. When, often by a fluke, she is promoted to a principalship in later life, her long years as a basic service professional in an organization stand her in good stead. She shows greater ability and self-confidence in directing the instructional program than men do simply because of her deeper understanding of the art of teaching, and she also demonstrates a high degree of ability in administering the school, the milieu in which she worked so long. Because again she is not seeking promotion from her present rank, she commits herself wholeheartedly to the role of principal and is able to master the job in a highly competent fashion. (pp. 336–337)

Of course, a fair number of men serve as principals of successful schools, too. Though the research is skimpy, a reasonable assertion is that these men bring to their practice a disposition, set of priorities, and leadership style that resembles their women counterparts. They view themselves, for example, more as "servants" to school purposes and to those who struggle with them to achieve these purposes. This is in contrast to the style of "superiors" who expect others to serve them. This assertion raises the thorny question of whether differences do indeed exist in the ways men and women manage and lead. The evidence for school administrators suggests that the answer to this question is yes. Moreover, the differences have something to say about the nature and content of educational administration preparation programs and about the whole issue of just how professionalized educational administration should become. As noted earlier, for example, professionalization, as now understood, may not serve women very well.

Meskin (1979) reviewed a number of studies that compared the behaviors of men and women principals. Her analysis of the Florida Leadership Project conducted in the 1950s led her to conclude that women tended to use both democratic behaviors and effective administration practices more frequently than men.

Meskin reviewed as well the landmark leadership research of Hemphill, Griffiths, and Fredericksen (1962). These investigators gave principals "in-baskets" filled with typical school problems to solve. Solutions were then evaluated by panels of experts that included both teachers and the principals' supervisors. Both groups displayed more positive attitudes toward the performances of women than those of men. With respect to specific categories of problems, women were judged better than men in "exchanging information," "maintaining organizational relationships," and "responding to outsiders." Men, on the other hand, fared better in "complying with suggestions made by others" and "analyzing the situation." Meskin (1979) observes that "women seem to be more thorough in their in-basket, use more information from the background materials, and discuss information more with superiors and subordinates. Men, on the other hand, made concluding decisions and followed pre-established structures to a greater degree in problem-solving and took more terminal actions" (p. 333).

It appears from this study that women outperformed men in interpersonal and informational aspects of leadership but that men were better bureaucratic managers. Other data from this study indicated that women were more concerned with the objectives of teaching, pupil progress, and the evaluation of learning than were men. Further, the principals' supervisors rated women as being better in evaluating the performance of new teachers and as more willing and able to provide instructional leadership. "In the important role of instructional leaders, women principals seem to far outshine their male colleagues" (Meskin, 1979, p. 331).

Another study reviewed by Meskin was that of Gross and Trask (1964). The indicators of effectiveness used in this study were teacher ratings of the principal's performance, teacher morale, and student academic performance. These investigators concluded that women's performance as elementary school principals was superior to that of men. In commenting on the study, Meskin (1979) states, "When educational values are considered, women principals showed a greater concern with individual differences and with the social and emotional development of the child than men principals. When evaluating teachers, women place greater stress on the teachers' technical skill and their responsibilities to the school organization than men. Women also tended to exert more supervisory control in their work and to worry less than male principals about their responsibilities" (p. 335).

In more recent studies, Shakeshaft and Perry (1995) found that women principals gave teachers more feedback about their teaching performance than did men principals. Further, this feedback included more detail about teaching and provided more specific recommendations for improvements. Lee, Smith, and Cioci (1993) investigated how high school principals' gender affects teachers' evaluations of their leadership. Men and women teachers assessed the leadership of male principals as being almost equally effective. By contrast, women teachers assessed the leadership of female principals as being very effective, but men considered female principals to be largely ineffective. The researchers suggest that men may be evaluating female principals poorly because they resist what is unfamiliar, are threatened by their more open and participatory style, are unsettled by the push to become more of a team player, and feel uncomfortable with the idea that one's teaching practice should be more visible. Further, men may feel that they have been well served by the present system that seems to favor them. Despite these differences in how men and women teachers evaluate male and female principals, both groups report higher levels of locus of control, self-efficacy, and staff influence over policy when working with female principals (Lee, Smith, & Cioci, 1993).

Using statistics from the 1993–1994 schools and staffing survey, Zheng (1996) examined teacher perceptions of the instructional leadership effectiveness of their principals. Roughly 12,000 public and private school principals and 55,000 teachers were included in his sample. Instructional leadership was measured by the extent to which teachers reported that their principals evaluated them fairly, let them know what was expected, were supportive and encouraging, included them in important educational decisions, provided resources to support teaching and learning, enforced school rules, talked to them about their teaching practice, communicated a vision, and developed clear goals and priorities for the school. Female principals were more positively rated as educational leaders by their teachers than were male principals.

From these and other studies, it seems appropriate to conclude that, as a group, female principals are more effective in providing instructional leadership than are male principals. Using the phrase "as a group" reminds us that many men would respond as women do and some women would respond as men do. To put it another way, if all that was known about two candidates competing for the same principalship position was that one was male and the other female, these studies suggest that, most of the time, the female would be a better bet.

The definitive work on the topic is Shakeshaft's (1987) *Women in Educational Administration*. She covers much of the same ground just presented but extends the discussion by providing a historical analysis and a biting critical commentary based on an examination of over 200 dissertations and 600 research articles. With respect to the question of whether differences exist in male and female styles, Shakeshaft concludes:*

1. *Relationships with others are central to all actions of women administrators.* Women spend more time with people, communicate more, care more about individual differences, are concerned more with teachers and marginal students, and motivate more. Not surprisingly, staffs of women administrators rate women higher, are more productive, and have higher morale. Students in schools with women principals also have higher morale and are more involved with student affairs. Further, parents are more favorable toward schools and districts run by women and thus are more involved in school life....

2. *Teaching and learning are the major foci of women administrators.* Women administrators are more instrumental in instructional learning than men and they exhibit greater knowledge of teaching methods and techniques. Women administrators not only emphasize achievement, they coordinate instructional programs and evaluate student progress. In these schools and districts, women administrators know their teachers and they know the academic progress of their students. Women are

*Charol Shakeshaft, *Women in Educational Administration*, p. 197. Copyright © 1987 by Sage Publications. Reprinted by permission of Corwin Press, Inc.

more likely to help new teachers and to supervise all teachers directly. Women also create a school climate more conducive to learning, one that is more orderly, safer, and quieter. Not surprisingly, academic achievement is higher in schools and districts in which women are administrators.

3. *Building community is an essential part of a woman administrator's style.* From speech patterns to decision-making styles, women exhibit a more democratic, participatory style that encourages inclusiveness rather than exclusiveness in schools. Women involve themselves more with staff and students, ask for and get higher participation, and maintain more closely knit organizations. Staffs of women principals have higher job satisfaction and are more engaged in their work than those of male administrators. These staffs are also more aware of and committed to the goals of learning, and the members of the staffs have more shared professional goals. These are schools and districts in which teachers receive a great deal of support from their female administrators. They are also districts and schools where achievement is emphasized. (p. 197)

More recently, Lee, Smith, and Cioci (1993, p. 156) found that, as a group, female principals use a more democratic and participatory style and evidence a style that is more personalized. Male principals, by contrast, were inclined to be more direct than autocratic and to use styles that were more impersonal and structured. Further, female principals focused more of their efforts on teaching and learning and on other academic concerns. Male principals were more inclined to be management oriented. The 2001 NASSP survey, for example, revealed that more women principals than men are likely to choose establishing a learning climate and curriculum leadership as the most important roles principals should play (68 percent versus 64 percent, and 46 percent versus 41 percent). By contrast, more men chose personnel and operational management (51 percent versus 45 percent, and 28 percent versus 15 percent).

When comparing themselves with their male counterparts, female principals viewed themselves as being more verbal, more concerned about personal relationships, and more cooperative. They viewed themselves as being the same as their male counterparts on such characteristics as aggressiveness, competence, and career and family orientations. They were less likely than men to be motivated by power (Gupton & Slick, 1996, p. xxxi).

The Woman's View

Shakeshaft (1995) found that gender seems also to be related to operational definitions of ethical behavior. Although both male and female superintendents value competence and trust (Garfinkel, 1988, cited in Shakeshaft), they give each a different priority. Female superintendents look for competence first in a team member. Male superintendents identify trust as their number-one priority, viewing competence as being much less important. In Shakeshaft's words, "Women saw things differently. Not only did women not code 'telling something' as disloyal, they said they expected subordinates to tell unless specifically instructed otherwise. They expected people to discuss conversations, actions and feelings with others" (p. 152). Men, by contrast, "said they assumed that if they told a subordinate something, the subordinate would not tell others unless he or she had been instructed to do so" (p. 152). Further, male team members reported that the way to show loyalty was not to disagree with the superintendent except in private. Female team members said that the way to show loyalty was to speak up when they disagreed. They thought that speaking up was a professional responsibility and that it would be immoral to go along with poor ideas. It appears from Shakeshaft's data that women felt the best way to serve their superintendents was to ensure that the best decisions were made by the superintendents for their schools.

The crux of the problem, according to Shakeshaft, is that existing theory and research in educational administration has been faulty because it too often has not accounted for the experiences of women. She argues that practices based on this research not only are slanted to the male world view but are less effective than would be practices based on theory and research that included the woman's experience. Her solution is to rewrite the literature and to restructure preparation programs. "Only when this is done will we be able to understand human behavior and organizations. Until then, we are writing a history and practice of males in school administration. As scholarship, this is shoddy and deficient. As practice, it is useful to only some practitioners" (Shakeshaft, 1987, p. 208).

Despite the problems that still must be surmounted before men and women enjoy equal access to leadership positions and before the discipline of educational administration respects the differences that women bring to their practice, a look ahead suggests that educational administration may have turned the corner and is heading in the right direction. Traditional approaches to administrative practice are giving way to a more responsive, situationally defined approach that is *women friendly*. The continuing march of teaching and learning to the center, the widespread interest in viewing schools as learning communities, and viewing faculties as communities of practice bound by a commitment to the common good, point in the right direction. The importance of caring and the belief that school leadership, teaching, and the process of schooling itself are moral enterprises are additional developments that suggest the acceptance of not only women, but their ideas, ways of knowing, and patterns of practice as the mainstream for the practice of educational administration.

REFERENCES

Beck, L. G. (1994). *Reclaiming educational administration as a caring profession.* New York: Teachers College Press.

Bell, C., & Chase, S. (1993). The underrepresentation of women in school leadership. In C. Marshall (Ed.), *The new politics of race and gender: The 1992 yearbook of the policies of educational association.* Washington, DC: Falmer.

Campbell, M., & Lam, D. (1993). Gender and public education: From mirrors to magnifying lenses. In S. K. Biklen & D. Polard (Eds.), *Gender and education* (pp. 204–220). 92nd yearbook of the National Society for the Study of Education, Part 1. Chicago: University of Chicago Press.

Carver, F. D. (1976). *Administrative-certification and training in Illinois.* Urbana, IL: Department of

Administration, Higher and Continuing Education. University of Illinois. Mimeographed document.

Doud, J. (1989). *The K–8 principal in 1988.* Alexandria, VA: National Association of Elementary School Principals.

Doud, J. L., and Keller, E. P. (1998). *A ten year study: The K–8 principal in 1998.* Alexandria, VA: National Association of Elementary School Principals.

Dwyer, D. C., Lee, G. V., Barnett, G. B., Filby, N. N., Rowan, B., Albert, B. R., & Kojimoto, C. (1985). *Understanding the principal's contribution to instruction: Seven principals, seven stories* (Vols. 1–8). San Francisco: Far West Laboratory for Educational Research and Development.

Feistritzer, C. E., et al. (1988). *Profile of school administrators in the U.S.* Washington, DC: National Center for Educational Information.

Garfinkel, E. (1988). *Ways men and women in school administration conceptualize the administrative team.* Unpublished doctoral dissertation, Hofstra University.

Glass, T. (1992). *The 1992 study of the American school superintendency.* Arlington, VA: American Association of School Administrators.

Glass, T., Björk, L., & Brunner, C. (2000). *The study of the American school superintendency 2000: A look at the superintendent of education in the new millennium.* Arlington, VA: American Association of School Administrators.

Gross, N., & Trask, A. E. (1964). *Staff leadership in the public schools: A sociological inquiry.* New York: John Wiley.

Gupton, S. L., & Slick, G. A. (1996). *Highly successful women administrators: The inside stories of how they got there.* Thousand Oaks, CA: Corwin Press.

Hemphill, J. K., Griffiths, D. E., & Fredericksen, N. (1962). *Administrative performance and personality.* New York: Teachers College, Columbia University.

Lee, V. E., Smith, J. B., & Cioci, M. (1993). Teachers and principals: Gender-related perceptions of leadership and power in secondary schools. *Educational Evaluation and Policy Analysis, 15*(2), 153–180.

Lipsitz, J. (1984). *Successful schools for young adolescents.* New Brunswick, NJ: Transaction Books.

McCleary, L., & Thomson, S. (1979). *The senior high school principalship* (Vol. 3). Reston, VA: National Association of Secondary School Principals.

Marshall, K., Patterson, J. A., Rogers, D. L., & Steele, J. R. (1996). Caring as career: An alternative perspective for educational administration. *Educational Administration Quarterly, 32*(2), 271–294.

Meskin, J. D. (1979). Women as principals: Their performance as educational administrators. In D. A. Erickson & T. L. Reller (Eds.), *The principal in metropolitan schools.* Berkeley, CA: McCutchan.

National Association of Elementary School Principals. (1998). Survey of school principals reveals more women, complex responsibilities, and concerns for the future of the profession. *NAESP News,* Alexandria, VA: National Association of Elementary School Principals.

National Association of Secondary School Principals. (2001). *Priorities and barriers in high school leadership: A survey of principals.* Reston, VA: National Associations of Secondary School Principals. *www.principals.org/pdf/HSSurvey.pdf*

National Center for Educational Statistics. (1995). *Digest of Educational Statistics 1995.* U.S. Department of Education, NCES 95–029.

National Council of Administrative Women in Education. (1973). *Wanted more women: Where are the women superintendents?* Arlington, VA: Author.

Noddings, S. N. (1992). *The challenge to care in schools: An alternative approach to education.* New York: Teachers College Press.

Pellicer, L. O., et al. (1988). *High school leaders and their schools.* Vol. 1: A national profile. Reston, VA: National Association of Secondary School Principals.

Pharis, W., & Zakariya, S. B. (1979). *The elementary school principalship in 1978.* Arlington, VA: National Association of Elementary School Principals.

Sadker, M., Sadker, D., & Klein, S. (1991). The issue of gender in elementary and secondary education. In G. Grant (Ed.), *Review of research in education* (Vol. 17). Washington, DC: American Educational Research Association.

Sergiovanni, T. J. (1994). *Building community in schools.* San Francisco: Jossey-Bass.

Shakeshaft, C. (1987). *Women in educational administration.* Beverly Hills, CA: Sage.

Shakeshaft, C. (1995). A cup half full: A gender critique of the knowledge base in educational administration. In R. Donmoyer, M. Imber, & J. J. Scheurich (Eds.), *The knowledge base in educational administration multiple perspectives.* Albany: State University of New York Press.

Shakeshaft, C., & Perry, A. (1995). The language of power versus the language of empowerment: Gender differences in administrative communication. In D. Corson (Ed.), *Discourse and power in educational organizations* (pp. 17–29). Cresskill, NJ: Hampton Press.

Skrla, L. (1999, April). Femininity/masculinity: Hegemonic normalizations in the public school superintendency. Paper presented at the annual conference of the American Educational Research Association, Montreal, Canada.

Stricherz, M. (2001, November 14). Study to profile secrets of 15 urban leaders' success. *Education Week, XXI*(11), 5.

U.S. Department of Health, Education, and Welfare. (1975). *The condition of education.* Washington, DC: National Center for Education Statistics.

Young, M. D., & McLeod, S. (2000). Flukes, opportunities, and planned interventions: Factors affecting women's decisions to become school administrators. *Educational Administration Quarterly, 37*(4), 462–502.

Zheng, H. P. Y. (1996). *School context, principal characteristics and instructional leadership effectiveness: A statistical analysis.* Paper presented at the annual meeting of the American Educational Research Association, New York City, April 8–12.

8 Students and Teachers Today

This chapter and the next two chapters look at the roles that teachers, students, principals, and superintendents play in schools today and the interdependence that exists among them. Clearly, the success of educational reform efforts will reflect the ability of reformers to recognize and respond to the dynamic, interlocking relationships that exist among all the various actors on the school stage. To ignore the impact of one of them—for example, how students and their relationships to their teachers and to the school can impact change efforts—is to jeopardize the success of those efforts.

The Role of Student

Educational reform proposals have largely ignored the role that students play in the success of efforts to increase academic excellence (Ericson & Ellett, 2002). This omission is unfortunate because, as key participants in teaching–learning initiatives, students have a profound influence on the success of those efforts. If students are not motivated and, thus, not engaged in the learning activity, then, no matter how otherwise well-conceived or well-intentioned the effort, it will not succeed. Most reform proposals have assumed that it is the teacher's and the school's responsibility to motivate and engage students. It is widely believed that good teaching always motivates and engages students and produces increased achievement. The rhetoric of the high-stakes testing movement, for example, clearly places the onus for raising student test scores on teachers and administrators. Either tacitly or explicitly, critics of the educational system often blame either teacher capacity or teacher effort for low student achievement (Ericson & Ellett, 2002, p. 3). More recently, however, some experts have begun to question those assumptions.

In their policy analysis, Ericson and Ellett (2002) raise a provocative question about educational reform: What is in it for the student? (p. 15). They answer by arguing that the structure of our educational system creates incentives for students that "undercut the intent of the reforms" (p. 2). Throughout our history, Americans have believed in the social and economic efficiency of education. Since public education's inception in the seventeenth century, as a people we have viewed it as a vehicle for social and economic advancement. Our democratic

175

belief in a meritocracy—that social and economic benefits will not be reserved for an elite but be available for all—depends on education to provide access to these benefits. More recently, the *A Nation At Risk* report, which was published in 1983 and which initiated the reform movement of the last two decades, cited a weakening of our economic competitiveness with other nations as the primary reason for strengthening education. According to Ericson and Ellett, we have defined the purposes of education, throughout our history, as getting ahead socially and economically for individuals and as providing the engine for economic progress for the nation as a whole.

Consistent with this structure and these purposes, according to Ericson and Ellett, the vast majority of students seek social status and wealth, rather than knowledge for its own sake, through education. To make this process efficient, as a society we have created a "medium of exchange"—grades, transcripts, degrees, and certifications—for students to use to gain their social and economic entitlements. These incentives, however, are extrinsic to education itself. Few rewards exist for students to value education for its intrinsic worth rather than for the external benefits to which it may lead. Our society has created an educational system that fosters this instrumental view of education in our young. Ericson and Ellett argue that it is quite "rational" for students, acting in their own self-interest, in this context to focus on getting good enough grades to "make it" in our society, and even to seek "shortcuts and end runs" in order to gain the credentials that they need (2002, p. 17). It is not necessarily in their self-interest as "rational" students to focus on developing the scholarly work habits and skills that can lead to academic excellence.

Ericson and Ellett believe that reformers have undercut their own efforts by reemphasizing social and economic purposes for education. By proposing rigorous academic improvements, for example, to strengthen the ability of our workforce to compete globally, they have reinforced for the vast majority of students that education is merely instrumental. Rather than committing themselves to the more rigorous scholarship that reform proposals demand, students will remain committed to doing whatever is necessary to getting by and getting ahead. Ericson and Ellett believe that this focus on the "credentialed symbols of educational achievement" rather than on academic excellence itself is "guaranteed to deliver marginal educational achievement and to create resistance to any real and meaningful educational reform" (2002, p. 17).

Ericson and Ellett do not suggest that all students are interested only in the social and economic benefits to be derived from education. In fact, they suggest an interesting typology of students. At the top of their rankings is the *ideal* student, a young scholar committed to the intrinsic value of pursuing knowledge for its own sake. These are quite rarely found in the system of education that we have created. Somewhat more frequently found is the *professional* student, someone whose motivation springs not intrinsically from the intellectual discipline itself but extrinsically from its value to a professional or career goal. A student committed to medical or legal study may fall into this category. A third type is the *status or wealth seeker* who, in the pursuit of rational self-interest, is strongly motivated by ambitions to social standing and money that are external to any intellectual discipline. An example is a medical student who does not deeply care about healing or curing but believes that medicine can provide an enviable lifestyle. The status and wealth seeker type is far more frequently found because the structure of our educational system encourages their development. The fourth category in Ericson and Ellett's typology, also frequently found, is the *indifferent/hostile* type who rejects both the value of education itself and the purported social and economic benefits. The indifferent/hostile student often only remains in school to high school completion because the social and economic penalty for dropping out earlier is so high.

Steinberg (1996) provides powerful support for the argument that the student disengagement from learning that Ericson and Ellett describe is a major problem in our educational system. Over a period of four years Steinberg studied 20,000 teenagers from nine high schools in California and Wisconsin, a sample that represented a diverse cross-section of the population. He found a pervasive lack of commitment to school work—nearly 40 percent indicated that they were "just going through the motions" in school (p. 67):

- *Many students do not take academic work seriously.* Two-thirds, for example, indicated that they had cheated on a test. Ninety percent said they copied homework from other students;
- *Outside activities compete with academic studies.* Two-thirds of students worked, and one-third of those "said they take easier classes so that their jobs won't hurt their grades." Nearly 40 percent of those who participate in an extracurricular activity at school said, "They are often so tired from it that they can't study."
- *The peer culture "demeans academic success and scorns students who try to do well in school."* Less than 20 percent of students have friends who value academic success. Nearly 20 percent acknowledge that they do not try as hard as they can because of fears about what friends will think. (pp. 18–19)

Earlier studies confirm the existence and power of an adolescent peer culture in schools with values that conflict with academic excellence. Allen (1986) asked how high school students come to understand how they are to behave in classrooms. Do students come to classrooms with some sort of an agenda? Having spent time in classrooms, students may well seek to shape classrooms to what they want. How do the events in classrooms shape the agendas of students? Students may be influenced by factors in the context of classrooms, such as what teachers seek to accomplish, assignments or tasks they are asked to do, and characteristics of other students. Allen was particularly interested in how student agendas and classroom events developed the students' viewpoint (perspective) to "make sense of their classrooms and assign meanings to their behaviors" (p. 438). He believed that previous research had attended to how students reacted to the teacher's agenda for the classroom, not to agendas that students might bring to the room.

To study this problem, Allen followed a typical 9th grade schedule in a high school in southern California that enrolled 600 students. He focused his attention on 100 students (mostly 9th graders) and four teachers assigned to five classes. These classes included agriculture, Spanish, health education, and English (two mini-courses). Allen observed classes for approximately sixteen weeks, interviewed students, and interviewed teachers.

What Allen found was that students did have a classroom agenda, but that this agenda was influenced by the context of the particular classroom. The agenda of students had two major classroom goals: socializing with other students and passing the course. To achieve these goals, students spent time in the first few days of a class figuring out the teacher. Figuring out the teacher meant determining the amount of socialization that would be tolerated and the amount of work that had to be accomplished. Students consciously sought to determine what the rules were for conduct and schoolwork and just how far these rules could be bent or broken.

After this initial period, classroom events became routine. Students sought to achieve the goal of socializing with others by having fun. Having fun included social talking, playing around, and humor. Students also sought to achieve the goal of passing the course by giving the teacher what the teacher wanted. Students worked on assignments and participated in classroom events. They also sought to increase the amount of time they could spend socializing by reducing the amount of work required to pass the course. They challenged the requirements of the teacher or copied the work of others.

Critical events occurred if the teacher's agenda conflicted with the students' agenda. If the teacher's agenda for passing the class was too easy or too hard, students became bored and increased their efforts at socializing with other students. In contrast to routine efforts at having fun, reducing boredom was often defiant or aggressive and sought to change the agenda the teacher was trying to set for the classroom. On the other hand, if the classroom became too noisy from socializing and the teacher began measures to gain control, students adjusted by trying to stay out of trouble by not talking or playing around.

The classroom teacher affected this general agenda of students. In agriculture class, for example, in-class academic activities were relatively unimportant and out-of-class activities were critical for passing the course. The teacher also stressed informal relationships with students, increasing opportunities for socializing. In Spanish, however, classroom instruction was structured, with high levels of academic expectation; classroom rules were rigidly enforced; and the teacher stressed formal relationships. Most students gave the teacher what the teacher wanted to pass the course and socialized the last few minutes of the class. In health education, class work was extensive but easy. Socializing had flexible limits, and the teacher stressed good rapport and cooperation with students. The teacher took a genuine interest in students inside and outside the health education classroom. For the students, each classroom was a different context that shaped their behaviors as they sought to fulfill their agenda.

The agenda of the students Allen observed is clearly consistent with the attitudes of disengagement. Steinberg describes as well as with the values of the status and wealth seeker and the indifferent/hostile types that Ericson and Ellett present. Clearly, making the most of an academic opportunity was not on the agenda of these students.

Canaan (1987) examined teenage cliques in schools and also provided evidence of the challenges that peer culture pose to instilling and developing values of academic excellence among students. Canaan conducted the research in a middle school with 634 students in 6th to 8th grades and a high school of 1,053 students in grades 9 to 12. The community of Sheepshead is a predominantly upper middle-class suburb with high per-pupil expenditures.

Canaan (1987) found that at middle school and high school, there is a three-tiered group-ranking system. The top group in the middle school—the "cool" group—is made up of boys and girls who are "athletically skilled and socially capable" (p. 386) of living by a set of rules. These rules include not admitting to liking school or getting good grades. The middle group of students in the middle school conforms "to the expectations of their teachers and parents and those of the cool group" (p. 386). Members of the middle group may be chided by a cool group member for studying too hard or following all the rules adults make. The lower group members are known for socially inappropriate behavior.

In the high school, the highest group is made up of two subgroups—jocks and freaks. Jocks excel in extracurricular athletic activities and dress and act with self-confidence. During the week, they follow coach's orders, but on weekends, they *party* by breaking these orders. Freaks defy adult values in and out of school. Both jocks and freaks are aware of what other members of the highest group are doing. The middle group is made up of various subgroups that are neither as cool as jocks and freaks nor as weird as the low group. Many in the middle group emulate the jocks and freaks. The low group in the high school is made up of several small groups whose "actions do not conform with cool notions of proper social action" (Canaan, 1987, p. 391).

The most visible groups in both schools are the top groups. They serve as model teenagers in both schools, defining what it means to be cool (what the appropriate values of a teenager are) and what the relationship of teenagers to school and adults should be (when and where it is appropriate to accept or reject adult values).

Through the perceptions of teachers, Antes and George (1990) also confirm the existence of a student subculture with values antithetical to academic achievement. In a survey of teachers in 276 schools in 87 communities, they found "completing assignments, attitude toward school, and classroom discipline all increase as problems as students progress through school" (no page number). Attitude toward school was seen as a serious problem by 21.1 percent of elementary teachers, 39.8 percent of junior high teachers, and 45.6 percent of secondary teachers (Antes & George, 1990).

In sum, these studies confirm the existence of a student peer culture and subcultures that increase in influence as students get older. The peer culture holds values that are often antithetical to those that the adult world of teachers and parents espouse. Teenagers may not agree with their teachers about what should be done in classrooms or with their parents about correct behavior. Teachers confront students with expectations about what it means to be a student, and parents confront their children with expectations about what is appropriate behavior.

Teachers and parents who contradict the norms of the student subculture encounter difficulties.

As cultural systems, schools are invented by society to initiate the young into that society. The young are not helpless, however. They respond to this adult invention by creating inventions of their own. They learn how to make it in the system and how to use the system to their own ends.

Although the ends that the peer culture seek may often appear to be in conflict with those of the adult world, as Ericson and Ellett suggest, children's values and behavior may actually be in tune with broader social messages about the purposes of education. All of these studies portray students, especially those in the upper grades, doing just enough academic work to get by, to pass the course, to please the teacher. In Ericson and Ellett's terms, they understand that *making it* in our society depends more on obtaining the certification symbols—grades, transcripts, and diplomas—than on superior scholarly achievements.

What do these studies, finally, suggest about school reform efforts? First, reformers must recognize that students are powerful agents for shaping what happens in schools. Answers to Ericson and Ellett's question: What's in it for students? must be included in reform proposals. Second, both Steinberg and Ericson and Ellett argue that parental, community, and social forces powerfully influence student attitudes toward school. Reform proposals must take these external forces on students' lives into account. Steinberg, for example, proposes to limit the number of hours that high school students work per week and to strengthen credentialing standards. Ericson and Ellett suggest that society create alternate pathways to schools "that feature practical, hands-on, experiential learning within a 'real world' context" for indifferent/hostile students to gain the adult knowledge and skills they will need to enter the workforce (2002, p. 22). These new pathways would eliminate the need for these students to remain in school just to gain the credential that the high school diploma provides.

The Role of Teacher

The rest of this chapter and the next two explore characteristics of the roles of teacher, principal, and superintendent as they have diverged and developed during the last 100 years. Differences in roles and responsibilities will be apparent, but so will striking similarities in the *dominant images* of the roles and in the kind of work that both teachers and administrators do. In brief, we shall see that the roles of both teachers and administrators have bureaucratic-rational and moral aspects and that they include instructional, managerial, and political responsibilities (Cuban, 1988, p. xviii).

The first school administrators in this country were also teachers. As schools grew and the bureaucratic demands increased during the nineteenth century, principal–teachers took on the responsibilities of administration while still teaching. Despite their common history and their common purpose to educate children, during the twentieth century, teaching and administering schools developed as distinctly different roles. Increasing role specialization widened the split as two separate career paths emerged—career teacher and career administrator (Cuban, 1988, p. xiii).

As a result of this separation, the roles of teacher and administrator today may appear dissimilar. Cuban (1988) suggests that this is because their daily work occurs in such different settings (p. xix)—teachers in classrooms juxtaposed against administrators in school office or district conference rooms. But, he sees strong similarities between the roles: "…teachers and administrators are both bosses and subordinates. They direct others while obeying orders. They are also solo practitioners. They prize autonomy. They manage conflict. They also are expected to lead" (p. xix).

Two Conceptions of the Teacher's Role

Two dominant conceptions of teachers have shaped the role in the last 200 years. Rooted in the growth of industrialization, one conception views schools like factories, mass producing students to become productive workers and contributing citizens. This *bureaucratic-rational* conception portrays the teacher as a technician who transmits knowledge following a prescribed curriculum, obeys and enforces rules and procedures handed down from above, and administers standardized tests designed to ensure that a uniform product emerges from the factory-school.

In contrast to the bureaucratic-rational conception, the *moral* conception portrays the teacher as an agent of change. Rooted in the cultural and religious traditions of the enlightenment and the belief in the development of a human's potential, the *moral* conception views the teacher as having a mission, not just transmitting knowledge, but transforming individuals. The teacher as moral agent must use independent judgment to determine what each child needs to reach his or her potential as a student and as a person and have considerable autonomy in making instructional decisions and assessing their value (Cuban, 1988, pp. 3–4).

These two conceptions have run through the fabric of public school teaching since its inception. Sometimes the technical view is ascendant, such as during the period of *scientific management* of schools. Sometimes the moral view is ascendant, such as during the progressive era when the view of schools as communities that transformed the hearts and minds of children became popular. Another example of this cycle occurred more recently. Immediately after publication of *A Nation At Risk* in 1983, the technical view of teachers as laborers whose work could be prescribed and controlled once again became prevalent. States and local districts mandated curriculum, competency tests for students, and new licensure requirements for teachers. When these prescriptive policies failed to achieve dramatic success, a second wave of reform assumed the moral conception of teachers. By the late 1980s, experts were advocating that teachers have more authority and autonomy for educational design. Reformers came to see teachers as the "agents rather than the object of school reform" (Johnson, 1990, p. xvii).

Sometimes, both conceptions can exist in the practice of the same teacher in what Cuban calls "uneasy equilibrium" (p. 5). Overall, however, from a study spanning ninety years, from 1890 to 1980, and including over 7,000 classrooms, Cuban concludes, "I found the persistent domination of teacher-centered practices before, during, and after each of the surges of reform aimed at installing student-centered approaches" (1988, p. 26). Teacher-centered practices would more likely be associated with the bureaucratic-rational conception of teaching and student-centered practices associated with the moral conception.

Cuban argues that these two conceptions of teaching become congruent in the "image of teacher as a professional" (p. 6). The professional must have mastery of technical skills and knowledge. So training and certification are essential. But the knowledge and skills acquired in training and experience and validated by certification are tools for the professional who uses them to achieve the larger, transformative mission of the moral agent.

Three Core Elements of the Role: Instruction, Management, and Politics

Whatever conception of the role a teacher enacts, three core elements—instruction, management, and politics—make up work responsibilities. As we discuss later, these same core elements make up the roles of principal and superintendent as well.

Instructional. The instructional role includes the typical teacher duties—planning lessons, deciding on instructional methods and materials, assessing students' learning. As experts have pointed out, historically a great deal of uncertainty has existed about what constitutes good instruction (Lortie, 1975; Cuban, 1988). Although research and the professional literature have identified promising practices, they have not validated universally accepted protocols for instruction. Without consensus, then, teachers enact the instructional role in widely diverse ways. Some teachers are content focused; some are child centered; others emphasize metacognitive skills—not just students learning but students learning how to learn. Within classrooms today, multiple permutations of these and other approaches are used.

Managerial. As Cuban points out, the managerial role is central to the bureaucratic-rational conception of the role (p. 30). Classroom management—routines that define student activity, rules that ensure orderly student behavior, procedures for attendance, homework, grading—is essential for any teacher to establish to accomplish instructional goals. In addition to serving this classroom purpose, the teacher's management of students also serves important socializing purposes, inculcating in students the importance and value of compliance with authority and teaching them how to live cooperatively in a community.

Political. Politics is also a facet of a teacher's role. Cuban (1988), for example, describes the teacher's political role within the classroom: "To the degree that teachers, for example, use their legitimate authority to allocate scarce resources to children, govern minors through a series of techniques, negotiate order, and bargain with members of the class, teachers act politically" (p. xix).

Ball (1987) describes the teacher's political role within the larger school community. Ball suggests that schools should be viewed as small political systems in which individual teachers, groups of teachers, departments, and administrators are seen negotiating for resources and power. These resources include prime classroom locations, space for storage or computers, particular students, certain classes, supplies, and requirements for students. Often these resources are seen as ways to enhance the prestige and power of an individual or department (math has more computers than business education) or to ease the burden of the work (only the smart kids take physics). Struggles over power include issues of who has the right to make decisions and whether these decisions are enforced or ignored. For instance, it may become part of the political order that although evaluations for nontenured teachers are important, evaluations for tenured teachers are pro forma or else the teachers of the building will demand that their association file a grievance against the principal.

This micropolitical view of the school stresses that the order of the school is constantly being negotiated and renegotiated. Under these conditions, the relative prestige and power of individuals—be they teachers, department chairs, or administrators—are in a state of flux and may differ from issue to issue.

Whether teachers enact the bureaucratic-rational or the moral conception of their role, or some combination of the two, they, like school administrators, perform job responsibilities in three core areas: instruction, management, and politics.

The Workplace for Teachers

The Teacher Shortage

A key question about the workplace of teachers is whether or not it can be sufficiently improved to attract and retain quality teachers. According to some estimates, U.S. schools will need 2.2 million teachers over the next ten years because of state and federal class-size reduction initiatives, student enrollment increases, and anticipated retirements of the current teaching force (National Commission on Mathematics and Science Teaching for the Twenty-first Century, 2000 as cited in National Science Foundation Program Solicitation, 2002). Enrollment is estimated to increase by 4 percent between 1997 and 2009. Since, as of 2002, the average teacher in the country is forty-four years of age, increasing retirements during this same time period will compound the problem (*Education Week on the Web*, 2002).

The issue is not just the quantity of teachers available for the nation's classrooms but their quality. Research tells us that teacher quality is the most significant variable in student achievement. Sanders and Rivers (1996) found that three years of ineffective teachers produced differences of up to 50 percentile points in test scores among otherwise comparable 5th graders than three years of effective teachers. Growing evidence, moreover, raises concerns about teacher preparation and quality. The National Center for Education Statistics, for example, found that in 2002 more than six out of ten high school students in history and specialized science courses such as chemistry were taught by teachers who did not major in those subjects in college and were not certified to teach them (Schouten, 2002). A 2001 California report indicated that 14 percent of California teachers were uncertified and, therefore, underprepared. More troubling, in California schools serving minority and economically disadvantaged students, 20 percent of teachers were uncredentialed (Solomon & Firetag, 2002). Recognizing the importance of teacher quality, President George W. Bush's education bill that Congress passed in 2002 called for a "highly qualified" teacher in every classroom by 2005 (Solomon & Firetag, 2002).

A growing controversy has developed about how to ensure that public schools have an adequate supply of the highly qualified teachers that President Bush wants. Pointing to the research on teacher quality, some experts have recommended that policymakers toughen standards and strengthen support programs for the training and induction of new teachers. As a result of these initiatives, by 2001, many states had established stronger minimum requirements for initial licensure, introduced induction and mentoring programs, and strengthened testing. Other education experts and observers, however, have argued that increasing requirements will only exacerbate the problem. In arguing for less stringent entry requirements, they point to the evidence that content knowledge is the key to teaching effectiveness and to the less compelling evidence of the value of pedagogical training. They advocate a market approach. Schools should be free to hire whomever they want to teach. Accountability demands from the schools' clients, parents, and students will ensure that only competent teachers are hired and retained (*Education Week on the Web,* 2002).

The Conditions of Teaching

Training and licensure are not the only issues in addressing the crisis in teacher quality. Attracting and retaining teachers depends on improving the conditions of the workplace. In her 1990 study of workplace conditions, Johnson pointed out, "Good teachers are in short supply. The most academically talented candidates never enter the classroom, and the best leave after only a short tenure" (p. xiv). In 2002, more than 20 percent of new teachers leave the profession within four years, adding significantly to turnover and to the loss of teaching capacity. Dissatisfaction with working conditions seems to be a key factor in these decisions to change careers (*Education Week on the Web,* 2002).

What Determines the Conditions of the Workplace

According to Johnson (1990), in teaching, like other professions, the nature of the work itself has in part shaped the workplace for teaching. She argues that the historic uncertainty about what constitutes good teaching that was mentioned earlier—disagreement about goals, lack of proven, widely accepted instructional strategies—and the ongoing variability that a teacher finds among students in any classroom are defining characteristics of teaching. These features of teaching necessitate that teachers claim substantial autonomy in the classroom and reduce the possibilities of effective supervision by administrators. The ill-defined nature of teaching also limits the level of specialization possible in work roles. Teachers confront the complexity of a *whole child* with a range of varying physical, emotional, intellectual, personal, and social needs to which they must respond.

Much of the uncertainty that teachers feel about their effectiveness also stems from the complexity that children always present. Today, the increasing diversity of students—in terms of readiness for schooling, assumed content knowledge and skills, and linguistic ability—compounds this uncertainty. McLaughlin and Talbert (2001) found that high school teachers in their study of sixteen high schools in California and Michigan over four years "often describe their work and see their professional rewards in terms of their relationships with students" (p. 6). In interviews, teachers emphasized the ways that today's students differ from yesterday's (p. 6): "Teachers experience today's students as changed in nearly every respect related to and predictive of academic success—family support, consistent attendance, attention to schoolwork, and social class and language compatible with school culture" (p. 8)

Historical and social forces have also shaped the workplace for teaching. Because women have historically made up the teaching force, teaching has remained low-status work with low pay and poor working conditions. Teachers, therefore, have always had to find intrinsic rewards for job satisfaction because few external rewards were available. The *egg crate* structure of school themselves—with separated classrooms of uniform size in a line along a corridor—reflects growth by accretion since the original one-room schoolhouse (Lortie, 1975, p. 14). This basic design has changed little in the last 100 years and contributes to the isolation that is one of the most significant workplace features in teaching. Finally, the scientific management of schools that began at the start of the twentieth century created an industrial image of teaching, with children as raw material subject to standardized procedures designed to produce uniform products. The legacies of this approach—in the bureaucratic structure of schools, the centralized curriculum development, standards and high-stakes testing—also define the workplace for teaching today (pp. 4–5).

What Key Elements of the Workplace Affect Teacher Satisfaction?

With these features, the workplace is more than a physical setting. It provides a context for teaching practice and influences it through a complex of elements. These include:

- Physical environment—safety and comfort, space, and resources
- Organizational structures—workload, centralized or decentralized authority, amount of autonomy, supervision, and level of interdependence and interaction

- Sociological elements—roles and relationships, characteristics of clients and peers, status
- Economic conditions—pay and benefits, job security
- Politics—access to resources, voice in governance, equity of treatment
- Culture—strength of norms and expectations, richness of history and tradition, supportiveness
- Psychological elements—meaningfulness of work, opportunities for learning, level of stress. (Johnson, 1990, pp. 12–21)

Johnson argues, "better workplaces are also better schools" (p. 26). Her study reveals that these workplace elements do affect teacher job satisfaction. Improving the workplace so that teachers feel they can do their job well is a key to attracting and retaining quality teachers.

While conceding that the relationship between job satisfaction and productivity is "elusive" (p. 24), Johnson cites Goodlad's (1984) research that showed a modest correlation between the level of satisfaction that teachers expressed with their working conditions and the judgment of those schools by parents and students. Schools that were rated more satisfying by teachers were more likely to be judged more positively by students and parents (p. 26).

Overall, the public schools that Johnson studied "proved to be deficient workplaces" (p. 326). However, some private schools were more satisfying workplaces for teachers. Although private schools generally pay even lower salaries than public schools, their better maintained facilities, smaller classes, stronger cultural traditions, greater autonomy, and generally smaller and less formal bureaucracy made them more attractive to many teachers (p. 329).

Fullan (2001) also suggests that workplace conditions for teachers are problematic. In fact, he believes that they have "deteriorated over the past two decades" (p. 115). Factors that have contributed to the worsening work environment are the decrease in esteem and respect from parents and community and the increase in stress caused by the overload of work responsibilities that have fallen to teachers. This heavier burden includes increased academic expectations, the growing range of family and social problems with which teachers must cope, and the imposition of mandates spawned by "multiple, disconnected reform efforts" (p. 115).

What Improvements Will Make a Difference?

Johnson (1990) recommends several significant workplace changes for public schools:

> Adequately funding and decentralizing schools, abandoning models of mass production, involving parents and developing systems of community support, and increasing the professional influence of teachers would enhance the quality of school as a workplace and make it possible for good teachers to do good work. (p. 338)

She cautions, however, that in order for an improved workplace to increase student learning, changes in attitude and role will be necessary. In her study, teachers seemed generally alienated from administrators, whom they often depicted as controlling figures making bureaucratic demands that became obstacles to effective teaching. Johnson suggests that to develop a healthier work environment for teachers, administrators will have to change. Central office administrators will have to assume a role that is more supportive and decentralizes decision making. Principals will have to share authority at the school level and place teaching and learning, rather than management and control, at the top of their priority lists (pp. 340–341).

According to Johnson, teachers, too, will have to change. In the face of adverse workplace conditions, many in her study had retreated into their classrooms and no longer participated in school-wide or district-wide reform efforts. However, to support a healthier work environment, they will have to be more willing to take school-wide responsibility and to be held accountable for their classroom performance. This last may prove to be a daunting challenge. Johnson notes that in her study, "Few challenged norms of noninterference that allowed staff to work behind closed doors, doors which sometimes concealed unprofessional practice. Few dared to violate norms of equity that dissuaded individual teachers from assuming leadership, displaying excellence, or presuming to advise their peers" (p. 342).

Fullan (2001), too, believes that the workplace must be improved to "energize teachers and reward accomplishments" in order to recruit and retain quality teachers. In fact, Fullan argues that this improvement is central to any serious school reform effort (p. 115).

The Impact of Teacher Isolation and Uncertainty

For most of the school day, most teachers in the nation are alone in a classroom with a group of children. Over the past quarter century, educational experts have studied and confirmed the isolation of teachers from other adults and the negative effects this lack of sustained professional contact can have on the efficacy of the teacher.

In his pioneering work using interviews and surveys, Lortie (1975) confirmed the "cellular" organization of schools into self-contained classrooms (p. 14). Teachers are individualistic because they are dropped into their classrooms and implicitly told to survive or to leave. What teachers come to realize is that each teacher must develop her or his own survival tactics. As a result of this isolation and these norms of independence, teachers have to solve their own problems and manage their own anxieties. No universally accepted techniques for classroom success exist (p. 134).

Lortie's study reveals other "endemic uncertainties" in teaching that can produce anxiety and self-doubt, thus reducing effectiveness (pp. 134–161). Goals in teaching often reflect broad and multiple purposes and are intangible. Assessment criteria may be equally unclear. When a child is successful, it is difficult to judge whether one teacher or another has had a primary influence. In these unstable circumstances, it is difficult for teachers to know with any assurance or confidence that they have done a good job.

Fullan (2001) cites two later studies that confirm that little has changed since Lortie's work. Goodlad (1984), too, in his study of teachers, confirmed that the pattern of isolation in teaching continued. He found that the teachers in his study were "virtually autonomous with respect to classroom decisions—selecting materials, determining class organization, choosing instructional materials" (as quoted in Fullan, 2001, p. 120). He also pointed out that "their autonomy seemed exercised in a context more of isolation than of rich professional dialogue" (as quoted in Fullan, 2001, p. 121). The majority of schools studied by Rosenholtz (1989) were "learning impoverished" and characterized by isolation, uncertainty about what and how to teach, and low job commitment (as cited in Fullan, pp. 121–122).

The Importance of Collaborative Work to Reform

Most experts today agree that creating a collaborative work culture for teachers that reduces isolation is essential to school improvement. Study after study confirms that substantial and lasting change in schools will only occur as a result of teachers embracing new beliefs about student learning and developing new practices to implement those beliefs. This kind of reculturing occurs as a result of personal growth that is thwarted or, at least, limited by workplace isolation but stimulated and supported by conditions of collegiality, in which teachers engage in substantive professional dialogue about the work they do. In a collaborative work culture, teachers can discuss the meaning of change and develop deeper personal understandings about it. They can develop more considered judgments about the value of a reform and also learn together how to implement the reform effectively (Fullan, p. 124).

Rosenholtz (1989), for example, identified positive effects of a collaborative work culture in "learning-enriched" or "moving" schools as distinguished from "learning-impoverished" or "stuck" schools. Among the key features of learning-enriched schools were collaboration between teachers and principals in goal setting and collegial work activity. This collaboration created more clarity and certainty about the efficacy of teaching practices and more commitment to them (as cited in Fullan, 2001, p. 126).

McLaughlin and Talbert (2001) also found the importance of reculturing to create collaborative professional communities of practice. They studied a cross-section of sixteen high schools in California and Michigan over four years, documenting the contexts or communities in which teachers work. They found that "all teacher communities play the same broad roles. They enact conceptions of practice and career and respond to 'shocks' from the broader system" (p. 93)—for example, changes in student demographics or new mandates. They also found, however, substantial differences among these communities. In most of the schools, they found teachers working in isolation, reflecting norms of autonomy. However, in several schools, they found that strong communities of professional practice, reflecting shared beliefs and norms of collaboration, had developed.

In the "weak communities" that exist in the majority of schools studied, McLaughlin and Talbert found that teachers work in private and their practice is highly individualized and idiosyncratic. Teachers respond to the enormous changes they experience in today's students by maintaining their past practice of trying to fill in gaps in student knowledge and skills or by watering down content (pp. 19–23). They often see the "nontraditional students" with whom they are dealing as deficient rather than different, when compared with the "ideal" student in the past (p. 40). Student learning experiences are "akin to an instructional lottery" (p. 64) that depends on the teacher they happen to draw in a given year.

In the "strong professional communities," in contrast, teachers have collaboratively developed "distinctive expectations for teachers' work and interactions with students." As a result of these shared agreements, teaching practices are much less varied; standards for student performance are not compromised; and student success is much less dependent on teacher quality. Teachers in these strong cultures often see today's students as different rather than deficient when compared with those in the past.

McLaughlin and Talbert (2001) also discovered that "within strong school and departmental communities in particular, alternative teaching practice and career patterns had evolved and were sustained" (p. 10). Whereas in weak communities, teachers perceive their careers to be in decline and blame the students, in the strong communities, teachers perceive and prize their "collective accomplishments," and feel the rewards of learning along with colleagues.

Interestingly, McLaughlin and Talbert also found that the strong communities were both "traditional" and "innovative." These differences reflect the two contrasting conceptions of teaching discussed earlier. In the traditional communities, curriculum was "predetermined"; instructional practices were teacher-centered; and collaboration focused on policies and procedures for testing and sorting students. The culture, in other words, reflects the bureaucratic-rational conception of the teacher.

In the "innovative" communities, in contrast, instructional practices were centered on the students; curriculum evolved to meet student needs without reducing expectations and emphasized student thinking and problem solving; and collaboration focused on shared responsibility among teachers for student achievement (p. 10, 11). This culture reflects the moral agent conception of the teacher.

As a result of their study, McLaughlin and Talbert conclude that creating strong communities of professional practice in American high schools is an issue of reculturing. "The ethos of teaching" must change "from individualism to collaboration, from conservatism to innovation." As Johnson does, they, too, believe that teachers must have the "vision and will to change their professional lives and practice" (p. 125). Otherwise, educational reform efforts will fail. Teachers must create "communities of practice…characterized by mutual engagement, joint enterprise, and shared repertoires of practice" (p. 127).

In conclusion, we have seen that the role of teacher is complex. Two contrasting conceptions—the bureaucratic-rational and the moral—have shaped the image of teaching over the last 100 years. Whatever image a teacher emulates, instructional, managerial, and, perhaps surprisingly, political functions must be performed effectively to be successful.

Attracting and retaining quality teachers to the classrooms of the twenty-first century and enabling them to enact this complex role will depend on improving the conditions of the workplace, including increasing pay and providing more and better physical, technical, and psychological support. Improving education, however, will also depend on replacing the historic culture of isolation with one of collaboration in which teachers join forces to confront and overcome the complex problems they face.

REFERENCES

Allen, J. D. (1986). Classroom management: Students, perspectives, goals, and strategies. *American Educational Research Journal, 19,* 437–459.

Antes, R. L., & George, G. (1990, April). *Teacher perception of students at risk.* Paper presented at the annual conference of the American Educational Research Association, Boston, MA.

Ball, S. (1987). *The Micropolitics of the School.* New York: Methuen.

Canaan, J. (1987). A comparative analysis of American suburban middle class, middle school, and high school teenage cliques. In G. Spindler & L. Spindler (Eds.), *Interpretive ethnography of education: At home and abroad* (pp. 385–406). Hillsdale, NJ: Lawrence Erlbaum.

Cuban, L. (1988). *The managerial imperative and the practice of leadership in schools.* Albany: State University of New York Press.

Education Week on the Web. (2002, June 19). Hot topics: Teacher quality. Retrieved June 20, 2002, from *http://www.edweek.org/context/topics/issues page.cfm?id=50.*

Ericson, D., & Ellett, F. (2002, July). The question of the student in educational reform. *Education Policy Analysis Archives, 10*(31),1–30.

Fullan, M. (2001). *The new meaning of educational change.* New York: Teachers College Press.

Goodlad, J. (1984). *A place called school: Prospects for the future.* New York: McGraw-Hill.

Johnson, S. (1990). *Teachers at work: Achieving success in our schools.* New York: Basic Books.

Lortie, D. C. (1975). *Schoolteacher.* Chicago: University of Chicago.

McLaughlin, M., & Talbert, J. (2001). *Professional communities and the work of high school teaching.* Chicago: University of Chicago Press.

National Commission on Mathematics and Science Teaching for the 21st Century. (2000). *Before it's too late.* Jessup, MD: Education Publications Center.

National Science Foundation. (2002). *Science, technology, engineering, and mathematics teacher preparation.* Program solicitation (NSF-02-130), p. 1.

Rosenholtz, S. (1989). *Teachers' workplace: The social organization of schools.* New York: Longman.

Sanders, W. L., & Rivers, J. (1996). Cumulative and residual effects of teachers on future student academic achievement. Report of the University of Tennessee Value-Added Research & Assessment Center, Knoxville, Tennessee.

Schouten, F. (2002, June 1). Feds: Out-of-field teaching persists. *The Arizona Republic,* 1–2.

Solomon, L., & Firetag, K. (2002, March 20). The road to teacher quality. *Education Week, 21*(27), 1–4.

Steinberg, L. (1996). *Beyond the classroom.* New York: Simon & Schuster.

9

The Principalship Today

Who are principals today? How do they see themselves? How did the role of principal develop historically and how has it changed over the years? This chapter explores answers to these and other questions in order to understand the obstacles and opportunities that challenge school leaders today and the new definitions of principal leadership that are emerging in the professional literature and in practice.

History of the Role

The role of principal has evolved and changed over the last 150 years. During the last half of the nineteenth century, as public schools grew in size and as state governments and national commissions and associations developed school standards, *principal–teachers* began to provide the managerial functions in schools that regulations required while still serving as teachers. By the 1920s, those duties had expanded to include the management of curriculum and the supervision of instruction. As a result, principals increasingly became professional administrators who taught no classes (Cuban, 1988, pp. 53–54). In the early decades of the twentieth century, the influence of Frederick Taylor's concepts of *scientific management* began to be felt in schools. The concept of principal as bureaucratic middle manager influenced how the role became formalized. Donaldson (2001) describes the bureaucratic leadership model that emerged for school leaders:

- Formal authority was vested in specific administrative roles to assure school-wide safety, orderliness, and productivity;
- The people in these roles organized a rational institutional process so that the school's core work with students was uniform and met state standards;
- Leaders were well informed, had access to governing and funding bodies, and were able to control personnel;
- Leaders shaped the school to meet emerging needs in the environment and among its students. (p. 4)

In this bureaucratic-rational conception of the role, the principal was first and foremost an administrator, ensuring that curriculum mandates, policies, and procedures decided by the school board or higher authorities were implemented in the school and that instruction was appropriately supervised. Hierarchical organization characterized by top-down bureaucratic control was the norm in public schools.

The principal, however, was not just to be an efficient bureaucrat following orders from above and ensuring that they were obeyed by those below. The principal was also to be a professional administrator with the expertise to supervise the instructional program of the school (Cuban, 1988, p. 59). Since the 1920s, this dual role—bureaucratic manager and instructional leader—has shaped the image of the school principal as defined in research literature and practice. Over seven decades, however, from 1911–1981, the evidence suggests that in reality "principals have spent most of their time on noninstructional tasks" (Cuban, 1988, p. 61).

In the second half of the twentieth century, schools experienced new demands and became far different places. Major social and political events—the civil rights movement, the Vietnam War, and Watergate—destabilized society. Parents of historically underserved students—the culturally and economically disadvantaged, racial and ethnic minorities, those with cognitive and emotional disabilities—began to demand that public schools provide for their children. In response to this advocacy, federal mandates for special education and for English Language Learners compelled schools to provide a free and appropriate education for all students.

As society demanded changes in schools, the conception of the principal also began to change. In 1983, the publication of *A Nation At Risk* began the most sustained and influential period of school reform in history. The standards and accountability movement that resulted has ratcheted up the pressure on school principals to provide the instructional leadership that will produce significant gains in student performance. The role of principal as "instructional leader" as well as manager began to emerge in the school effectiveness literature of the 1970s (Donaldson, 2001, p. 4).

By the 1980s, the ideal principal was an instructional leader who defined the school's mission and set clear goals; coordinated and supervised curriculum and instruction; established an academic climate that set high academic expectations and standards; and fostered a healthy, safe school culture for both students and teachers. "In short, the tendency during this era was to place the burden for improvement upon the principal as the individual 'strong instructional leader' in the organization" (Marsh, 2000, p. 127). The image of leadership emphasized "top-down decision making by a strong, technically adept leader" (Lashway, 1995, p. 1).

During the 1990s, the role of the principal changed rapidly and dramatically. The scale of expected change grew and its pace accelerated (Marsh, 2000, p. 127). Demands on principals narrowed from broad expectations for efficient and effective school operation to a more specific focus on accountability for student performance, especially as measured by standardized tests (Doud & Keller, 1998, p. 1). In the 1990s, the pressure on principals "to be accountable for meeting performance standards increased, and that accountability was reinforced through performance-based funding" (Doud & Keller, 1998, p. xi).

An organizational consequence of increased accountability was the movement to more decentralized decision making so that individual school faculties and principals were more "directly responsible for instructional decisions that affect their schools" (Doud & Keller, 1998, p. 1). At the same time that accountability and high-stakes testing required principals to have strong, technical skills for management tasks, the movement toward participatory management required that they have strong interpersonal skills for organizational culture-building tasks. Instead of working in an environment that expected and accepted unilaterally exercised authority, principals now functioned in a school world in which power was fractured and divided among various participants in the schooling enterprise.

The result of these complex and rapid changes of the 1990s has been a sense of "role ambiguity and role overload" (Marsh, 2000, p. 127) that many principals experience as overwhelming. As a consequence, new definitions of the role are evolving in both the professional literature and practice. The role of the principal as "the solitary instructional leader" (Marsh, 2000, p. 129) no longer is tenable. The new image of school leadership is "one of empowering and building capacity" (Marsh, 2000, p. 130) in others. In the collaborative world of the twenty-first century school, the principal is no longer, if he or she ever was, the organizational expert. The new challenges and demands require the creation of new knowledge and skills for enhancing teaching and learning. "Acquiring the knowledge is more a matter of culture and reflection than technical skills" (Marsh, 2000, p. 131).

In summary, the role of principal has evolved and changed over 150 years. During the twentieth century, professional literature and practice identified both instructional leadership and bureaucratic management as core role elements. During the last twenty years, however, school reform initiatives have dramatically expanded and transformed the role. New definitions emphasize the principal as a collaborative leader focused on developing the culture of the school. These definitions are further developed and explored in the rest of the chapter.

Who Principals Are Today

In spite of an increase in retirements, the average age of principals today is older than in the past. According to the 1998 National Association of Elementary School Principals (NAESP) Ten-Year Study (Doud & Keller, 1998), the median age of elementary principals in 1998 was fifty, three years older than the median age in 1988 and the oldest median age since NAESP began issuing these ten-year studies in 1928 (p. 78). NAESP also reports that this aging of principals occurred in spite of an approximate 42 percent turnover from 1988–1998 (p. 117). "It is apparent that many of the principals who were appointed to replace those who retired or left the principalship during the last decade had considerably more years of teaching experience prior to assuming their first principalship" (p. 37). NAESP concludes that the pool of applicants for elementary principalships is older and more experienced than in the past (p. 38).

The 2000 National Association of Secondary School Principals (NASSP) survey, too, concludes that principals are aging. A higher percentage (28 percent) of high school principals reported having more than fifteen years experience as a principal than in previous surveys. The comparative figures were 23 percent in 1988 and 21 percent in 1978.

Although the workforce is older, it is increasingly female. A dramatic gender shift appears to be occurring in school leadership at both the elementary and high school levels. According to the NAESP survey, women now occupy 42 percent of K–8 principalships, compared with 20 percent in 1988 (Doud & Keller, 1998, p. x). Similarly, NASSP reports that women now make up 20 percent of high school principals, compared with 12 percent in 1988 and 7 percent in 1978.

Women and people of color, nevertheless, continue to be underrepresented among principals. "Educational administration is highly stratified by race and gender" (Banks, 2000, p. 242). Although 75 percent of teachers are women, and although teaching remains the primary career gateway to administration, a much smaller fraction of women teachers than men become principals. Despite the high turnover rate reported by NAESP, 95 percent of respondents to their 1998 survey were white—an *increase* of 5 percent over 1988. Only 2.6 percent were black; less than 1 percent were Hispanic (p. 81). In 1993–1994, of the approximately 80,000 public school principals in the country, only 10 percent were African Americans, 4 percent were Hispanic, and less than 1 percent were Asian American or American Indian (Fiore, Curtin, & Hammer, 1997 as cited in American Association of Colleges of Teacher Education white paper, p. 3).

As Banks (2000) points out, underrepresentation of both groups "is embedded in a compelling historical context" (p. 230). For example, school professionals with teaching experience compose the pool of candidates for most principalships. But teaching opportunities for African Americans declined in the 1960s and 1970s. When the courts integrated schools, black schools in the south closed; and many black teachers lost their jobs. In the case of women, in 1905 over 60 percent of elementary principals across the nation were women. After World War II, however, the number of men entering education as a career increased. "During that period, school boards tended to limit new hires to heads of households" and to replace retiring female principals with men (pp. 229–230). For both women and people of color, then, the pool of potential administrators today is smaller because of these historical factors.

The issue of the projected shortage of school leaders is reported widely and regularly these days in the media and in the professional literature. Substantial evidence exists for the concern and not just in the United States. "More and more principals in almost every Western country are retiring early" (Fullan, 2001, p. 141). Most experts predict continued high turnover in the principalship over the next decade. The U.S. Bureau of Labor Statistics projects that in the first decade of the twenty-first century 80,000 principals will retire or leave the profession (Hertling, 1999, p. 1). NAESP also predicts that at least 40 percent of current principals will leave their jobs.

A crucial issue, then, is identifying, recruiting, and hiring qualified replacements. This challenge is made doubly difficult by job conditions as reported by current principals. Two-thirds of respondents to the NAESP survey expressed concern about attracting qualified replacements because of increased work-related stress and low salaries (Doud & Keller, 1998, p. 114). Fullan (2001) agrees that "more and more potential teacher leaders are concluding that it is simply not worth it to take on the leadership of schools" (p. 141). In a survey conducted by the Connecticut principals' association, 91 percent of responding districts said that experienced teachers were not interested in pursuing a principal's career (Olson, 1999, p. 4).

In summary, despite many principals reaching retirement age and leaving, principals on the whole are getting older. One explanation is that districts are hiring older replacements with considerable teaching experience. Although the workforce is increasingly female, the majority of principals are still male; and the overwhelming majority is white.

How Principals See Their Jobs

Increased Workload

In many ways, today's principals see themselves as hurried, overburdened, and frustrated by their inability to meet expectations. Ninety percent of principals in Toronto, Canada, in a 1997 survey said the demands on their time had increased in the previous five years. Ninety-one percent indicated that they could not fulfill all assigned responsibilities (Fullan, 2001, p. 139). Reporting on interviews with elementary principals in 2002, *Education Week* said they "described a position whose job description had no bounds" as they dealt with the increasing social and personal needs of their students and families, the pressure of new legal mandates, especially in special education, in addition to an expanding list of regular job responsibilities (Archer, 2002).

The unremitting and varied pressures of today's school environments have expanded and intensified the workload for all principals. Federal, state, and local law and policy, parent, and community demands, and "ubiquitous technology have all stormed the walls of the school" (Pierce, 2000, p. 2). These forces, as well as high-stakes testing and accountability and other school reform initiatives, have made new demands on principals' time. Yet, "almost none of the daily expectations and challenges have been reduced or transferred to other staff" (Peterson, 2001, p. 1).

Recent national surveys of principals confirm the expansion of the role and the consequence that principals cannot accomplish all that is expected, especially in instructional leadership. The 2001 Public Agenda report, *Trying to Stay Ahead of the Game,* concludes from its survey that principals have an "overcrowded agenda" (p. 11) and warns school reformers that they must address this issue before increasing expectations even further. Seventy percent of NAESP survey respondents perceive increased responsibility for marketing/politics to generate support for education over the previous three years. This change may reflect the increased pressure that schools and school districts feel from both accountability demands and the school choice movement. Sixty-six percent report increased contact with social service agencies over this same period. Again, this change appears to mirror the increasing personal and social needs that children bring to their schooling experience. Other areas in which significant numbers of NAESP survey respondents note increased responsibilities included working with site-based councils (61.6 percent), planning/implementation of site-based staff development (65.5 percent), and curriculum development (62.4 percent) (p. 2). When asked how they spend their time, however, these same respondents rank staff development near the bottom of their time priority lists (p. 10). This is a troubling finding given the perception of increased responsibility among principals themselves and the importance of staff development documented by research.

The NASSP survey produced similar findings—too much to do and too little time in which to do it all. The average high school principal spends over sixty-two hours working each week. Yet, "The results of this survey confirm what is commonly said about the job of a high school principal: there is not enough time to do everything that needs to be done" (p. 8). Although high school principals in the survey believe their most important responsibilities are in areas of curriculum and instruction, "they report spending much of their time and energy carrying out functions that have little to do with student learning, effective teaching, or creating a climate conducive to both of these" (p. 31). NASSP's survey of middle school principals indicates that 50 percent of respondents also work sixty hours per week or more. In 1965, the comparable number was just 12 percent (Archer, 2002).

Frustrations with Politics and Bureaucracy

As much as increasing responsibilities and lack of time, the obstacles posed by politics and bureaucracy are major frustrations for principals. Public Agenda (2001) concludes that organizational red tape and political maneuvering are perceived as much greater problems by principals than any other concern—including funding, high-stakes testing, and ineffective teachers. Nearly half of the principals think that politics and bureaucracy are the primary reasons that colleagues leave the principalship (p. 8). Seventy percent say that "managing harsh public criticism and political heat has become a routine part" of the job (p. 35). An equal number feel that managing power relationships among vested interest groups is an "absolutely essential" performance characteristic (p. 10). From one-on-one interviews, focus groups, as well as responses to survey questions, Deborah Wadsworth of Public Agenda writes, "To hear them tell it, glitches, hurdles, delays, and second-guessing seem to bedevil even the most ordinary of tasks." She describes a "mind-boggling array of political tangles and bureaucratic encumbrances" that principals have to negotiate to accomplish anything successfully (p. 32).

More Responsibility, Less Authority

Although the role has expanded, authority to accomplish the new duties has not. According to NAESP, principals do perceive a shifting of responsibility and authority, away from shared involvement with central office and toward more collaboration with staff. For example, just 29.2 percent indicated that they shared teacher selection responsibility with central office, compared with 54 percent ten years earlier. Moreover, nearly 75 percent of principals in the NAESP survey report that in the last three years "moderate to substantial authority had been delegated to them for making decisions at the school site" (p. 23). Yet that authority is exercised in a much more participatory environment. In teacher supervision and evaluation, for example, the NAESP analysis indicates that, "It appears that collaborative structures...are more common in 1998 than they were in 1988" (p. 14).

According to Public Agenda (2001), the lack of authority to match increased responsibility is a key concern. Only a few principals feel they have adequate authority to reward outstanding performance by teachers (p. 13). A clear majority of principals (68 percent) feel that they do not have enough authority to "remove ineffective teachers from the classroom" (p. 13). And nearly all principals (95 percent) surveyed by Public Agenda feel that giving principals the authority to remove poor teachers, even those with tenure, would make their leadership more effective. Many principals, especially in large, urban districts complain that they have little or no real involvement in decisions about hiring teachers for their schools, yet they are held accountable for those teachers performance (Pierce, 2000, p. 3). Fullan, too, reports that 84 percent of principals in his survey report a decrease in authority (2001, p. 139).

Decreased Effectiveness

A consequence of this double bind—more responsibility, less perceived authority—is that many principals feel their efficacy has diminished. In the Fullan study, for example, 61 percent of principals reported a decrease in their effectiveness. They only have time for the urgent management issues that demand their immediate attention but not for the important instructional concerns. Pierce (2000) summarizes the problem, "Creating a learning community requires planned pursuit, yet principals can easily be consumed by everyday 'urgent but unimportant' matters" (p. 1). NASSP findings sound the same theme in describing work conditions that decrease effectiveness:

> The role of the principal, as presently structured, is reported by the survey respondents to be that of a manager mostly engaged in urgent activities.... Being an instructional leader requires the purposeful and intentional action of principals spending significant time doing those things that are important, but often not urgent: planning, team building, teacher development, and relationship building. (p. 31)

Mixed Feeling about Standards and Accountability

The standards and accountability movement may be the most powerful and important external force that principals today confront. Yet they are not fully committed to the direction in which it is pushing public schools. The Public Agenda (2001) survey results suggest that principals feel considerable ambivalence and frustration about the importance and value of the standards and accountability movement. For example, 30 percent think that standardized tests "are a seriously flawed measure of student achievement." Twenty-five percent think that the tests are important but that there are "serious problems with how they are currently used in my district." On the other hand, more than 40 percent of principals think the tests both are important and well used at the district level (p. 15). Forty-four percent think that unreasonable pressure from the standards and accountability movement is driving talented people from the field. But 34 percent think that this pressure only drives out "less able" principals (p. 16).

Increased Stress

Ample evidence suggests that the working conditions described here have increased the level of stress that principals feel. Expanded work that leaves principals fatigued and forced to compromise priorities in their personal lives certainly produces stress. In a Montana study, principals said that "long working hours" were their top stressor (Pierce, 2000, p. 2). In the Public Agenda report, 83 percent of principals surveyed said that "the enormous demands of their job have forced them to make serious compromises in terms of their family and personal life" (2001, p. 26).

Other stressors include the tumultuous school environment in which new demands incessantly intrude and require immediate attention from the principal. The NAESP study reports that 75 percent of principals feel that fragmentation of time in their jobs has increased with the burgeoning workload and that this is a major concern for them. Coupled with other change factors—increased pressure to improve student achievement, to raise money to supplement inadequate budget allotments, to develop and implement site-based decision-making councils—this increased fragmentation of time has resulted in "higher levels of job-related stress" (p. 121). Public Agenda reports that 92 percent of principals feel that the time, responsibilities, and "strain of their day-to-day workload not only heightens burnout" but discourages talented people from becoming administrators (p. 26).

The strains of increased accountability have left many principals feeling more exposed, vulnerable, and stressed. Olson (1999) comments that, "More accountability has also meant more stress—and lots of it. Too often, they complain, they feel out on a limb with little support or recognition from their school systems" (p. 3). One source of accountability-induced stress may be a superintendent's negative perception of the principal's performance. Public Agenda reports that superintendents have serious concerns about principals' knowledge and skills. Only half of superintendents surveyed in 2001 indicate that they are happy with the overall performance of their principals. Their responses in rating their principals on thirteen specific leadership qualities are even more negative. Only one superintendent in three indicates happiness with principals' abilities to recruit and develop teachers, make tough decisions, delegate authority, involve teachers in decision making, and use money wisely (2001, pp. 23–24).

Early Retirement

The frustrations described here—long hours, overwhelming workload, increased stress, higher expectations, strained relationships with central office—may be why more principals see themselves retiring early. More than 60 percent of 1998 NAESP respondents say that they will retire at their earliest eligible retirement date (p. 87). The mean projected retirement age is 57. In 1988, the mean age was 58 (p. 93). The 1998 Educational Research Service study of this issue reported that 62 percent of principals surveyed intend to retire in their 50s (American Association of Colleges of Teacher Education, 2001, p. 2).

The Brighter Side

It is perhaps surprising, given the realities of job expansion and their negative perceptions of work conditions, but today's principals generally feel positive about their jobs and what they can accomplish in them. The Public Agenda (2001) report states that principals "evince a strong can-do spirit, a confidence that they can make a difference" (p. 7). So strong is their belief in the importance and value of the principal that 97 percent of Public Agenda respondents indicate that, "Behind every great school is a great principal" (p. 7). Despite the frustration and stress of increased workload and fragmented time, the NAESP study reports that morale among elementary principals is excellent. Thirty-eight percent of respondents describe their morale as excellent. "Fewer than one in a hundred said their morale was very bad" (p. 66). In addition, the survey results indicate that, despite increased pressures for improved student achievement, principals generally do not have job security worries. When asked if they would choose to be elementary principals if they were beginning their careers again, 84.5 percent indicated that they either certainly or probably would make the same career choice (p. 84). Public Agenda reports a similar finding with a less substantial majority. Sixty-six percent of principals surveyed said they would choose the same line of work (p. 30).

In summary, principals see themselves as overloaded with work and feel frustrated by their inability to meet all the expectations, especially in instructional areas. Bureaucratic red tape and political machinations are also major sources of frustration. Principals feel caught in a double bind—expanded responsibility without a concomitant expansion of authority. The resulting feelings of ineffectiveness often cause them a great deal of stress. In spite of it all, principals seem resilient and hopeful. They believe in themselves and in their capacity to be successful.

The Role Today

As principals' self-perceptions suggest, role overload and ambiguity are endemic problems for principals in practice today. Fullan (2001) provides a powerful summary of the conditions of the role today:

> With the move toward self-management of schools, the principal appears to have the worst of both worlds. The old world is still around with expectations to run a smooth school, and to be responsive to all; simultaneously the new world rains down on schools with disconnected demands, expecting that at the end of the day the school should be constantly showing better test results, and ideally becoming a learning organization. (pp. 138–139)

Leadership, Management, Politics, and Culture

The professional literature has traditionally identified instructional leadership and school management as core elements of a principal's role. To find ways to manage the complexity, ambiguity, and expansion of the role, today's principal, though, must be proficient in at least two additional roles—politics and organizational culture.

Because of the negative perceptions that politics and politicians often provoke in society, it is easy to ignore the vital role the principals have in constructive politics. Cuban (1988), among others, argues for the importance of political activity in the principal's core roles. He defines *political* as "to sense and transform public expectations (which is another way of saying *values*) into formal school decisions and authoritative actions in order to achieve both organizational and personal goals." Every time a principal proceeds to "persuade, deflect, and enlist teachers, parents, or district officials to build support or overcome opposition to what administrators desire," he or she is acting politically (p. 76).

Bolman and Deal (2000) concur with this analysis. They argue that three basic conditions define the necessity of constructive political activity:

- *Enduring differences* that produce value disagreements that need to be adjudicated or negotiated;
- *Scarce resources* that mean no individual or group can ever get all they want and that priority decisions among competing interests have to be made;
- *Interdependence* that means people in the organization need each other. They cannot simply go their separate ways when conflicts occur. (pp. 164–165)

To be effective in a world characterized by these conditions—diversity of values, scarcity of resources, and conflict—leaders need three skills:

- *Agenda setting:* the ability to create a vision and a strategy for change that takes into account the needs and concerns of others;
- *Networking and forming coalitions:* the ability to develop support among people for the vision and strategy;
- *Bargaining and negotiating:* the ability to resolve conflicts and maintain support without compromising the vision. (Bolman & Deal, pp. 166–179)

Recognizing that the role of the principal has "become dramatically more complex, overloaded, and unclear over the past decade," Fullan (2001), among others, advocates another element of the principal's role, reculturing the school organization (p. 137). The kind of change necessary to improve schools is "deeper" and more complex than most people think. It involves reculturing schools. "Any other changes are superficial and nonlasting." Citing Bryk et al. (1998), he notes that short-term improvement in standardized test scores "are neither deep (what is learned is not transferable) nor lasting" (p. 147).

Fullan is concerned, however, that role overload may foster passivity and dependency in principals at the very time when reformers call for initiative and independence. Fullan argues that the conditions under which principals operate foster this dependency. Principals find themselves constantly "on the receiving end of externally initiated changes" that bombard them, often in chaotic fashion. In response, principals often seek "the latest recipes for success" in the form of someone else's product. This illusion of some external solution or "silver bullet" is destined to fail because lasting change depends on reculturing an organization—that is, changing how people relate to each other and to their mutual work (2001, pp. 157–158).

Describing these four distinct elements separately and analytically does not portray their dynamic and integrated relationships. The actions and results in one dimension often shape and are shaped by actions and results in the others. Experts have long recognized, for example, the interrelationships between leadership and management. John Gardner (2000) once commented that "Every time I encounter utterly first-class managers they turn out to have quite a lot of leader in them" (p. 6). Peterson (2001) also advocates the integration of the leadership and management dimensions. He calls for principals who are "bifocal leaders" who "manage by leading and lead by managing" (p. 5). Culture building and leadership also have a symbiotic relationship. Principals must be able somehow to clarify tangible instructional goals from the ambiguity of collaborative work (Lashway, 1995, p. 2).

Person in the Middle

Perhaps the most powerful image of the principal today is that of the person in the middle beset by the kinds of conflicts and dilemmas that appear in most human triangles (Fullan, 2001, p. 137). Cuban (1988) describes principals as "sandwiched between what state and district policymakers intend, what the superintendent directs, what parents expect, what teachers need, and what students want" (p. 76). In this unenviable position, the principal lives with these conflicts and dilemmas: the responsibility to produce results often exceeds the authority to make something happen, allegiance is split between the school and district and other external powers, professional needs and concerns and political realities may be at odds, and the demands for change may undermine the responsibility for maintaining stability (p. 61).

As the person in the middle, the principal may be whipsawed between demands for more school accountability and the movement to site-based decision making. Olson (1999) notes that a "decentralized governance structure gives principals greater freedom, but also more responsibility." In many participatory management schemes, principals share authority with others but maintain singular responsibility. Site-based councils have a collective voice in school management and control over how problems are solved and resources allocated. Yet the principal remains individually responsible and accountable for school performance in the eyes of parents, community, and even superintendents and school boards. From her focus group research, Orr (2001) notes that superintendents, commenting on the principal's role, "pointed out the tension created between school accountability and participatory decision making, and the rise in conflict that comes from greater public participation in educational matters, all of which affect the principalship" (p. 14). Press coverage of test results may also increase the accountability pressure principals feel (Orr, pp. 15–16).

Realities of School Leadership

The working conditions described here certainly challenge a principal's ability to enact effectively these four role elements. What complicates a principal's work even more are obstacles in school life that a principal must confront and overcome.

One of these obstacles is the difficulty of finding opportunities to work with others, who are busy with their own priorities. Teachers spend the bulk of their days engaged with students in classrooms. Thus, they are not available to the principal for school-wide leadership activities, except at limited times—before and after school or at lunch. And at those times, they are often distracted by what they perceive as the more important priorities involved with teaching their students, debilitated by fatigue, or skeptical of the value of the school-wide activities when weighed against their own priorities. Donaldson (2001) describes a "conspiracy of busyness" in schools. "Teachers' attentions, then, are riveted within their classrooms." Their focus is on their students because it is student success that is the source of their satisfaction and fulfillment (p. 24).

Ironically, the more engaged teachers are with their students, the less available they are to the principal for direct leadership activity. As a result, much leadership activity has to occur "on the fly"—in hallways between classes, in the main office before school, and in faculty rooms at lunchtime. This phenomenon further intensifies the fragmentation of time that the leader experiences (p. 13). Furthermore, when asked to engage with school-wide leadership challenges, to embrace change proposals, teachers will first ask, implicitly if not explicitly, "How will all of 'that' affect my success with 'this'?" (Donaldson, 2001, p. 20).

Another obstacle to leadership is what Donaldson describes as the "individualistic ethos" that characterizes the culture of teachers and teaching in most schools. In a classroom world in which student needs are diverse and highly variable, few universally clear and accepted protocols exist for teaching, and considerable disagreement exists about how to assess success, teachers have learned to rely on their individual judgment and intuition. Teachers' embrace of this individuality "sets up a counterforce to classical leadership." Quite naturally, in school culture teachers resist efforts by principals to "coordinate, restructure, and monitor" their work (2001, p. 25).

A third obstacle is teacher expectation for the role of principal. Consistent with the individuality and autonomy prized by teachers is their belief that the principal's job is to perform a "buffer-and-support function" (Donaldson, 2001, p. 29). That is, from teachers' perspectives, a primary role of the principal is to shield them from district or community conflict and to protect them from organizational intrusions into their domains so that they can do the important work of teaching undisturbed. "The net effect of this 'leave it to the administration' phenomenon is that many teachers and other school staff remain reticent to engage in organizational decisions or challenges" (p. 29).

A final obstacle is the bureaucratic-rational model of the principal's role. When principals were only or primarily managers or administrators, the bureaucratic-rational model of hierarchical, top-down behavior may have sufficed. With today's complex expectations for instructional leadership, what Donaldson calls "the classical leadership model" no longer works. It conflicts directly with the beliefs, norms, and behaviors that define life for teachers in schools (2001, p. 35). Norms of teacher autonomy, especially in matters of curriculum and instruction, for example, ensure that the formal authority of the principal often does not carry beyond the closed classroom door, unless a teacher decides to cooperate. Moreover, for the classical leadership model to be effective, the principal, who controls decisions, has to be the expert who knows more than teachers. The reality of schools today, however, is that "the staff are the most informed and the most expert with the children they teach" (p. 36). Finally, the bureaucratic-rational leadership model puts a premium on standardization and uniformity, conditions that are impossible to obtain in today's highly individualized and varied school environments (pp. 35–37).

In summary, the conditions of the role as defined in the professional literature confirm principals' self-perceptions. The role has expanded and become more complex. The principal is in the middle, at the vortex of powerful influences that enable and inhibit the principal's ability to perform successfully. External forces, especially accountability demands and expectations for the principal's singular leadership, exert a powerful pressure. But so do internal conditions—teacher autonomy, lack of time, teacher expectations for leadership that differ from the external expectations, and the traditional structure of the role. Skills in politics and organizational culture development are now as essential to successful role enactment under these complex and dynamic conditions as the traditional core elements of instructional leadership and bureaucratic management.

The Role in the Future

The Key to Change

There is every reason to believe that, despite the daunting challenges the principal's role presents, effective principals will continue to be critical to school improvement. This understanding is not new. Since the 1960s, studies of school effectiveness, conducted by Ron Edmonds of Harvard and others, have regularly identified the principal's leadership as a key if not the key factor in school improvement (Sammons, 1999, as referenced in Fullan, p. 141; Olson, 2000, p. 4). Beginning in the 1980s, experts such as Madeline Hunter began to advocate the centrality of the principal as instructional leader who could coach teachers and help them become skilled at more effective instructional practices (Olson, 2000, p. 4). Today, Fullan (2001), among others, says that every improving school he knows of has a principal "good at leading improvement" (p. 141).

Dealing with the Shortage

As discussed previously, the current and projected shortage of school principals has been widely reported. Because of the recognized importance of the principal's leadership in schools, a diverse and powerful group of policymakers and funding agencies have recognized the crisis in leadership that the nation faces (Olson, 2000). They include professional groups, universities, foundations, government agencies, as well as elected officials. Responses to this critical problem tend to fall into three categories: changing labor market conditions to create a larger pool of candidates, splitting the position between leadership and management duties, and redefining the nature of the role to make it more attractive. An obvious labor market approach is to increase principal salaries. Olson (1999) points out that salary schedule compression means that in many districts a high school teacher with some extracurricular assignments can earn as much in ten months as a new principal can earn working the full year. The Educational Research Service estimates that the daily rate of pay for a new elementary school assistant principal is less than 5 percent higher than that of an experienced teacher (Archer, 2002, p. 4).

Other examples of labor market approaches include that the school systems develop a pool of internal candidates for principalships by creating career ladders (Anderson, 1991, as cited in Hertling, 1999, p. 1); and that districts recruit teachers internally through training programs and administrative internships. Many school districts, especially larger ones, have undertaken either or both of these approaches.

Another labor market approach to the shortage is to refocus school districts on the pool of candidates traditionally overlooked in principal searches—women and people of color. Some experts recommend that districts revamp mentoring programs to give more access to candidates from underrepresented groups as well as reform hiring practices that may reflect ethnic, racial, and gender bias (Grogan, 1997, as cited in Orr, 2001, p. 4).

Among the approaches to splitting the position is the idea of job sharing—dividing the traditional duties of the principal between two different individuals who have different skill sets. For example, one might handle supervision of instruction while the other handles student discipline and building management. Because this approach could be costly, it might only be feasible in a situation in which a veteran principal could share a job with a novice in an intern role (Muffs & Schmitz, 1999, as cited in Hertling, 2001, p. 2). In England and Wales, some schools have responded to the overload issue by recognizing the traditional dichotomy in role between manager and leader. "School heads work in tandem with business managers, called bursars" (Hertling, 2001, p. 3). Pierce suggests a "two leader" approach—"a principal teacher and a principal administrator" (p. 4).

New Definitions of the Principal's Role

In advocating a new definition of the principal's role, Orr (2001) argues that the new demands and changing expectations have so expanded the principal's responsibilities that the job may no longer be tenable (p. 11). "Greatly expanding demands and pressures for accountability overwhelm the principalship, like public schooling generally" (p. 12). She believes that the nature of the role itself is "the largest deterrent to recruiting and retaining well-qualified school leaders" (p. 23). Based on her research, Orr has four recommendations for school district leaders who wish to redefine how the role is conceived and supported. They must:

- "Establish expectations for the primacy of instructional…change-oriented… and organizational-learning leadership" in the principal's role;
- Support principals in learning the knowledge and skills that these forms of leadership will require;
- Clarify to the community these new expectations;
- Enable "more distributed leadership for the vast array" of management responsibilities. (pp. 25–26)

Limitations of the Heroic Model of Leadership

Other new definitions of leadership begin with the agreement that leadership is not a set of personal qualities with which certain individuals are imbued and which enable them to sweep into a school, clear away disorder and confusion, and lead the school through the sheer force of personality. Gardner (2000) commented, "In curious ways, people tend to aggrandize the role of leaders. They tend to exaggerate the capacity of leaders to influence events" (p. 9). Donaldson (2001) states that the conception of leaders as heroic "violates, when applied to public schools, the democratic value system and distributed power arrangements we find there" (p. 40). Elmore (2000), finally, says, "Contrary to the myth of visionary leadership that pervades American culture, most leaders in all sectors of society are creatures of the organizations they lead." He believes this phenomenon is particularly true in public schools, where leaders almost exclusively come from the ranks of teachers and, therefore, are "well socialized" into the status quo of the current school organization (p. 2).

Elmore (2000) argues that we need to "de-romanticize" leadership to make large-scale improvements in school organizations. Rather than the illusion of the all-powerful personality who can "embody all the traits and skills that remedy all the defects" (p. 14), he suggests a definition of leadership that focuses on improvement in instruction and that distributes leadership throughout the organization.

The new definition of school leadership that Elmore advocates, though, does not conform to the traditional bureaucratic-rational conception of the role. In the classic leadership model described earlier, the principal controls specific functions in the organization. In the school committed to instructional improvement, "most of the knowledge required for improvement must inevitably reside in the people who deliver instruction, not in the people who manage them." Therefore, the principal cannot *control* teaching and learning. Elmore believes that, instead, the principal's role is to guide and direct them through the processes of distributive leadership (p. 14).

A Distributed Leadership Model

In the bureaucratic-rational model, leadership resides in a few top-echelon positions in the organization. In an institutional, systemic model, leadership is distributed throughout the organization (Ogawa & Bossert, 1995, p. 41). It does not reside in particular roles or individuals but in the relationships that develop between the individuals in the roles. So, leadership becomes a social and cultural phenomenon.

The need to reconstitute leadership in this way has long been recognized by experts. Gardner, for example, said in 1990, "Our high level leaders will be more effective in every way if the systems over which they preside are made vital by dispersed leadership.... No individual has all the skills—and certainly not the time—to carry out all the complex tasks of contemporary leadership" (Gardner, 2000, pp. 11–12).

Ogawa and Bossert (1995) developed this image of distributed leadership:

> We offer a view of leadership that does not treat it as the province of a few people in certain parts of the organization. Rather, we treat leadership as a quality of organizations—a systemic characteristic.... Leadership flows through the networks of roles that comprise organizations. The medium and the currency of leadership lie in the personal resources of people. And, leadership shapes the systems that produce patterns of interactions and meanings that other participants attach to organizational events." (p. 39)

Elmore (2000), however, offers the most developed model of distributed leadership. The basic challenge in developing a distributed leadership model is "organizing diverse competencies" so people either have the knowledge and skills they need to do their jobs or can gain what they need from a colleague inside or from an expert outside the organization. A work culture that prizes collegiality and collaborative problem solving, then, is essential to the success of distributed leadership. If, through collaborative learning, a match exists between the knowledge and skills people have and the competencies that they need to perform their job, then they and the organization will be successful in improving student learning. But because teaching and learning are so complex, the responsibility for the leadership of this activity—guiding and directing the collaborative enhancement of everyone's knowledge and skills—must be widely distributed across the organization. A crucial role for the principal and other administrative leaders in Elmore's conception is to ensure that this process remains coherent through the development of a "common culture—or a set of values, symbols and rituals" (p. 15). Clear instructional goals and collective values that a common culture provides keep the distributed leadership model productive and coherent.

Elmore offers five principles for a distributed leadership model:

1. *Improvement of instruction is central to the leader's role.* School leaders may be adept in management, politics, or culture building. But, if these skills are not focused on large-scale improvement of instruction, then nothing will change.

2. *Leaders must promote the value of continuous collective as well as individual learning.* The autonomy and isolation that have characterized professional practice must be replaced by an ethic of collective review and scrutiny.

3. *Leaders must model the centrality of learning that they expect from others.*

4. *The expertise required for learning and improvement determines the roles and activities of leadership.* In this model, authority resides primarily in knowledge and expertise and not in an institutional position.

5. *"The exercise of authority requires reciprocity of accountability and capacity.* If the formal authority of my role does require that I hold you accountable for some action of outcome, then I have an equal and complementary responsibility to assure that you have the capacity to do what I am asking you to do." (Elmore, 2000, pp. 20–21)

Three-Stream Model of Leadership

Donaldson (2001), too, argues that we need a new leadership model. His *three stream* model incorporates some of the elements of the distributed leadership model and is built on a recognition and acceptance of the structure and culture of American schools: "American public schools are unusual types of organization. They function more on moral conviction and professional judgment than they do on tightly prescribed goals and technical rationality; their power is distributed, and the citizen can potentially influence policy more than the educator" (p. 39).

In Donaldson's model, the school leader is not the heroic, preeminent figure overshadowing faculty and staff. The principal, instead, is someone who "seeks to lead" (p. 46) by establishing "a collective relationship" among faculty, staff, and himself or herself. The relationship that Donaldson envisions, which is the first stream in his model, develops from trust, openness, honesty, and affirmation. It is characterized by mutuality and reciprocity. All adults in the school community are full partners who influence and are influenced by each other. The health and vitality of this collective relationship then can serve to motivate and focus the adult community on renewing and revitalizing their sense of moral purpose. This explicit, acknowledged, collective purpose is the second stream of leadership. Finally, in Donaldson's conception, the community, buoyed by the strength of their relationships and motivated by their mission, purpose, or direction, mobilizes to address tough challenges that will improve the lives of students. This "action-in-common" is the third stream of leadership (pp. 39–54).

Accountability

The reality of the principal's work in the early twenty-first century is that the national shift to a results-focused environment is likely to continue for some time. Heightened accountability for students' results will necessitate focused attention on reshaping the school organization to meet achievement expectations. This pressure potentially creates tension and conflict for the school leader who may be held singularly responsible for improvement in student performance while working collaboratively with staff and parents in the kind of participatory school environment that the new definitions of leadership envision. According to Marsh (2000), principals will, first, have to be transformational leaders who can lead from the middle and develop a collaborative work culture that empowers faculty to invent new approaches to strengthen student learning. However, principals will also have to focus their schools on results so that "high performance work teams" are accountable for enabling all students to reach high standards. And they will have to provide the management support—through technology and the allocation of personnel and budgetary resources—to support the strategic directions that they have set with their faculties (p. 143).

Elmore's analysis of the accountability problem that principals face is that American schools have a "weak technical core." No universally clear, proven, accepted, and implemented teaching strategies define what top-quality professionals do in the classroom. He contrasts this condition with the "strong technical core" in other professions, such as medicine, in which clear, specific protocols define, for example, how surgeons perform an operation. As a result of the lack of clarity and agreement about what constitutes good teaching practice, schools and school leaders currently lack the capacity to respond effectively to the performance pressure of the accountability movement. Consistent with the "weak technical core," schools have weak internal accountability systems. He argues that the school leader's challenge is to clarify with faculty an ambitious student learning target, specify the instructional practices that are likely to produce it, enable faculty and staff to increase knowledge and strengthen skills, and then hold teachers accountable for meeting these performance standards and professional expectations (Elmore, 2002, pp. 1–4). The principal must create a "common culture of expectations around the use of those skills and knowledge…holding individuals accountable for their contributions to the collective result" (Elmore, 2000, p. 15).

In summary, new definitions of the principal's role are emerging in literature and practice in response to the role overload and ambiguity that principals today experience. The classic model of leadership that concentrated authority and responsibility in a charismatic principal is clearly inadequate in meeting today's demands and will likely be even more so in the future. A more systemic model of collective leadership is emerging that locates authority and responsibility in roles and relationships throughout the school. Nevertheless, in a results-oriented, accountability-driven environment, that collective leadership will have to demonstrate that student learning is improving,

Conclusion

Whatever the future holds for schools and principals, effective leadership will not be enacted in formulaic fashion. There are and will be no recipes for success. Leadership theory has long recognized that leadership is contextual. "Acts of leadership take place in an unimaginable variety of settings, and the setting does much to determine the kinds of leaders that emerge and how they play their roles" (Gardner, 2000, p. 8).

Effective principals in the twenty-first century will have different characteristics depending on the context they are in—for example, the phase of the change process. Fullan (2001) suggests that failing schools need more assertive leadership, whereas more successful schools may require a more participatory approach (p. 148). In addition, as the context changes—as a school in crisis becomes more stable, for example—the principal's leadership will also have to change—from more assertive to more participatory, for example.

Although no formulas or recipes exist for a principal's leadership that will guarantee success, there are emerging characteristics of successful principals in the literature and in practice that improve the odds of success. The effective twenty-first century principal will integrate high-quality performance in diverse dimensions of the role—educational leader, manager, politician, and organizational culture expert. The effective twenty-first century principal will not be a detached authority figure. He or she will be linked in a web of relationships through which authority and responsibility are distributed throughout the adults in the school. The effective twenty-first century principal will build strong, trusting relationships with staff. In collaboration with them, the principal will foster a culture of learning that sets clear and high expectations for everyone's performance, adults and students, enables everyone to gain the knowledge and skills they need to be successful, and embraces authentic and appropriate forms of accountability.

REFERENCES

American Association of Colleges of Teacher Education. (2001). *PK–12 educational leadership and administration: A white paper.* Washington, DC: AACTE.

Anderson, M. (1991). *Principals: How to train, recruit, select, induct, and evaluate leaders for America's schools.* Eugene: ERIC Clearinghouse on Educational Management.

Archer, J. (2002, April 17). Principals: So much to do, so little time. *Education Week on the Web,* 1–6.

Banks, C. McGee. (2000). Gender and race as factors in educational leadership. In *The Jossey Bass Reader on Educational Leadership* (pp. 217–256). San Francisco: Jossey-Bass.

Bolman, L., & Deal, T. (2000). The manager as politician. In *The Jossey Bass Reader on Educational Leadership* (pp. 164–181). San Francisco: Jossey-Bass.

Bryk, A., Sebring, P., Rollow, S., & Easton, J. (1998). *Charting Chicago school reform.* Boulder, CO: Westview Press.

Cuban, L. (1988). *The managerial imperative and the practice of leadership in schools.* Albany: State University of New York Press.

Donaldson, G. A. (2001). *Cultivating leadership in the schools.* New York: Teachers College Press.

Doud, J., & Keller, E. (1998). *A ten-year study: The K–8 principal in 1998.* Alexandria, VA: National Association of Elementary School Principals.

Elmore, R. (2000). *Building a new structure for school leadership.* Washington, DC: The Albert Shanker Institute.

Elmore, R. (2002, January). The limits of "change." *Harvard Education Letter: Research Online,* 1–4.

Fiore, T., Curtin, T., & Hammer, C. (1997). *Public and private high school principals in the United States: A statistical profile, 1987–88 to 1993–94.* Washington, DC: National Center for Educational Statistics, U.S. Department of Education.

Fullan, M. (2001). *The new meaning of educational change.* New York: Teachers College Press.

Gardner, J. (2000). The nature of leadership. In *The Jossey Bass Reader on Educational Leadership* (pp. 3–12). San Francisco: Jossey-Bass.

Grogan, M. (1997). Equity/equality issues of gender, race, and class. *Educational Administration Quarterly, 32,* 5–44.

Hertling, E. (1999). *Conducting a principal search.* (ERIC Digest Number 133). Eugene: ERIC Clearinghouse on Educational Management.

Hertling, E. (2001). *Retaining principals.* (ERIC Digest Number 147). Eugene: ERIC Clearinghouse on Educational Management.

Lashway, L. (1995). *Can instructional leaders be facilitative leaders?* (ERIC Digest Number 95). Eugene: ERIC Clearinghouse on Educational Management.

Marsh, D. (2000). Educational leadership for the twenty-first century: Integrating three essential perspectives. In *The Jossey Bass Reader on Educational Leadership* (pp. 126–146). San Francisco: Jossey-Bass.

Muffs, M., & Schmitz, L. (1999, November). Job sharing for administrators: A consideration for public schools. *NASSP Bulletin, 83*(610), 70–73.

National Association of Secondary School Principals. (2001). *Priorities and barriers in high school leadership: A survey of principals.* Reston, VA: National Association of Secondary School Principals.

Ogawa, R., & Bossert, S. (1995). Leadership as an organizational quality. In *The Jossey Bass Reader on Educational Leadership* (pp. 38–58). San Francisco: Jossey-Bass.

Olson, L. (1999, March 3). Demand for principals growing, but candidates aren't applying. *Education Week on the Web,* Retrieved June 4, 2002, from *http://www.edweek.org/ew/vol-18/25prin.h18.*

Olson, L. (2000, January 12). Policy focus converges on leadership. *Education Week on the Web,* Retrieved June 4, 2002, from *http://www.edweek.org/ew/ewstory.cfm?slug=17lead.h19.*

Orr, M. T. (2001). *Rethinking the principalship: Shortages as opportunities for leadership reform.* Unpublished manuscript. New York: Teachers College, Columbia University, Department of Organization and Learning.

Peterson, K. (2001, Winter). The roar of complexity: A principal's day is built on fragments of tasks and decisions. *Journal of Staff Development, 22* (1), 1–5.

Pierce, M. (2000, September). Portrait of the 'super principal.' *Harvard Education Letter: Research Online.*

Public Agenda. (2001). *Trying to stay ahead of the game.* New York: Public Agenda.

Sammons, P. (1999). *School effectiveness.* Lisse, The Netherlands: Swetz & Zeitlinger.

10 The Superintendency Today

The role of the superintendent is dynamic, shaped and reshaped by social, political, and economic forces. It has evolved and changed historically since its advent in the early nineteenth century—from clerks for powerful boards in the first half of the nineteenth century, to professional educational leaders like Horace Mann in the late nineteenth century, to corporate CEOs in the era of scientific management of schools in the first half of the twentieth century. Profound social, political, and economic changes have occurred in the last decades of the twentieth century—for example, the Supreme Court decision outlawing segregation in schools, the Vietnam War and Watergate, globalization, and the information-based economy. These changes have resulted in educational reforms—the standards and accountability movement, teacher empowerment, parent involvement in decision making, site-based management, and school choice. These reforms have further transformed conceptions of the superintendent's authority and leadership.

As the role has evolved, three major leadership dimensions consistently emerge in the practice of successful superintendents today. They are influential educational leaders, effective politicians, and efficient managers. What is more, the best superintendents integrate their skills in performing in these dimensions in a dynamic, responsive enactment of their roles.

History and Evolution of the Role

In the first half of the twentieth century, faith in the efficiency benefits of scientific management was widespread. The factory model of schooling prevailed—"large classes, rigid schedules, and uniform approaches to instruction" (Johnson, 1996, p. 271)—with its emphasis on providing suitable workers for industrial America and its values of efficiency, competition, and standardization. School systems were simpler than they are today. Before the 1960s, hierarchical organizations characterized by top-down bureaucratic control were the norm in public schools. The environment for public schooling then was more predictable and stable. Boards of education, composed largely of businessmen, gave superintendents wide authority to exercise monolithic authority if they were credentialed, experienced, and seemed reasonable. Blumberg (1985) tells us that, after bitter and public struggles for power between superintendents and boards at the end of the nineteenth century, the balance of power swung to superintendents (p. 59). A corporate model of school system management flourished in which boards met infrequently, made broad policy decisions, and left the day-to-day management of the schools to the superintendent. Parents and teachers respected the expertise of professional school administrators. Superintendents could make decisions unilaterally and expect them to be carried out.

In the second half of the twentieth century, school systems became far different. Major social and political events—the desegregation of schools, Vietnam, and later Watergate—destabilized our society. Student demographic diversity exploded; the personal and social needs they brought to schools increased; the federal mandates for special education and English Language Learning to meet their diverse needs proliferated. Students were no longer, if they ever were, "raw materials ready to be processed in an education factory" (Johnson, 1996, p. 272). District staffs expanded in response to new laws and regulations, their roles became more complex and specialized, and they were less easily managed and controlled by superintendents.

As the sorting and selecting mission of factory schools became increasingly untenable, clarity and consensus about the purposes of schooling no longer existed. Boards of education became far more diverse in racial, gender, and socioeconomic composition and far less accepting of the superintendents' authority. The increasing ethnic, racial, and linguistic diversity among parents and students, too, increased the difficulty of any ready consensus emerging among competing factions about what educational goals to adopt or what educational practices to follow (Johnson, 1996, p. 154). The dilemma between *equity*—the belief in equal education for all children, regardless of the disadvantages or disabilities they bring to school—and *excellence*—the need for all children to reach high standards—caused tension and conflict in public debate.

The social and political environment also changed radically. The publication of *A Nation at Risk* in 1983 began the most sustained period of school reform in our history. According to the 2000 American Association of School Administrators (AASA) Ten-Year Study, the standards and accountability movement of the last twenty years permeated schools more than any earlier reforms including scientific management, progressive education, or even the Sputnik-induced curriculum changes of the late 1950s. As anxiety grew about America's ability to compete in a global economy, school reform became a national priority, and a steady drumbeat of media criticism of the performance of public schools increased public skepticism. Superintendents and other school staff no longer could wear the mantel of professional authority. People no longer accepted the underlying assumption of professionalism—that school people had special knowledge and skills not possessed by the general public (Owen, 1998, p. 4). As Johnson points out: "In response to alarming reports of the schools' failings, there is an increasing conviction that public education is, indeed, the province of the public rather than professionals" (1996, p. 154).

The expectations of communities changed as the desire to participate more actively in the education of its children increased. Everyone—parents, teachers, board members—became an educational expert.

Throughout the last decades of the twentieth century, the expectations of parents about the school's role in educating children also changed dramatically. No longer were parents content to drop their children at the schoolhouse door and trust their education to school staff. Dramatic and widely publicized incidents of school violence, such as the killings at Columbine High School, undermined the faith that children were even physically safe at school. Parents no longer saw themselves as clients of the school (Owen, 1998, p. 3). Now, more and more parents, too, expected to be full partners in educational decisions that affected their children.

Other changes also transformed the environment and altered the authority of the superintendent. In the 1960s, collective bargaining laws began to transform the internal power relationships in school districts. Not only salary and benefits but also working conditions gradually became subject to mutual agreement. On paper, organizational charts continued to show superintendents as chief supervisors of district staff. In reality, union leaders became at least as powerful in directing staff action. By the end of the century, few superintendents could manage their day-to-day work without copies of collective bargaining agreements, sometimes running to fifty or more pages, on their desks. In contrast to earlier eras, when the most important group with which the superintendent worked was the board of education, Blumberg (1985) describes twin primary focuses of the superintendents in his study: working with school boards and working with unions.

Instead of working in an environment that expected and accepted unilaterally exercised authority, superintendents now function in a school world in which power has fractured and divided among the various participants in the schooling enterprise. "Many actors both inside and outside of school districts now claim the right to say what is taught, how it is taught, and how it is assessed" (Johnson, 1996, p. 154). Blumberg states that, beginning in the mid-1960s, we have seen "diminished power of the superintendent.... If there ever was such a thing as the 'Imperial Superintendent,'...the concept is no longer in vogue" (pp. 60–61). Superintendents can no longer issue orders. They must persuade and cajole. The insight "that you can't be a leader unless you have followers" became a catch phrase because it was universally true.

In summary, a host of social, political, and economic forces have impacted the role of superintendent during the last decades of the twentieth century. These influences have created a much more complex environment in which superintendents must work and transformed the authority of the role.

Who Superintendents Are Today

We know curiously little about superintendents. In reporting the dearth of demographic information, Hodgkinson and Montenegro (1999) call them the "invisible CEOs" and decry the irony that so little attention is paid to a group in public education who are so important to the quality of schools (p. 5).

One group that has regularly surveyed superintendents since the 1920s is the AASA. The 2000 AASA Ten-Year Study reports significant demographic trends that pertain to the future of the position. The AASA Study finds that superintendents are aging. In the latest study, the average age had increased to 52.5, the oldest median age in any study this century (p. 19). However, current superintendents have served an average of 8.5 years in the superintendency and consider themselves at mid-career. As a result, in contrast to media reports in recent years that have forecast a shortage of superintendents to replace the existing cadre as they retire, the AASA study concludes that "the predicted mass exodus of superintendents in the coming decade will probably not occur" (p. 22). A similar demographic study in New York State in 2000, however, found that more than 57 percent of current superintendents intend to retire within five years. This study also cites the diminishing applicant pools reported by school districts across the state as they seek new superintendents (New York State Council of School Superintendents, 2001, pp. 4, 5).

Again contrary to media reports that describe superintendent tenure as under three years, the latest AASA data indicate that the tenure of superintendents is five to six years per district served. Urban superintendents, however, have markedly different demographic characteristics. The latest data available from the Council of Great City Schools (2001) indicate that the average tenure for an urban superintendent in their sample (forty-four of fifty-six member districts) is two and a half years, up from two and one-third years in 1999. In contrast to all superintendents, urban superintendents have a much higher representation of both minorities (51.8 percent) and women (30.4 percent). The figure for women represents a 10 percent increase from 1999.

The AASA study also finds that the vast majority of superintendents continue to be white and male, but the number of female superintendents has grown in the last decade from 6.6 percent in 1992 to 13.2 percent in 2000. Despite this increase, over the last century the number of female superintendents has remained essentially the same (p. 77). The number of minority superintendents also increased from 3.9 percent to 5.1 percent during the same period (p. 15). Other studies, cited by Hodgkinson and Montenegro, generally confirm these figures. The current statistics "leave the nation far behind in attempting to more closely reflect in public school leadership the gender and racial make-up of its students" (Hodgkinson & Montenegro, 1999, p. 19).

Bjork (1999) observes that according to U.S. Department of Labor statistics, the public schools superintendency is the most male-dominated executive position in the United States (Bjork in Skrla, 1999, p. 3). Although 75 percent of teachers are women, and although teaching remains the primary career gateway to the superintendency, a much smaller fraction of women teachers than men teachers become superintendents. Despite widespread and now long-term understanding of the problem, by some estimates men are still forty times as likely as women to advance from teaching to the superintendency (Skrla, 1999, p. 3).

When a woman does advance to the superintendency, because of the powerful but often invisible sexism in society, she frequently finds herself in a classic double bind: "Everything she does to enhance her assertiveness risks undercutting her femininity, in the eyes of others. And everything she does to fit the expectations of how a woman should talk risks undercutting the impression of competence that she makes" (Skrla, 1998, p. 8). This no-win situation appears to exist despite evidence that, especially in today's collaborative superintendency with its emphasis on interpersonal relationships, women may be more successful than men (Skrla, 1999, p. 3).

The AASA study indicates that female superintendents tend to have fewer overall years in education but more years as classroom teachers than their male counterparts. A majority comes from elementary school backgrounds and began administrative careers in elementary schools, in contrast to male counterparts, who more often come from high school backgrounds (2000, p. vii).

Women superintendents (76.9 percent) are much more likely than men (46.8 percent) in the AASA study to feel that a *good old boy/girl* network has helped them to get their jobs (p. 87). Women are also four times as likely to think that discriminatory practices were barriers to women in getting superintendencies. Factors identified included perceptions of board members that women are not strong managers, do not understand finance and budget issues, and would allow emotions to influence decisions (p. 88).

Overall, despite dramatic changes in the superintendent's role, the demographic profile of those serving in it has not changed. The overwhelming majority of superintendents are white men over fifty years of age. Despite the increasing diversity of school districts, minorities and women are seriously underrepresented, except in urban districts where the majority of superintendents are men of color.

How Superintendents See Their Jobs

In the last two decades, the national spotlight on the shortcomings of public schools has eroded public confidence and increased demands for demonstrable improvement. The resulting calls for accountability and the legal requirements that districts publicly report and compare test scores have increased pressure on superintendents to prove that they can improve student learning. Despite these pressures, superintendents appear both confident and optimistic about their abilities to meet this challenge. The Public Agenda's report (2001) *Trying to Stay Ahead of the Game*, details the results of a national survey in 2001 and states that seven out of ten superintendents believe that "even the most troubled districts can be turned around" (p. 7). Eight out of ten also believe that standardized tests are important, and more than half feel that their districts are making appropriate use of them (p. 15).

Despite the daunting challenges of their jobs, superintendents continue to find their jobs satisfying and fulfilling. The AASA study finds that superintendents across America view their job as "a very viable and rewarding career" (2000, p. iii). Public Agenda confirms that superintendents are generally satisfied with their career choice and, indeed, would make the same choice again if given the opportunity (2001, p. 33).

Despite these positive feeling, superintendents express strong frustration with the red tape in their jobs, and with the increasing constraints that new laws and regulations impose on school governance. Public Agenda reports that nearly 90 percent of superintendents feel that dealing with local, state, and federal mandates demands far too much of their time (2001, p. 9). They complain of additional responsibilities being added to their workload over the last decade that over-whelm their daily agenda (p. 5).

A primary responsibility of superintendents is to plan and manage school dis-trict budgets. In survey responses, interviews, and focus groups, superintendents indicate that funding issues constitute their major headache. Public Agenda reports that two thirds of superintendents feel that insufficient funding is more of an obsta-cle to their efforts to improve schools than is the lack of parent involvement or poor teacher and administrator quality. Overwhelming majorities of superintendents (more than 80 percent) feel that unfunded state and federal mandates and dispro-portionate increases in the costs of special education create severe budget problems.

A key relationship for all superintendents, historically and currently, is with the school board. Perceptions of the state of these relationships today appear mixed. Public Agenda finds that nearly 70 percent of superintendents responding to their survey complain about board interference in their work. Almost two thirds agree that boards too often seek to hire superintendents whom they can control (2001, p. 9). On the other hand, the AASA study findings suggest a more positive tenor to board-superintendent relations. Ninety-one percent of superintendents report receiving either excellent or good evaluations from their school boards. Nearly two thirds indicate that their boards' views are aligned with community in-terests (p. 59). Superintendents also report that board members accepted their policy recommendations almost all of the time (p. 64). Superintendents, interest-ingly, give boards lower evaluations than they receive from them. Thirty percent say that some board members are "not qualified" to carry out their duties (p. iv).

Despite their overall job satisfaction, the level of stress that superintendents report in their jobs is noteworthy. The AASA study states that 51 percent of re-spondents indicate that they feel "very great" or "considerable" stress in their po-sitions. The figure a decade ago, however, was not much different—a total of 50.1 percent in 1992 felt these high levels of stress. Public Agenda reports that an over-whelming majority of superintendents surveyed (over 80 percent) feel that "man-aging harsh political criticism and political heat" is an everyday job activity. A similar majority believes that their positions have forced them to make serious compromises in their personal and family lives. An even greater majority (over 90 percent) feels that the demands of the job discourage highly talented people from seeking it (2001, p. 26).

Evaluating the implications of this information is difficult. A complex lead-ership position such as the superintendency will presumably always produce stress in individuals. But do these findings suggest a problematic level of stress or not? Overall, the number of superintendents in the AASA study who feel "consid-erable fulfillment" in their jobs is 56 percent, down by 5 percent from 1992 figures (p. vi). Nevertheless the study concludes, "This is topic that needs much further study" (p. v).

The superintendents in Blumberg's 1985 study felt quite positive about their jobs. In general, "they liked what they were doing, felt challenged, had fun, and often were simply quite excited by their personal and professional prospects" (p. 137). Yet, Blumberg also comments that, "the people who hold this office seem to be becoming increasingly aware of the emotional costs involved" (p. 155). He describes several sources of their growing distress: "the slowness of the decision-making process; boredom; loneliness; feelings of inadequacy; concern over compromises of ethics; and feelings of personal stress" (p. 138).

Blumberg describes one unique stressor for superintendents in America—the perception in their communities that they are "public property" (1985, p. 156). This characterization, which was identified and confirmed by participants in the study but not by others in their communities, does not refer to community expectations about the multiple public and visible aspects of the superintendent's role—attending school sporting events, plays, and concerts; attending community events; marching in the parades, and so forth. Instead, in their perception that they are public property, superintendents were referring to the community expectations that they will be accessible and available on any day at any time; that community members feel they can intrude on the superintendent's personal and family life; and that, as the custodian of the community's educational values for its children, the superintendent's personal conduct should be above reproach (p. 156).

Interestingly, Blumberg portrays superintendents responding in widely varied ways to these pressures. Some resent and resist them and attempt to establish clear boundaries between personal and professional lives. Others appear to welcome them as opportunities to demonstrate their constant concern for the welfare of the community and its children.

Overall, in their perceptions of their jobs, superintendents seem highly resilient. They acknowledge the increasing complexities, frustrations, and stresses in the work, but do not appear daunted by them. On the contrary, they are optimistic and hopeful about their abilities to improve learning for children.

Three Dimensions of the Role

How are the pressures of the educational reform movement of the last twenty years impacting on the three dimensions of the superintendent's role—educational, managerial, and political leadership? In studies, a dynamic, integrated image of the role that successful superintendents play begins to emerge. A reciprocal relationship between the superintendent and the context affects the enactment of the three dimensions of the role. In her qualitative, in-depth study of twelve superintendents, Johnson (1996) finds that all three dimensions must be "connected and balanced," with actions in one dimension complementing and supporting those in another. "Constituents looked to superintendents for leadership in these three dimensions, and they often withheld support if it was lacking" (p. 24).

Johnson (1996) also suggests that the superintendency is highly contextualized. She identifies three "embedded contexts" in which superintendents function:

- *The context of the times*—"the times create possibilities for action, they also shape leaders by encouraging certain approaches and discouraging others" (p. 15);

- *The context of locale*—financial conditions of a community, social class structure, community values;
- *The context of the organization*—the cultures and norms of the school system itself, its unique history (pp. 14–16).

The reciprocal relationship between superintendent and context affects the emphasis a superintendent places on each of the three dimensions. The superintendent first must understand these contexts as fully and quickly as possible. Then the superintendent acts to change the context. But then, to continue to be effective, the superintendent must also then change his or her responses. So, in effect, the superintendent is also changed by the context. "Having altered the local context, the superintendent's approach to leadership must also change" (Johnson, 1996, p. 118).

Blumberg also confirms this reciprocal relationship between superintendent and context. Citing Bakke, he describes the "fusion process" through which a match develops between the individual superintendent's style and approach and the needs and goals of the organization in which he or she works. He suggests that the "good fit" that may develop is itself constantly changing as the individual and the organization react and respond to each other and, thus, change themselves (1985, p. 44).

Because of contextual factors, then, the three elements—educational leader, politician, and manager—may not receive equal emphasis. In her interviews with constituents in the districts she studied, Owen (1998) found that the three roles do not hold equal weight. The superintendent's political role was "most visible to them and was most frequently mentioned by them" (p. 16). In contrast, Peterson (1998) suggests that the role may be in flux because accountability pressures in the national context are forcing all superintendents to pay more and closer attention to their roles as educational leaders (p. 3).

Today's superintendent, then, enacts the three dimensions of the role differently depending on factors in the local, state, and national contexts. As those contexts change, so does the superintendent's response.

The Myth of Heroic Leadership

In describing the leadership provided by a superintendent, many people, frustrated by complexity and confusion, yearn for the heroic leader who can come into a district, clean up, and lead the district forward through the sheer force of his (usually in this image) personality. Johnson describes heroic leaders as those who "clarify problems, create order, inspire confidence, and make things right" (1996, p. 7). She suggests this image of leadership is unrealistic for several reasons including the limitations on the positional power of today's superintendent, the fact that heroic leadership does not inspire in others the sustained commitment to reform necessary for successful change, and the increased complexity of school organizations.

Elmore (2000) also sees heroic leadership as a myth. He point outs that there are only a few "larger than life" leaders in any society and that, "Few visionary leaders have had any effect on the dominant institutional patterns of American education" (p. 2). He also suggests another reason that people in school yearn for heroic leaders. Because educators believe that the core of teaching and learning is ineffable—that is, magical, mystical, artistic—and not reducible to rational formulation, organization, or management, they also believe that leadership should be "loosely-coupled" to the technical core of teaching and learning. In this conception, leadership only influences the school organization by personality characteristics, not by competence in organizational and management skills (p. 8).

Collaborative Leadership

Instead of believing in the myth of heroic leadership, Elmore (2000) argues that distributive leadership is the only way to accomplish the complex work of large-scale instructional improvement (p. 15). Johnson also depicts a more collaborative style of effective superintendent leadership. "The emerging conception of leadership is one of reciprocal influence, through which individuals holding different roles collaborate to improve education" (1996, p. 13).

Today's effective superintendent practices a style of collaborative leadership that is both top-down—that is, articulating core values, establishing accountability structures—and bottom-up—that is, including all constituents meaningfully and developing leadership in others. In this process, leadership is less hierarchical. The superintendent's role has shifted from the top of the organizational structure to the hub of a complex network of interpersonal relationships (Peterson & Short, 2001, p. 539).

Effective external leadership also is more collaborative, less heroic. The Annenburg Institute studied communities that came together around shared goals to improve their schools. In describing several examples of successful public engagement, Kimpton and Considine (1999) state, "Leadership isn't about pulling people along anymore. It is much more about orchestrating ideas, people, visions, potential and diverse organization into a cohesive program of education improvement" (p. 5).

Vision Setting

One of the primary ways that superintendents exercise instructional leadership is through the formulation of a vision for the district. A school district vision involves the collaborative process of articulating beliefs about the education of children, defining goals for the school organization that enact those beliefs, and developing plans to reach the goals. As this definition suggests, the *how* of developing a vision seems to be at least as important as the *what*. Johnson finds that developing an effective vision involves a "delicate balance of control and collaboration" (1996, p. 82). Superintendents who develop their vision independently risk political criticism of being unilateral and not taking into account the local context. However, a superintendent who develops a collaborative vision risks being viewed as weak and ineffective as the power of the vision becomes diluted by committees and compromises.

The most effective superintendents in Johnson's study are able to articulate their educational values with "clarity and conviction" (p. 86) and yet adapt them to the needs of the context. In collaboration with others, they are able to put their personal imprint on a vision that, at the same time, convinces others that the vision is addressing important local needs, and they enhance their credibility by not only stating their values but acting on them as well.

Bringing about Educational Change

The measure of the effectiveness of the educational leadership of the superintendent is the educational change produced. Superintendents are key players in any school improvement process. Successful school systems almost never have poorly performing superintendents (Owen, 1998, p. 13). Clark and his colleagues observe "District-wide change is not possible without the support, encouragement, and involvement of the superintendent" (cited in Owen, 1998, p. 7). In assuming their roles, superintendents expect to bring about change. Few enter the job planning to maintain the status quo (Johnson, 1996, p. 119).

Bringing about educational change in a school system, nevertheless, can be a daunting challenge. Johnson describes how teachers and administrators are inured to a new cycle of change with the advent of a new superintendent because of decades of school reform activity characterized by finger pointing, failed promises, and lack of follow through. She says that superintendent turnover makes staff especially skeptical and mistrustful of yet another initiative. Staff cynics cite the metaphor of the *revolving door* of administrative change to justify their inaction.

Johnson suggests three characteristics of a successful change process initiated by a superintendent:

> First, constituents must be convinced that the proposed reform is educationally worthwhile and locally warranted, that it provides promising answers to important problems. Second, the strategy for implementing the reform must be viable, taking into account the expectations and experiences of those in the district. Third, teachers and principals must believe that the new superintendent advancing reforms is credible, trustworthy, and ready to see change through. (1996, p. 93)

Transactional versus Transformational Leadership

Leadership theorists, beginning with James MacGregor Burns (1978) have contrasted transactional and transformational leadership. Transactional leadership maintains the status quo through an exchange. The leader meets the needs of followers, and they give the leader the support necessary to continue. Organizational equilibrium remains undisturbed. Transformational leadership produces change by developing commitment to shared values and capacity to translate those values into action. Organizational equilibrium shifts.

Educational change requires transformational rather than traditional transactional leadership. In her study, Johnson finds, however, that superintendents have first to meet the transactional expectations of constituents before transformational leadership is possible. The expectations for new superintendents are distinctly transactional at first. Teachers and principals feel that if the superintendent responds to their needs—for budget support, facilities maintenance, and other basics—then they might be willing to comply with the superintendent's initiatives. However, although meeting basic needs at this transactional level is necessary, it is not, Johnson finds, sufficient to produce a more transformational, a more reciprocal relationship, in which mutual commitment to change can occur. Superintendents have first to prove that what is happening in classrooms is important and valuable to them. In her study, superintendents accomplish this through substantive classroom visits and dialogue with teachers and principals about teaching and learning issues. They have to establish their "credibility as educators" (p. 131). When staff comes to trust the superintendent as an educator, one important consequence is that they are not only more likely to commit to, rather than comply with, change efforts, but are also more likely to take a broader system-wide view of their work. These superintendents are able to "enlarge the field of attention" of teachers and principals (p. 144).

In Johnson's study, few superintendents significantly affect educational practice in their districts; few achieve the level of transformational leadership. The obstacles are formidable: teacher fear, distrust, suspicion, cynicism of the new and unknown in contrast to the security of the familiar and predictable world of their classrooms. Many superintendents fail to overcome these obstacles. But those who do meet the basic needs of staff win their confidence and respect by being credible educators and then engage staff in meaningful dialogue about school improvement (1996, p. 149).

Personal versus Positional Authority

In today's world of collaborative leadership, superintendents who do win the respect and confidence of their constituents and achieve transformational leadership make effective use of personal authority: their interpersonal skills, social attractiveness, and charisma. Positional authority, the power that comes with the role, may have been sufficient to bring about educational change in the days of scientific management when the hierarchy of the school organization functioned effectively. But positional authority no longer is sufficient. Who the superintendent is as a person matters. "Superintendents' capacity to lead rests in part on their own moral purposes, their commitment to education, and their courage to stand up for what they believe" (Johnson, 1996, p. 281).

Superintendents establish who they are and what they believe in through being involved and engaged in the work of the organization. Johnson states that the collaborative leadership model that emerged as most effective in her study requires significant one-to-one relationships between the superintendent and members of the school community. "Before personally investing in a superintendent's initiatives, constituents wanted to know about the person behind the initiatives" (1996, p. 283).

Like Johnson, Peterson (1998) also finds that personal visibility matters. Through frequent school visits, superintendents signal their instructional commitment. Visits also offer the opportunity, through observing teachers and reviewing student work, to demonstrate the value and importance of district instructional goals (p. 12).

The Superintendent as Teacher

As a collaborative leader, who depends on personal authority as much or more than positional authority to persuade and influence others, the superintendent today has, in Johnson's words, "a teaching mission" (1996, p. 275):

> Thus, it was through their roles as teachers that these superintendents convinced others to lead with them—to participate in shaping a vision for change, to take principled stands about important issues, to accept responsibility for defining and solving problems, and to engage colleagues in finding better approaches to schooling (1996, p. 278).

The Centrality of Politics

To enact their educational mission effectively, superintendents must possess political acumen. Most researchers and observers agree that political leadership, the second major dimension of the role, is central to the work of today's superintendent. Blumberg says:

> What is important is to understand that being a superintendent inevitably involves the manipulation and exercise of organizational power. This is essentially a political activity, as are, of course, the mobilization of community support and the management of conflict, activities that require a great deal of a superintendent's time and concern. (1985, p. 46)

Elmore (2000) suggests that politics is the bedrock of the superintendency. Citing Madison's *Federalist Papers*, he reminds us that "institutions of government exist to play the interests of competing factions against each other, so as to prevent the tyranny of one faction over all others" (p. 18). Competing factions, jockeying for more power, are "hardwired into the culture and institutional structure" (p. 18). Blumberg, too, states that, "The institutionalized right of individuals and groups to oppose a superintendent's proposals is embedded in our democratic system" (1985, p. 48).

Superintendents and Political Conflict

The conflictual nature of the position is not a new phenomenon, although it may have been exacerbated by the social upheaval of the late twentieth century. At its essence, the superintendent's role has evolved through political conflicts with boards of education over the power that superintendents would have to run schools. Blumberg (1985) traces conflicts over the superintendent's role from the nineteenth century and earlier. In describing the early predilection of school boards to make day-to-day educational decisions, he cites the "antiexecutive" tradition in colonial history (p. 20). "Ceding public powers to a single individual is simply against the American tradition" (p. 74). Much of the conflict centered on the struggle for power over educational decision making that superintendents ultimately won with the rise of scientific management and professionalism in the superintendency at the beginning of the twentieth century as well as the growing complexity of school systems themselves. But, as Blumberg, points out, that ascendancy came at a price—continuing conflict over the extent of the superintendent's power over community finances and its values for its children.

Blumberg says that changes in the superintendency over the last 100 years have less to do with substantive differences in the problems faced (in fact, he gives pertinent examples to suggest that the problems have tended to re-cycle through history) and more to do with changes in the politics of the positions. Superintendents today have to be skillful at maintaining a balance among the various conflicting forces in the school arena for this more diverse, open system to function effectively.

Because politics are so embedded in the role, the conflict that results is a function of the position, not the person. "It comes with the territory" (Blumberg, 1985, p. 1). Superintendents today often describe themselves in no-win positions, in which any significant decision they make alienate and upset someone or some group. Unlike other visible public leaders, such as elected politicians, they do not have partisan coalitions on whom to rely for support in times of trouble. And, unlike politicians, who cannot be easily removed from office until the next election, superintendents serve at the pleasure of the school board and can be removed at any time.

To be an effective educational leader amidst this conflict and complexity, a superintendent today must indeed be an adept political leader—building coalitions and alliances among the various actors who have power in school decision making, negotiating effective compromises, and forcing and trading concessions when necessary (Johnson, 1996, p. 153).

Johnson identifies three different kinds of political contexts in districts— *partisan politics* in which discrete political alliances are ascendant; *participatory politics* in which affiliations in groups vary according to the issue at stake, and *patronage politics* in which long-standing loyalties defined by family, race, ethnicity, or neighborhood determine decisions including the allocation of resources. Successful superintendents recognize the differences in context and have versatile skills to adapt and respond.

Although politics, the art of jockeying for power and influence, come into play in a superintendent's relationships with all constituent groups, the two major political challenges are the board of education and the unions. Because of the conflicts inherent in the relationship with the board, to be effective any superintendent must find a balance point that establishes the boundaries of the working relationship between the board and the school district. The equilibrium that the superintendent seeks empowers the board to do its job of setting broad policy and reflecting community interests and concerns without intruding on the day-to-day leadership and management in classrooms or in school and district offices. In attaining this balance, an effective superintendent will be successful at "avoiding destructive public conflict, framing problems in ways that would elicit attention and action, promoting orderly and constructive decision-making, converting political opponents to allies, and fostering collaboration among adversaries" (Johnson, 1996, p. 169).

The other major political challenge is working with unions, especially the teachers' union. Johnson finds that it is essential for superintendents to establish firm, fair, and respectful relationships with union leaders (1996, p. 185). Blumberg's study reveals that maintaining such a sound and positive relationship is a complex and delicate endeavor. As the *man in the middle* between the board and the union, the superintendent must balance their often conflicting interests. In the starkest terms, the relationship with the union is a struggle for power and authority over who is going to make educational decisions. In the history of collective bargaining in schools, negotiated contracts have steadily expanded beyond salary, benefits, and basic working conditions and encroached on issues of curriculum, pedagogy, and organization. This struggle for power necessarily makes the relationship adversarial. But the superintendent cannot afford to treat union leaders as enemies. In the politics of the school system, he or she will sooner or later need their support or at least their acquiescence. At the same time, the board is watching and judging the performance with the union. Inherently, they are jealous of their management prerogatives, and, as Blumberg points out, they may, as laymen, be suspicious of an "unholy alliance" developing between their professional administrator and the professional educators in the union (1985, p. 98).

Studies of the superintendency reveal important caveats about political leadership. Johnson asserts that it is essential that the superintendent's political decisions be guided by clear and obvious educational principles and purposes. In her study, the criticism of superintendents' political leadership took two forms—their political ineptness or their political emptiness, that is "playing politics" for their own sake with no larger educational purpose (1996, p. 186)

Blumberg suggests that superintendents' political acumen requires that they take a broad, conceptual, somewhat detached view of the politics of their domain. This overview enables them not only to see the various forces, factions, and interest groups but also to understand how they interact and influence each other. This intellectualized perspective is key to making sense of a disorderly, even chaotic, series of events and to developing a plan of action to control it. The detachment is also is a way for the superintendent to maintain *sanity* in what can appear at times to be an insane school world.

> The highly political and conflictual world of the superintendent appears to be randomized, irrational, and uncontrollable. To the extent that the superintendent can understand the complex web of events that he confronts and subject that under-

standing to his own intellectual analysis, he is better able to order the world, control it, and maintain his own sense of self. (Blumberg, 1985, p. 57)

Notwithstanding the centrality of politics in their roles and their recognition of its importance, superintendents still express strong frustration with politics and red tape in their jobs. Eight of ten superintendents who responded to the Public Agenda survey, for example, felt that "politics and bureaucracy" were the key factor in decisions by talented people to leave the field (2001, p. 8).

In summary, politics and conflict are embedded in the role. To be effective, a superintendent must respond to the unique political context of the district and establish viable working relationships with all political players, especially the board and the unions.

Integration of Leadership and Management

Managerial leadership has often been described as a separate function from educational and political leadership. In its domain is the "mundane work of making a bureaucracy work" (March, 1978 as quoted in Johnson, 1996, p. 219). Although there is certainly a reality to this view, it does not capture the more complex interrelationship that appears to exist today between effective management and the other dimensions of leadership. Johnson argues that the separation of leadership and management is a social construct that is misleading and inaccurate. In her study, successful superintendents do both simultaneously. "In no district did we find evidence of effective leadership without effective management." In fact, they manage in order to lead, or to put it another way, they lead through managing:

> They were deliberate in their use of authority, calculating in their delivery and receipt of information, and purposeful in their demands for accountability. They pay attention to the routines and structure of the organization in order to accomplish larger goals. They did not, however, manage rigidly; instead they used authority and structure to further strategic goals. Once again, how they managed varied according to the context. Some effectively reasserted more central control, for example in a district amidst crisis and chaos; others decentralized control, for example in a stable district where site-based empowerment made sense. (Johnson, 1996, pp. 239–240)

Issues of Centralization and Decentralization

In today's more complex school world, superintendents are involved in what most observers describe as a series of delicate balancing acts. They "must walk a fine line" between promoting change and the discomfort it can create and yet respecting the climate and culture of the organization (Owen, 1998, p. 6). Often, they employ management strategies to strike the balance. A key managerial priority is finding the appropriate balance between controlling decisions at the central office far from the classroom and allowing teachers and principals to make decisions closer to the point of instruction. Superintendents today face the dilemma between need for more coordination of curriculum and instruction across grades and levels in the interest of improved student learning and the benefit of encouraging and empowering individuals and schools sites in the interest of building their capacity to make more effective decisions about student learning. Most of the superintendents in Johnson's study attempt to acknowledge the tensions involved in this dilemma by "two seemingly different directions"—both greater site-based autonomy and greater public accountability (1996, p. 246).

Johnson (1996) describes "managerial levers" (pp. 246–267) that superintendents employ to accomplish this balancing act, including:

- Coordinating district activities through the articulation and institutionalization of a set of core educational values;
- Attempting to make the central office more responsive to school needs and to establish closer relationships between central office and the schools;
- Playing an active role in principal selection to ensure that building leadership is loyal and aligned;
- Supervising principals directly to maintain and strengthen those relationships and to ensure that the principal's vision and the superintendent's are consonant. Peterson's study confirms the importance of this tactic of personal supervisions of principals to ensure the vision is integrated throughout the organization. (1998, p. 17)

Elmore (2000), too, describes the balancing act that superintendents must master between the control necessary for ensuring system-wide improvement and the autonomy that teachers and principals need to be able to achieve improvement. Elmore suggests that the word *control* itself is problematic because it implies that the controller knows what the controllee should do. In bringing about instructional improvement, however, the knowledge of what to do "must inevitably reside in the people who deliver instruction." This reality is the main reason for Elmore's call to distribute leadership throughout the organization. In his model of distributed knowledge and leadership, district leadership can provide guidance and direction by clarifying the "glue of a common task or goal—instructional leadership" and by strengthening the culture—the commitment to a common set of values and beliefs. Superintendent leadership initiatives in these two will help ensure the necessary coordination and standardization for improvement to be consistent across the system (p. 15).

In summary, effective superintendents today provide educational leadership through management strategies that further instructional goals. These include decisions about organizational structure, the delegation of authority to the site level, strengthened accountability measures, the degree of centralization in curriculum and instruction, and personal involvement in administrative hiring and supervision.

Conclusion

The role of the superintendent in twenty-first century school districts appears to be highly contextualized. Although many of the challenges the superintendents face—for example, budget shortfalls, state and federal red tape, eroding positional authority—are similar from district to district, and the culture of the districts and the context in which the superintendent works are very different. All successful twenty-first century superintendents must integrate high performance in all three dimensions of the role—educational leader, politician, and manager. However, how the effective superintendent enacts the three dimensions of the role in one district may be substantially different from the equally effective work of a superintendent in another district. Indeed, to remain successful, each of these effective twenty-first century superintendents will have to change and modify their approaches to respond to changes in the districts. Context appears to matter that much and to change that much.

The effective twenty-first century superintendent is not a detached authority figure at the top of the bureaucratic hierarchy. In the complex and turbulent environment in which today's schools exist, the superintendent is at the hub of networks of others—staff, parents, board and community members, and students. The successful school system itself is a flexible organization in which leadership recognizes the necessary interdependence of the whole organization with its surrounding environment—government, social agencies, parents, and business groups— and its internal interdependence as well. In such a fluid and dynamic school world, leadership authority will not just reside in the positional leaders, such as the superintendent, but will be distributed throughout the organization. In this less hierarchical, more informal organizational structure, collaboration in the interest of creative problem solving will be prized and rewarded. These dynamic relationships will unleash energy that strengthens commitment and purpose and ultimately produces sustained improvement of instruction (Johnson, 1996, p. 275).

REFERENCES

American Association of School Administrators. (2000). *The 2000 study of the American school superintendency.* Arlington, VA: The Association.

Bjork, L. G. (1999). Collaborative research on the superintendency. *AERA Research on the Superintendency SIG Bulletin, 2*(1), 1–4.

Blumberg, A. (1985). *The school superintendent: Living with conflict.* New York: Teachers College Press.

Burns, J. M. (1978). *Leadership.* New York: Harper & Row.

Council of Great City Schools. (2001). *Urban school superintendents: Characteristics, tenure, and salary.* Washington, DC: The Council.

Elmore, R. (2000). *Building a new structure for school leadership.* Washington, DC: The Albert Shanker Institute.

Hodgkinson, H., & Montenegro, X. (1999). *The U.S. school superintendent: The invisible CEO.* Washington, DC: The Institute for Educational Leadership.

Johnson, S. (1996). *Leading to change: The challenge of the new superintendency.* San Francisco: Jossey-Bass.

Kimpton, J. S., & Considine, J. W. (1999, September). The tough sledding of district-led engagement. *The School Administrator Web Edition.* Retrieved March 2, 2002, from *http://www.aasa.org/publications/sa/1999_09/kimpton.htm.*

March, J. G. (1978). American public school administration: A short analysis. *School Review, 86*(2), 217–250.

New York State Council of School Superintendents. (2001). *Snapshot 2000: A study of school superintendents in New York state.* Albany, NY: New York State Council of School Superintendents.

Owen, J. (1998). *The roles of the superintendent in creating a community climate for educational improvement.* Paper presented at the Annual Conference of the American Educational Research Association, San Diego, CA.

Peterson, G. (1998). *Demonstrated actions of instructional leaders: A case study of five superintendents.* Paper presented at the Annual Conference of the American Educational Research Association, San Diego, Calif.

Peterson, G., & Short, P. (2001). The school board president's perception of the district superintendent: Applying the lenses of social influence and social style. *Educational Administration Quarterly, 37,* 533–570.

Public Agenda. (2001). *Trying to stay ahead of the game.* New York, NY: Public Agenda.

Skrla, L. (1998). *The social construction of gender in the superintendency.* Paper presented at the Annual Conference of the American Educational Research Association, San Diego, CA.

Skrla, L. (1999). *Femininity/masculinity: Hegemonic normalizations in the public school superintendency.* Paper presented at the Annual Conference of the American Educational Research Association, Montreal, Quebec.

11 Schools as Political Systems

This introduction sets out interwoven themes that focus on the realities of education and power within the United States. Understanding these realities involves the use of *concepts*, that is, ways of thinking about the complexity of life. The concepts used here are applicable to any large systems—economic, political, social—but they are made relevant in Part Four of this book for local, state, or national systems of schooling.

System Shock

Regardless of level, one major reality of education today is the presence of a widespread set of challenges directed against purported failures in public education. To understand what is happening we need to think of a *system* undergoing *shock* where before it had known only regularities of behavior and belief.

System Regularity

Any system is composed of a set of *routines*, that is, regular ways of acting and thinking about significant values in life. These routines have a major purpose, namely, to further the values that the system carries out for those it serves. These routines have several uses:

- They reflect the system's norms (i.e., values and outcomes) that are made evident in its activities.
- They socialize new members to the norms of the system.
- They specify detailed behaviors to carry out tasks.
- They provide all adherents with psychological security linked to the certainties of regularities.

As a particular example of this larger concept of systems, think again about the familiar aspect of professional instruction, namely, lesson plans. Much time in training, and even more in later preparation, are given to this task. Its purpose is to focus the teacher's mind on precise learning objectives that can be linked to reading and lecture resources. With these in hand, the teacher has a comforting guide to class work and a satisfying sense that broader objectives of the system are being met. In turn, these plans also provide the principal with an oversight of how well the system's tasks are being met, and for the superintendent with a sense that all is going well down in the trenches of teaching. All these constitute a system that, across this and many other routines, indicates the goals and operations.

System Shock

Against the settled nature of system and routines, there is a contrast in yet another concept, namely, *system shock*. This term designates a disruption of routines due to external events in society that create system challenges with resultant reactions. These disruptions arise outside the system and are traceable to major stresses in society, such as war, depression, or general dissatisfaction with government policies. At the heart of these stresses is an imbalance between human needs and wants, both of which are expansive, often without limit. However, it often occurs that the resources to treat both needs and wants are limited, and such limitations invite conflict over who gets what, when, and how from the system. In this way, imbalance creates stress among citizens and even societal institutions. A system undergoing this stress can find that its basic routines, indeed even its underlying values, are challenged by those dissatisfied with existing policies. Such challenges can lead to members within the system having to adopt new values and new routines that will carry out a new agenda of activity.

A major example of these concepts was the southern school desegregation after 1956. Briefly, when the U.S. Supreme Court (*Brown v. Topeka*, 1957) and a later act of Congress (Civil Rights Act of 1964) overturned the decades old, racially segregated schools, southern school officials found that community and personal senses were deeply upset. They had to accommodate this ban to meet Constitutional goals and to receive federal funds. In later decades, many aspects of southern education were changed, and, despite a later Court reversal of this ban, new practices and attitudes came into public education (Wirt, 1997).

The resulting new agenda caused by system shock brings new definitions of the values that the system will serve, a reordering. With this change new routines redefine the system's purposes, four of which were set out previously. This reordering is not abrupt, for it can take decades. In all this change, system members come over time to accept as normal the values and behavior that had been earlier opposed.

In southern desegregation, for example, several decades after the federal Civil Rights Law, a new curriculum had been adopted by the states about the role of African Americans in our history. Further, local school boards began hiring African Americans as professionals, and teachers reappraised their lesson plans to accommodate this new challenge to the segregated system. Attendant on the reordering was a great emotional conflict because the old and new systems reflected different, basic values about race and living in communities. Some opponents of the change even went so far as to flee the public schools for private or *deseg* academies; that proportion was much less than the attendant publicity.

Relevance of These Concepts to American Education

As this book points out, America's schooling has undergone a system shock, not only recently but throughout its history. The introduction 160 years ago of Horace Mann's new idea of free, public education, and the efforts early in the twentieth century to provide technical education are historical examples that illustrate system shock. As pointed out above, a similar system shock emerged during the last half-century when waves of reform sought to alter, patterns of segregation. The chapters that follow show how this shock and response theme applies to different levels of governance in the United States. In the following section we discuss another large-scale way of thinking about education that is tied to a different concept, namely, the power to make school decisions.

Decisional Power

As if educational problems were not enough for professionals, another brand of problems is suggested by two fairly common questions that arise in local schools:

1. Why is the local music curriculum typically the first to be chopped in a budget crunch?
On the one hand, music teachers are very experienced in teaching technology, and everyone knows that learning music can add significantly to the quality of life. On the other hand, these teachers appear quite weak in generating community support for their instruction beyond an athletic band. It is these teachers' weakness in public support that leads to their budget being cut.

2. Among all teacher competencies, why do coaches more often become principals?
Football involves substantial community contact through team members or by a larger adult interest in winning—"We are number 1!" The coach, especially if successful, gains much support from the community. After all, other than in athletics, few other teachers put their products on public display to the community. Given this context, when a school board looks for a new principal, it will find that those community bonds can generate outside support for such an appointment.

Clearly this case seems the reverse of the first, but both have one common factor, namely, the presence or absence of community support. So something other than experience in teaching or administration is needed to understand policymaking by local boards. This view of education policymaking is rooted in the concept of *power,* particularly political power.

To grasp this concept, a series of subconcepts will illustrate what is involved, with their details found in later chapters. *The key to understanding the major concept of political power lies in the understanding that a* public *policy is linked to the role of the* public. Education, like many other policies, shares this linkage. However, the public is not of a single mind; people differ over what education is for or about.

Over a century ago, a philosopher, when asked about the emergence of a new educational system, asked, "Education for *what*?" Since then, answering this query has been the center of much school controversy. Let us review these subconcepts.

Dominance in Decision Making

Because differences exist over which of many values in education is to predominate, conflict is a natural part of the policy scene. Conflict can only be resolved in the form of public policy that reflects the values of one group that has power and other resources to realize these values. In much of the twentieth century, that dominance rested with school professionals. The history of American education shows clearly that those trained in *ed schools* received the authority to define *the best* in schooling practices (Clifford & Guthrie, 1988). Of course, there were school boards at state and local levels to make formal decisions, but mostly they reflected basic support of professional decisions. Locally, parents had pretty much accepted what professionals were doing, thereby providing support for the dominance of professional policies. Moreover, state and national governments were little involved in local schooling, thereby reinforcing the dominance of local control of schools. For much of the last century, then, the key to control rested with the local superintendents. Superintendents were regarded as officials who were scientifically proficient and who set curriculum and other schooling policies (Kerr, 1964; Tyack, 1974).

In the last forty years, however, other groups have emerged to challenge this professional dominance. On the one hand, many new local groups arose, such as teacher unions, ethnic groups, and parents. There was also the rise in the external authority of the state and national governments by which local groups could challenge professional views. This shift provided alternative political arenas in which to set new school policy that had been blocked at the local level, that is, courts and legislatures.*

When asked the question "Education for *what*?" each group answered with its own agenda. Thus, a wide range of educational matters were challenged for reform: curriculum, organization, governance, and finances. The result was a mélange of new policies designed to forward different group agendas. Underlying much of this change was a basic, public dissatisfaction with public school services.

Consider the following review of challenges by recent decades. There was concern about "why Johnny can't read" in the 1950s, support of school desegregation in the 1960s and 1970s, reform of local control of school sites in the 1980s, clamor for voucher or charter schools in the 1990s, and the adoption of statewide standards-based accountability systems in the 2000s. Combined, these waves of complaints and subsequent reforms constituted a widespread rebuttal of the old pattern of professional dominance of school policy. Indeed, most critics had used some feature of that dominance as a key weakness in schools that needed reform.

---

*To review other agencies, see Frances Berry, "Sizing Up State Policy Innovation Research," *Policy Studies Journal* 22 (1994): 442–56; David Kirp and Donald Jensen, eds., *School Days, Rule Days*. Philadelphia: Falmer, 1986.

Conflict Resolution of Policymaking

In that context, however, this host of new issues had internal contradictions. In a common local conflict, namely, teacher union's demands for better salaries versus a school board's limited budget, some method is needed to resolve the conflict to produce a public policy that keeps education ongoing.

What are the methods used for conflict resolution on school policies? In the first two thirds of the twentieth century, the methods employed were decisions made by the superintendent backed by the profession's norm of improving school quality and efficiency. Even before that, in the nineteenth century, decisions were typically made by a local board of largely male farmers with a limited view of schooling. These decisional methods reflected an underlying value in American democracy, namely, that decisions involving allocation of resources or values must be made either by those elected or by appointments by those elected.

In today's world, by contrast, there are many stakeholders seeking multiple values, all of which create a condition of turbulence in policymaking. Administrators or school boards are confronted by a wide variety of individual parents or groups seeking often clashing views of the basic question: Schooling for what? Today, superintendents spend much of their time in public relations activity, seeking to shape community views of the school system. Their earlier role of creating and organizing professional goals is now shifted to more work with many local groups—or with higher governments (see for example, Cuban, 1985). Here, the administrator must work amid this conflict of views to seek compromises in public policy. That can be accomplished only by more community contact—that is, public relations—to resolve this conflict. Nor should it be a surprise that amid this current turbulence the personal stress of the job increases, which may account for the shorter tenure of superintendents. By the end of the 1990s, three years was the average for big city superintendents, and a little over double that for suburban positions; moreover, a shortage of principals was also emerging as many incumbents retired early.

This brief description of decisional power suggests that the new role of the administrator is quite literally described as a *politician*. Indeed, the context in which the policymaker now operates is what political scientists would term a *political* context. Like the traditional politician, one is faced with different viewpoints on policy. Here, one must seek a compromise. When compromise is successful, no one gets everything, no one loses everything, but everyone gets something. This new role of decision making for school administrators means that the usually *evil* notion of politics is abjured to focus on practical ways to set goals and get things done.

Dual Role of the Professional

These two broader concepts—system shock and power—of the working context within education today suggest that both may be in conflict. On the one hand, the political aspect of conflict resolution is a concept that permeates all aspects of education today (Wirt & Kirst, 2001). On the other hand, the work of teacher and administrator is primarily that of being an educator, another concept that shapes one's work. Given both concepts of work, the educator faces two questions:

- How to teach and administer effectively by professional norms?
- How to protect against competing claims of nonprofessionals who legitimately use the political context to further their aims?

In short, whether as teacher or administrator, one must be both an educator and a politician.

Politics and School Policy

As noted throughout this book, the educational orientation of schools has been increasingly dominated by political aspects at different levels of policymaking. Although the original Constitution and later amendments did not refer to education, that task was *reserved* by implication to the states. Those units, however, did little with schooling until starting about the mid-nineteenth century with the policy of free public schooling. What that history means was that overseeing and providing education was primarily a local function, although constitutionally a state power. That condition prevailed for nearly a century, until events of the last of the twentieth century brought both federal and state levels increasingly into local schooling. Succeeding chapters cover each of these levels in local, state, and federal governments, namely, the political characteristics of American education.

Politics, Government, and Challenge

It would be useful to define two key terms used throughout this section, namely, politics and governance. It is necessary to drop the widespread popular notions of these terms and focus rather on the behavior they describe. By *politics* we refer to one form of dealing with social conflict rooted in groups that differ in their values and goals about using public policy. By *governance* we refer to a constitutional mechanism for resolving this group conflict by creating and implementing public resources in the form of policy. Those meanings are generic in that they apply to a wide range of public policies, from whether the local city council should increase police pay to the congressional decision to declare war.

These two terms assume some important aspects of American life. They presume that our nation is formed of many groups having different values about important matters. Many groups seek to enlist governance to support their values and interest through use of public resources. Moreover, some of these values can be in conflict, and so as to reduce the stress in society from these confrontations, a conflict resolution mechanism is needed. One of these may be the use of social institutions to reduce stress, and one of these is the political system whose policies can resolve this conflict.

Behind that understanding is that we reflect a great variety, often diverse, of values, and so a real possibility exists that these values may contradict. That realization is a starting point to understanding the political aspects. As one example, note the phenomenon of immigration. Most of us, except Native Americans, came to this continent from other places, possessing values about serious matters. More important, those values led to differences in opinion about the allocation of public resources. Note the historical reaction of new and old immigrant groups to newcomers:

- Middle of the nineteenth century Yankee disgust at the Irish
- Late nineteenth century distaste of both Italians and Slavs
- Twentieth century distaste by many at the rise of Hispanic and African Americans

Nor has that ethnic conflict ended. In 1995 Hodgkinson reported U.S. Census Bureau estimates that by 2010 African American and Hispanic populations would be equal in size. He predicted that by 2025 only one half of American youth will be white and one half "minority," and by 2050 whites will be the "majority minority" among other minorities (Hodgkinson, 1995). By 2001, the Hispanic population was 36,972,000 and the African American population was 36,247,000, with the gap widening in favor of Hispanics (U.S. Census Bureau, 2002). In a recent analysis of U.S. census data, Cortez concludes that "Hispanic student enrollment in U.S. schools has doubled over the last decade. More than 9 million Hispanic children are of school age. One in every six children enrolled in public schools is of HIspanic origin" (Cortez, 2003, p. 2). Given these changes, conflict increased among different groups over school policies. For example, differences over bilingual education and English only have led to political contests in numerous states during the 1990s.

At the heart of social change are values that affect common questions about school policy. For example:

- *What should be taught?* For much of the nineteenth century the answer was simple—reading, writing, 'rithmetic, as an old song defined it. Over time, however, school professionals have determined other and more detailed curricula, usually by working through state laws. Washington came into the picture in the late 1950s with funds for improving the teaching of science and mathematics. However, any change in the curriculum gave rise to controversy, such as adding a state requirement for sex education (Portner, 1994).
- *When to teach at different stages of student life?* Are social studies taught early in life or later in adolescence? Should there be a sequence of learning mathematics from simple arithmetic to calculus, or should components of all kinds be introduced early on and added to? Again, any changes fostered considerable controversy, such as the *new math* innovation in the 1970s.
- *Who should teach?* During the nineteenth century, as education became more professional, teachers first had to be trained in *normal* schools. But later, with blessings from the profession, even more training was required for certification

by the state. A teacher was defined by college courses set first by professionals and then by state law. Only at the end of the 1990s did some states permit limited teaching by those without certification.

■ *Who should be accountable for the student's learning?* From the earliest days of American education, it was the teacher who answered that question and was judged by others on the basis of tests. However, what if student failures were traceable less to teachers and more to lack of parental support, limited school resources, or indifference by administrators? In the last of the twentieth century more attention had been paid to these alternative causes, namely, those outside the classroom. With the Bush administration in 2002, federal law supported national grading for select grades. However, for most parents, it is the teacher who is still held responsible for answering this persistent question.

A Paradigm of Educational Policymaking

Amid such controversy, how is it possible to provide some understanding to these turbulent policy demands? We suggest that underlying it all is a simple paradigm, or explanation, of interactions over school policy. It is sketched in Figure 11.1. Each component of this figure is an idealized version of reality that helps to distinguish stages of this process. Moreover, some stages occur in different sequences. But overall this paradigm can help us understand stages in the educational policy-making process.

Public Dissatisfaction

As is often the case in a democracy, policy change arises over dissatisfaction by the public over what government does (Iannaccone & Lutz, 1970). A major problem in society is first perceived, and then remedies are proposed to correct the problem. Here is how the paradigm works. Either a *crisis* arises or else a widespread awareness arises over a problem. Neither case arises very often in the flow of governance; much of policy life is repetitive, dealing with minor matters. Nevertheless, on some policy changes a reaction of widespread disappointment appears. During the 1990s this was the case for such issues as:

■ Improved curriculum in science and mathematics
■ Site-based management
■ Student testing
■ Improved teacher training and testing
■ Desegregation changes

Political Pressure

This policy stage gives rise to pressure exerted on decision-making agencies, such as school boards or, in the end, state or federal legislatures. The form of pressure

FIGURE 11.1   A Paradigm of Educational Policymaking

Policy Stages	Time Stages
Public Dissatisfaction	1

Political Pressure
Protests
Pressure group activity
Elections:
    Referendum
    School board
	2

Authoritative Decision Making
Interactions of:
    Legislative body
    Executive
    Central office and superintendent
Public policy authorized
	3

Administration/Implementation	4
Evaluation of Policy Effects	5
Impact on Group Concerns	6

involves group protests to such agencies, pressure group activity on individual policymakers, and using referenda or electing new officials.

In this process in education, groups once quiescent over schools have become quite active on a range of policy issues. Table 11.1 notes the presence of such groups energized during the last of the twentieth century (Wirt & Kirst,

TABLE 11.1   New Groups and New Issues in School Policymaking

Parents: local control of making school policy
Teachers: collective bargaining for salaries and working conditions
Students: civil rights on youth issues, e.g., expression, dress
Taxpayers: reform local financing to shift costs to the state
Minorities: desegregation, special education
State-federal agencies: guidelines, mandates, court orders on new policies

1997). This description of group pressure is brief even though it is quite complex, for here are interwoven the often hectic interactions of many stakeholders in education. Clearly, this stage is a highly visible aspect of school policy, featured often in the news media and regularly accompanied by research reports on dissatisfactions and remedies. Moreover, the process is not time-bound. It is spread over many years, as with changing desegregation policy through court action.

Authoritative Decision Making

At this stage, the issue may have stimulated latent, political ideologies among public and policy actors. For example, the effort by the Clinton administration in the 1990s and more recently the Bush administration to create national standards on curricula objectives, such as history or reading, generated a states-rights opposition against such centralization.

In other policy initiatives that are realized, it is as if different *streams* of politics, policy, and problems finally come together, creating windows of opportunity for change (Kingdon, 1995). Indeed, a set of these broad reform streams appeared in state policy in the 1980s and 1990s, as earlier chapters pointed out (Mazzoni, 1995). Thus, in the 1980s there were widespread state reforms of top-down policies designed to increase the value of quality by setting specific state goals. Then, in the 1990s a smaller wave of locally directed, bottom-up reforms occurred that emphasized the values of quality and choice. It is at this stage of policymaking that most observers, professional and citizen, think that the process is criticized as *political*. Yet, as noted in preceding chapters, different stages in Figure 11.1 can also be seen as political, by which is meant contending over competing demands for resources or values for school policy.

Administration and Implementation

The next stage involves an effective method for carrying out public policy. As we have seen in earlier chapters, *administration* refers to the use of personnel and material resources into an organization designed to carry out the policy's purposes. On the other hand, *implementation* refers to the operations to carry out those purposes. While administration is relatively brief in setting up the policy system, implementation can be extended for many years. By and large, the broad purpose of this stage is to make effective the actions sought by those dissatisfied with existing policy. Descriptively these functions involve a new set of authority located in the central office of local schools or in the state and federal bureaucracies.

Evaluation

A final stage of making policy can become highly political, namely, evaluation of the effectiveness of the policy's implementation. In this stage, specialized personnel evaluate the goals of the policy, the means employed to meet them, and the results of the policy on students. Much of this is highly quantitative, consisting of statistical tables and formulas to provide evidence to answer an old question: Did this policy work?

The political aspects of this stage lie both in how the evaluation is set up and conducted, and in what happens to stakeholders faced with these results. As to the latter, some see it as a success. Yet others see in the evaluation the results that are needed to change that policy into some more effective form. Others, however, may claim the result is a failure and hence the need to reinstate an earlier policy. Whatever the judgments, they are often used to reinvigorate the entire policy process in order to begin again. It is as if in Figure 11.1 a new line should be added to show its ongoing nature. Someone once said that the process of governing consists of doing nothing, then adjusting to it, and next waiting until someone next complains about the adjustment, and so on *ad infinitum.*

The policymaking process sketched briefly in Figure 11.1 and in the text describes a political system. It interweaves actors with institutions to create public policies that are then carried out. Such a political system includes partisans of those seeking change or accepting what exists. It is also a process that brings in political parties, particularly at the state and national levels, as we will see in later chapters.

It is this political process that at the end of the twentieth century made school policy the subject of so much conflict over many issues. The barrage of these challenges constituted the system shock discussed earlier in the introduction to this section. Moreover, the process also was far from the neutral orientation of school professionals who earlier had sought to educate students without such conflict. For contrast, we need to grasp the earlier image of school policy that had characterized much of the last century. That image was seen as an ideal world that many school people now think has been lost—to the detriment of effective schooling.

The Apolitical Myth of Schooling

Amid school professionals there exists to this day a belief that schools are not political and that their decisions are not politically motivated. In some respects, this attitude is a myth, a term drawn from the social sciences. This concept means that many people believe something to be true but without much rational evaluation of whether it is. For example, the myth of the *golden past* suggests that people and life at an earlier period was much better than the present. In education, this myth is not about the substance of educating but about the process of making school decisions. What is this myth, a concept contrasting with school politics of the last half of the twentieth century?

Components of the Myth

At the core of this myth is the belief, shared by professionals and citizens alike, that politics and education should *not* be mixed. Indeed, education is apolitical, that is, not political. "There is no Republican or Democratic way to teach long division" is the way a wag once put it. Holding aside that problematic belief, why would this myth be accepted by educators? First, to be thought political might well bring disfavor from citizens who share a wide dislike of politics and politicians. Second, by holding this view educators provide a seemingly neutral view on a wide range of school matters and in questions of taxes and spending. That stance contrasts with that of agencies for other local departments seeking more resources.

What was the source of this apolitical myth? Early in the last century, a national political reform movement (i.e., Progressives) sought to eliminate the evils of local parties and politics (Goldman, 1956). In that period, it was a scene shot through with *bosses* and *machines,* loaded with patronage jobs and corrupt contracts. That movement had major results in changing party activity, and it also meant that some school stakeholders wanted to disassociate themselves from other public services with their political bases. In that period, teachers, administrators, and school board members were appointed through party leaders on the basis of loyalty, not honesty or competence, and that is patronage.

Many in the emerging profession of education had sought to isolate themselves from such control. Professionals gave great commitment to honesty, efficiency, and quality—unknown values to party partisans. Deans of education schools, university presidents, and others worked across the nation to create a new kind of schooling—a "closed system" (Iannaccone, 1967). Here, the model would be one of a *scientific* profession in which its members would be protected against the depredations of party life. The argument used widely was that teaching the young was not something left to the incompetence of party leaders, but made safe in the hands of neutral professionals.

This model adopted a new form of organization that was centralized, unlike the widespread decentralized school systems of big cities. Leadership in this new system would be the superintendent who headed the organization by seeking education reforms that had been developed in *ed schools* or in practice by leading superintendents. That leader was subject to a contract from a citywide board of education (many cities had numerous local boards then), and both sides would appoint the principals, and they would appoint the teachers. Note that this organizational model was borrowed from the corporation model emerging in large-scale business, with a chief executive officer, board of directors, plant managers, workers, and so on. All of this activity was carried out without reference to any aspect of political parties. The new model was not only *nonpartisan* but emphasized professionalism, which meant it led to efficiency and quality. That system would fend off corruption, dishonesty, favoritism, and so on.

Viewed from the perspective of political science, all of this was simply another model of control, even though it was urged as being nonpolitical. For much of the last century, this model dominated American education, and its source emanated from the requirements of ed schools, administrator groups, teacher colleges, and so on. Further, its textbooks for trainees urged this model as the only path to salvation of the soul of education. Behind the sheen of professionalism was a method of controlling all aspects of schooling with a structure of educational ideology. It is control that needs focusing on here, and it is this quality that suggests a myth of being nonpolitical.

More pragmatically, relative advantages existed for professionals holding this attitude for there was much to gain from it. The higher status and salaries that members achieved from the public became evident over time; by 2000 superintendent salaries typically exceeded that of other local officials, sometimes more than the state governor. Also, the tighter control of its members and students had strengthened its organizational unity. The myth that only schools had this unique function of nonpartisan decision making stood in contrast with the eager search for public funds from voters or local governments by other municipal agencies. Given the practical factors behind this myth, it is no surprise that public education had a continuing support from the public and professionals alike for much of the twentieth century.

Voter Support and Professional Control

Why would this set of attitudes be termed a myth? Partly, the reason lies in the realization that this model was itself a method of control—namely, professional control of resources and values within the school system. Just as the old party control model had defined who got certain resources, so the new model substituted yet another. Recall that in both models decisions were made about the distribution of funds and personnel and the emphasis focused on special values (loyalty versus proficiency). Earlier we noted that control of values and policies were the central *political* aspects of decision making. Progressive reformers had urged support of this new model in terms of honesty, efficiency, quality, and nonpartisanship. However, this emphasis did not change the fact that it was still a political model of decision making. That is why a myth is sometimes defined as being true—or not.

A second problem with this myth lies in the potential for democratic control that could be exercised against professionals through the voters in elections to boards or referenda. This was a possible entry into decision making through the voters themselves. The potential in school referenda was often steered by professionals' views of what was best for voters' children. At school board elections, those elected were primarily supporters of professional views of schooling, and they were responsive to what they were told. The outcome was that a professional model of control over education policy settled in across the thousands of American school districts.

Challenges to the Myth

However, in decades of the twentieth century, other groups appeared with other views of schooling such as those noted in Table 11.1. Different issues and differing stands raised by these stakeholders challenged professional decisions. In the resulting turbulence, these new groups thrust themselves forward through referenda or board elections at the local level or through legislation at the state and federal levels. Combined, these new forces constituted the system shock phenomenon discussed earlier. Where once superintendents were benevolent autocrats, where educators alone defined state curricula, and where teachers narrowly defined the societal world of students, others now appeared—both professional and citizen—to offer a wider view of control over such issues. Professionals, who once held a unitary view of their work, split asunder into teacher, principal, and superintendent organizations; some of these even became supporters of some reform due to their disappointment with existing school policies.

In this pattern of challenge across the nation after 1960, not all districts or states acted in unison. However, one by one most underwent a change that constituted a system shock. These patterns of challenge may be seen in the following model that developed through time:

- A citizen's disappointment expressed to a teacher over a policy's operations, say poor reading tests is discounted by the teacher.
- Group mobilization of such disappointment over reading is presented to local boards, but reform proposals are discounted by the superintendent.
- Groups coalesce to urge the state legislature to change reading practices to enhance students' ability: State lobbies of teachers, administrators, and reading specialists object because most students are doing well, but some reading teachers do agree that change is needed based on their experiences.
- Citizen losers at the state level appeal for a new federal law or new regulations of the U.S. Department of Education designed to enhance reading abilities: Some professional groups appear to challenge such change, and other teachers support this change.
- At some stage, state or federal laws emerge changing reading practices: Changes emerge in ed schools for new trainees in coursework and textbooks, local and state curricula are altered to meet this change, and some appear as champions of the change.

This simplified model of only one change typifies the political interaction of the earlier model of change: policy disappointment, citizen challenge, new policy, and administration/implementation into practices. Clearly, though, not all challenges followed precisely these stages, for much interactive effect occured from one stage to another. However, if this change is seen as being multiplied many times across many policy areas, we can understand the scope of this system shock that shattered the professional myth. In this process, professional control was intermixed with citizen influences working through the normal, democratic channels of policymaking.

A Look Ahead

The end result in the twenty-first century on controlling school policy is unclear. From the perspective of the superintendent or school board, their decisional powers are squeezed from the top by state and federal oversight over an ever increasing array of school policies. On the other hand, they are also squeezed from the bottom by the power of teacher organizations, by the actions of community groups, and by the resulting turbulence over the question of education for what. Even this dilution of professional power is affected by the turbulence coming from local politics. Thus, an appointment by one board is later diluted by the election of a different board with different goals, catching the administrator between cross-currents of opinion from different groups. As noted earlier, one sign of such turbulence is the increasing turnover in holding office.

Yet the professional model has not disappeared from the scene. Their voices are heard, if not always followed, at all arenas for making decisions. Locally, an effective superintendent can lead the community to accept new programs, if limited, or can play the political game among many groups in order to mobilize them behind his or her goals. Principals can introduce a new program by an effective outreach to the community, as can teachers. The professional views of such groups are heard at state and federal levels when new policies are under consideration, especially when they are combined. Their experience administering new policies provides an empirical basis for evaluating them in reality that is studied by scholars or bureaucrats. So the picture is not just one of nonprofessional control, but rather one of strong professional leadership mixed with considerable input by citizen groups.

This mixed model of educational decision making is similar to what has happened to professions other than education in recent decades. For lawyers, doctors, planners, or child care specialists, citizen or consumer input has become a regular source in making policy and in evaluating it. Consequently, citizen voices are now heard, not ignored, and their judgments of effects are a significant indicator of policy success or failure.

Summary

It is clear from this introductory chapter that the concept of understanding the making of school policy is now much more complicated than it was forty to fifty years ago. Under the older myth of being apolitical, professionals today face a complex of sources of opinion on the who, what, when, and how of schooling. Education policymaking has come to fit the norm of policymaking for *other* types of policy (Wirt, 1981). If a president wished to cure cancer with federal programs within the next decade, he would have to listen to power holders in private and public realms of the American society: oncologists and cancer patients, private research firms, pharmaceutical companies, state health officials, hospital directors—the list goes on of those needed to consult to achieve agreement. The result is that unlike the conditions early in the last century, when there was a singular view of education, today a multitude of voices with some authority is attempting to define this policy. It is a vision, not from a single voice, but a cacophony of sounds, signifying and accomplishing much. In that context then, educational decision making at different levels of government shares this political outlook in which professional and citizen views intermix.

REFERENCES

Clifford, G., & Guthrie, J. (1988). *Ed school.* Chicago: University of Chicago Press.

Cortez, A. (2003, January). The emerging majority, *IDRA Newsletter,* XXX, 1–2.

Cuban, L. (1985). Conflict and leadership in the superintendency. *Phi Delta Kappan, 67,* 28–30.

Goldman, E. (1956). *Rendezvous with destiny.* New York: Vintage.

Hodgkinson, H. (1995, January 18). A true nation of the world. *Education Week,* p. 32.

Iannaccone, L. (1967). *Politics in education.* New York: Center for Applied Research in Education.

Iannaccone, L., & Lutz, F. (1970). *Politics, power, and policy.* Columbus, OH: Merrill.

Kerr, N. (1964). The school board as an agency of legitimacy. *Sociology of Education, 38,* 34–59.

Kingdon, J. (1995). *Agendas, alternatives, and public policies* (2nd ed.). New York: Harper Collins.

Mazzoni, T. (1995). State policymaking and school reform. In J. Scribner & D. Layton (Eds.), *The study of educational politics* (pp. 53–74). London: Falmer.

Portner, J. (1994, October 12). Grassroots warrior waging battle over sex-ed curriculum. *Education Week,* p. 5.

Tyack, D. (1974). *The one best system.* Cambridge, MA: Harvard University Press.

U.S. Census Bureau (2002). *Statistical Abstract of the United States.* Washington, DC: U.S. Census Bureau.

Wirt, F. (1981). Professionalism and political conflict: A developmental model. *Journal of Public Policy, 1,* 1–23.

Wirt, F. (1997). *We isn't what we was: Civil rights in the new south.* Durham, NC: Duke University Press, Part II.

Wirt, F., & Kirst, M. (1997). *The political dynamics of American education.* Berkeley, CA: McCutchan.

Wirt, F., & Kirst, M. (2001). *The political dynamics of American education* (2nd ed.). Berkeley, CA: McCutchan.

12 The Local System of Policymaking

This chapter is the first of three to examine policymaking at three levels—local, state, and national. How the levels of policymaking are alike and different are reviewed throughout. Yet it is clear that at each level there are distinctive approaches to understanding educational policymaking, just as there are some similarities. In this chapter, we focus on four aspects of local school politics: individual access to policy, group access, school boards, and school-site politics. In short, we examine voting, pressure groups, board activities, and *micropolitics.*

Individual Access to Decision Making

Models of how decisions are made in political systems are roughly of three types: populist, elite, and a mixture. The *populist* model is a view that most Americans hold of their democracy; namely, the people vote to select representatives who will reflect their policy viewpoints. The *elite* model is that of small groups, knowledgeable about the policy system, who restrict popular input in order to forward their own views. Finally, there is a third model in which citizen and elite interact collaboratively to make policy.

To review the role of citizens on policymaking, we focus first on the populist model that has long been linked to two uses in school politics: school board elections and referenda. Each use incorporates the basic democratic process of voting to carry out the beliefs of "education for what."

School Board Elections

For this model to be valid in operation, there should be a considerable turnout by voters to elect candidates to the school boards. In this fashion, the board should be the pivot between the professional and the parents. However, research on voting overwhelmingly agreed: *Most eligible citizens do not vote in these elections.* Indeed, election turnout is weak for all levels of government. The presidential contest is about 50 percent, and then the figures decrease in a cascade down through congressional, state, and local government—and then school boards. At this level, the turnout figure is about 12 percent, although an especially heated contest, say over desegregation or school failures, increases that figure—but not by much. Research also shows that turnout increases with the status level of a district, that is, the higher figure in one is linked to a higher figure in the other. As with other studies in political science, higher status means higher interest in politics, higher turnout, and more use of other political means to affect the nature of the policy system.

How could that be for school elections? Political science explanations differ. The nonpartisan quality of such elections provides no political parties that could provide a cue for voters. Another reason may be that voters prefer the professionals to run the schools and thus think they need little help from the voter. A third reason is that issues around school elections have limited visibility or interest to most voters, and thus their indifference results in low turnout. A final reason may be that the candidates are not well enough known for voters to decide whom to support. Clearly then, this populist model lacks validity in reality when far too many citizens do not participate; we return later to condition this conclusion (Teixeira, 1992).

How do we find candidates for board elections? All political systems require a recruitment process to select leadership. This process is not random, for there is a winnowing process, so that few are called to seek office. Laws restrict entry only to those above a certain age and to those holding district residence—massive barriers to recruitment. Getting past these, however, requires access to certain resources, partly campaign money, of course, but also awareness and knowledge about school issues. So few citizens possess these qualities, and especially important is a record of community activity in civic affairs, business, politics, or schools. Again, such activities are most often linked to higher status, all of which provide training grounds for participation.

The qualities described previously inhere mostly in the middle class or higher status groups with little involvement by workers or the poor. When the Progressive movement early in the last century adopted election reforms for schools, worker representation dropped substantially within several decades; George Counts' (1927) classic study in 1920 demonstrated that shift. These restraints continued in the decades since. As Table 12.1 shows, board qualities at the end of the twentieth century were not much different. The qualities of the members were male (but declining proportion), white, over 40 years of age, and higher income. In short, this table shows that unrepresentative boards are pervasive, thereby raising questions about the validity of the populist model. It would seem that schools would reflect only the views of this one group, always a minority in the total population.

That judgment is problematic, however. Despite these qualities, boards have shown themselves open to dealing with large-scale frustrations by citizens. Regularly, advocates of new ideas have emerged to create the waves of reforms on a range of policies. For example, note reform waves for choice, charter, curricula changes, family values, and so on. Indeed, this increased policy activity by boards had led in part to the challenge to superintendents that produced higher turnover, as noted in the previous chapter. Indeed, the worst situation for the superintendent is to find the board that selected him has been changed by a succeeding election to those with different, if not contrary, views on school policy.

TABLE 12.1 Demographics of American School Board Members

	1987 to 1988	1997 to 1998
Gender		
Male	61.0	54.1
Female	39.0	39.1
No response	n/a	6.8
Ethnic background		
African American	3.6	6.5
White	94.4	81.3
Hispanic	1.5	3.1
American Indian	0.1	1.0
Asian	0.2	0.3
Other/no response	0.2	7.8
Age		
Under 25	0.1	0.7
26–35	6.9	3.7
36–40	19.4	6.1
41–50	41.8	46.6
51–60	20.9	24.2
Over 60	10.9	14.6
No response	n/a	4.1
Income		
Under $20,000	5.0	0.3
$20,000–$39,999	28.0	10.6
$40,000–$59,999	32.4	15.3
$60,000–$79,999	18.4	21.0
$80,000–$99,999	6.3	17.3
More than $100,000	9.4	28.0
No response	n/a	7.5
Where board members live		
Small town	28.6	24.5
Suburb	27.6	37.4
Rural area	25.9	15.7
Urban area	11.0	7.1
Mixed (combination of responses checked)	n/a	13.6
Other	n/a	0.7
No response	n/a	0.7

Viewing the total picture of board elections, though, it is clear that it is used little by voters in elections, although a sudden outburst of feeling can be transferred into these elections. However, if there is grave dissatisfaction about educational services, the board provides a channel for funneling it into creating new policies and members. For example, as Iannaccone and Lutz (1970) found in the years after World War II in the suburbs of Los Angeles, new arrivals found opposition from superintendents and boards to their ideas about better education. The newcomers were ignored until they had enough votes to replace, first, the board and then the superintendent with new personnel reflecting the views of the new arrivals. In most cases, though, voters see these elections as having low visibility and the voters have low interest in the whole process.

We can combine the Los Angeles story and the general finding by noting the differences within communities over schools faced by conflict. What are the theoretical conditions for board and superintendent? As Table 12.2 shows, when dissatisfaction is high with the board but not the superintendent, the outcome most likely leads to board member changes. However, if dissatisfaction is high or moderate with these policy agents, the board shifts to an arena in which differences are worked out. Finally, though, when dissatisfaction is high with these two agencies, the outcome is superintendent turnover. The last case describes the Los Angeles suburb noted previously.

If we shift the focus from the board to the voters, why do they participate, if at all? Despite the general finding of voter disinterest, there was a great interest in citizen participation in making school policy at the end of the twentieth century. This participation was not simply in voting but also in group activity. Of those who participated, many sought *instrumental* changes, that is, specific policy changes. Typical was the reaction by African American or Hispanic parents to get more of their groups on these boards so as to influence the school system. Another example was the effort to obtain a school choice program to deal with the alleged problems of public education.

That surge, however, did not reflect the usual norm of inactivity of citizens and of voting on school matters. Citizens may have opinions on a range of issues,

TABLE 12.2   Dissatisfaction and Challenge: Three Outcomes

Focus of Dissatisfaction			
Board	Superintendent and Board	Superintendent	**Outcome**
High	High	Low	Board turnover
High	High	Moderate	Arena-like decisions
Low	High	High	Involuntary superintendent turnover

Source: Modified from Roger Rada, "Community Dissatisfaction and School Governance," originally published in *Planning and Changing,* 15 (1984): 246 and reprinted with permission of *Planning and Changing.*

as reflected every August in the Gallup Poll reported in the *Phi Delta Kappan*. Yet that does not mean they *act* on them; indeed, the evidence that they do much of anything at all is found in records of their weak voting. Of course, community dissatisfaction may lead to an occasional uprising of "Throw the rascals out!" but not that often.

A more subtle interpretation of these data appears in the insight of Boyd (1976), namely, that sophisticated boards and superintendents seek to avoid the outcomes noted in Table 12.2. They do this by adopting an awareness of the subtle existence of a "zone of tolerance" about their activities within which they are free to act, but beyond which the community objects and causes problems. Within that zone, these agents can operate with minimum voter input or challenge. However, to move beyond the zone of tolerance, to take stands on issues that affront many in the community, gives rise to challenge. Knowing this, these agents seek to avoid voter criticism and avoid losing office. The theory seems satisfying, but it is hard to prove or disprove as it rests on the cognitive dimensions of both voter and school members.

If the evidence is true about the school-world nonparticipation, what of the small groups who do participate in school policy, either by voting or by running for and serving on school boards? For those who do participate the experience has many positive effects. A review of those participating in school work, especially on boards, found there was a positive effect that was cumulative. That is, "the more people participate, the greater will be the impact on them, and the greater the impact, the more likely it will take the form of enhanced growth and development" (Salisbury, 1980, p. 177). This group seems to reach beyond the personal agenda of work and play to serve the community, although most are drawn from the more educated population. Yet at the neighborhood level, participation in school policymaking by those less schooled also seems to have an enhancing effect on their lives.

Referenda and Policymaking

The American practice of letting citizens vote on policy issues, an anomaly in world democracies, varies considerably among the states, but it is much more widespread on voting for school bond or levy issues at the local level. Involvement here provides a record of citizen moods about schools. Historically, support for such financial issues in referenda has been substantial, reflecting again the traditional public support of schools. In the last third of the twentieth century, however, that mood changed abruptly to rejection of such referenda. Where in 1965 across the states, three in four financial referenda were approved, two decades later in 1986 only one in three passed (Wirt & Kirst, 1997, p. 116). This drying up of local support has been one of many signals of the system shock for education.

There is an historical irony here, for the origin of the school referenda was the Progressive movement that sought to counter the corrupt party control of schools. "The cure for democracy is more democracy" was their battle cry, and thus letting voters decide on school finances would bypass party leaders. Also, some business conservatives thought it important to control this democratic zeal by requiring that such bond issues require an extraordinary majority to pass. By the century's end, however, that hope of broad citizen support of finances fell afoul of the challenges we have noted earlier.

Another issue in referenda is, Why do citizens vote and who are they? Answering such queries leads to differences in motivations, for they show that voting is dependent on several factors of the person or the group qualities:

- Group characteristics, such as status—higher status equals more support
- Personal qualities, such as age—younger equals more support
- School district qualities, such as amount of politicization—greater means lower support
- Psychological characteristics, such as alienation from schools—higher means lower support

We explore just one of these qualities in this section. In recent years, evidence grew that *older* voters opposed school referenda. It was not surprising that in areas with large proportions of the elderly, such as Florida, school referenda are overwhelmingly defeated. Explanations are various:

- Rationally, the elders may find that in their life cycle they now have little use for schools and so withdraw support. "I paid my taxes while the kids grew up, but now I don't need schools for them."
- They may be responding to the widely publicized alienation over hearing about the *failures* of public schools. "Schools were so much better in my time than today."
- They may subscribe to the growing distrust of government itself, an issue pushed strongly by many conservative politicians. "Private education in the schools of my choice does much better than do public schools."
- The economic explanation may be that at this stage of life they have less disposable income except for their own lives. "I live on a fixed income in retirement with just so much income that can't cover school taxes."

Voter support for schools thus presents a contradiction. There still exists an underlying support for public schools. Polls in the 1990s reported this support in general, while noting also that such support was even higher for one's own local schools (reviewed later). Indeed, when school leaders were compared with those from other institutions, schools outranked all others except for doctors (Piele, 1983). However, the audience for public schools is shrinking traceable to three populations with few if any children: the singles, the young married without children, and the elderly. Moreover, the small number of children removed from public schools to enter choice or charter systems also shrinks that audience. School support for referenda, then, is still high with middle-class or more affluent parents, but we are some distance removed from the scene after World War II and before when professionals could count on a large, satisfied audience for public schools.

The Pressure Group Context of Local Schools

In the normal context of policymaking, the individual means less than the group to which he or she belongs. The individual alone may mean little to policymakers, but many individuals clearly do think they mean much. A farmer complaining about a rule from the U.S. Department of Agriculture may not be able to change it, but spokespersons for the Farm Bureau on the same matter may well cause its change. In short, while advocates of the democratic system speak well of the individual whose interests are to be met in policymaking, it is more likely that the group's interests are heard and acted on. This concept is the pressure group context of local school politics. More broadly, the pressure group serves to funnel group interests into the policy system. Even more, they also transform such pressure by reshaping it to mobilize support of officials; indeed, they can also provide information for evaluation of a policy down the road.

Rise of Narrow Interests

There are intriguing questions about this pressure context. Why do individuals join such groups? Clearly they get something from it; indeed, some may benefit from pressure activity *without* joining, namely the *free rider* problem (Olson, 1965). Others, however, may join the group to share other benefits, that is, receiving health care. Many others may join just for solidarity, namely, the psychological reward from belonging to a group of like-minded members. However, the interest for most joiners lies mainly with this *quid pro quo* of shared benefits.

Not surprisingly, the number of educational pressure groups has expanded during the last of the twentieth century. Before that time, such groups were focused on a single source, the National Education Association. It originally shared concerns for both administrators and teachers, reflecting a *unitary* value that underlay the professional syndrome discussed in the previous chapter. However, that unitary interest faded about 1960 when superintendents, principals, and other administrators were excluded from membership. Teachers organized for collective bargaining and others sought different benefits. That breakup of the old National Educational Association contributed to the turbulence of educational policies we have noted. From this unitary pressure for making policy, a pluralism of diverse groups has arisen that is focused on much narrower issues.

The reforms in school policy noted earlier had developed such narrow groups, for example, desegregation, bilingual, compensatory, and special education programs. The support of any such group is not for education in general, but for the special program. A similar growth also emerged for ideological pressure groups, seeking to maintain a set of values that should be part of school operations. These groups constitute what scholars define as *social movements,* large-scale organizations designed to further goals set in class, religion, or race. They include the women's liberation movement and such organizations as National Organization for Women. Others include Christian Coalition groups supporting school prayer, opposing certain library books, or teaching evolution. While national in organization, these ideological groups focus on local cases to achieve their goals; they do so by linking their ideas to sympathetic members of the local community. Older groups supporting education in general, such as the Parent Teacher Association and American Association of University Women, have declined in numbers while those for the narrower groups have increased.

This spread of narrow groups context and specific goals increases the number of advocates in policymaking that face the local administrator or teacher. Where once these professionals dealt with a Parent Teacher Association made up of sympathetic supporters and dealt with minor issues, today they must face a kaleidoscope of multiple but narrow demands for the schools to act on *now*. In the process, the administrator becomes a political negotiator among those competing claims for values and resources from groups that share little unitary interest in education.

Behind all these changes lies another understanding of education. The variety of groups now on the scene reflect the variety of American values that often clash in policymaking. For example, both civil libertarians and church groups are diametrically opposed over the provision on religious worship. Further, given this difference and its potential for conflict, there is the need in policymaking for making coalitions of small groups in order to win. That function, found also in nonschool policy, often relies on political parties to resolve conflict through compromise. However, political parties have taken little interest in school, yet the need for conflict resolution still exists. That need is often met by school officials and local groups. The administrator needs to negotiate among such groups to achieve not a consensus—that is 100 percent—but a majority in the form of a compromise policy for the schools.

Superintendents, Pressures, and Outcomes

Superintendents were aware of the rise in prominence of such community groups. Their awareness of this growth is reflected in Table 12.3, which summarizes a national survey of superintendents that reflects "more" or "much more" demands from three types of groups: traditional (e.g., teacher organizations), citizens (e.g.,

TABLE 12.3   Superintendents Saying More or Much More to Increased Demands on the Office

Group Type	Percent	Group Type	Percent	Group Type	Percent
Traditional		*Citizen*		*Officials*	
Business	48	Clientele	52	Elected local	34
Labor	62	Minorities	50	State	50
		Citizen opinion	61	Federal	54

Source: Frederick Wirt and Leslie Christovich, "Administrators' Perceptions of Policy Influence: Conflict Management Styles and Roles," *Educational Administration Quarterly*, Vol. 25, No. 1, pp. 5–35, copyright © 1989 by the University Council for Educational Administration. Reprinted by Permission of Sage Publications, Inc.

need to improve reading), and officials (e.g., state inspection of local school affairs). This study also noted that when superintendents were asked to specify exactly how many groups increased demands on them, the modal number was six of ten possibilities.

It follows that when community conflict arises from many local groups, the superintendent's position is quite different than when they are quiescent. One variable is the intensity of this official's views on matters involving community conflict. Not being a blank tablet on which the community can write, the administrator can interact. Table 12.4 suggests the likely outcomes of superintendent–community interactions. This official most likely is overcome (i.e., loses) when she or he opposes what the community is seeking; all other outcomes mean that one's own values are sustained (i.e., win option). If one's intensity is high, while the community's is also high and opposed, the superintendent's removal is a likely outcome. One is better off when one's intensity is low. For if the community group's intensity is high, one can simple comply in its implementation; if the community intensity is low, one is left alone to focus on internal routines.

Finally, the superintendent's stance toward conflict is shaped by his or her personal reaction to it. As with any conflict in human behavior, whether a schoolyard conflict or one between nations, one can either fight or flee from that confrontation. First, the superintendent seeking to avoid confrontation can simply preside over the conflict without taking any stance. Second, if one is assertive in taking stands, one can fight to reflect the professional view of school leadership. Finally, one can seek a compromise between oneself and the community to facilitate policy resolution.

We know little of how these roles work out in reality. How many fall into which type? Does it differ with the kind of community? With the kind of policy issue? With the age of the superintendent? Further, the role taken in the theoretical analysis assumes a broad community view, when in reality the local scene may be a series of narrow policy conflicts on which different segments of the community

TABLE 12.4 Superintendent Outcomes versus Community Values

Superintendent Value Intensity	Community Conflict	
	High	*Low*
High		
Outcome		
Complies	Win	Win
Opposes	Lose	Win
Low		
Outcome		
Complies	Win	Win
Opposes	Win	Win

are involved. For this official, the pressure of local opinion is a matter of juggling among different balls held by these community segments. Letting one fall may not be disastrous, but too many falls may well lead to a fall from office.

In sum, this increasingly complex, local policymaking in the pressure context comes close to a more sophisticated model of democracy. Working through local group associations, not through political parties, citizens can mobilize support from others, can link to state and national affiliates concerned with this policy, and can use all the standard methods of arousing community concern to achieve a policy solution. The professional can no longer introduce new ideas and expect community support. Rather, she or he must negotiate among these groups to arrive at a policy that allows some role in introducing new ideas. In that regard, the role has become political in terms described earlier. Members may be disgusted at this change (those reported in Table 12.3 were consistently) and may yearn for the earlier day of the benevolent autocrat. Nevertheless, the democratic impulses of our society in recent decades have reached into this policy area. Anyhow, the earlier superintendents did not think they were autocrats, and their citizens may not have thought of them as benevolent.

The School Board Context of Policy

Amid the community, rural or city, the school board is the pivot of formal policymaking between professionals and citizens. We need to review this board's composition, decisional rules, and recent criticisms as an ineffective institution. After all, school boards have presided over the alleged failures of public schools in recent decades, so at some point questions can be raised about their utility.

Board History and Composition

The recent characteristics of backgrounds of American school board members in Table 12.1 show that boards are not representative of the American people. The Progressive reforms eliminated much of the American variety, replacing it with people who were middle class, not workers, with good incomes, and white. Yet these boards serve several major purposes. One of these is that the perception of the school may not be that of the professionals, as Table 12.5 points out. Superintendents think better of schools in general or locally than do board presidents or the general public. Even when the focus shifts to one's local schools, all grading improves for all three groups, but are still different.

That difference of opinion opens the way for democratic policymaking. Where once the board position was almost symbolic, today its members must learn about a wide range of matters in the schools' finances, programs and curricula, buildings, and so on. Where once school boards accepted and even legitimated professional decisions, today they are deeply involved in conflict and often querulous about what the professional is doing. Where before at best they created an implicit zone of tolerance outside which professionals should not traverse,

TABLE 12.5   Board and Superintendent Grading of Schools

Grade	Percent Giving Grade		
	Board President	Superintendent	General Public
Grades for national public schools as a whole			
A	2	5	3
B	31	66	20
C	51	25	48
D	9	1	13
Fail	2	—	3
Don't know	5	3	13
Grades for public schools in your community			
A	23	32	9
B	56	58	31
C	18	8	34
D	1	1	10
Fail	0	—	4
Don't know	1	—	12

Source: National Center for Education Information, "Profiles of School Board Presidents in the U.S." Washington, DC: U.S. Department of Education, 1989.

today they cover the waterfront in great detail on most matters. All this makes for a messy picture of school policymaking compared with the earlier professional control, but there is nothing neat about other democratic matters either.

Criticism and Support of School Boards

In time, some observers came to question this board's utility as they were seen as weakening in the face of reform efforts and the increasing turbulence of policy demands. The problem with this criticism is selective perception, that is, seeing only one part of a larger system. The sense of alleged failure stems from individual problems faced, sometimes by a few schools, which is extrapolated to the whole system. Voters, moved by this perception—and perceptions are more important than realities in political life—seek to change the school board. Of course, as the problem may be massive, a new board can do little. That outcome produces even more voter dissatisfaction. Consequently, across the nation at the end of the twentieth century this kind of frustrating cycle was found in many policy areas.

On the other hand, did schools *fail* if they were judged by other than media stories? Student test results, a very complex picture indeed, suggest strongly that any decrease in the 1960s gave way to stronger results in later decades, of which the public knew very little (Berliner & Biddle, 1995). Another source of information on schools comes from those both close to and removed from school operations, namely, the general public. That survey of attitudes is found in a 1989 national survey by the U.S. Department of Education reported in Table 12.5. The attitudes about grading schools by board presidents, superintendents, and the general public in general versus local schools suggest some important points. The superintendent thinks better of schools, whether national or local, than do the boards. Further, and possibly just as significant, is that when evaluating "schools in your own community," the appreciation improves significantly. Where only one in three board presidents gave high grades to schools nationally, the figure is four in five for one's own schools; the figures for superintendents are seven in ten versus nine in ten. Compare much of that support from those closest to schools with the general lack of support for schools in the nation and at home. The last finding would be most affected by the episodic accounts of schools found in the media; after all, those who are closer to local schools find them much better. Finally, scholars' evaluations, while critical in some part, do support the utility of these boards in transferring citizen preferences into local policymaking (First & Walberg, 1992; Danzberger, Kirst, & Usdam, 1992).

Board Decision Making

How is policymaking actually carried out? There are three rough categories of demands for policies facing any decisional group, public or private. Some demands get no action at all due to lack of supporters or of officials' need for action. Another type of demand consists of negotiations among interested parties to reach a compromise. The third demand, however, requires a prompt response, either because there is a crisis that must be acted on immediately, or because these demands are simply formal authorization of decisions made earlier.

Focusing on the most contentious of the demands, namely that involving a negotiation, and assuming that the board has heard all subcommittee reports and interested individuals, how does the board make the decision? That query may sound as if there are many answers, but in reality there are probably only two ways of doing it. Peterson (1976), in evaluating Chicago school policies, has described these as the "pluralist" and the "unitary." The essential themes and basic components of each are set out in Table 12.6.

Essentially these two methods focus on political and ideological interests. In pluralist bargaining, a school organization or an electoral group involves broad community group issues such as race or class. While this decisional method focuses on diversity and opposition, the second decisional mode—unitary—presumes that the group shares much in common that reflects a unity of spirit and action. This method has often been contrasted in the theories of organizational or rational decision making and is featured in that literature.

This more complex view of school boards suggests that the institution continues to have a key role in local decision making. Increasingly, though, many observers who favor the unitary view of decisions are faced with the rancor and

TABLE 12.6 **Dual Decision Modes for School Boards**

Pluralist: A contest among groups sharing little in common
Pluralist mode: Each board member represents a narrow group, intent on defending the interests of that group, e.g., budget making
Ideological mode: A contest among those representing a broad group to defend a class or race, e.g., principal appointments

Unitary: A union among groups sharing some qualities
Organizational: Decisions from board members desiring to promote broad objectives of the school, e.g., maintain professional standards against challenge by citizens
Rational: Decision by board members agreeing on school objectives to be used later to judge new policies, e.g., definition of non-discipline.

Source: Abstracted from Paul Peterson, *School Politics: Chicago Style.* Chicago: University of Chicago Press, 1976.

division of pluralist bargaining, especially in big cities. For this and other reasons, the waves of reform noted throughout this book gave little attention to their role. Such reforms have focused more on substantive policies and structures and less on process. Sometimes boards are seen as part of the problem needing reform; some even argue that boards should be removed from the policy process, because they are said to block state reforms. As a result, recent reforms focused either on the state or on the local school site, bypassing and omitting the board's role. Yet many boards have begun to enact many reforms on their own before state action.

Positive Roles of the Board

Moreover, the continuing use of citizens of this institution cannot be ignored in recognizing the worth of this institution. At one level, it reflects the traditional ways that citizens think about governing, for they exhibit legislative, executive, and judicial behavior. Legislatively, they annually adopt budgets, pass regulations, and make other policies, as noted previously. They also provide another legislative connection with the citizen who needs a service, namely the board's *complaint catching.* In executive terms, they oversee the execution of school policy, such as approving contracts for services or materials. Further, as executives they gather information on how well a policy is doing, an evaluation function. Judicially, they deal with student discipline problems (i.e., suspensions and expulsions); often it is the last appeal body before parents go to the courts.

To become more effective in the face of numerous problems suggested by the reform waves, boards might well reform certain aspects that had been set a century earlier in the Progressive era (Carol et al., 1986). Some problems clearly require a change to meet new policy needs, for example:

- Providing children with services linked to municipal governing agencies;
- Linking state curriculum reform based on national standards to local capacities;

- Periodic review of the board's abilities to meet emerging policy needs;
- Movement toward election at-large, rather than by districts (in 1996, 53,000 were selected by the first and 30,000 by the latter);
- The role of the board in personnel matters, including the role of teacher organizations.

Micropolitics within Local Schools

Across the complexities of local policymaking, it is important to recall that the same prevails *within* the school site itself. Recall the earlier definition of politics as a competition over public resources in order to reinforce particular values. We have seen this political process detailed in this chapter, but it will be helpful to note that the same competition arises within the school site itself among the different stakeholders in that school. For example, with only limited funds, what department gets more of the new book budget—social studies or science? With budgets for only a few paraprofessionals, which faculty members get them? Of the principal's limited agenda, where would one want the support of the Parent Teacher Association? Among the Parent Teacher Association and community groups, what preference should exist to hire different ethnic members as faculty?

Basic Concept of Micropolitics

Some salient points exist in these illustrative questions. They involve site-based decisions over allocations in situations in which resources are limited, not expansive. Each stakeholder has a clear set of reasons—or interests—to support an answer. Such matters involve a kind of politics at this level, limited resources fought over by a few people who feel very intensely about the matter. These participants include principal, teachers, parents, students, and others (e.g., central office). Finally, the policymaking agency may be diverse—a principal, a faculty subcommittee, an entire faculty, parents, and so on—but a decision must be made.

In these illustrations we get a glimpse of the concept of *micropolitics,* namely resource conflict among limited participants pitched to the school-site level (Ball, 1987; Blasé & Anderson, 1995). As with the broader type of politics discussed in this chapter, common qualities exist at the site level. There are different stakes, interactions, strategies, and styles of play—all to optimize winning in policies.

At the core of micropolitics is the process of personal negotiation without using the force of public authority. Local politics elsewhere involves votes in elections or at board meetings that authoritatively settle disagreements over resources and values. In the case of micropolitics, however, two stakeholders exist, for example, each wanting some resource from the other, to be obtained not by authority but by trading one's own resources. This policymaking consists of interpersonal exchanges of offers and counteroffers, and the purpose is to minimize what one surrenders to secure the optimum from the other. An agreed policy then involves both sides getting some goods by mutual acceptance.

To illustrate this, let us focus on the most common interaction found between principal and teachers. What does the principal want and what do teachers have to offer? In general, the principal wants professional material resources (e.g., carrying out the lesson plans), while the teachers want esteem for their work. The first seeks recognition from some agency outside the site, while the second can support that goal. Or the principal seeks recognition of his leadership within the school site, and teachers can provide support. The administrator seeks autonomy in carrying out professional work, while teachers want autonomy within their classrooms. The leader wishes not to enforce district rules too harshly, while teachers want some freedom from them.

In short, at the heart of the interactions that follow a set of *exchanges* takes place. How do they proceed? For example, the principal wants to be sure that teachers are carrying out their instructional responsibilities through some kind of evaluation system; but teachers quite often resist the process as an intrusion on their autonomy. The result of a negotiation, often implied, may be that the principal pays little attention to the evaluation while the teachers support him in his leadership endeavors. The result has been competing interests yielding through negotiation into a compromise involving optimal (not maximal) outcomes that both sides accept.

Several implications are inherent in this exchange:

- Public resources have been informally allocated by decisions—the core essence of politics;
- This interaction focuses on negotiating competing interests through the process of persuasion;
- Each side uses strategies to achieve their goals;
- The result is a compromise acceptable to both;
- Finally, in most micropolitics, someone other than these two stakeholders may well have to pay an additional cost for the decision. Thus, the incompetent teacher is allowed to stay in the classroom (i.e., students pay the cost), while central office and superintendent do not know of this cost.

The Principal: Pressure and Leadership

As noted previously, the principal sits amid a flow of pressures. The central office and superintendent impose directives that can limit site discretion or autonomy. Neighborhood groups want something—often vague—that is imposed on the principal to handle. Teachers focus on better pay and working conditions. External professional standards of administration set goals about good education. These groups may well have divergent goals that the principal is expected to achieve, and some he cannot escape (e.g., attendance reports). The unsurprising outcome is that many principals modify their own goals to compromise with the local pressure of school groups.

Consequently, the principal has to create strategies to cope with such pressures, that is, to manipulate the micropolitical environment to his or her goals. The principal may divide his or her opponents—classic strategy of all leadership. Contenders can be co-opted to weaken them. New issues may be raised—*red herrings*—to deflect these pressures. One can also control the information within the site; that is, knowledge is also power. Some other specific strategies are involved, for example:

- Control the agenda items
- Divert or postpone contrary recommendations
- Recruit the neutral stakeholders
- Create a false consensus by rearranging the arguments
- Even alter the minutes of group meetings

It should be clear from this listing that reform efforts from other levels can be checked or modified if the principal is reluctant. If the reforms are accepted, however, he or she can use these and the process of negotiation to move reforms along. However, imagine the difficulties of trying to control these subtle efforts by issuing mandates from the state or central office.

Leadership and the Principal

On the other hand, some principals shape their environment despite such pressures but are still able to lead their schools. *Leadership* refers to moving others to adopt one's own values or programs that change the system's goals. A relatively recent complex analysis (Wirt & Krug, 1998) in a national poll of principals sought to distinguish between leaders who follow the organization (i.e., the "maintainers") and those who seek to change school goals (the "leaders"). The study, using a range of dimensions of school policy and varied by personal qualities, found that leaders had distinctive qualities. Regardless of size of site or of personal qualities, they work harder, recruit faculty support for their goals, and work closely with superintendents having similar goals.

Beyond this world of maintainers and leaders are those principals who are burned out. The complexity of their tasks and strategies often leads to frustration, despite their best efforts. Also, growing community opinion about alleged failures is another weakening factor. On any given day, the barrage of requests for resources that are unmet, the proliferation of new demands that need to be explored, the push from the central office, all lead to frustration. Not surprising, then, many get out, not only from the school, but the educational system itself through early retirement; by 2000, there was a national shortage of persons to fill these principalships.

There are other actors in this micropolitical world of the school site, which we can only mention briefly here. Note that all are involved in the negotiations over exchanges of valued goods, along with attendant strategies. Figure 12.1 suggests the range of interactions among stakeholders. Imagine a line drawn as a linkage between a pair of them, such as, parents and teacher groups, and then add more lines between other pairs. When completed, such a graph would be very

School Board

Superintendent

Principal

Individual Teacher   Students

Teacher Groups —————————— Parents

Paraprofessionals   Neighborhood Groups

FIGURE 12.1   The Web of Interactions among Local Stakeholders

confusing, but it would also demonstrate the highly varied lines of political interaction in even the smallest school. Imagine further the kinds of useful strategies
that might inhere to enhance each partner in this dual relation. This *web* of site relationships forms the basis of the concept of micropolitics. Further, imagine such a
web across time, so that partners at an earlier period are in a different power relationship at a later time. This realization makes the politics of education, even at
the local school site, a complex analysis of school life.

Summary

It is striking to note that the diverse forms of local politics sketched in this chapter
are found in every 1 of the 14,000 school districts in the nation. Not surprising,
there are different patterns, for localities are not simply the result of cookie cutters.
Yet this diversity has two utilities, one for the principal or superintendent and another for the scholar of school politics. First, for any one seeking a principalship or
superintendency, it is important to receive ahead of time a rough sketch of these
forms of local school politics. That information, like all knowledge, provides a
map of how to use one's resources to be successful. For the scholar, though, this
diversity provides a great opportunity to test differences among these levels to
forward theory. Chapters 9 and 10 pick up the theme of superintendents and principals at work in today's society.

REFERENCES

Ball, S. (1987). *The micro politics of school management.*
London: Methuen.

Berliner, D., & Biddle, B. (1995). *The manufactured crisis.* Reading, MA: Addison-Wesley.

Blasé, J., & Anderson, G. (1995). *The micropolitics of
educational leadership.* New York: Teachers College Press.

Boyd, W. (1976). The public, the professionals, and
education policy making: Who governs? *Teachers College Record, 77,* 539–577.

Carol, L., Danzberger, J. McCloud, B., Cunningham,
L., Kirst, M., & Usdan, M. (1986). *School Boards:
Improving grassroots leadership.* Washington, DC:
Institute for Educational Leadership.

Counts, G. (1927). *The social composition of boards of education.* Chicago: University of Chicago Press.

Danzberger, J., Kirst, M., & Usdan, M. (1992). *Governing public schools.* Washington, DC: Institute for Educational Leadership.

First, P., & Walberg, H. (1992). *School boards.* Berkeley, CA: McCutchan.

Iannaccone, L., & Lutz, F. (Eds.). (1970). *Politics, powers, and policy.* Columbus, OH: Merrill.

Olson, M. (1965). *The logic of collective action.* New York: Schocken.

Peterson, P. (1976). *School politics: Chicago style.* Chicago: University of Chicago Press.

Piele, P. (1983). Public support for public schools: The past, the future, and the federal role. *Teachers College Record, 84*(3), 690–707.

Salisbury, R. (1980). *Citizen participation in the public schools.* Lexington, MA: Lexington.

Teixeira, R. (1992). *The disappearing American voter.* Washington, DC: Brookings.

Wirt, F., & Kirst, M. (1997). *The political dynamics of American education.* Berkeley, CA: McCutchan.

Wirt, F., & Krug, S. (1998). From leadership behavior to cognitions: A constructivist theory of U.S. principals. *Journal of Educational Administration, 36*(3), 229–248.

13 The State Level of Policymaking

While the variety of decision making at the local level seems complex, the state level is simpler to describe despite its recent growth. The constitutional key to education policy lies with the American states, not at the local level. When the original Constitution was accepted in 1789, there was no reference to school policy, nor was there any mention of such policy in state documents. What little schooling there was fell to churches or families designed to prepare the young to read the *Bible* or do simple arithmetic. Little of this was set out in public law.

However, over a half century later, when reforms were sought to make education compulsory, it was the states that initiated this policy. The state was exercising one of its *reserved* powers, left for the states and implied in the Tenth Amendment of the U.S. Constitution. For over a century after that, the state did remarkably little other than issuing broad goals and providing meager financial or material support. Even the chief state school officer was often a patronage appointment given to a long-time local superintendent. In short, from the mid-nineteenth century on, it was up to the local district to design and carry out schooling. The 1900 song about "School Days, school days, good old golden rule days...." was focused on a local school, most often the one-room type.

Against that picture of little action by the states, today the state is involved in setting specific goals, or *mandates,* employing a state bureaucracy closely linked to local schools that regularly reported to the state capitol on what they were doing. That state growth created an entire policymaking system in which the many interest groups of education are closely involved. Indeed, the states do so much for education that a comparison of their policies is a useful index to education in America. This framework of state growth of policymaking, new participants, regular implementation, and state comparisons forms the basis of this chapter.

Growth of the State System

The growth of the states in schooling proceeded at an uneven pace; even the acceptance of free public education as a state goal, introduced by Horace Mann in the 1840s, was not accepted by the last state until Mississippi agreed in 1918. From the once vague state goal, there has emerged over time many detailed requirements that now constitute a large volume of state law on education.

State–Local Levels Equate to Equity-Choice Values

The reasons for this growth are shortly reviewed, but it is important to note that the growth was linked to the acceptance of some new and basic values in schooling. As professionalism grew during the nineteenth century and expanded in the last century, the values at the core of this concept rested on the need to standardize instruction and school resources. That standardization was also linked to the need to provide the funds to ensure the presence of equity in the distribution of resources. In short, quality and equity were basic values at the state level. Regularly opposing such state laws, however, were local citizens with other values to be maintained through local control. This alternative value system emphasized that there was no uniform law that could cover all varieties of local schooling, even within a state. Consequently, it was necessary to insist that each district should make its own choice in schooling. An early conflict was over the number of days that schooling was compulsory; typically a farming nation wanted their children available for labor early and late in the school year. They resisted the state effort to increase the school year. Of course, if this thinking dominated, the result would be a proliferation of local schooling, ranged by differences in choice-focused schooling in matters such as financial sources, personnel, and days of compulsory attendance.

Over time the choice theme lost out to the professionals' interest in equity through standardization at the state level. Yet local control never disappeared, as advocates won by insisting on financing most of the costs through local taxes. That victory contributed to the enormous spread of the quality of resources and personnel among the 14,000 school districts today (as shown later).

In short, the level chosen to focus school authority was tied to different values, each of which frustrated the thrust of other levels. More quality and equity, it was urged by professionals, would be sought at the state level. Yet its success weakened choice at the local level, but to do otherwise, it was argued, would weaken state values.

Growth Forces

Another central factor in this state development has been the increase in the capacities of states to intervene locally in schooling. For a century or more after the 1840s, state action involved legislatures usually meeting only every other year, governors disinterested in local school policy, and a minimal bureaucracy designed only to receive, not issue, local reports. However, after World War II, legislatures met annually, legislative staff grew, state research activities appeared (usually in *ed schools*), governors slowly became aware of the cost of schooling, and an increase began in state funds for local schooling. These changes, only sketched here, typified a new state capacity to be involved in school policy.

Other changes were attributable to new laws in the last of the twentieth century. One of these was the growth in federal grants for local education (reviewed in the next chapter) that led to the states overseeing their implementation to the local level. Another factor was that states became the focus of different reform movements to increase quality and improve student learning; these focused on curriculum requirements and testing. Typically, the recent drive to improve student achievement led to the development of a centralized testing system in order to compare results. For example, children with special educational needs became a central issue in recent decades. However, those needs required special personnel that most local districts lacked, thereby opening the way for state help.

A recent force for state growth was the increased role of the federal government, especially in federal grants. These moneys began with grants to train teachers in 1958 and expanded considerably in 1965 with federal aid to education under the Elementary and Secondary Education Act of 1965. If federal legislators thought that money should go for education of special groups or an educational cause, then 1 percent of the grant was set aside for state assistance and oversight. In effect, Washington induced the states to assist in administering the federal funds and programs.

As a result, state staffs grew to provide this bureaucratic oversight, while other state staffs created a new evaluation to judge test results. For example, a 1983 federal law sought to reform schools through evaluation of student learning that required state experts in testing and curricula. That evaluation movement escalated with a 2001 federal law designed to test all students on two subjects at different grade levels and do so on a continuous basis.

If the top of the governing system contributed to the state growth, so did the bottom level, namely, the school district. The central problem was the increased inability of local systems to respond to the flood of criticisms cited throughout this book. Those included widely reported failures of student learning, and the constant feuding by local stakeholders (reviewed in the previous chapter). These publicized incapacities at the local level left a vacuum of control over schooling. As *nature abhors a vacuum,* so this political vacuum opened the way for more state involvement.

As if that was not bad enough for local control advocates, there were changes in the states' tax revenues for schooling. In the last of the twentieth century, states took on new sets of taxes (e.g., personal and corporate income, sales). This larger pool of state revenue was a target for local schools to siphon off for local needs. The result was that a larger share of local costs came from the state, and what was more, it came with state oversight. By the mid-1980s, the states on the average were providing about half the local school costs; by 2000, though, that percentage had dropped, but everywhere it was greater than it had been twenty-five years before.

In short, the internal dynamics of a federal system had led advocates to rearrange resources and authority so that locally more authority and funds were drawn from higher sources, along with more state and federal mandates on programs and goals. At the personal level, the teacher and administrator today find a larger amount of their time spent in dealing with these mandates and funding sources that had been designed to meet a greater variety of educational needs.

State Differences in School Policy

It would be a serious mistake to conceptualize the state role in a singular fashion, for it is clear that within the web of federalism the state–local interaction varies considerably. In this section we explore not only those differences but also the reasons for them. In this picture of diversity we learn much about how the educational cultures shaped the variety of schooling that exists within the nation.

The core measure of education's effort is partly quantitative, namely, the amount of student learning. However, the amount of money provided is another key measure, whether it comes from the state, district, or federal level. By reviewing per capita spending on education by the states, we find two major characteristics of state education. These are, first, the increased state role in finances, and second, the great variation among the states in this and many other school policies.

First, a shift took place in the relative contribution at each level. As noted, the state's share of local costs has increased considerably, despite variation among the states. Fifty years ago, the local district had by far the largest percentage share for funding schooling (roughly two thirds), while the states had a much smaller share, and Washington had almost none (except near military bases). Today, that state share has grown, in some states bearing over one half the local costs (e.g., California); the federal share has grown to about 6 percent, while the district share has shrunk accordingly. That change in percentages is the result of growing pressures among all states to increase both state and federal funding for local costs. As big cities have an extraordinary share of poor students who need special education funds to educate them, the federal percentage is considerably higher. As most federal funds go for this special purpose, a city such as Chicago may have 40 percent or more of its costs for special education borne by Washington. These new funds not only assisted many districts but also increased the state and federal capacity to get more involved, as noted.

A second finding is that, if we were to group states into similar patterns of funding or other school policies, we would note a clustering, often on a regional norm. The pattern suggests the differences that exist among states in what values they emphasize in school policies. In Table 13.1, the education laws of two states were subject to analysis of their contents. That analysis was focused around how the laws fit four basic values (quality, equity, efficiency, and choice)* as these applied to seven different types of school policy. The analysis was applied to two seemingly similar states, but the results showed that there were substantial differences for many types of policy.

For example, in the key area of finance laws, Illinois paid much more attention than Wisconsin to emphasizing the value of efficiency. Typically, such laws involved how local budgets had to be prepared and what kinds of levies were possible. That emphasis is a limitation on local boards, possibly reflecting an earlier tradition of inefficiency. The same contrast appeared in the value of quality for

---

*These values are similar to the values of excellence, equity, efficiency, and choice discussed in Chapter 1.

TABLE 13.1   State Policy Values in Illinois and Wisconsin Laws

Policy Area	Quality		Equity		Efficiency		Choice	
	IL	WI	IL	WI	IL	WI	IL	WI
Finance	7	9	12	17	31	17	27	18
Personnel	30	12	14	8	6	8	6	1
Testing/assessment	4	—	4	3	—	2	1	—
Program definition	26	53	22	40	5	23	22	38
Organization/governance	19	15	34	19	51	43	25	33
Curriculum materials	3	1	5	—	1	—	3	3
Buildings/facilities	12	9	10	6	5	6	16	6

Source: Frederick Wirt, et al. (1988). "Analyzing Values in State Policy Systems," *Educational Evaluation and Policy Analysis.* Vol. 10, No. 4, p. 278. Copyright 1988 by the American Educational Research Association. Reprinted with the permission of the Publisher.

personnel, such as the qualifications of school teachers. On the other hand, there was considerable agreement on many items in this table, reflecting the commonalities of the professional educational system. Nevertheless, there are also many minor differences on other policies that are always value based.

At a larger level of analysis, these distinctions reveal the underlying American value of individualism that works its way out through local and state political cultures. A *culture* is a regular way of thinking and acting about matters that are important in life. In matters of governance, *political culture* refers to matters involving ideas and behavior about politics and policies. In the classic work on this concept (Elazar, 1984), political cultures necessarily differ due to the states' diverse origins in population, religion, and later events. These cultures, it is argued, shape the states' political institutions and public policies in ways that are distinctive among American regions. Much work in political science has been dedicated to tracing these cultural effects among the states in different public policies and political behavior. Even physical discipline in schools was harsher in some states (the South) than elsewhere (Wirt, 1991; Vandenbosch, 1991).

An effort was made to see if these political culture differences were linked to educational policy differences (Marshall, Mitchell, & Wirt, 1989). State school elites in six states of differing cultures were interviewed for their judgments on a range of school policies, and the analysis then showed whether they fit these political cultures. Of the school programs explored, ranging over seven policy areas (see Table 13.1), twenty-four of thirty-three programs met the expected cultural types.

One familiar example of cultural differences may suffice in the Confederacy states and the Yankee states of the northeast. Loss in the Civil War had so gutted southern state and local resources that little public funds existed, then and since, to finance much schooling. These states rank low in most fifty-state comparisons across a wide range of policies, including schooling. On the other hand, in the northeast, the dominant role of the Puritan church's emphasis on education led to early adoption of state education laws that were well financed. Recall that Massachusetts was the first state to require school attendance (1852) and Mississippi the last (1918). By any measure of student achievement or of state taxes, these two regions were widely disparate over the last 160 years.

Thus, history permeates existing state institutions for schooling, reflecting differing backgrounds of religion, resources, and events. With school reforms of the last decades of the twentieth century, those states with the lowest schooling outcomes adopted far more reforms than those with better schools. Thus, of the eight states adopting the most reforms, seven were located in the old Confederacy (Shin & Van Der Slik, 1985).

In short, there are multiple state reactions to system-wide problems in schooling. These states and their many districts vary in many dimensions besides history. Districts range in size from the giant New York City to a rural one-room school in North Dakota. That variety means that with any systemic school problem the state policy response will vary. In short, there is no such thing as a *state policy process,* but rather differing responses to common problems within diverse political systems that produce different school policies. Not surprisingly, after some finance reforms, Hawaii in 1996 provided 92 percent of all school costs (its royal tradition led to centralized oversight of local schools), while New Hampshire contributed only 11 percent. That difference was not much changed from before the reforms, as the rankings of states (see later) not only vary but also show little change over time.

School Policymaking Process of the States

We suggest that there are common elements to the *process* of making policy, despite the many differences among states in its details. There often arise common problems with which schools must deal. Similar needs and problems running across the variety of states make possible some common processes, but also create some differences.

For example, among six states of varying cultural resources in the mid-1980s, most state elites found that school finances were the most important school problem facing them (Marshall, Mitchell, & Wirt, 1989). The options they could employ for finances were also common, namely, either equalize funds among the districts or create an overall funding level drawn from the state for the districts. In short, the problem and the agreement among policy options were both common, and with this background, state legislators turned to making new laws.

The Policymaking Process

Most state policies originate in statutory law, although their legal basis lies in the state constitution; most statutes end up in bureaucratic regulations. A state policy arises due to a common dissatisfaction over a service that is *mal*-administered, *mis*-administered, or *un*-administered; that is, a practice is done corruptly, poorly, or not at all. The public dissatisfaction leads to getting a policy issue on the government's agenda. To do that, however, state legislators must *notice* the problem before considering it, and it is often surprising how a problem is not noticed until a crisis brings it to lawmakers' attention. Then, the authoritative method of passing a law, not detailed here, takes place by accepting the problem and providing its resolution as legitimate public policy. Its subsequent implementation requires bureaucracies to reorder their resources to encompass it. That means creating a staff that will protect and implement the law, often with necessary regulations.

All of these steps take time. Just noticing the problem may take years, as many citizens must organize the relevant issues in order to maintain and justify its existence. Of course, from time to time, an abrupt issue suddenly arises, creating much more public attention, which in turn attracts wide support that leads to new legislation. However, these abrupt adoptions can constitute a further problem. Thus, California in the late 1990s had so many school reforms suddenly thrust on state administration that it was hard to discover which reform was working well.

For example, in the late 1990s, the drive to reduce classroom size was widely accepted and publicized in the media and became law in many states. However, by late 2001 a first test on a national survey of teachers and parents in such schools showed some problems with the practice (Jacobson, 2001). That finding is difficult to understand given all the reforms working on the school site at the same time; there still remains evidence that student achievement improves.

These reform movements demonstrate another nonschool factor at work, namely, the role of the mass media in getting school issues on the agenda and in securing adoption (Kingdon, 1995). Ideas get political acceptance if they are floated first in the mainstream of American life and so give rise to conflict. The media are not neutral in this process; often their owners see themselves as part of a state elite seeking to improve the state through improved education.

What can the media do in the policy process? They can act as a pressure group, namely:

- Educate legislators and the general public to a new problem and possible remedies
- Transmit the views of both advocates and critics
- Report educational research that explains the problem or demonstrates successful efforts in other states
- In short, encourage the legislators to recognize "an issue whose time has come"

Besides the media acting as an interest group, there are many other interest groups in education policy, more at the state level than locally. Such groups can evaluate how a proposed policy will affect them. Thus, publicity and knowledge of the issue are generated to legislators and the media. Arrayed around particular issues is a set of groups whose influence varies considerably.

All groups are of equal importance in democratic theory, but some are more equal than others, to judge from knowledgeable observers. That may be seen in the judgment of state education elites in six states who ranked the influence of state interest groups in education, seen in Table 13.2. The *insiders* included a small set of actors: legislators, the entire legislature, the chief state school officer, and all education interest groups combined. It is clear that education elites see the formal legislative authority as the key to making school policy. Some other groups come close in influence, such as teacher organizations, a few occasionally come into view, while yet others are usually ranked quite low in influence. The ranking of courts in this table is surprising, for decisions here have caused upheavals in entire educational systems. Recall the original desegregation decisions of *Brown vs. Topeka*, or a later West Virginia case that led to an entire reorganization and funding of schooling over the issue of desegregation.

Pressure Groups

Other aspects of pressure groups, besides their agenda or their influence, provide several dimensions of understanding policymaking. At the deepest level they are

TABLE 13.2   Policy Influentials in Six States, Mid-1980s

Group	Six State Rank	Policy Type
Insiders	1	Individual legislators
	2	Entire legislature
	3	Chief state school officer
	4	All education interest groups combined
Near circle	5	Teacher organizations
	6	Governor/executive staff
	7	Legislative staff
Far circle		
Player	8	State board of education
	9	Others (commissions)
	10	School boards association
	11	State administrator association
Forgotten players	12	Courts
	13	Federal policy mandates
	14	Noneducation interest groups
	15	Citizen groups
	16	Education researcher organizations
	17	Referenda
	18	Producers of educational materials

Source: Catherine Marshall, Douglas Mitchell, & Frederick Wirt. (1989). *Culture and Education Policy in the American States*. New York: Falmer, p. 23.

in contention over just four basic values—quality or excellence, efficiency, equity, and choice. At the political level they serve to focus many individuals with a particular goal seeking action from government. Those dimensions operate within the structure of a policy environment in which there is often conflict. That conflict is tied to a common quality of politics, namely, there are not enough resources to meet all demands. As the old Appalachian phrase puts it, "They ain't enough of the good things of life to go around." Hence the political friction of policymaking over limited resources is common.

These groups are not simply about policies, for they also reflect a wider range of values in the American ideology. In the nineteenth century and later, the professionals used the National Education Association (NEA) to define one set of values. These were the values of the "best system" for schooling (Tyack, 1974), exemplifying quality and efficiency through standardization of the school services. In the last of the twentieth century, however, the NEA splintered into special programs and professional interests. Thus, California may have twenty major associations focused on education, involving separate groups for teachers, districts, administrators, and so on (Wirt & Kirst, 1997, p. 81).

At another level, a pressure group can offer selective benefits that are urged upon followers by those seeking to alter school practices. For example, some groups seek to define the curriculum so that their values are fortified within the schooling of young Americans. These efforts may be seen in recent changes in curricula to emphasize the values of women, minorities, Christians, capitalists, and others (Marshall, 1992). Even the politically correct terms for these groups are urged on students, exemplified by the use of the term, *The War Between the States,* in the South, and the term, *The Civil War,* outside that region.

One group may be used to illustrate pressure activity at the state level, namely, teachers. The NEA once dominated interests for this and other groups, but went through a reorganization after 1960 due to a challenge from the rise of another group—the American Federation of Teachers (AFT). Before 1960, the NEA spoke for the benefits of education in general, assuming that the interests of teachers and administrators were always the same. It emphasized standards of quality or efficiency through its many reports. While much of its attention was focused on Washington, there were powerful state affiliates of the NEA. After the challenge from the AFT, from a focus mostly on administrators, the NEA then paid more attention to state requirements for teachers in about 8,500 district units. It urged legislators and local boards to listen to teacher requests, but it did not support their strikes or collective bargaining.

The challenge to the NEA came from the AFT, which was organized much more tightly because it did not seek to cover the nation. Its focus was on teachers mostly in the big cities and worked in one half the states—and it did urge strikes. Those factors gave rise to numerous strikes during the 1960s and later, although the rate diminished in later decades as local school boards learned to live with their demands. The AFT's argument was that education was not unitary, for the requirements of teacher and administrators could often be in conflict, especially on salaries. Its success with strikes led to larger enrollment in the AFT and indeed moved the NEA to become more affirmative in seeking collective bargaining for teachers.

Where once teachers had no spokespersons at the local level, or at the state level, this interaction of the two interest groups over the last forty-five years made teachers politically strong at all levels. These groups endorsed presidential candidates, their state laws enhanced collective bargaining, and at the district level their voices were heard clearly—if not always followed. The success of both interest groups was indicated earlier in Table 13.2. Education interest groups were ranked fourth in policy influence among the six states, preceded only by constitutional authorities.

Among the influence of nonschool groups, the role of business groups would be the greatest. They have moved to a national focus in recent decades, forming such national lobbies as the Committee for Economic Development, National Alliance of Business, and the Business Roundtable. These groups are important for the intensive reports they publish on the conditions within American schools. At the state and local levels, the chambers of commerce carried a powerful interest linked to the requirement of taxes for education. Many of these business groups were the backers of state reforms, primarily with a focus on the values of efficiency and quality. At the local level these voices emphasize taxes and school quality.

Despite these special interest groups, there has been a decline in groups supporting a general loyalty to the public schools. The Parent Teacher Association and American Association of University Women were known for this support. These general benefit groups have lost the special attention of policymakers, confronted as they are by the more numerous special interest groups.

Finally, this brief review of general and special interest groups in education emphasizes the importance of group life in the policy world, particularly if it has a narrow agenda and organizational focus. The individual may generate a new policy idea, but it takes group action to coalesce support to transmit to the legislature. This analysis reflects the new pattern of pluralistic demands arising from the pressure system that has contributed in part to the system shock that education now knows—or endures.

Policy Authorization

The details of making law are not our concern here, but there are several aspects of that process that are uniform. One deals with the perceptual context of how legislators make decisions, and the second deals with the question of how agendas are created.

The Cognitive World of Policymakers

Different cognitive factors operate among the lawmakers that shape their behavior. Not every policy proposal is heard, or if heard, not acted upon. Even within the same law-making body, perceptual differences emerge that define what is relevant for action or inaction. These attitudes have been termed the *assumptive worlds* of policymakers that form screens against the flow of policy demands (Marshall, 1985). These perceptions are not printed rules but are deduced from law-makers' actions.

In brief, these perceptions work upon lawmakers to determine:

- Which persons can effectively initiate policy to which others will pay attention;
- Who can decide what is not acceptable as policy;
- Who can accept what is appropriate for action now or later.

Although this may seem a subjective process, those involved know about these rules as part of a working world of policy. The newcomer clearly learns what those rules are in order to be effective in the legislature or in the home district. He or she learns quickly "who is the man you have to go to" for action on your bills. There is a larger, institutional purpose to such assumptions. They keep the policy world predictable to its participants, and they make possible the creation of coali-tions that ultimately produce public policy.

Setting the Agenda

The *agenda* refers to the specific issues that lawmakers agree to deal with; not all, but only some get on the agenda. How do the favored issues get on this agenda? As shown earlier, the media of communication can signal interests by reports on that issue found in other states or districts. After all, for policymakers these are signals of dissatisfaction with some aspect of schooling. A further stimulus to the agenda is the pressure of interest groups that can confront lawmakers with a clear recognition of a problem to be considered. National lobbies, or "policy issue net-works," provide a wide sweep across the states or nationally (Kirst, Meister, & Rowley, 1984). Further, research organizations, like those in ed schools or business groups, can also provide surveys of the problem and its causes or remedies.

Although all states have a standard process for lawmaking, that process is subject to different impulses to get onto the agenda. For example, a sudden crisis can cause the process to be overwhelmed so as to produce laws quickly. An exam-ple is the addition of state-required curricula seen in the *wave* of reform in the 1980s. Alternatively, a sustained campaign over time can slowly lead to negotia-tions leading to a policy, for example, the decades-long movement to recognize collective bargaining for teachers. A final impulse to action lies in minor additions to existing law, for example, a new reporting form from district to the state agency.

Consequently, lawmaking among the states has a common quality, yet that is overlain by a great variety in the assumptions and recognitions of lawmakers that lead to different paces of effort by legislatures. Confronting this rush of issues is a subjective factor, namely, differing views of what is significant, of who may partic-ipate in lawmaking, and what the pace of policy change will be.

Administration and Implementation of Policy

The next stage of the policy process moves from authorization to the carrying out of such decisions. That stage involves both administration (the structuring of resources and personnel) as well as implementation (operations designed to meet the policy's goals). We focus first on administration.

Four state agencies oversee the administration of schools in America: chief state school officer (CSSO), state board of education (SBE), state education agency (SEA), and the governor's office. While these are common in all states, they differ in methods of appointment and the range of duties. For example, voters may elect the SBE and CSSO, they may be appointed by the governor, or the legislature may appoint the SBE who appoints the SEA. In 1996, the CSSO was appointed in half the states, a decrease in recent decades, while the SBE was appointed in thirty-six states and its size ranged from few to many members. However they were selected, these officials were ultimately responsible to two sources, the legislature and governor, who set their agenda, and to the huge bureaucracy whose work they oversaw.

Administration is more fragmented within the SEA, so it is hard to generalize about its authority. Sometimes the SEA appoints the CSSO and may be elected or appointed; rare, however, is a unified single school system, except for the New York Board of Regents. As Table 13.2 showed, the CSSO influence was stronger than even the governor, but it was just below that of the legislature. The CSSO regularly provides publicity about schooling and offers a strong legislative connection. He or she may also administer the SEA in carrying out state legislation. An analysis in 1982 (McDonnell & McLaughlin, 1982) found this influence was linked to the state's political culture (noted later): Some states focus on local control and others on state control.

The actual implementation of state policy rests with the SEA. Its size and local influence have grown along with that in state education policy. Indeed, this agency oversees a broad range of state and federal policies that run from direct control to indirect persuasion. In effect, the SEA is a cluster of experts who help carry out state laws with linkages to the local district.

So extensive has this authority of the SEA become that a reaction set in against it, taking the form of deregulation or devolution. In 1995, thirty states considered such deregulation; Texas repealed one third of its areas of oversight and limited the SEA to just six functions. Similarly, charter schools in some states were released from state supervision of schooling (Wirt & Kirst, 1997, p. 241). This reaction demonstrates once again the theme of popular dissatisfaction and policy reaction in the creation of school policies. In this case, dissatisfaction arose from local control advocates who were unhappy with state intervention that was designed to enforce state mandates. At this time, little is known of how this shift will affect curriculum, staff, student learning, and other school matters. What this movement demonstrates is that centralized and decentralized impulses constantly run through American federalism.

Recent Evaluations of State Reforms

To demonstrate the considerable variety of state implementation, we can array the states along constant measures of education policy. *Education Week* has regularly summarized state-by-state indicators of their capacities and student results in such an analysis. A recent report (Meyer, Orlofsky, Skinner, & Spicer, 2002) enables us to evaluate this variety in state education. Table 13.3 provides a measure of resources that each state applied to schooling, drawn from scores of other variables. This table emphasizes the enormous diversity among the American states, such that a student in one state receives an education that is considerably less than that in other states.

Note, for example, the measure on the state's share of instructional costs. From the highest spending state (New Jersey) to the lowest (Mississippi), a student in the former received twice as much state help as the latter; in New Jersey there were two dollars spent for every dollar in Mississippi. As more available funding

TABLE 13.3 Ranking of States' Resources and Finances

State	Resource Adequacy		Instructional Cost	Teacher Training	
NJ	A	97	10,787	C+	78
WY	A	97	7,928	F	57
NY	A	96	9,935	C	76
WV	A	95	7,565	C	76
WI	A	94	8,363	D+	68
VT	A	93	8,527	C+	78
DE	A–	91	8,752	D+	69
MI	A–	91	8,045	C–	70
RI	A–	91	9,515	D+	67
IN	A–	90	7,754	C+	78
CT	A–	90	10,135	B+	87
ME	B+	89	7,656	D	65
MN	B+	89	8,453	C	74
PA	B+	87	8,321	C–	71
OK	C	74	5,943	B–	81
AR	C	73	5,269	B–	82
NM	C	73	6,463	C–	71
CO	C	73	6,085	C	76
NV	C–	72	5,632	C–	71
FL	C–	71	5,982	D+	67
ID	C–	70	5,386	D	64
TN	D+	69	5,733	C	75
MS	D+	67	5,283	C	73
CA	F	59	6,255	C	74
UT	F	57	4,372	D	66
AZ	F	55	4,968	D	65
U.S.			7,079		

Source: Data for this table drawn from Meyer, Lori, et al., (2002, January 10). "The State of the States." *Education Week,* pp. 68–90.

leads to more educational resources or better trained personnel, the measure of spending separates the schools from best to least for students.

Note certain qualities of the high spending states (i.e., $9,000), namely, New Jersey, New York, Connecticut, and Massachusetts. As shown later, these states are part of an older moralist political culture linked to the Puritan religion. That linkage is also seen in the ten states within the next lower range ($7,000); these ten are dominated by the same political cultures (except for West Virginia). On the other hand, among the low spending states are the rural imprints of the South and West. Of the eleven lowest states ($3,800 to $5,400), five had been in the Confederacy, and the others have small populations in large territories.

Does this state money influence the quality of its school programs? In Table 13.3 we find another ranking in the first two columns. These are the measure of the *adequacy* of school resources that is designed to overcome regional differences in costs. Those states at the top did the best, and those at the bottom the worst. Looking for patterns, again we see that the states with the highest grades (B+ and above) are rooted in the moralist political culture of New England, except for Indiana and Wyoming. At the bottom of these measures, the states share the traditionalist political culture, heavily rooted in the South. The glaring exception is California where the rush of immigrants has strained even its resources. In short, it seems that the highest spending states seem to have the highest grades on adequacy of its resources for schooling. The cognitive structures such as cultures may lie behind these spending patterns, an influence to be studied shortly.

How does that connection work when it comes to a particular school program, one illustrated by the training of teachers? The evaluation in Table 13.3 shows little relationship of the kind found previously. Thus, the highest grade given was just a C+ for New Jersey, also seen earlier as the highest on resources provided. There is trace evidence of the connection of political culture in the fact that Connecticut and Massachusetts had the highest grades but in that rank North Carolina was also included, which was the highest of all states in this ranking. At the lowest end of that scale (F on teacher training) were states small in population within a large territory (e.g., Wyoming, North Dakota, Kansas, and South Dakota).

Other examples of mismatched rankings are seen; for example, Texas is middling on other measures but D+ on teacher training. Or California, which has the fifth largest economy in the entire world, is middling on resources provided and even weaker on other measures. Such contradictions would require a state-by-state review to help determine why particular rankings appeared (seen in Meyer, Orlofsky, Skinner, & Spicer, 2002, pp. 95–169).

Given these variations among the states, we cannot find any simple measure to distinguish them. Wealth of the state or population size might explain differences on resources and policies. Yet that is not so for a large California population or a limited population in Vermont or Delaware; the last two loom large in the measures seen in Table 13.3. The ratio of land size to population might explain matters, as it seems to account for some of the rural states noted previously. Yet how to account for the differing outcome measures of similarly small populations in Vermont and New Hampshire?

In sum, we return to the clear factor of dramatic differences in resources among the fifty American states, although explaining them, especially on particular programs, is less clear. It may be that the political culture explanation may help account for this, and to that explanation we next turn.

Political Culture and State Results

Earlier we noted that the most states seeking reform in the 1980s were found in the traditionalist political culture of the southern states. Differences were noted in which school values got priority between two states. We also noted in a national survey that there were points of cultural differences among states' school resources and expenditures. Moving from this rough clustering of states we need to explore the reasons for these differences more fully.

The work of Elazar concluded that there were three broad groupings of political ideas and behaviors in American history (Elazar, 1984). In the South was a "traditionalist" culture in which public policy is limited, party completion is absent, and life operates under an agricultural elite that eschews parties. A second culture, the "moralist," was rooted in the Puritan tradition in New England and across the northern belt of states. This culture saw government as one way of improving the "commonweal" of life and should be used for those ends with an active and competitive party life. Finally, a third culture, the "individualist," viewed government as simply a "marketplace" in which one sought and obtained policies to further economic development. This outlook means politicians respond to demands and use the party to meet individual needs. Its supporters—usually in big cities—operated amid a host of favors and often corrupt legal practices. The roots of all three cultures lay in religions and ethnic origins with different outlooks that constituted a culture.

Hints of those distinctions were earlier suggested, and now we need to review how a set of six states, two from the three cultures, each typified a particular culture. Education policy elites in those states were asked their view of what the state's public thought about a range of school policies; the test of the study was to see if their views clustered with their respective cultures. Figure 13.1 uses a scattergram of the central measures of these elite views of citizens' attitudes for each state to test this difference. This figure shows statistically central attitudes in each state as they appear along two sets of attitudes (their wording is not included here).

Clearly there are different clusters, and roughly they are in the direction of the posited political cultures. Thus, Wisconsin is the most moralist on Elazar's analysis and so it appears here on citizen attitudes as elites judged them. Illinois, the most individualist on that same scale, also rates low on the same scale. Pennsylvania is similar to Illinois but also shows more moralistic views. However, elite views of citizens in the other three states are not that helpful, particularly for the southern states. While these scores are mixed, however, they are located roughly on the same cultural line that would fit this cultural theme.

For those with an interest in comparing the school qualities of the American states, this political perspective suggests many opportunities for study. Researchers

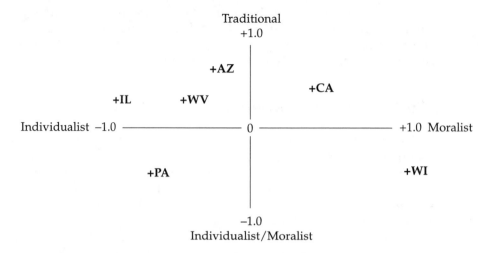

FIGURE 13.1   Political Culture and Elite Views of Citizens on School Policy

Source: Catherine Marshall, Douglas Mitchell, & Frederick Wirt. (1989). *Culture and Education Policy in the American States.* New York: Falmer, p. 117.

over the last two decades have set out a substantial basis of how that culture affects differences in policy of all kinds. For example, in a review school principals in a national sample were tested for the influence of such political cultures (Wirt & Krug, 1998). It demonstrated that there exists a national administrative culture, with little variance among the fifty states. On many other issues, however, considerable variation exists among the states. The first finding rejects any cultural influence, while the second suggests that culture may play a part in principals' attitudes.

Summary

The state level of policymaking shows considerable agreement but also great variation, so that there is no simple model of this process. Throughout this book the great variety of policies and behaviors are seen that is the hallmark of American education.

One of the common findings is that there is not only great variation but also a new growth of the state's role in shaping and administering educational policy. That also means great growth in overseeing local schooling through state mandates. The state variation in school policy suggests that there are roughly two kinds of education provided students in this nation, very good and very weak. The growth of the American states is partly attributed to citizens seeking more help for local schools, as well as by growing dissatisfaction over schooling services. The state assistance takes the form of legal mandates and increased funding of local costs. That growth, however, may be undergoing change as local resistance to mandates has moved some states to reduce them.

While the legal process of state policymaking is rather standard, there are great variations in how it is shaped by the differing attitudes of policymakers themselves. That cognitive factor can account for why policies vary among the states, but another explanation may lie in a background of different political cultures that shape expectations and goals of those who make policy. It is also clear that the outcome is a state pattern of great variation in how education is conceived and supported within what Walt Whitman once termed America as being "a nation of nations."

REFERENCES

Elazar, D. (1984). *American federalism.* New York: Harper & Row.

Jacobson, L. (2001, October 3). Survey finds mixed views on smaller schools. *Education Week, 21*(5), 5.

Kingdon, J. (1995). *Agendas, alternatives, and public policies* (2nd ed.). New York: Harper Collins.

Kirst, M., Meister, G., & Rowley, S. (1984). Policy issue networks: Their influence on state policymaking. *Policy Studies Journal, 13*(2), 247–264.

Marshall, C. (1985). Assumptive worlds of education policy makers. *Peabody Journal of Education, 62*(4), 90–115.

Marshall, C. (Ed.). (1992). *The new politics of race and gender.* Philadelphia: Falmer.

Marshall, C., Mitchell, D., & Wirt, F. (1989). *Culture and education policy among the American states.* New York: Falmer.

McDonnell, L., & McLaughlin, M. (1982). *Education policy and the role of the states.* Santa Monica, CA: Rand.

Meyer, L., Orlofsky, G., Skinner, R., & Spicer, S. (2002, January 10). The state of the states. *Education Week, 27*(17), 68–90.

Shin, D., & Van Der Slik. (1985). Legislative efforts to improve the quality of public education in the American states: A comparative analysis. Paper presented to the Annual Convention of the American Political Science Association, New Orleans, p. 36.

Tyack, D. (1974). *The one best system.* Cambridge, MA: Harvard University Press.

Vandenbosch, S. (1991). Political culture and corporal punishment in public schools. *Publius: The Journal of Federalism, 213,* 117–122.

Wirt, F. (Ed.). (1991 Spring). Symposium on empirical aspects of political cultures among the American states. *Publius: The Journal of Federalism, 21,*(2), 1–14.

Wirt, F., & Kirst, M. (1997). *The political dynamics of American education* (2nd ed.). Berkeley, CA: McCutchan.

Wirt, F., & Krug, S. (1998). From leadership behavior to cognitions: A constructivist theory. *Journal of Educational Administration, 36*(3) 229–248.

14 The Federal Level of Policymaking

The states' picture of growth in education has been matched at the federal level. Where once their only contributions were research reports on schooling or providing tax substitutes near military bases, today Washington provides a wide range of programs and revenues. In this chapter we review that history, analyze federal methods of interaction with schools, examine a set of national policies, and evaluate the role of courts in setting new parameters of educational values.

History of Federal Education Policy

The expanded role of Washington in school policy reflects one of the many changed aspects of American federalism. That expansion has emerged during the last fifty years, while the scene before that was one of a far away agency in the national capitol with which local schools had no contact. This abrupt change is one facet from the old world of state–local professional control. Today, even local administrators must necessarily have some links to Washington, while teachers are involved in adopting their policy activities.

The Early Silence of Washington

The reason for Washington's absence from the education scene was constitutional. Reviewing Article 1, Section 8, of the U.S. Constitution of 1789, these express powers of the national government had no reference to education at all. Indeed, that same omission occurred for all state constitutions at that time. The reason was that the concept of public education did not exist. There was schooling, of course, but primarily it was scattered in private hands of family and church.

As the previous chapter pointed out, a slow growth of constitutional provisions for education occurred, not in Washington, but in the states. The reason was the slow adoption of a *state* provision for public education and compulsory attendance after 1840. However, that state adoption did not mean much specifically, for it expressed only a statutory belief that, in the interest of a better society, there was a need for local units to provide this service. No state requirements existed about funding, curriculum, and governance; it was simply a matter of local control. At no point was the federal government involved; indeed, it was not until well after the Civil War that a federal agency was created generally to assist education by reporting on improving instruction. Later in the twentieth century Congress permitted local districts to receive federal funds in lieu of taxes for educating children from nearby military bases.

If we skip over that period of a limited state government and dominant local control, there are decades in which Washington did very little. It was also a period when the locality dominated schools so much that it became an ongoing part of American values. Even in recent years, an Organization for Economic Cooperation and Development survey of many democracies found the United States the most heavily supportive of localism on many matters (Organization for Economic Cooperation and Development, 1993, p. 134).

Beginning after World War II, however, some leaders called for a policy termed "federal aid to education." The constitutional passage that would make this possible was the provision "to tax and spend for the general welfare" (Art. I, Sec. 8). For years, such a concept would be passed in one house of Congress and defeated in the other; at one point it was the national debate topic for high school. The blocking of this policy came from two questions that were so controversial no compromise seemed possible. How to provide federal funds to segregated schools or to parochial schools? The first part of the question split support of the Democratic party; southern Democrats approved, but northern Democrats and Republicans did not. The second part of the question ran afoul of the First Amendment's ban against congressional support for religions; here, the split ran the other way—southerners said no, and northerners said yes.

Sputnik to 1972

What broke this deadlock had nothing to do with either issue but with the jarring realization by the American public in the late 1950s that the Russians could put up an orbital space vehicle while we could not. That Sputnik action struck so deeply into public opinion that in turn it generated a psychological sense of a national crisis on the quality of our schools compared with the Russians'. From that event came a crash program to provide federal funding to train teachers in mathematics and science. This policy marked the first large increase in federal programs and funds for improving schools. The problems of segregation and religion were not raised, masked as they were by the national crisis.

The years of the Kennedy and Johnson administrations (1961 to 1968) were marked by an even greater increase in federal funding in social welfare and school desegregation. Both initiatives were focused on the value of equity, that is, the need to remove inequities in American life, particularly for those less favored by social resources. The welfare effort was so successful that by the twenty-first century social programs were an accepted part of federal policies, debated only over small changes. The desegregation program, discussed later, was assisted by the Emergency School Assistance Act of 1972, but was eventually turned aside after several decades of strong opposition.

The main program of federal policy in this era and later came from the use of federal funds for local schooling. The forces seeking change in the social basis of American society during the 1960s provided not simply the Civil Rights Act of 1964 but the Elementary and Secondary Education Act (ESEA) of that same year. While the Civil Rights Act sought to remove restrictions against voting by southern African Americans (among other changes), the ESEA prohibited the use of federal money for segregated schools.

Both laws were directed primarily against the South, where the biggest problems were evident. The efforts of whites in that region to maintain the traditional political and schooling practices were challenged in federal courts by investigators from federal agencies for education and justice. Federal court decisions supported both the Civil Rights Act and ESEA when challenged by southerners, and this barrage of federal efforts signaled to southern practitioners that change was needed. Changing one's culture is never easy, and as noted in the previous chapter, resistance can persist over time. Now, however, southern local school and political figures were faced with a difficult bind; without policy change, there would be heavy costs in court cases they would likely lose. Slowly adjustments took place, a process noted later.

However, for the rest of the nation the core of the ESEA was the provision of money from federal programs to improve learning in the public schools. From a little to a lot of federal aid to education for most schools, the federal thrust began in the 1960s and expanded in later decades. New and later laws expanded federal oversight of how states and localities used them. From the perspective of a typical superintendent by the end of the 1970s, one was surrounded by a set of *picket fences* of federal programs. The programs each had their own directors who were involved in state and national agencies and who used their information base to administer local activities. While the superintendent was officially responsible for administering such programs, in reality that authority had been devolved into a complex net of picket fences.

We review some of these federal programs, but note how over time these federal laws were backed by special groups. We have noted the help for those seeking desegregation. Title I of ESEA in time had become a center for special education, which meant big cities and minority students with poor school records. The same equity orientation is seen in later laws designed to equalize local funds for women athletes in high schools and universities. A similar protection was seen in a federal law to provide privacy to children, thereby overturning a set of controls that administrators and teachers had once known.

The Last Quarter Century

This change in Washington's policies had consequences for the state of public opinion. From the earliest days of the Sputnik crisis, education was ranked in the top three issues of leading concern for most Americans. By 2000, it was the leading issue; shortly after the dreadful World Trade Center attack in September 2001, while terrorism was most highly rated, education became the highest ranked only four months later. One effect of federal policy was that it raised educational problems to national attention, providing citizens with the belief that there were problems in the public schools and suggesting that Washington could improve these conditions. Many professional and private groups contributed to this surge of opinion after 1972, and some who studied student learning seemed to confirm it. On the other hand, though, that belief about "school failures" in achievement, despite its breadth, was poorly supported by evidence (Berliner & Biddle, 1995).

As a result, more federal policies appeared to remedy the problems. Both political parties came to endorse the need for such policies, although often they debated only over the pace or total cost of the program. However, efforts by a conservative Republican majority and President Ronald Reagan in the 1980s and later to abolish the U.S. Department of Education failed primarily due to grassroots pressure. By the time of the second Bush administration in 2001, the Republican was a reluctant supporter of expanded funds for the ESEA. With renewal of the ESEA in 2002 (termed by Bush as the No Child Left Behind Act), a majority of both parties supported an increase in its funds, despite intense in-fighting in Congress. That law was heartily endorsed by the president and his Democratic opponent on other policies, Senator Ted Kennedy.

By 2002, the federal picture was symptomatic of the new shape of the politics of education in which all other levels were involved. Larger shares of local costs had emerged from the states (despite some reductions in the 1990s). The federal percentage in the 1960s started out at 9 percent but fell steadily and remained at 6 percent nationally; big cities did even better, as they had so many needing special education, where just under one half of local costs came from Title I. What were these federal programs and how did they interact with state and local levels?

Federal Education Policies

The growth in Washington in education policy is associated with a growth also in the variety of groups seeking funds and programs. This growth applies not simply to public education but also to a variety of other kinds of schooling by the national government. For example:

- The U.S. Department of the Interior educates Native Americans
- The U.S. Department of Defense schools children of military personnel abroad and sends members to universities
- All agencies have in-service training programs to update personnel quality

Federal assistance to public schools is our focus here, though, and to get a sense of the variety of programs and of clientele, Table 14.1 shows abbreviated estimates that suggest several important facts about the federal level. Clearly, many programs provided for many kinds of clientele across American education. Historically, little of this support existed before 1960. In this budget, the size of clientele served ranges from Native Americans (smallest cost) to student financial aid

TABLE 14.1   2002 Appropriations for Federal Education Policies

Program	(Million $)	Number of Programs
Disadvantaged	12,347	21
Title I	12,309	19
Migrant	38	2
Impact aid	1,144	5
School improvements	7,837	41
Indian	120	1
Bilingual and immigrant	665	1
Special education & rehabilitative	11,785	13
Special	8,673	9
Rehab: Service and disability research	2,946	1
Vocational and adult	1,934	11
Student financial aid	12,286	6
Other	3,899	3
Postsecondary	2,270	3
Research, statistics	444	5
Total education department	53,534	—

Source: Condensed from *Education Week,* January 30, 2002, pp. 26–27.

(largest cost). These items also cover nonschool aid such as professional training, technology developments, and research activities.

Finally, many items are earmarked for special projects favored by congressmen (Robelen, 2002). These may include a special program for children in Cleveland's Rock and Roll Hall, or for bringing airline representatives to local schools to talk about their business. Over 750 earmarks appeared in the budget shown in Table 14.1; however, its $440 million cost is only a small fraction of the $53 billion budget. Yet these actions serve to link legislators to the Department of Education, a part of the *iron triangle* of federal policymaking.

Holding aside this one-year budget estimate, over time the largest expenditures for a single program has been for special education, namely, assistance to the poorest and mostly minority children. That item has contributed greatly to big-city schools, much larger than the average 6 percent for all American public schools. It has developed its own network of supporters that make it immune to budget cuts.

Federal Uses of Funds

The transfer of funds from Washington has been accompanied by several kinds of influence. That transfer shows directly how Washington agencies seek to influence the goals at the state–local level. These methods of influence run a range from suggestive to coercive, with a focus on the middle range.

The oldest method has been generating and distributing knowledge about education, often reports or statistical analyses. The National Center for Education

Statistics is the most recent agency with this focus. Recall that amid such provisions of data lies the possibility of proposals for change, even though state or local education systems can use or ignore such a service. At the other end of federal methods is the more coercive use of regulations for which federal moneys are to be used, complete with auditing or program reviews. The method of accountability is to hold officials responsible for use of federal money by reporting on activities: Federal funds are withheld for noncompliance. Yet it is clear that there is considerable evasion of such requirements by state–local officials.

Closely allied with this method of influence has been the creation of categories of programs, or *categorical grants,* to use federal money for specific purposes set out by federal law. The federal funds may be matched by state–local resources, or federal money may be used only, both designed to provide special educational services. The core of this influence of the ESEA has been the use of different funds for different program goals; in recent years, President Clinton's Goals 2000 and President Bush's No Child Left Behind are typical. On a broader scale of methods of federal influence is general aid to education, involving few requirements for use by states as found in a more recent requirement for *bloc grants.* Starting with President Reagan in the 1980s and carried out in later programs by Clinton and Bush, categorical grants have been collapsed into bloc grants, one for a major purpose that was then turned over to the states to meet their special educational needs. The assumptions here are twofold: to remove federal control over local matters, and to believe that state–local officials know their own distinctive needs best. A final method of federal influence lies in services as consultants on special problems. Early in desegregation, under the School Emergency Act of 1973, federal officials assisted districts undergoing this change. Later, the introduction of an all-computer curriculum in local schools could rely on the federal consulting assistance.

Finally, one other method, quite intangible but real, involves how the president identifies and proposes visions of improved schooling to the nation. Better known as the *bully pulpit* from President Theodore Roosevelt, this method specifies national problems and suggests likely remedies. His audience now becomes national and helps focus opinion on one set of ideas. In education, this function, new in the last decades of the twentieth century, has the president raising a major problem among public schools and then setting out plans to correct it. For example, President Reagan appointed a commission of educational leaders whose report in 1983, *A Nation at Risk,* condemned the existing state of public education and called for major reforms. Widely publicized, this report was the stimulus for many state reforms that followed in that decade that increased students' curriculum requirements and tested teachers' abilities.

The Politics of Federal Aid

Moving beyond this brief description of federal policies, it is significant to understand that such programs are covered by a thick web of political activity. Each of the programs and subprograms shown in Table 14.1 has developed supporters whose aim is to protect programs and to increase the budget. Understanding the politics of the matter involves both political parties and pressure groups.

At one level, the politics of federal aid is partisan. The initial growth in the 1960s started that way. A liberal Democratic president, Lyndon Johnson, and a Democratic majority in both houses introduced the ESEA and has since backed it at every renewal. One indicator of this partisanship is hinted at in Table 14.1. Every program but one found the House budget lower than the Senate, while the Senate increased these estimates. Behind these numbers was a Republican-controlled House seeking to challenge Democratic President Clinton's education budget. The previous year's total had been almost $33 million that the GOP House cut down to almost $27.4 million, but the influence of the Democrats in the Senate upped the total again to $28.8 million. The result overall was a 2 percent cut in these programs. On such tiny percentages do the parties fight tooth and nail for advantages to their supporters.

The larger story here is that the Democrats have supported larger education budgets and have innovated more new programs. The Republicans, however, have sought to reduce these appropriations and, in one failed effort, sought to abolish the entire Department of Education. Part of this division is ideological. Many Democrats are low-income parents who need more money to school their children, while Republicans with larger incomes can take care of their own education—and dislike paying taxes for others. Part of this clash also involves votes for these parties. Teachers are one part of the Democratic voters, and they show it by their donations. In the three years from 1989 to 1993, according to a Federal Elections Commission report of 1993, the Democrats received five to six times more contributions than Republicans (as reported in Wirt & Kirst, 1997, p. 255). Thus, the National Education Association donated over $6.6 million to the Democrats but only $123,000 to the Republicans. Similarly, the American Federation of Teachers showed the same difference: $3.4 million versus $60,000.

At another level of understanding, the role of pressure groups is important for continued federal policies. Note the number of particular programs listed in Table 14.1, each of which involves a particular beneficiary, for example, special education for poor children (Kirst, 1988). Over time, each group of supporters had formed protective associations in Washington to ensure that its budget did not get cut. Over the years, this *hardening* of each category of aid occurred with a linkage of a pressure group to an administrative subagency within the Department of Education and to a subcommittee in the education committees of Congress. These triple forces of pressure group, agency, and Congress, called the *iron triangle* of policy power (Heclo, 1978), meant that to protect the beneficiaries a separate clientele could unify the separate powers under the Constitution. Each year, that combination made sure that a budget request for this program was upheld. While there were partisan differences in Washington over such programs, of course, the pressure linkages shown here can overcome them to support their beneficiaries.

Multiply that political force for one group with the many other beneficiaries of policy that are suggested in Table 14.1, and we can see the considerable national force on educational legislation that has been sustained for some decades. Even with a recent devolution of federal funds from Washington to the states in bloc grants, it is the total budget settled in Congress that gets passed down to the states. That pressure linkage works especially well for one program, Title I of ESEA. Its supporters were so opposed to being included in a bloc grant that it would cost presidents too much energy, even if successful. With the renewal of ESEA in 2002 and despite a new focus on testing students, Title I remained the largest single program cost. Thousands of employees at local, state, and national levels need these funds to realize their objectives, thereby providing a political backing to sustain that goal.

Consequently, the political context briefly described here constitutes a force of inertia that acts to maintain this pattern of policymaking. Further, this political context also implies that innovation on any large scale is to be avoided because big change carries potential threats to many interests. As a result, only a *tinkering* with small changes takes place (Tyack & Cuban, 1995). In short, this politics of federal grants protects the interests of those involved through a process of coalition-building and policy incrementalism, a familiar story for a range of other public policies in Washington.

The Limits of Federal Aid

If one asks, did these federal aid programs work, that is, realize their professed goals, the answer depends on definitions of *work*. From the perspective of special interest groups, their successful search for larger budgets suggests that they do believe this is the case. For them, *work* means a continuing policy life rooted in Washington. However, if the definition of *work* means did the school clientele receive services that benefited their education, the answer is not all that clear.

In one sense, Washington is like the emperor without any clothes, that is, despite the concept of federal power, their agents cannot force state and local boards to comply with all requirements of federal law, despite the range of methods noted earlier. The problem is that state–local agencies are not without power of their own that can deflect or ignore federal mandates without cost to them. Their representatives in Congress and state legislatures can defend the interests of clientele if reports are not handed in. It is different if the process involves financial corruption, but most of these interactions are not of that kind. For example, local agencies may issue reports on their use of a program and its budget, but they may not always focus on the evaluation that Washington seeks. That in turn leads to another sequence of paperwork that may not meet the requirements. Further, there is no single agency overlooking all programs noted in Table 14.1, but rather a large set of evaluators and so no common standards of compliance exist. One gets a picture of many evaluation reports going up to Washington with little effort at federal compliance. Most local officials, in the phrase often used, "take the money and run." Even if under Title I those reports continue to indicate poor student learning (often the case), to cut this program in part or whole is politically unthinkable.

What has often occurred is that the goals of these laws have become not only institutionalized in the iron triangle of Washington but in the state and local personnel. These constitute separate organisms having their own goals, procedures, and measures of success. Nor is it possible to hold responsible a local board or superintendent when they are faced with this picket fence of separate authorities, particularly for vocational and special education.

Note also that state–local governments are embedded in a long historical tradition of separate loyalties and laws, the essence of states rights, that creates a separate political culture. We explored these in the previous chapter. Those political elements can forestall what is often judged to be Washington's *interference* with local schooling. In short, the dual appeals to states rights and local control counterbalance centralized thrusts of Washington.

Technical Evaluation

Despite the political qualities that weaken the accountability of federal programs, a second factor is found in the technical problems of attempting to implement policies across 14,000 districts and fifty states. Not all federal programs contain this quality (e.g., Native American education), but the presence of this complexity suggests how difficult it is to undertake reform on a national basis.

As an example, we focus on innovations in the teaching of science. Since the 1958 program to improve teaching in math and science, a reflection of the Sputnik crisis, many millions of dollars have been spent by Washington, hundreds of university staff have generated curriculum innovations, and new courses have been developed by many hundreds of teachers (Dow, 1991). Did this curriculum innovation work?

Large-scale reform takes time just to get underway. In the 1960s scientists developed a strong program in earth sciences, physical science, biology, chemistry, and engineering. Many schools were adopting some of the new curricula, although enrollment peaked in the mid-1970s, and then slowed down as the momentum for reform weakened. Indeed, by the early 1980s there was a decrease in all subjects at local schools except for biology.

Evaluating progress requires answering several questions. Was the curricular material of high quality? It is clear that the new program possessed the best knowledge from the best scientists. Did more teachers use the materials? Despite the publicity and professional encouragement, no more than one quarter of the teachers used the relevant physical science textbook, while other curricula found only a 15 percent adoption rate. Evaluators then concluded that "other than the content, length, and difficulty of class, little had changed" (Yee & Kirst, 1994). A final question—the most significant—was: Did more students enroll in these science classes and did they learn from them? The problems were considerable. It turns out that districts did not require these courses for all students but used them only as alternatives. Moreover, students using them were regarded as college-bound, and thus the courses were rejected by those in general or other course sequences. Even worse, evaluations showed few gains in students' knowledge of science.

A final question then arises. Why did the innovation not work? The problem may lie in the fact that the providers and users of the new curriculum had different technical expectations of the changes. The scientists were not teachers in public schools and so failed to understand that such teachers might adapt changes to fit their own teaching methods. Thus, the new work required longer classes and more teacher preparation than was possible in the local schools. Moreover, teachers had not been trained enough in the new sciences, and so found the curriculum difficult to understand or to teach. Consequently, the pressure was not to adapt the new but to stick with the familiar. The best outcome was found in improved textbooks, but too little contact with students by unprepared teachers meant it was only a success in affluent schools with good facilities and prepared teachers.

This example of technical reasons for federal programs not working due to the superimposition of one set of expectations on another is typical of problems arising within an intergovernmental system. What works locally may fail if expanded to more governments, as the energy in the first weakens with the many. Or, assumptions about the real world of public schools may clash with contrary assumptions held elsewhere. This federal effort to create a national set of goals for a curriculum, for example, history in the Clinton administration, sets off condemnations by others whose ideological assumptions are contrary to the reformers. Given these constraints of an intergovernmental system, it is surprising that as much was carried out.

Summary

This account suggests important dimensions of the intergovernmental relations in federal education policy. Across a wide array of constituents, these policies add a dimension of funding and programs not known before. For any policy, it has become a defensive and formidable political support system. Its personnel penetrate all intergovernmental levels of policymaking, regardless of the branch in which they serve. Its clientele—the students—may well benefit from all this policy effort, although separating out the independent influences of different policy opens a can of worms about causation. Some policies may take large sums and many personnel to implement, but the improvement of student learning is not that clear.

However, from the perspective of professionals, it is also clear that Washington has become a major partner in schooling children since 1960 and will continue to do so. Efforts in the 1990s to remove this federal force left programs about the same, even if funds were devolved to the states. Much of this federal money goes into special education of Title I in which there is still little evidence of overall changes in student learning. Nevertheless, that policy effort continues, partly for political reasons; the large corps of intergovernmental personnel supporting it makes it immune from alterations, much less killing it. That support also rests on the belief of many who are working out an equity ideal about the need for government to improve those who need help. For the practitioners of Washington policy, it may be that participation itself has the highest value in seeking to achieve social and moral goals.

The Courts as an Arena for Policymaking

So used are we to the legislatures making policy that it is often a surprise to learn that the judicial branch is also involved in that function, a theme of Part Four of this book. Indeed, its decisions give rise to further action by these legislatures and by other levels of government. For those who see the judges as austere declarers of basic principles of justice, it is important to understand exactly how the courts relate to policy.

Courts, Politics, and Policy

This awareness is not a new matter. In the 1840s, a careful French observer of the new American democracy, Alexis de Tocqueville, noted that, "scarcely any political question arises in the United States that is not resolved, sooner or later, into a judicial question" (1955, p. 290). That American tendency to go to court to settle conflicts, a tendency far greater here than in other democracies, has generated great volumes of litigation. Some of it involves personal matters—divorce, auto accidents, and so on. However, another and more political part of it arises over the question of public policy. A good part of education policy is rooted in part on court decisions. In the last half of the twentieth century such questions arose over desegregation (*Brown v. Board of Education of Topeka*) and at the state level over school finances (*Serrano v. Priest*). Both stimulated considerable reforms in state and local levels, as a later section in this chapter and the chapter on finances point out.

What then is the political nature of the courts that is relevant to policymaking? Any court decision involves settling a dispute between two or more parties. When the local court approves a divorce between Jane and Joe Doe, the decision is of relevance only to those two and their families. The policy implication is quite limited, as the judge is simply following existing statutory law. However, if the U.S. Supreme Court outlaws southern desegregation, the decision does not involve simply the plaintiff Brown and the defendant Topeka school board. The outcome is that the decision rested on a principle (i.e., the "equal protection of the laws" in the Constitution), one that is applicable to all other similar cases. Such a decision opens the way for further litigation from those similar types, and indeed, it may well stimulate legislatures to change the law. In short, a decision in the particular becomes a decision in the general, and as such it can precipitate a new and principled public policy.

That general principle of courts and policy is well illustrated in education in the decades before 2000. Religion in the schools is a contemporary example. Separate cases were seen in state and federal courts regarding Bible reading in classrooms or use of schools for religious meetings, required prayers in classes or on football fields, transportation of students to parochial schools, teaching of evolution, banning of school library books, and so on. Early in 2002, the U.S. Supreme Court heard arguments over Ohio's policy of funding alternative schools in which Cleveland's parents then sent their children mostly to religious schools. That result was challenged by those who supported the First Amendment's ban on government support of religion. The law's supporters argued that the state gave money to parents, and it was their choice—not the state's—to attend religious schools. The challengers said that regardless of the origins, religion was receiving governmental support.

The principle of courts and education policy is manifest here, regardless of the particular cases (Kirp & Yudof, 1987). Whether administrators can search student lockers or ban prayers at commencement (they can), the political process is the same. The court is thus an arena to which contestants come to argue conflicting interests in how schools should operate. The lobbyists of the legislatures are omitted here, but lawyers are a substitute in presenting the cases. Such policies have an additional force, that of legitimacy. Some citizens may seek to avoid this force, as with Southern reaction to school desegregation. But this was the force that compelled local change. Further, the decision allocates the distribution of *public* policy resources, just as is the case in legislatures. The school must use its resources to carry out a court's decision. That is the essence of policymaking.

Finally, another political aspect of the judiciary is that its members are not neutral in making such decisions. One theme of political science has been to trace the degree to which the justices vote together on particular issues and to judge them from a conservative or liberal perspective. For example, we have seen several courts in the last decades that challenged desegregation and upheld most efforts to enforce it. Then, with the Reagan appointments to the Supreme Court in the 1980s, the bench began to alter on this matter, as the new judges raised serious questions about when desegregation was completed. In 1992, that Court, with a conservative majority, held that if demography causes segregation, there was no barrier to it, especially if the record shows no intent of local officials to segregate. A majority of the justices ignored a court brief from fifty-eight leading scholars of the topic that desegregation was not a failure as alleged and was thus a proper exercise of school policy. That decision set off elimination of desegregation court orders across the nation.

In short, the decisions by one kind of majority about desegregation were overturned by another kind of majority. We can argue about the rights or wrongs of both cases, but the thrust of the issue is that different people with different evaluations of the schooling policy decided differently. That is one other sense to the political concept of judicial actions on policymaking.

Courts, Regulation, and Rights

Another perspective on the role of the courts is that their actions are designed to control the behavior of citizens and of government. This regulative function leads to the creation of certain rights of citizens that are to be protected against other private individuals and protected against government. One of these civil rights may be to define a specific action, such as telling an arrested person his or her rights, as immune from encroachment by government or others. That definition may well lead legislatures to accept and expand this definition by application of statutory law.

Such rights can cover not only a substantive matter but can also apply to a process that is designed to protect citizens and their rights. Clearly, due process of law is one of these, indeed, an ancient one that goes back to the Magna Carta in 1215 AD and was found in the Constitution. The difficulty is that the Supreme Court over its history has reviewed more cases defining this right than on any other part of the Constitution. A set of procedures must be defined that government must follow, for without it a citizen's other rights are voided. The clearest case in education is the creation of complex rules for suspensions and dismissals by school authorities. Each rule defines a proper way for the authority to act that leads to such a decision. Rules on this authority were limited decades ago, but today they fill many pages. Another case is the process for educating handicapped children through adoption of a clear principle of action with requirements for appeal from educator's decisions.

In all this change, the Supreme Court has been a leader, often defining substantive rights derived from the Constitution. In the process, citizens came to have a larger legal *quiver* of protections against alleged arbitrary action by school officials. Even more protective, these rights were written into state and federal law— indeed, into corporate personnel policy. For example, was removal from a job due to economic reasons or to discrimination based on age, gender, or skin color? All this constituted an institutionalization of civil rights against not only government but also corporations.

Another political dimension to this role of the courts is found in a network of pressure groups that seek to protect not simply substantive rights, but also procedural aspects. Even at the local level, awareness of these protections and the availability of pressure groups can move groups to challenge local actions as violations of their rights. In short, this is another aspect to the dimension of system shock affecting all of education, namely, the challenge to the one-time authority of superintendents and boards. Finally, this dimension of judicial regulation may well act as a barrier to reform of school practices. As noted in the Ohio case previously, an effort to provide funds for school choice caused citizens to challenge the action in courts. Even if successful with the Supreme Court, the advocates have undergone considerable expense of money and time to validate this reform measure.

Summary

The expansion of judicial power over education in the last decades of the twentieth century reminds us that the courts always had the latent power to review interactions of government and citizens. However, that role was expanded due to citizens seeking to change existing practices because their *rights* were invaded.

Note this aspect of major reforms in desegregation, finances, use of authority by school people, and, overall, in redefinitions of the nature of rights under law. Finally, the use of the courts as an arena of school policymaking is not over, as shown by the Ohio case over religious aid in 2002.

Courts in Action: Desegregation

The unspoken assumption in the foregoing discussion is the great power of the Supreme Court in initiating and maintaining change in public policy. That has been the case for a variety of new civil rights, but, as we discuss, that is not always the case. It is useful to reexamine the role of the courts in the case of school desegregation, for more than changes in personnel and opinions occur as the nation adapts to social change.

In the last century there were two massive social experiments by the national government, social welfare and desegregation (Merelman, 2002). Social welfare consisted of entitlements for health, social security, unemployment compensation, minimum wage, and support for the needy. These entitlements show a major change of equity in public policy to meet the needs of the disadvantaged. Moreover, these programs are backed by a large array of clientele served by such laws and by pressure groups. That combination makes it extremely hard for opponents to do anything more than challenge fund increases—but never to overturn them. Like all western democracies, the United States has joined the list of *big governments* in this policy—although often underfunded compared with the other nations. Note, however, that the defense of these programs rests in Congress and in its networks of iron triangles; behind these laws is a large group of beneficiaries who can be mobilized if threatened.

Compare that policy condition with the failure of racial integration in the public schools. We have summarized part of this account earlier, but the discussion here addresses the action and reaction among courts and beneficiaries. When the *Brown v. Topeka* case was implemented in the Civil Rights Act and ESEA of 1964, most southern schools needed federal funds to deal with a weakened and segregated educational system.

In the matter of schooling, however, southern officials could not obtain federal school funds unless their schools became desegregated. As close observers noted (Wirt, 1997; Orfield, 1978), a few years were taken up with the reaction of this traditional political culture to such a devastating change, not only for their schools but also for voting and other racial practices. As local officials slowly worked their way to this change, they felt the federal influences of the Office of Education, the Department of Justice, and federal courts. The last consistently provided support for administrative policies designed to desegregate; even whole state systems were overturned by federal courts. While most districts made some change, about 10 percent of the whites abandoned them for private or *deseg* academies. In this fashion they avoided the federal responsibility to change their racial practices. Many implied that if Washington wanted to educate African Americans, it could do so in local public schools.

As a consequence of this federal pressure, the proportion of African Americans in newly desegregated schools increased strongly until the late 1970s and then held steady (Orfield, 1987). One rough measure of the change is the decreased proportion of African Americans in formerly all-black schools. By the 1980s, however, the proportion of African Americans in mostly minority schools dropped, especially in formerly heavily African American schools, and all-white schools fell to less than half. Of course, there was variation within the region.

If such figures were a measure of success for this national policy, it ignores the growing opposition by white southerners and many other Americans, and ultimately by some African American leaders and citizens. In summary, over these last decades the political support evaporated and then disappeared. Majorities in Congress, presidents of both parties, and ultimately a newly constituted Supreme Court opposed desegregation, as did a majority of whites on opinion polls. For many, the term *busing* was a civil evil that needed to be thrown out; note that the opposition affected not simply the South but also the North. That attitude was also reflected by citizens *voting with their feet* in a *white flight* away from living near African Americans, whether in neighborhoods or schools. By 2000, the racial picture of most big cities was like a bull's-eye target, black in the center and white around it; the term *apartheid* was regularly used to describe the change. In the South, there was also a return to having large proportions of African American students in schools.

In policy terms, matters also changed. In 1982, President Reagan and Congress repealed the Emergency School Aid Act of 1972, the main instrument for enforcing desegregation. Reagan's appointments began to fill the Supreme Court with conservative members, and, as noted earlier, in 1992 it overthrew the *Brown v. Topeka Board of Education* decision. A majority of the Supreme Court had heard an appeal from local schools against continuing desegregation. Due to these demographic changes, it was argued, there were few whites left in the big cities to alter racial proportions in schools. Moreover, it was claimed, local officials could not be blamed if they did nothing to promote segregation. On the other hand, as argued by a group of social scientists who had studied desegregation over several decades, desegregation was not a failure as many alleged. In the end though, the Supreme Court overturned the *Brown* decision of over thirty years on the grounds that if demography led to segregation, and if officials did not officially segregate, then there was no barrier to continuing this new segregation. In the few years of the 1990s thereafter, many big cities moved to drop desegregation plans—including Topeka.

What are we to make of this political struggle over social policy? Was it the fault of the media, who, it was claimed, reported only on the failure of desegregation in big-city schools? A close analysis of newspaper coverage for the 1990s revealed quite the contrary; almost all newspaper stories were not critical (Merelman, 2002). Was it the growth of a conservative movement in America since President Reagan's election that generated the impression of failure drawn from studies in think tanks and related books? Clearly, the evidence supports this movement's growth in groups and writings, but it is problematical that it influenced legislators or judges who were not already of that mind. The underlying explanation lies in the growing belief of many citizens that desegregation was a misguided movement. The grounds for this belief may lie with adverse publicity, personal experiences, and racist outlooks. That is a supposition, and it is equally problematical because there is no test of where the attitudes came from or how people shaped their own opinions.

Note that the desegregation supporters lacked the continuing support of an organized set of beneficiaries, as was the case with social policy. The National Association for the Advancement of Colored People, the original stimulant of the *Brown* decision and others, was the only support group. By the end, though, many African American parents came to believe that a school limited to their race would be beneficial to their children's learning; that view was heard even in the National Association for the Advancement of Colored People and elsewhere. Again, this lack of an organized political support, facing a growing opposition of public opinion, meant that in a political system—in which politicians know that large opinion sets had better be paid attention to—these leaders changed their minds. As they looked around, elements of the political system at all levels, and the Supreme Court reflecting conservative views, approved this policy change. In short, there was only limited support of the beneficiaries for this national program, and so, unlike that for welfare, it failed. Critics may well charge racism for the outcome, but the opposition was larger and louder, and in democracies that works.

In the preceding analysis we have suggested the many qualities of the political nature of court action. We dealt in depth with only one issue, desegregation, as it deals with the rise and fall of political opinions working through constitutional agencies. That, too, demonstrated finally the ultimate political nature of court actions as they affect educational systems.

REFERENCES

Berliner, D., & Biddle, B. (1995). *The manufactured crisis.* Reading, MA: Addison-Wesley.

de Tocqueville, A. (1955). *Democracy in America. The Henry Reeve text as revised by Francis Bowen now further corrected and edited with a historical essay, editorial notes, and bibliographies by Philip Bradley.* New York: Vintage Books.

Dow, P. (1991). *Schoolhouse politics.* Cambridge: Harvard University Press.

Heclo, H. (1978). Issue networks and the executive establishment. In A. King (Ed.), *The new american political system.* Washington, DC: American Enterprise Institute.

Kirp, D., & Yudof, M. (1987). *Education policy and the law.* Berkeley, CA: McCutchan.

Kirst, M. (1988). The federal role and chapter I. In D. Doyle & B. Cooper (Eds.), *Federal aid to the disadvantaged.* Berkeley, CA: McCutchan, pp. 97–118.

Merelman, R. (2002, February 6). Dis-integrating American public schools: Our new social myths and their consequences. *Education Week, 52,* 36.

Orfield, G. (1978). *Must we bus? Segregated schools and national policy.* Washington, DC: Brookings Institution.

Orfield, G. (1987). *Public school desegregation in the United States, 1968–1980.* Washington, DC: Joint Center for Political Studies.

Organization for Economic Cooperation and Development. (1993). *Education at a glance.* Paris: OECD.

Robelen, E. (2002, January 30). Spending plan for 2002 laden with "earmarks." *Education Week, 23,* 27.

Tyack, D., & Cuban, L. (1995). *Tinkering toward Utopia.* Cambridge, MA: Harvard University Press.

Wirt, F. (1997). *We ain't what we was: Law and civil rights in the new south.* Durham, NC: Duke University Press.

Wirt, F., & Kirst, M. (1997). *The political dynamics of American education* (2nd ed.). Berkeley, CA: McCutchan.

Yee, G., & Kirst, M. (1994). Lessons from the new science curriculum of the 1950s and 1960s. *Education and Urban Society, 26*(2), 158–171.

15 The Legal Foundation for Public Education: An Overview

Legal mandates governing public schools emanate from a combination of federal and state constitutions, laws, and regulations; contractual provisions; and judicial decisions. Although some may think that the term *school law* refers to a body of knowledge separate from the law in general, this is not the case. For example, contracts in school settings must conform to the basic principles governing all contracts. Likewise, constitutional principles must be followed whether in a public school or other government agency. Granted, there are some unique features of the school environment that may influence how legal provisions are applied and how courts interpret the mandates, but the legal principles are not suspended simply because the setting is a school.

Given the multiple sources of law and the variety of participants in public school systems—school boards, district and building administrators, teachers, support staff, parents, and students—some uncertainty exists about the scope of the various actors' authority. The different levels and branches of government often confuse school personnel as they attempt to carry out their jobs in conformance with the law. This chapter provides an overview of the legal framework of public education, including the sources of legal requirements, the delegation of authority to administrative agencies, and the role of the courts in interpreting constitutional and statutory provisions.

Constitutional Provisions

A constitution provides the fundamental laws governing a nation or state. Public schools are significantly influenced by both the United States Constitution and their respective state constitution. Although we have fifty separate state constitutions in our nation, they reflect considerable similarities.

Federal Constitution

The U.S. Constitution is the ultimate law of the land in our country. This document describes the relationship between the states and the federal government and provides for the protection of individual rights. The United States is unique among nations in that the Constitution has endured for more than two centuries with only twenty-seven amendments. A hallmark of our Constitution is the separation of powers among the executive, judicial, and legislative branches of government to form a system of checks and balances.

A basic principle of our legal system is that all statutes, regulations, and policies generated by any level of government must conform to the federal Constitution. The judiciary is empowered to interpret the meaning of constitutional provisions and to judge whether challenged statutes, regulations, and government practices impair constitutional rights. During the 1960s and 1970s, an activist U.S. Supreme Court expansively interpreted the federal Constitution, articulating individual rights and protections that had not previously existed. These constitutional rights placed limitations on the authority of state legislatures, school boards, school leaders, and other school personnel.

While public school policies and practices must conform to all parts of the federal Constitution, some provisions have an especially significant impact on the school environment. For example, the General Welfare Clause (Article I, Section 8, Clause 1) empowers Congress to tax and spend monies for the common defense and general welfare of the nation. The framers of the Constitution realized that they could not anticipate all the needs of the nation, so the General Welfare Clause provides flexibility for adjustments in these needs. The Supreme Court recognized in 1937: "Needs that were narrow or parochial a century ago may be interwoven in our day with the well-being of the nation. What is critical or urgent changes with the times" (*Helvering v. Davis*, p. 641). The scope of congressional power under the General Welfare Clause has been controversial, but this provision nonetheless has enabled Congress to allocate funds for a range of educational purposes. For example, Congress has enacted legislation providing federal aid for disadvantaged students, the school lunch program, loans and other aid for postsecondary students, educational research and development, services for children with disabilities, vocational education, and many other targeted programs. Congress has also used this provision to enact laws protecting student privacy in recordkeeping practices and ensuring parental access to their children's records. It has also enacted a number of other laws designed to protect subjects involved in research studies, place responsibilities on school districts in connection with asbestos removal and related environmental concerns, and address numerous other issues that affect schools and their clientele.

Another constitutional provision with a significant impact on school policies and practices is the Commerce Clause (Article I, Section 8, Clause 3). This provision empowers Congress to regulate commerce among states and with foreign nations. This clause may become increasingly important because of efforts to regulate materials accessible to children over the Internet (see Chapter 16). Also, Article I, Section 10, has a major impact on schools in its prohibition on governmental action impairing the obligation of contracts. All school employees are protected by individual contracts and in most cases by master contracts that are negotiated between the school board and the collective bargaining unit. As discussed later in this chapter, school boards also enter into contracts with a variety of businesses and individuals for instructional and support services.

Other constitutional provisions that protect personal freedoms have implications for the organization and administration of schools. Although individuals do not have an inherent right to an education simply because of U.S. citizenship (*San Antonio v. Rodriguez*, 1973), the Bill of Rights and other constitutional amendments contain important individual rights that are shielded from governmental intrusions. Legal developments pertaining to some of these provisions are addressed in the next chapter (e.g., freedom of expression, protection against arbitrary searches), so the constitutional amendments guaranteeing individual rights are mentioned only briefly here.

Some of the most significant personal freedoms are contained in the First Amendment's guarantee of religious liberties and its protection of free speech and press as well as the right to assemble and petition the government. These provisions have generated a large amount of school litigation involving student attire, distribution of literature, electronic expression, student-initiated devotional activities, meetings of student and community groups in public schools, government aid to religious schools, curriculum censorship, academic freedom, teachers' political expression, and a host of other concerns.

Although not equaling the First Amendment's volume of litigation, the Fourth Amendment's protection against unreasonable searches and seizures has been the basis for a number of significant judicial rulings involving drug-testing programs for students and teachers and searches of lockers, cars, and individuals at school. Also, the Ninth Amendment, which stipulates that "the enumeration in the Constitution, of certain rights, shall not be construed to deny or disparage others retained by the people," has been the basis for some educational litigation. Students and teachers have asserted that protected unenumerated rights include the rights to govern their appearance and to privacy outside the classroom (see Cambron-McCabe, McCarthy, & Thomas, 2004).

The constitutional provision most often used in school cases is the Fourteenth Amendment, because it directly addresses state action, whereas the protections in the Bill of Rights place limitations on the federal government. The Fourteenth Amendment in part protects individuals' life, liberty, and property rights against state encroachment without due process of law, and since the mid-twentieth century, the Supreme Court has interpreted protected liberties as incorporating the personal freedoms contained in the Bill of Rights (*Cantwell v. Connecticut*, 1940; *Gitlow v. New York*, 1925). By applying the first ten amendments' restrictions on congressional action to state action as well, this incorporation doctrine is especially significant in school controversies that are governed by state law.

In addition to incorporating the guarantees in the Bill of Rights and making them applicable to state action, the Fourteenth Amendment contains other significant protections against state encroachments. The Equal Protection Clause, prohibiting states from denying equal protection of the laws to their citizens, has been used to challenge a broad range of discriminatory practices. Indeed, when the Supreme Court relied on the Equal Protection Clause in 1954 to rule that separate schools for black and white children are inherently unequal (*Brown v. Board of Education*), it started a trend of judicial activism that will never be completely reversed. Before *Brown*, federal courts had reviewed only 300 school cases (Hogan, 1985); most legal controversies involving schools dealt instead with state laws pertaining to contractual concerns or pupil injuries. But following *Brown*, federal litigation escalated until it reached its high point in the late 1970s and early 1980s. Although federal litigation involving schools has leveled off, thousands of school cases are initiated in federal courts each year. The principles announced in *Brown* have affected equal protection litigation challenging discrimination based on gender, ethnic background, native language, disabilities, and other characteristics, as well as race. Some school finance litigation, addressed in Chapter 17, also has been based on the Equal Protection Clause or comparable state provisions.

The Fourteenth Amendment's Due Process Clause prohibits states from depriving citizens of life, liberty, or property without due process of law. This provision contains both procedural and substantive aspects. Procedural due process ensures that individuals are provided notice of the charges against them and an opportunity to refute the charges in a fair hearing prior to the government depriving them of their life, liberty, or property rights. Minor deprivations require only informal procedures (see *Goss v. Lopez*, 1975), but significant impairments (e.g., student expulsions, teacher dismissals) require more formal procedures, with the opportunity for the accused to be represented by an attorney and to confront adverse witnesses.

Substantive due process protects individuals against arbitrary government action threatening life, liberty, or property rights by requiring such action to "be based on a valid objective with means reasonably related to attaining the objective" (Cambron-McCabe, McCarthy, & Thomas, 2004, p. 14). Constitutional standards define minimal levels of acceptable conduct, and statutes and regulations can provide more extensive procedural and substantive safeguards beyond the constitutional minimums.

State Constitutions

Under the Tenth Amendment to the U.S. Constitution, "powers not delegated to the United States by the Constitution, nor prohibited by it to the states, are reserved to the states respectively, or to the people." Because education is not mentioned in the federal Constitution, it is one of the reserved powers of the states. All state constitutions require their respective legislative bodies to establish a system of free public education for children residing within the state. The state constitution usually places an obligation on the legislature to enact laws that will ensure a uniform, thorough and efficient, suitable, or adequate system of free schooling. The most common term across state education clauses is *uniform system*. Indiana's constitutional provision is typical:

> Knowledge and learning, generally diffused throughout a community, being essential to the preservation of a free government; it shall be the duty of the General

Assembly to encourage, by all suitable means, moral, intellectual, scientific, and agricultural improvement; and to provide, by law, for a general and uniform system of Common Schools, wherein tuition shall be without charge, and equally open to all. (Article 8, Section 1)

Also common is for states to charge the legislature with providing a "thorough and efficient" educational system, illustrated by the wording in Ohio's education clause: "The general assembly shall make such provisions, by taxation, or otherwise, as, with the income arising from the school trust fund, will secure a thorough and efficient system of common schools throughout the state...." (Article VI, Section 2).

In addition to placing a duty on legislative bodies to provide a system of schooling, most state constitutions also contain antidiscrimination provisions and measures similar to the federal Bill of Rights to protect individual liberties. In some instances, state constitutions may be more protective of personal rights than the federal Constitution, for example, in protecting individuals against governmental searches without individualized suspicion (see *Theodore v. Delaware Valley School District,* 2000). Also, some state constitutions are more restrictive than the federal Constitution in prohibiting the use of public funds for religious purposes. To illustrate, the Florida voucher program for students attending failing public schools, which allows state vouchers to be redeemed in religious schools, has been struck down under the Florida Constitution, but not under the Establishment Clause of the First Amendment (see *Holmes v. Bush,* 2002). A few state constitutions include specific curriculum mandates, but usually they charge the legislature with providing for education, which includes making curricular determinations.

Statutory Provisions

In a democracy, the legislative branch of government enacts laws that are intended to reflect the preferences of the citizenry; such laws must be consistent with constitutional grants of power and restrictions on legislative authority. Within these constraints, elected legislative bodies in our country have considerable latitude in operationalizing constitutional guarantees and in providing for the general welfare. Bills become laws after being signed by the chief executive (i.e., the President for federal laws and the Governor for state laws). Federal laws can be located in the *United States Code,* and state statutes can be found in each state's code.

Federal Legislation

Congress has the authority to enact laws that embody the aims of the United States Constitution. Under the Supremacy Clause (Article VI, Section 2), the federal Constitution as well as laws made pursuant to the Constitution supercede any inconsistent state laws. Yet, because education is not a fundamental right under the federal Constitution (*San Antonio Independent School District v. Rodriguez,* 1973), congressional influence on education has often been indirect. Basically two types of federal laws have a significant impact on public schools: funding laws and civil rights laws.

Funding Laws.   Some laws enacted under Congress' general welfare powers tie federal aid to particular initiatives designed to enhance the welfare of the nation. States have discretion as to whether to participate in such programs. However, if states accept the federal funds, they must satisfy the accompanying regulations.

Federal legislation actually provided land grants to states for the maintenance of public schools before ratification of the U.S. Constitution, but the significant legislative role in providing aid to stimulate targeted school reforms started in the 1960s. The Elementary and Secondary Education Act of 1965 (ESEA) was the most extensive educational funding law; a central provision of the ESEA provided support for compensatory education programs for economically disadvantaged students. The ESEA signaled a huge shift in federal education policy, and federal aid to education doubled with passage of this law. For the next fifteen years, the federal government's contribution to education steadily increased until it reached over 9 percent of total public education revenues in 1981. As addressed in Chapter 17, the federal share of education aid was about 7.3 percent in the 2000 to 2001 academic year (National Education Association, 2002).

However, the federal share of education revenue is expected to increase because of the No Child Left Behind (NCLB) Act, signed into law in 2002. This 670-page law is the most comprehensive reauthorization of the ESEA since 1965. It holds schools accountable for annual testing of all students based on academic standards (by 2005 to 2006 in reading or language arts and mathematics in grades 3 to 8 and by 2007 to 2008 in science at designated grade levels). Also, high school students must take a test covering the core curriculum at least once during grades 10 to 12. Each school must establish annual progress objectives to ensure that all students reach proficiency within twelve years (by 2013 to 2014), must narrow the test-score gap between disadvantaged and advantaged students, and must ensure that all teachers are of high quality.

The NCLB Act requires school districts to provide educational options to students who attend Title I schools that for two consecutive years have not made adequate yearly progress in key subject areas. To avoid sanctions, a school must meet its annual objectives for all subgroups specified in the law (i.e., major ethnic/racial groups, economically disadvantaged students, limited English proficient students, and students with disabilities). Most school districts initially are providing public school options for students assigned to schools rated as deficient, but each year the educational options must increase. After five years of failure to make adequate yearly progress for all groups, the school will be reconstituted with a new staff, converted into a charter school, operated by a private firm, or taken over by the state.

The reauthorization of the Individuals with Disabilities Education Act (IDEA) also is expected to increase the federal share of funding special services for children with disabilities. All states currently participate in the IDEA funding program, which requires them to comply with extensive regulations pertaining to the provision of appropriate programs for children with disabilities. Congress originally authorized this federal law (formerly the Education for All Handicapped Children Act of 1975) to provide up to 40 percent of the excess costs of special services for these children, but appropriations have not yet come close to that percentage.

The IDEA provides extensive protections to children with disabilities including the development of an individualized education program by a planning team of regular and special educators and the child's parents; procedural protections in placement decisions and in administering discipline, with the guarantee that services will not be terminated for disciplinary reasons; and placement with nondisabled children to the maximum extent appropriate (least restrictive environment), which means bringing services to the child in the regular classroom when possible. In addition to their entitlement to special education, children with disabilities must be provided related services (e.g., transportation, physical therapy) that are necessary for them to benefit from the educational program. Given the substantial costs associated with providing appropriate programs for children with disabilities, considerable IDEA litigation has focused on who has the fiscal responsibility for particular programs and placements for such children (see Mayes & Zirkel, 2000).

While the NCLB and the IDEA are two of the most significant federal laws that affect education, other categorical funding laws have influenced school policies and practices through the regulations that must be satisfied as a condition of receiving the aid. Many categorical aid programs enacted as part of the War on Poverty in the 1960s and 1970s focused on equity goals and improving educational programs for disadvantaged students (e.g., aid to desegregate schools and provide bilingual education). Congress began moving away from categorical programs in the 1980s, although some aid, such as support for children with disabilities, has remained categorical. The current emphasis in federal aid initiatives is on reading in early grades, school accountability for student performance, and elimination of the achievement gap among various groups of children. Some movement has been made toward providing state and local education agencies more discretion in selecting strategies to satisfy standards as long as they are demonstrating accountability for student academic progress measured on statewide tests.

Civil Rights Laws. Congress is empowered to enact legislation to implement constitutional protections. Whereas state and local education agencies can decline to participate in federal funding programs, they must comply with civil rights laws. Some civil rights laws have general application, whereas others apply to federally assisted entities. As addressed in Chapter 16, individuals can bring private lawsuits to compel compliance with some of these civil rights laws. Other laws state explicitly that the sole remedies are administrative, or they have been judicially interpreted as precluding private suits for damages. The most common administrative remedy included in legislation affecting education is for the Department of Education to withdraw federal aid from the noncomplying institution. The threat of such sanctions has caused school districts to alter policies and practices, but rarely have federal funds been withheld.

A number of important laws were enacted during the civil rights movement of the 1960s, and these measures protect citizens from discrimination on various characteristics, such as race, national origin, gender, age, disability, and religion. Courts have often been called on to interpret these laws and clarify the scope of individuals' statutory protections against discrimination.

In addition to substantive rights guaranteed by specific laws, individuals can use a civil rights law enacted in 1871 to secure monetary damages for violations of their constitutional rights and in some instances for impairments of other federally protected rights. This law, referred to as Section 1983, was originally intended to protect the rights of African American citizens, but it has become prominent in the last several decades as a vehicle for other individuals to get damages for federal deprivations. Thus, school employees and students have used Section 1983 to seek damages if school policies and practices have violated their federal rights. However, suits cannot be brought under Section 1983 if the federal law at issue has been interpreted as precluding such private suits (see *Gonzaga v. Doe*, 2002; Chapter 16).

The meaning of some laws may be ambiguous, so courts must illuminate legislative intent. If the judiciary misinterprets a law, Congress can clarify its meaning through an amendment, unless the law has been invalidated as abridging federal constitutional provisions. Such amendments have been enacted on several occasions after the Supreme Court has interpreted a law in a manner that does not reflect legislative intent. For example, after the Supreme Court interpreted Title VII of the Civil Rights Act of 1964 as allowing employers to omit pregnancy-related disabilities from employee disability packages (*General Electric v. Gilbert*, 1976), Congress responded by amending Title VII with the Pregnancy Discrimination Act of 1978 that specifically prohibits employment practices that discriminate against pregnant employees. Also, after the Supreme Court ruled that the Education for All Handicapped Children Act (now the IDEA) did not allow successful plaintiffs to be awarded attorneys' fees (*Smith v. Robinson*, 1984), Congress responded by amending the law to make explicit provision for the award of attorneys' fees.

State Legislation

Whereas Congress can influence education only indirectly through its general welfare and other enumerated powers, state legislatures have comprehensive authority "to prescribe and control conduct in the schools" as long as actions and policies conform to the federal Constitution (*Tinker v. Des Moines*, 1969, p. 507). Thus, state legislatures have considerable discretion to enact laws pertaining to all aspects of the educational enterprise from regulating personnel licensure and the instructional program to raising revenue and distributing school funds. State legislatures even have the authority to abolish local school districts, but given the reverence for local school control in our nation, such action seems unlikely. Before local school boards could be eliminated, other conflicting state statutes would have to be altered, such as provisions entitling citizens to vote on school district boundary changes that result in annexations (see *State v. Board of Education*, 1987).

State legislatures legally can regulate detailed aspects of public schools, but most have not found it feasible to do so. They also are empowered to delegate authority to make rules and regulations to state administrative agencies or local boards of education, although their lawmaking powers cannot be delegated. There has been a trend toward more explicit state legislation accompanying an increase in the state's contribution in funding public schools (see Chapter 17). In some states, such as California and Florida, legislative directives are quite extensive, leaving little flexibility at the district level. But in other states with a greater commitment to local control of education (e.g., Colorado, New Hampshire), local boards have been delegated a great deal of authority to make operational decisions within broad legislative guidelines.

State law attaches conditions to public school employment, such as requirements that public school teachers must satisfy to receive teaching licenses. State laws also specify dismissal procedures for tenured and nontenured teachers; the specifics of state retirement plans; the scope, if any, of collective bargaining for public employees; and whether principals and other administrators will be given some type of job security beyond their status as a teacher (e.g., two-year contracts).

As with employees, state laws also govern many aspects of students' relationships with public schools. The most important stipulation is that all children between specified ages (usually six to sixteen) must attend a public or private school or receive an equivalent education. Compulsory attendance laws are designed to ensure an educated citizenry, which is considered essential in a democracy. After the Supreme Court struck down state-imposed school segregation (*Brown v. Board of Education,* 1954), a few southern states eliminated their compulsory education laws, but all states now make education mandatory. States vary as to exceptions they allow to compulsory education (e.g., married students, students with valid work permits who are at least fourteen years old), and the Supreme Court has recognized a religious exemption for Amish youth who have completed eighth grade (*Wisconsin v. Yoder,* 1972). Beyond mandating that all children be educated, states have broad discretion to prescribe courses of study, instructional materials, graduation requirements, assessment practices, and most features of school operations.

At the same time that federal support for education declined in the 1980s and the Supreme Court became less assertive in expanding individual rights, state legislatures were increasing their oversight of local school boards through a number of educational reform measures. Indeed, following distribution of *A Nation at Risk* (1983), education assumed a prominent place on state political agendas, and during the next decade practically every state adopted a major school reform package. This reform legislation tended to increase the state's oversight role and place additional responsibilities on local districts and school leaders.

Accountability laws making schools responsible for students meeting academic standards measured by test scores currently are at the forefront of state education legislation (and federal legislation as well). The mandates across states focus on aligning curriculum and assessments to rigorous academic standards, implementing high-stakes testing, and publicly reporting test results by school and grade level. These accountability laws often include the dissemination of school rankings and the provision of assistance and sanctions for low-performing schools. In addition, many state laws focus specifically on educational personnel and establish standards and tests for teacher and administrator licensure, teacher and leadership academies to provide professional development, alternative recruitment and preparation routes for nontraditional teacher and administrative candidates, teacher and administrative mentoring and induction programs, and targeted recruitment for educators that focuses on minority populations (see Anthes, 2001).

Legislatures also are authorizing alternative school governance arrangements, which include waivers of specific laws and regulations that apply to public schools. This is apparently in response to criticism about the high degree of legislative control over public education and the desire to nurture more innovation and an entrepreneurial spirit toward the operation of public schools.

The most striking trend in this regard is the charter school movement, which has spread rapidly across states. In 1992, only two states authorized charter schools that operate outside many state regulations on the basis of a charter granted by state or local education agencies, universities, or other entities specified in the legislation. A decade later, thirty-nine states, the District of Columbia, and Puerto Rico had charter school laws (Center for Education Reform, 2002). Most of these laws limit the number of charters granted to existing public or private schools or groups starting new schools. The degree that these schools are exempt from state regulations varies widely across states. For example, several charter school laws allow such schools to be exempt from most state and local district curriculum and personnel requirements, but the majority of states allow waivers from a more limited set of rules and regulations, some of which might be negotiated as part of the charter approval process.

State legislatures have the legal authority to regulate alternatives to public education, although they cannot force all children to enroll in public schools. The Supreme Court ruled in 1925 that parents have a constitutional right to choose private education for their children (*Pierce v. Society of Sisters*, 1925). The Court declared that "the fundamental theory of liberty upon which all governments in this union repose excludes any general power of the state to standardize its children by forcing them to accept instruction from public teachers only" (p. 535). Although states retain the authority to regulate education to ensure an educated citizenry, there has been a trend toward deregulating home education and private schools in terms of input standards and satisfying the state's interests by assessing student performance (see Dare, 2001). If students in a certain school or home education program consistently score poorly on statewide tests, courts may rule that the specific school or program can no longer satisfy compulsory attendance mandates.

Similar to controversies over federal laws, courts may be called on to interpret state statutes if their meanings are not clear. State legislatures can amend a given law if the judiciary misinterprets legislative intent, unless the court concludes that the law abridges state or federal constitutions or civil rights laws.

Administrative Rules and Regulations

Laws cannot include every single detail necessary to implement legislative will, so Congress and state legislatures have delegated some authority to administrative agencies to develop rules and regulations to implement the laws within statutory specifications. But as noted, the legislative branch of government cannot delegate its lawmaking powers to administrative agencies, which would dilute legislative autonomy and threaten the basic principle of maintaining a separation of powers that is central to the constitutional system in the United States. In addition, such a transfer would put the administrative decision makers out of reach of the electorate, the important political check that exists in the country's democratic system.

Nonetheless, delegated administrative authority can be substantial, and administrative rules and regulations provide a significant source of legal requirements. In the school context, regulations adopted to implement statutory provisions often have a far greater impact on school personnel and educational practices than do the laws themselves.

If questions are raised as to whether an agency is exercising lawfully delegated authority, courts search the enabling statutes for reasonably precise guidelines that might describe the policy objectives of the legislature or guide administrator discretion in implementing the legislative goal. In general, the delegation is valid if the statutory guidelines limit the discretion of the administrators and do not allow administrative judgment to be substituted for that of the elected legislators (*A.L.A. Schechter Poultry Corporation v. United States,* 1935). Administrative regulations are legally binding unless challenged and found beyond the scope of delegated authority or in conflict with statutory or constitutional interpretations.

Federal Agencies

The Department of Education and other federal agencies play an important role in interpreting congressional enactments through the regulations they promulgate. Since its creation in 1980, the Department has functioned under the direction of the Secretary of Education, who is a member of the President's cabinet. When an education bill is signed into law, the Department designs regulations, which are reviewed by Congress following public hearings.

Sometimes federal regulations go beyond congressional intent or at least beyond what the Supreme Court has determined congressional intent to be. As noted previously, if the Court has erroneously interpreted the law or its regulations, Congress can pass an amendment to clarify the law's meaning. And if the federal agency has misinterpreted the law's intent, Congress can withhold approval during its review of the administrative regulations. Conflicts can, and often do, arise between judicial and agency interpretations of given laws; such conflicts are particularly troublesome if no legislative action is taken to resolve them. For example, as addressed in Chapter 16, the Supreme Court's interpretation of the standard to use in assessing sexual harassment claims under Title IX of the Education Amendments of 1972 (*Davis v. Monroe County,* 1999; *Gebser v. Lago Vista,* 1998) conflicted with the detailed regulations issued by the Office for Civil Rights (OCR) in the Department of Education. The subsequent revision of the OCR's *Sexual Harassment Guidance* (2001) distinguishes the Court's standards applied to private lawsuits against educational institutions to secure damages under Title IX and the

OCR's standards for administrative enforcement (withholding federal aid from noncomplying institutions). Of course, if the Supreme Court or the OCR has misinterpreted congressional intent, Congress can amend the language of Title IX to clarify its meaning.

State Agencies

Like Congress, state legislatures also can delegate to administrative agencies rule-making authority, but not lawmaking power. States vary greatly in the delegation of such administrative authority. Some prescribe detailed standards that must be followed by state and local education agencies, whereas others include general directions in state laws and delegate authority for state and local boards of education to formulate the specific guidelines for schools to follow.

All states except Wisconsin have established a state board of education, a policymaking body, that provides rules and regulations to implement laws affecting education. The state board of education must always operate within legislative directives, and therefore, has only the authority expressly or implicitly delegated by state law. Members of the state board of education usually are appointed by the governor or elected by the citizenry (Cambron-McCabe, McCarthy, & Thomas, 2004).

State boards of education generally oversee school accreditation, which traditionally has required schools to satisfy various curriculum, facility, and personnel requirements. There is a recent trend for states to shift from such input standards to performance-based accreditation, reflecting the movement in this direction among regional and other accrediting agencies. Under the newer models, schools are judged based on various student performance standards. State boards also often monitor teacher licensure, although a number of states recently have established professional standards boards to handle teacher and administrator licensure. In some states, the professional standards board functions independently from the state board of education.

Each state has a chief state school officer (CSSO), often called the state superintendent of instruction, who functions in an executive capacity and often chairs the state board. The CSSO generally provides leadership for statewide school reform efforts, monitors implementation of education policies, and gathers data on the condition of education in the state. In some states, the CSSO plays a role in resolving educational controversies, and individuals cannot initiate a lawsuit for a grievance pertaining to internal school operations until they have exhausted such administrative appeals (Cambron-McCabe, McCarthy, & Thomas, 2004). Courts show considerable deference to decisions of CSSOs unless they have acted arbitrarily or disregarded the evidence presented (*Botti v. S. W. Butler*, 1987; *Eisbruck v. New York*, 1987). A state education department usually reports to the CSSO and provides consultation to the state and local school boards, engages in research and development activities to improve educational practices, and assists the CSSO in gathering data and monitoring school activities.

State boards can adopt rules and regulations that govern a range of school operations, as long as they function within legislative parameters. Broad legislative guidelines are often considered adequate authorization for administrative action (Valente & Valente, 2001). In some states, rules pertaining to such matters as proficiency testing for students and programs for children with disabilities are embodied in state board rules rather than state law. For example, Indiana legislative mandates regarding the education of children with disabilities are quite broad, whereas the state board has adopted extensive administrative rules that school districts must follow in the identification and education of these children (511 IAC 7-17 through 7-31, 2002).

Courts may be called on to determine whether the administrative body has acted beyond its express or implied delegated powers. At times, there is a fine line between legitimate implied authority to carry out its educational function and a non-delegated illegal activity, but courts generally have upheld decisions made by state boards of education. For example, the Kansas State Board of Education attracted national attention in 1999 when it rejected proposed science standards emphasizing evolution and instead adopted an alternative set eliminating the requirement that local school districts teach or test students about evolution (Hemenway, 1999). Although considerable concern was voiced about the wisdom of this decision, the board was acting within its delegated authority to make curricular determinations. The success of antievolution forces in Kansas was short lived, however, as there was a shift in power to create a moderate majority on the state board, which approved new science standards in 2000, reinstating the study of evolution.

Occasionally, a conflict will arise when one administrative agency seeks to take action that impinges on the authority of another administrative agency. In this highly regulated world during a period of rapidly changing circumstances, such jurisdictional conflicts are not unusual. Courts normally resolve these disputes by identifying the particular activity and determining which administrative agency has the more central responsibility. As an example, an Illinois dispute arose over the authority of a county health department to make sanitation and health inspections of public school cafeterias. The school district argued that this authority to inspect the schools resided exclusively in the regional superintendent of schools. The appellate court, analyzing the appropriate statutes, determined that the regional superintendent did not have exclusive authority. Because the legislature delegated to county health departments general authority for sanitation and health inspections, the Illinois appeals court concluded that the county health department was authorized to inspect school cafeterias, even though regional superintendents had general inspection authority for school buildings (*County of Macon v. Board of Education*, 1987).

Local School Boards

Webb, Metha, and Jordan (2003) have observed that public education in our nation "is a state responsibility, a local function, and a federal concern" (p. 408). Although public schools are legally controlled by the state, they are administered locally. Hawaii is the only state that has not established local school boards to administer public schools. The amount of administrative authority delegated to local districts varies widely across states as does the number of districts established. The southeastern part of the nation tends to have larger school districts, and thus a smaller number of them, whereas districts in New England and the Midwest tend to be small except in large urban centers. Several states with smaller districts have intermediate administrative units that perform regulatory or service activities for a group of local districts. Some states have separate school districts for elementary and secondary students, but more commonly, districts include all pre-K–12 students in a given geographic area. A couple of states have fewer than twenty school districts, whereas a few have more than 700 districts, and districts range in size from a handful of students to several hundred thousand (see Webb, Metha, & Jordan, 2003). There are approximately 14,900 local districts nationwide and about 600 special districts operated by federal and state agencies.

Many erroneously believe that local school boards control public education in this nation; local boards have only the authority that the state legislature delegates to them. The legislature determines whether a local board's discretionary powers are quite extensive or narrowly prescribed by state law. As with state administrative agencies, local school boards' delegated authority can be directly specified or implied. The operation of public schools has become so routine that there is seldom a question of appropriate exercise of authority. But when a school district faces a new problem and wants to develop a policy that goes beyond anything that has been done before, questions may arise about whether legislative authorization exists for such action. Likewise, when a school district takes an action that upsets the district's constituency, school patrons may consider legal challenges, alleging that the district has exceeded its authority.

Because the locus of legal responsibility for education remains with the state, the legislature can restrict the discretion of local boards through legislation, which has happened with recent school accountability laws. Nonetheless, in most states, school boards retain considerable latitude to make policies governing schools, which are legally binding on employees and students as long as they are adopted pursuant to statutory authority. Courts are reluctant to overturn decisions made by school boards unless the board action is arbitrary, capricious, or outside its legal authority. Local boards' delegated powers generally encompass the authority to purchase equipment and materials needed to operate the schools; to build and maintain facilities; to hire, assign, and terminate personnel; and to determine the curriculum and other aspects of the educational program within statutory guidelines. Even without explicit legislation, local boards have discretionary authority to make decisions necessary to run the schools. To illustrate, courts have upheld local school boards' authority to establish prerequisites to receipt of a high school diploma, such as a proficiency test and community service requirement, without specific legislation in this regard (see *Brookhart v. Illinois State Board of Education*, 1983; *Herndon v. Chapel Hill-Carrboro City Board of Education*, 1996). Also, school boards can place conditions on employment (e.g., continuing education requirements, residency requirements) beyond state minimums, unless prohibited by law (see *Harrah Independent School District v. Martin*, 1979; *Meyers v. Newport School District*, 1982).

Some local boards' decisions have been challenged as beyond their lawful scope of authority. For example, a North Carolina case involved a challenge about the authority of a school district to initiate an extended day-care program to better accommodate the home arrangements of many of its latchkey students. The school district initiated an extended-day program that charged a fee for activities after school for children who might not have parents at home at the end of the normal school day. The only costs to the school district were for fuel and lighting associated with use of the building. A coalition of day-care-center operators challenged the authority of the school district to initiate such a program. A North Carolina appeals court in *Kiddie Korner Day Schools v. Charlotte-Mecklenburg Board of Education* (1981) held that the school district had the authority under state statute to operate such a program for latchkey children. Additionally, the court upheld the school district's authority to expend money for heating and lighting the building to benefit these extended-day pupils. Concluding that the school board had the authority to absorb the fuel and electricity costs of the program that advanced the public purpose of improving the educational achievements of latchkey children, the court rejected the contention that the expenditure must be approved by the voters in a referendum.

Whereas public school administrators are school employees, board members are considered public school officers with some of the state's sovereign power. Generally, school board members are elected by residents of their districts, but board members in a few states are appointed by the mayor, city council, or other agency. Procedures used to elect board members cannot disenfranchise qualified voters. Violations of the federal Voting Rights Act might be found if *at-large* elections significantly dilute the minority vote (see *Johnson v. Desoto County*, 2000). Yet, the Supreme Court also has struck down congressional redistricting plans drawn on the basis of race as abridging the Fourteenth Amendment's Equal Protection Clause (*Bush v. Vera*, 1996; *Shaw v. Hunt*, 1996), so it is doubtful that race-based voting districts to elect school board members would be constitutional (see *Cannon v. North Carolina State Board*, 1996).

State law usually specifies the terms, qualifications, and grounds for dismissal of board members as well as some of local boards' operating procedures. An important operating principle is that school board meetings and records must be open to the public to ensure that citizens are fully informed regarding board activities and decisions. State law can specify certain exceptions to *sunshine* provisions, such as allowing boards to meet in executive session to discuss personnel and property matters, collective bargaining, and other sensitive issues that pertain to lawsuits or public safety. Even matters that can be discussed in executive session must be brought to public meetings for any formal actions to be taken (see Cambron-McCabe, McCarthy, & Thomas, 2004; Valente & Valente, 2001). In making these decisions, individual board members cannot act on behalf of the board; a school board must act as a unit. Also, school administrators can make recommendations to the board, but they have no authority to make decisions that become official board policies.

School-Based Councils

School-based councils have become popular since the 1980s in an effort to democ-ratize school decisions and increase community ownership of public schools. Wohlstetter and Van Kirk (1995) have argued that high-involvement, decentral-ized management is desirable for schools and will result in improved organiza-tional effectiveness and productivity if power, information, knowledge, and rewards are decentralized. Indeed, the school site has increasingly become the focus of school reform and accountability initiatives. Some arrangements estab-lishing school-based councils have generated litigation, and the legal relationship between such councils and local school boards is still evolving.

The Supreme Court declined to review a Seventh Circuit decision in which the appeals court upheld Illinois legislation authorizing the creation of elected school councils in Chicago public schools. These councils have the authority to hire school personnel and approve budgets and programs. The appeals court re-jected the school principals' assertion that removal of administrative tenure im-paired their rights. Also, the court held that the election of school council members did not impair voting rights of nonparent residents who had only two places on the council, whereas six seats were reserved for parents (*Pittman v. Chi-cago Board*, 1995).

Statewide efforts in Kentucky to create local school councils have generated some questions about their jurisdiction. After a local board required school-based councils to obtain board approval for school improvement plans, several teachers challenged this action. Recognizing some overlap in duties between local boards and school councils, the Kentucky Supreme Court ruled that local boards were not delegated authority to approve school-based council decisions pertaining to school improvement plans (*Board of Education v. Bushee*, 1994).

The judiciary will invalidate actions of school-based councils only if the coun-cils act beyond their scope of authority or impair protected rights. With federal and state mandates placing more responsibilities on local schools to make adequate yearly progress toward performance objectives coupled with more emphasis on school report cards and school rankings, the importance of local school councils may increase.

Contractual Provisions

State legislation grants school districts the authority to enter into a range of con-tracts for educational goods and services. School contracts must contain the basic elements of all legal contracts (i.e., offer and acceptance; competent parties; con-sideration, such as salary in exchange for services; legal subject matter; and proper form; see Alexander & Alexander, 2001). Only the school board can enter into em-ployment contracts; as noted previously, the superintendent can make personnel recommendations but is not authorized to consummate employment contracts. Most certified school employees enter into term contracts (for a designated period of time such as one year) or continuing contracts that can be terminated only for a cause specified in the law.

In addition to individual contracts with school district employees, many school boards also have signed master contracts that are bargained with one or more groups of employees. Individual employment contracts usually specify that their terms include all provisions of the collective bargaining agreement. In most states, the collective bargaining process between the school district and its employee groups is carefully controlled by statutes and administrative regulations. There are detailed requirements about who is covered in the collective bargaining process, the scope of the negotiations, appropriate actions of each party during negotiations, and the availability of various options when impasse is reached. All school leaders need to be aware of applicable bargaining requirements for public employees as well as the provisions of the negotiated agreements.

Contracts can be formed only according to the specific standards stated in law. If an individual accepts a school position without a valid contract, the person serves as a volunteer. A South Dakota school district, for example, had an unexpected resignation in late August. The position vacancy was announced, and a candidate visited the district and interviewed for the position. The candidate was told he would have a two-week trial period, as the board was not scheduled to meet before then. The candidate refused to take the position on a trial basis, so the contract was prepared, and he signed it. Before the contract was signed by the appropriate parties representing the school district, the new teacher had trouble with his class, and the board refused to approve the contract after the teacher had taught for nine days. The South Dakota Supreme Court held that no contract existed because the contract had not been signed by the appropriate district representatives as required by law, which in this case were the president of the school board and business manager of the school district (*Sutera v. Sully Buttes School District*, 1984).

While employment contracts (individual and collectively bargained agreements) are school districts' major contractual obligations, schools are businesses and enter into contracts with a variety of vendors to provide goods and services that support the educational program. These range from milk contracts and textbook contracts to contracts for new school buildings. Some school districts are exploring more broadly the services that they can purchase through contractual agreements. Whereas transportation services have been contracted for decades, contracting for custodial services and food services from private vendors is becoming more popular. The current climate seems hospitable toward contracting for a range of goods and services in public education.

A controversial issue, which is revisited in Chapter 17, is for private contractors to provide instructional services or to operate entire schools. In recent years, corporations such as Education Alternatives, Inc., and the Edison Project have attracted substantial attention because of their contracts to manage public schools and school districts (see Gewertz, 2002). Also, a number of companies, such as Sylvan Learning Systems and Britannica Learning Centers, have more limited contracts with public school districts to provide intensive tutoring or specialized instruction. School boards may feel that they have little to lose by entering into these contracts, because the companies are paid only if the contractual provisions are met, usually specified in terms of student achievement gains. The judiciary may be called on to evaluate the validity of a given contract or to assess whether a party has breached its contractual obligations. In most instances, contractual arrangements to provide instructional services or to manage schools have been considered lawful contracts between school boards and companies (see McCarthy, 2000).

Also, contracts for commercial activities in schools are becoming more prevalent, and some of these contracts have generated legal controversies. Courts generally have upheld local boards' authority to contract with companies to advertise in public schools in return for equipment or revenue. To illustrate, the North Carolina Supreme Court held that the state board of education's prohibition on local board contracts with Whittle Communications to show Channel One's news program with advertisements interfered with school boards' statutory authority to enter into contracts for supplementary materials (*State v. Whittle Communications*, 1991).

Other contracts pertaining to student activities raise interesting questions about who has the authority to enter into contracts representing the school district. For example, in *Community Projects for Students v. Wilder* (1982), a state appeals court held that a supplier of merchandise for sale by students could not sue the school district for the value of unsold and unreturned merchandise because the school board had not signed the contract. The court articulated who had the authority to make contracts: "Under the system of public education in this state, local school boards alone have the duty or authority to enter into or authorize purchases of supplies and equipment for the respective local school systems" (p. 435). The court rejected an argument that the principal had apparent authority to bind the board of education to the contract.

Judicial Role

The term *common law* refers to judicially created legal principles (Cambron-McCabe, McCarthy, & Thomas, 2004). Courts do not enact laws, but they play an important role in shaping the law through their powers of judicial review. In settling disputes they often give meaning to legislative and constitutional provisions. Many phrases in the federal and state constitutions, such as "equal protection" and "cruel and unusual punishment," or in laws, such as "equivalent instruction" or "thorough and efficient," are not self-explanatory, and courts have developed various criteria to assess whether the constitutional and statutory provisions have been breached. These judicially created standards can be as important as the constitutional or statutory provisions themselves, and, therefore, much of the study of school law focuses on judicial rulings. It is imperative for school leaders to understand the function and structure of the judicial system in our nation and be able to locate pertinent cases (Exhibit 15.1).

Courts do not provide advisory opinions; there must be a genuine dispute between parties affected by the policy or practice for a court to hear arguments and render an opinion. Also, the judiciary relies on precedents in that it applies

---

EXHIBIT **15.1**

Locating Cases (*Lee v. Weisman*, 505 U.S. 577 (1992)

Cases are often cited in support of a proposition, and the citation communicates how the case can be easily located in its entirety. Cases are collected according to reporter systems, each of which has its own title and abbreviation. The number in front of the reporter identification is the volume; the number following the reporter is the page number where the decision can be found. Therefore, the Supreme Court decision in *Lee v. Weisman,* 505 U.S. 577, 112 S. Ct. 2649 (1992), can be found on page 577 of volume 505 of the *United States Reporter.* A decision may appear in more than one reporter. Supreme Court opinions, because of their importance, are published in several reporters. The official reporter for the Supreme Court, the *United States Reporter,* is listed first in citation. The second citation is for the *Supreme Court Reporter,* often cited because it is published more quickly after a decision than the official reporter. Very recent opinions will not yet be cited in any reporter due to delays in publishing. These recent opinions can be found, however, in either LEXIS or Westlaw, two computerized legal research companies that provide online opinions within twenty-four hours of a released decision. The LEXIS cite to the *Weisman* decision is 1992 LEXIS 4364. The Westlaw cite to oral arguments before the Supreme Court in *Weisman* is 1991 WL 636285. Computerized research can provide access to much more information than the mere published opinion (i.e., briefs and transcripts of arguments). Federal district court decisions are available in the Federal Supplement, abbreviated F. Supp. and F. Supp. 2d, and opinions of the federal circuit courts of appeal are available in the Federal Reporter, abbreviated F., F.2d, and F.3d. The *Weisman* district court decision is reported at 728 F. Supp. 68 (D.R.I. 1990), and the First Circuit decision is reported at 908 F.2d 1090 (1st Cir. 1990).

State court decisions are not collected for courts of general jurisdiction (the lowest level), but state appellate courts are available either in the official state reporter (e.g., the *Illinois Reporter*) or in a regional reporter. West Group Publishing Company publishes state opinions by regions. For example, the *Atlantic Reporter,* Second Series, abbreviated A.2d, reports cases from Connecticut, Delaware, Maine, Maryland, New Hampshire, New Jersey, Pennsylvania, Rhode Island, and Vermont. There are seven regional reporters—Atlantic, Northeastern, Northwestern, Pacific, Southeastern, Southern, and Southwestern—that report cases from all fifty states. Also, West Group publishes separate reporters for New York (abbreviated N.Y.S.2d) and California (abbreviated Cal. Rptr.) because of the volume of cases in those states, and it collects cases in some specialty reporters according to subject area. Since 1982, it has been collecting education cases reported in various regional and federal reporters in a single source entitled the *Education Law Reporter.* The *Weisman* Supreme Court decision is reported in the *Educational Law Reporter* at 75 Ed. Law Rep. 43 (1992).

---

principles of law established in previous cases with similar factual situations. Although the Supreme Court has overturned its precedents, it does so only when absolutely necessary. For example, when it rendered *Brown v. Board of Education* (1954), declaring that *de jure* school segregation violates the Fourteenth Amendment, it overturned the "separate but equal" doctrine it had established in *Plessey v. Furguson* (1896). More recently, when the Court ruled that public school personnel could provide remedial services for students in religious schools (*Agostini v. Felton*, 1997), it overturned a precedent established only twelve years earlier (*Aguilar v. Felton*, 1985).

If a case can be decided on statutory grounds, the Supreme Court will avoid constitutional interpretations. For example, in *Lau v. Nichols* (1974) the Supreme Court ruled that students with English language deficiencies were entitled to special assistance under Title VI of the Civil Rights Act of 1964 that bars discrimination on the basis of race, color, or national origin in federally assisted programs. Because relief could be provided under federal law, the Court did not have to address the claim that the school district's treatment of English-deficient students violated the Fourteenth Amendment's Equal Protection Clause. When a constitutional interpretation is necessary, the U.S. Supreme Court has final authority to decide what constitutional provisions mean. The only way to override a Supreme Court interpretation is to amend the Constitution.

Whereas a statute is usually couched in general terms and attempts to deal with future circumstances, a judicial decision by necessity deals with interpreting a statute, contract, regulation, or constitution in the context of a particular dispute. Judges apply the judicial standard that pertains to a particular set of facts, and as noted, they attempt to adhere to precedents established in prior cases. One complex aspect of determining the importance of a court decision is deciding how broadly the legal standard and result reached in one decision can be applied to other circumstances.

A fundamental principle of the federalist system is the dual authority enjoyed by the state and federal governments. Because the source of a decision has bearing on its significance, it is important to understand the structure of state and federal court systems.

The Three-Tiered State Judicial System

Most states have a three-tiered judicial system that includes a court of general jurisdiction, a court of intermediate review, and a court of last resort (Figure 15.1). The name given to each of these levels differs considerably from state to state and can be a source of some confusion. The court of general jurisdiction may be called a district court or circuit court, but New York's courts of general jurisdiction are called supreme courts. Courts at this level are usually organized on a county basis, and the judge or magistrate is not required to issue a written opinion. Decisions at this level often are not published and have precedential value only in the specific jurisdiction.

The party who loses at the trial court level can appeal to an appellate court. Each state has a single high court often called the state supreme court, but several states use other names, such as the court of appeals. These courts of last resort at the state level can choose to accept cases on appeal. This process of selective appeal, known as *certiorari*, protects the highest court from minor or routine cases that could result in case overload. State courts have jurisdiction over disputes in-

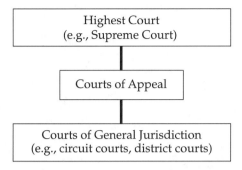

**FIGURE 15.1   Typical Three-Tiered
State Judicial Structure**

volving the respective state's constitution and laws; cases involving both state and federal issues can be filed in state or federal courts. The highest state court has the final authority in interpreting the meaning of state laws and the state constitution, but interpretations of the federal Constitution can be appealed to the U.S. Supreme Court. In addition to this three-tiered system, states usually have courts of special jurisdiction, such as small claims courts and probate courts.

The Three-Tiered Federal Judicial System

The three-tiered federal court system entails district courts, circuit courts of appeal, and the United States Supreme Court. Federal district courts have general jurisdictional requirements that must be satisfied to use that forum. Federal courts enjoy jurisdiction over disputes involving federal legislation and the U.S. Constitution and parties residing in different states. It is possible for federal constitutional questions to move from state courts to federal courts. Beyond this, the systems try to protect the jurisdictional autonomy implicit in the notion of federalism. The number of federal district courts in a state is based on population, and every state has at least one.

Appeals from federal district courts are made to the circuit courts of appeal. Figure 15.2 provides the boundaries for twelve of the circuits; the Thirteenth Circuit has national jurisdiction over limited claims such as customs, copyrights, and patents. Circuit decisions usually are rendered by a three-judge panel, but the entire court (*en banc*) will agree to rehear some cases. Circuit rulings can be appealed to the U.S. Supreme Court. At least four of the nine Supreme Court justices must agree to review a case before it will be heard by the Court. The criteria justices generally use in granting *certiorari* include the case's potential for developing a more precise interpretation of the law and for resolving conflicts between appellate courts in different circuits. The Supreme Court renders an opinion in only about 5 percent of the cases seeking review.

The Supreme Court provides binding authority for the United States, and Supreme Court decisions have shaped substantive law in a number of constitutional

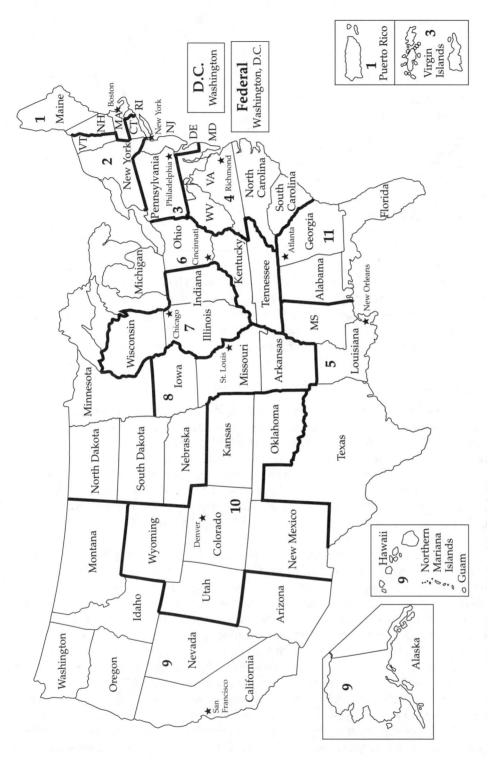

FIGURE 15.2 The Thirteen Federal Judicial Circuits

Source: Reprinted with permission from *West's Federal Reporter*, Third Series, Vol. 309 (2003). Copyright 2003 by West Group. All rights reserved.

areas affecting schools. For example, as a result of desegregation litigation, the racial composition of student bodies and staffs in many schools throughout the nation has changed significantly, and some desegregation remedies have been implemented across school district boundaries (see *Missouri v. Jenkins,* 1995). Also, school practices have changed as a result of Establishment Clause decisions striking down daily devotional activities sponsored by public schools (see *School District of Abington Township v. Schempp,* 1963).

Courts can offer various types of relief in situations when protected rights are impaired. The judiciary can order declaratory relief (establishing rights without providing enforcement), injunctive relief (ordering the unlawful practice to cease), reinstatement, removal of material from school records and personnel files, damages to compensate for injuries incurred, punitive damages if deprivations have been willful or reckless, and attorneys' fees.

Interaction of Courts and Legislative Bodies

If the Supreme Court has interpreted the federal Constitution as *prohibiting* a specific public school activity, all school laws and policies must comply with the national standard. But if the federal Constitution has been interpreted as *permitting* the practice, states have latitude to restrict it, which causes legal standards to vary across states. Indeed, a permissive Supreme Court decision stimulates legislative action, whereas the reverse is true when the Court definitively rules that a particular practice is not allowed. To illustrate, when the Supreme Court declared that the use of corporal punishment in public schools does not abridge the federal Constitution (*Ingraham v. Wright,* 1977), only one state restricted this practice. Now, however, more than half of the states by law have placed constraints on the use of corporal punishment or have prohibited it altogether in public schools. As discussed previously, legislative bodies have some discretion to amend laws if judicial interpretations of the provisions are inconsistent with the lawmakers' intent, but the Supreme Court has the final word in interpreting whether the legislative act conforms to the U.S. Constitution.

The notion of *federalism* and limitations on the powers of the federal government to impose constraints on state action have received considerable attention recently. In several decisions, the Supreme Court has expanded state immunity under the Eleventh Amendment from federal lawsuits initiated under civil rights laws (see *Board of Trustees v. Garrett,* 2001; *Kimel v. Florida Board of Regents,* 2000). These decisions have tipped the balance in favor of states' rights. The Court has reasoned that for suits against states to be authorized, the federal laws must be explicit in abrogating such immunity under very narrow circumstances to enforce constitutional rights.

Preventive Law

Litigation is costly in terms of time and other resources. Many, if not most, school controversies can be resolved through mediation or administrative appeals, thus avoiding lengthy judicial proceedings. School leaders should be knowledgeable of avenues available to handle disputes and should educate their staff members regarding alternative approaches to conflict resolution. Some laws make provisions for mediators to be involved if disputes arise or specify other procedures to be followed in an effort to resolve differences before they become very adversarial. For example, the IDEA of 1990 entitles parents to mediation as the first step in dispute resolution if they are dissatisfied with the school district's proposed placement for their child with disabilities. The intent is for mediators to facilitate the identification of acceptable options so that parents and school personnel can avoid adversarial proceedings.

But despite their efforts to keep controversies from escalating into litigation, school leaders cannot ensure that their actions will not be challenged in lawsuits. They can, however, take steps to guard against successful challenges. Because new legislation and judicial action frequently change the law, school leaders need to stay abreast of developments. They should regularly review school policies in light of changing legal standards and be certain that all school practices are consistent with current law (see Hawkins, 1986). Such periodic reviews can also enable administrators to anticipate and rectify situations that might cause legal vulnerability.

School leaders need to know when to consult with counsel and what questions to ask, and, most importantly, they need to have enough legal background to evaluate the worth of the information that the attorney provides. A school leader should ask as many questions as necessary to understand the reasoning behind the attorney's advice, including questions about the strength of the judicial precedent, the effective date of statutes, and the extent to which the facts of the case in question match those of the case upon which the attorney may be relying. A school attorney will be able to answer an administrator's legal questions only to the extent that the law in the particular area is settled. Legal standards are not always clear and most evolve over time. Neither attorneys nor school leaders are expected to anticipate future legal developments, but they are expected to understand clearly established law (see *Wood v. Strickland*, 1975).

Despite the many overlapping and, at times, conflicting legal requirements emanating from constitutional provisions, statutory enactments, administrative rules and regulations, contractual provisions, and judicial decisions interpreting legal mandates, school personnel at all levels of the educational enterprise retain discretion to make decisions as long as they act consistently with higher authority. Not only will knowledge of the law help school leaders in identifying potential legal liabilities, but also it can assist in ensuring that actions are reasonable and fair. School leaders should engage in regular communication with staff members, school constituents, and students regarding the fundamental values guiding our legal system and how they relate to the educational philosophy of the district.

Many educational practitioners erroneously view the law as an external force that dictates what they can and cannot do, a prescription that limits professional autonomy rather than a framework for expressing public values and making decisions (Bull & McCarthy, 1995). It is common to view the law as a series of standards or rules with the school leader responsible for conveying these rules to the district or school. To regard school law as a prescription for proper behavior or as a set of boundaries within which behavior is acceptable is to treat law as static and unresponsive to the ongoing changes in the society it is designed to regulate. A more enlightened view is to regard knowledge of the law as relevant to administrative actions because it provides insights that will improve the quality of decision making and performance.

Administrators' decisions affecting such things as student welfare, learning climate, and work environment can be informed by a legal perspective. At one level, this perspective offers an understanding of the subtleties of legal authority and liability. At another level, the law provides a set of aspirations, many of which are embedded in constitutional principles, such as due process, equal protection, and free speech. The ways in which these principles are translated into legal standards are explored in more detail in the next chapter.

Notwithstanding the significance of the law, it is important to understand that legal standards do not necessarily define best educational practice. A practice may be lawful, such as using peers to grade assignments and call out classmates' scores for the teacher to record (*Owasso v. Falvo,* 2002), but the practice may not seem educationally sound in a given situation. Simply because a practice will not trigger legal liability does not mean that the practice should be used. It is educators, not courts or legislatures, who must determine what actions are reasonable and appropriate in most school situations (Bull & McCarthy, 1995). Legal knowledge is important and can be very helpful, but it is not a substitute for an educational philosophy.

REFERENCES

A.L.A. Schechter Poultry Corporation v. United States, 295 U.S. 495 (1935).

Agostini v. Felton, U.S. (1997).

Aguilar v. Felton, U.S. (1985).

Alexander, S. K., & Alexander, M. D. (2001). *American public school law* (5th ed.). Belmont, CA: West/Thomson Learning.

Anthes, K. (2001). *ESEA 2001 policy brief: School and district leadership.* Denver: Education Commission of the States.

Board of Education v. Bushee, 889 S.W.2d 809 (Ky. 1994).

Board of Trustees v. Garrett, 531 U.S. 356 (2001).

Botti v. S. W. Butler County School District, 529 A.2d 1206 (Pa. Commw. Ct. 1987).

Brookhart v. Illinois State Board of Education, 697 F.2d 179 (7th Cir. 1983).

Brown v. Board of Education of Topeka, 347 U.S. 483 (1954).

Bull, B., & McCarthy, M. (1995). Reflections on the knowledge base in law and ethics for educational leaders. *Educational Administration Quarterly, 31,* 612–630.

Bush v. Vera, 517 U.S. 952 (1996).

Cambron-McCabe, N., McCarthy, M., & Thomas, S. (2004). *Public school law: Teachers' and students' rights.* Boston: Allyn and Bacon.

Cannon v. North Carolina State Board of Education, 917 F. Supp. 387 (E.D.N.C. 1996).

Cantwell v. Connecticut, 310 U.S. 296 (1940).

Center for Education Reform (2002). *Charter school highlights and statistics. http://edreform.com/pubs/chglance.htm.*

Civil Rights Act of 1871, 42 U.S.C. §1983 (2002).

Community Projects for Students v. Wilder, 298 S.E.2d 434 (N.C. Ct. App. 1982).

County of Macon v. Board of Education, 518 N.E.2d 653 (Ill. App. Ct. 1987).

Dare, M. J. (2001). *The tensions of the home school movement: A legal/political analysis.* Unpublished Ed.D. dissertation. Bloomington: Indiana University.

Davis v. Monroe County Board of Education, 526 U.S. 629 (1999).

Eisbruck v. N.Y. State Education Department, 520 N.Y.S.2d 138 (Sup. Ct. 1987).

Gebser v. Lago Vista Independent School District, 524 U.S. 274 (1998).

General Electric Company v. Gilbert, 429 U.S. 125 (1976).

Gewertz, G. (2002, April 2). Takeover team picked in Philadelphia. *Education Week,* 1, 20, 21.

Gitlow v. New York, 268 U.S. 652 (1925).

Gonzaga University v. Doe, 536 U.S. 273 (2002).

Goss v. Lopez, 419 U.S. 565 (1975).

Harrah Independent School District v. Martin, 440 U.S. 194 (1979).

Hawkins, H. L. (1986). *Preventive law: Strategies for avoidance of litigation in public schools.* UCEA Monograph Series. Tempe, AZ: University Council for Educational Administration.

Helvering v. Davis, 301 U.S. 619 (1937).

Hemenway, R. (1999, October 29). The evolution of a controversy in Kansas shows why scientists must defend the search for truth. *The Chronicle of Higher Education, 46*(10), B7.

Herndon v. Chapel Hill-Carrboro City Board of Education, 89 F.3d 174 (4th Cir. 1996).

Hogan, J. (1985). *The schools, the courts, and the public interest.* Lexington, MA: D.C. Heath.

Holmes v. Bush, No. CV 99-3370, 2002 WL 1809079 (Fla. Cir. Ct. Aug. 5, 2002).

Individuals with Disabilities Education Act, 20 U.S.C. §1401 (2002).

Ingraham v. Wright, 430 U.S. 651 (1977).

Johnson v. Desoto County Board of Commoners, 204 F.3d 1335 (11th Cir. 2000).

Kiddie Korner Day Schools v. Charlotte-Mecklenburg Board of Education, 285 S.E.2d 110 (N.C. App. 1981).

Kimel v. Florida Board of Regents, 528 U.S. 62 (2000).

Lau v. Nichols, 414 U.S. 563 (1974).

Mayes, T., & Zirkel, P. (2000). State educational agencies and special education: Obligations and liabilities. *Boston Public Interest Law Journal, 10,* 62–90.

McCarthy, M. (2000). Privatization of education: Marketplace models. In B. Jones (Ed.), *Educational administration: Policy dimensions in the twenty-first century,* pp. 21–40. Greenwich, CT: Ablex.

Meyers v. Newport Consolidated Joint School District, 639 P.2d 853 (Wash. Ct. App. 1982).

Missouri v. Jenkins, 515 U.S. 70 (1995).

National Commission on Excellence in Education. (1983). *A nation at risk: The imperative for educational reform.* Washington, DC: Government Printing Office.

National Education Association. (2002). *Rankings and estimates.* Annapolis: NEA.

No Child Left Behind Act of 2001, 20 U.S.C. § 6301 et seq. (2002).

Office for Civil Rights. (2001). *Sexual harassment guidance: Harassment of students by school employees, other students, and third parties.* Washington, DC: Department of Education.

Owasso Independent School District v. Falvo, 534 U.S. 426 (2002).

Pierce v. Society of Sisters, 268 U.S. 510 (1925).

Pittman v. Chicago Board of Education, 64 F.3d 1098 (7th Cir. 1995).

Plessy v. Ferguson, 163 U.S. 537 (1896).

Pregnancy Discrimination Act of Title VII of the Civil Rights Act of 1964, 42 U.S.C. § 2000e(k) (2002).

San Antonio Independent School District v. Rodriguez, 411 U.S. 1 (1973).

School District of Abington Township v. Schempp, 374 U.S. 203 (1963).

Shaw v. Hunt, 517 U.S. 899 (1996).

Smith v. Robinson, 468 U.S. 992 (1984).

State v. Board of Education, 741 S.W.2d 747 (Mo. Ct. App. 1987).

State v. Whittle Communications & Thomasville City Board of Education, 402 S.E.2d 556 (N.C. 1991), *reh'g denied,* 404 S.E.2d 878 (N.C. 1991).

Sutera v. Sully Buttes School District, 351 N.W.2d 457 (S.D. 1984).

Theodore v. Delaware Valley School District, 761 A.2d 652 (Pa. Commw. Ct. 2000).

Tinker v. Des Moines Independent School District, 393 U.S. 503 (1969).

Valente, W., & Valente, C. (2001). *Law in the schools* (5th ed.). Columbus: Merrill/Prentice Hall.

Voting Rights Act, 42 U.S.C. §1971, et seq. (2002).

Webb, L. D., Metha, A., & Jordan, K. F. (2003). *Foundations of American education* (4th ed.). Upper Saddle River, NJ: Prentice Hall.

Wisconsin v. Yoder, 406 U.S. 205 (1972).

Wohlstetter, P., & Van Kirk, A. (1996). Redefining school-based budgeting for high-involvement. In L. O. Picus (Ed.), *Where does the money go: Resource allocation in elementary and secondary schools* (pp. 212–235). Newbury Park, CA: Corwin Press.

Wood v. Strickland, 420 U.S. 308 (1975).

Zelman v. Simmons-Harris, 536 U.S. 639 (2002).

16 Leading Public Schools: Legal Considerations

The law influences most facets of school operations and interactions, so it is important for school leaders to be knowledgeable of legal principles and their underlying values. This introduction to substantive aspects of the law is not intended to be a comprehensive treatment of all legal principles that have an impact on education; volumes have been written on this topic (see, for example, Alexander & Alexander, 2001; Cambron-McCabe, McCarthy, & Thomas, 2004; Valente & Valente, 2001). Rather, the focus here is on broad generalizations that depict the evolving law governing education and the relationship between legal standards and educational policymaking. These legal standards provide a framework, but considerable latitude exists in translating educational philosophy into policies that shape practices in schools and school districts.

The first part of this chapter presents several legal generalizations, and the next section addresses selected topics in more detail. The chapter concludes with a brief treatment of potential liability of school districts and school personnel. In some areas explored in this chapter, legal precedents are clearly established, but the law is still evolving in others. The most taxing situations are those without specific legislative or judicial guidance, that force public school personnel to make judgments based on their professional preparation and knowledge of the law (see Cambron-McCabe, McCarthy, & Thomas, 2004).

Legal Principles

Certain principles permeate the law. A thorough grounding in these central beliefs can guide educators' actions in areas where the status of the law is unclear. Principles are highlighted here that have particular implications for public schools and their students, patrons, and personnel.

Ensuring That All Policies and Practices Are Reasonable

A cornerstone of the legal foundation of education is that reasonable actions and policies will be upheld if legally challenged, whereas unreasonable actions and policies can evoke adverse legal consequences including monetary damages. Public educators are expected to be familiar with the law and to act reasonably in complying with legal requirements. They are presumed to understand pertinent federal and state constitutional and statutory provisions, agency regulations, and judicial interpretations of these mandates. In connection with constitutional impairments, the Supreme Court has emphasized that educators cannot plead ignorance of the law as a defense for violating clearly established rights (*Wood v. Strickland*, 1975).

The expectation of reasonable actions also pertains to educators' behavior in supervising students. Unreasonable actions in this regard can result in awards of damages for negligence. As addressed in more detail in the last section of this chapter, a claimant can prevail in a negligence suit by establishing that the actor causing the injury owed a duty to protect others from harm and breached that duty by exercising an inadequate standard of care under the circumstances. Most education litigation focused on negligence claims until the mid-twentieth century, and school law instruction dealt primarily with tort liability and contracts until the 1960s. Negligence suits continue to be steady producers of school cases, even though other topics (e.g., rights of children with disabilities) may generate more cases during a specific period of time.

Teachers and administrators are also expected to act reasonably in their instructional roles. Although no instructional negligence (malpractice) suit has yet been successful (see *Brantley v. District of Columbia*, 1994; *Hoffman v. Board of Education*, 1979; *Suriano v. Hyde Park*, 1994), it is conceivable that educators in the future could be found liable for failing to (1) identify students' needs, (2) place them in appropriate instructional programs, or (3) accurately report students' progress to their parents (Cambron-McCabe, McCarthy, & Thomas, 2004). Educators also are expected to exercise reasonable judgment in selecting materials and approaches that are appropriate for instructional objectives and the level and maturity of their students (see *Boring v. Buncombe*, 1996; *Fowler v. Board of Education*, 1987). It is not considered reasonable judgment to use the classroom as a forum to proselytize students (see *Palmer v. Board of Education*, 1979; *Roberts v. Madigan*, 1990).

Students and their parents can also presume that public school personnel will make reasonable choices in disciplinary matters by selecting strategies that are appropriate for the offense and the child's characteristics. Unreasonable disciplinary practices can result in sanctions against school employees and possibly monetary awards for the students (see *Doe v. Renfrow*, 1980; *Hall v. Tawney*, 1980).

In addition to exercising reasonable care in classroom activities, public educators are expected to make reasonable choices in their personal lives. They are held to a higher standard of discretion than is the general citizenry, given their important role in modeling behavior and transmitting values to our nation's youth. Nonetheless, public school personnel retain some rights in their private activities; courts usually require evidence that educators' choices have a negative impact on teaching effectiveness or the management of the school for disciplinary action to be upheld (see *Melzer v. Board of Education*, 2002; *Weaver v. Nebo School District*, 1998). An educator's involvement in a divorce or an adulterous relationship would not be sufficient alone to warrant dismissal or other adverse consequences (see *Littlejohn v. Rose,* 1985; *Sherburne v. School Board,* 1984). However, teachers who have engaged in public sexual acts or have advocated gay rights in the classroom have not been protected from dismissal, and, in some instances, mere choice of an unorthodox lifestyle has been found to adversely impact teaching effectiveness (see *National Gay Task Force v. Board of Education,* 1984; *Rowland v. Mad River Local School District,* 1984).

Promoting Fairness in Government Actions

Fairness and justice are prominent values in American jurisprudence. The Fifth Amendment originally placed due process restrictions on Congress, and the post–Civil War Fourteenth Amendment expanded due process protections to restrict state power as well. As described in Chapter 15, substantive due process protects individuals against arbitrary government action infringing on life, liberty, or property interests, and procedural due process ensures that any government impairment of these interests is carried out in a fundamentally fair manner.

The determination of what procedures, if any, are constitutionally required in a given school controversy involves a two-step analysis. It must be determined whether there has been a deprivation of a liberty or property interest, and if so, what procedural safeguards are necessary to protect the interest at stake. At a minimum, individuals are entitled to notice of the charges and a hearing before a fair tribunal when facing deprivations of liberty or property rights. Part of the notice requirement is that regulations including penalties for infractions are well publicized. School leaders would be wise to have handbooks for students and employees that clearly specify what behaviors will evoke disciplinary actions.

A property interest exists when a person has some objective claim to a government job or other benefit. Compulsory education statutes, for example, entitle students to attend public school, and this entitlement cannot be denied for even a short period of time without procedural due process (*Goss v. Lopez,* 1975). The primary sources of a property right to employment for school personnel derive from individual contracts, state tenure laws (continuous contract status), and other legislative or school board action that creates a mutual expectation of continued employment with dismissal only for specified reasons. Consequently, a tenured teacher cannot be dismissed at any time without procedural safeguards to ascertain the legitimacy of the charges, and a nontenured teacher must be provided procedural due process if dismissed during the contract term.

A liberty interest for students or employees is implicated when the government's action impairs fundamental constitutional rights (e.g., freedom of speech or association), significantly damages an individual's reputation, or forecloses the opportunity for an employee to obtain another position (Cambron-McCabe, McCarthy, & Thomas, 2004). It is difficult to establish that an individual has been stigmatized to the extent that it would implicate a constitutional liberty right. For example, courts have not found the nonrenewal of nontenured teachers' contracts to impair a liberty interest, regardless of whether people in the community might view it as evidence of incompetency. Also, students facing reasonable corporal punishment do not have a liberty right at stake, despite the embarrassment accompanying this form of discipline.

The constitutional inquiry ends if there is no governmental impairment of a liberty or property interest, and procedural safeguards are not required. Conversely, if a liberty or property deprivation is found, the Court then must move to the second step and assess the level of procedural safeguards necessary to protect the threatened interests. The government still can discipline or dismiss the individual; it simply must do so in a fair manner. No mechanical formula exists to determine the appropriate procedural safeguards. The key is for all involved to have an opportunity to present their evidence that might change the decision or at least illuminate the record. As noted in Chapter 15, the nature of the proceedings depends on the deprivation involved. With minor deprivations, an informal hearing often is sufficient for all sides to be heard before the decision is made. For example, if a student is suspended from class for less than one day, notice of why the punishment seems warranted and an oral hearing for the student to refute the charges would satisfy due process requirements. The punishment can be administered immediately unless there are questions about the veracity of the charges. As the deprivation becomes more serious, such as an expulsion, the procedural safeguards should also be more elaborate.

The two-step analysis provides the framework for understanding what minimal procedures are constitutionally required. School leaders also need to stay abreast of procedural safeguards required by federal and state laws, contractual agreements, and school board policies that often go beyond constitutional minimums to ensure fairness in government actions. For example, state tenure laws often provide detailed procedures that must be followed in dismissal actions. Tenured teachers usually can expect written notice of the dismissal charges, an impartial hearing with representation by counsel, the right to present testimony and to cross examine adverse witnesses, and a decision based solely on the evidence presented in the hearing.

Federal and state laws similarly provide additional procedural safeguards for students. For example, a number of states by law specify procedures that must be followed before any students can be expelled, and these go beyond constitutional minimums. Also, the federal Individuals with Disabilities Education Act includes detailed procedural protections for children with disabilities in placement decisions. Such children are entitled to stay in their current placements pending meetings of their planning teams to assess whether placement changes are necessary (*Honig v. Doe*, 1988). Each level of the education enterprise (e.g., classroom, building, school district) can go beyond requirements imposed by higher authority in providing additional procedural safeguards, but they cannot dip below minimums imposed from above.

Justice Frankfurter described the notion of due process as fairness: "It is not a technical conception with fixed content unrelated to time, place and circumstances...due process is not a mechanical instrument. It is not a yardstick.... It is a delicate process of adjustment" (*Joint Anti-Fascist Refugee Committee v. McGrath*, 1951). Understanding the essence of due process as fundamental fairness can provide an important perspective for school leaders in handling school situations and transmitting to staff members and students a commitment to ensure reasonable and impartial school actions. Many schools are introducing peer mediation and conflict resolution training for teachers and students to help them address conflicts in productive ways and to instill a desire to be fair in dealing with others (see Girard & Koch, 1996; Johnson & Johnson, 1995; Robinson, Smith, & Daunic, 2000).

Although procedural safeguards may appear onerous, state and federal courts are not interpreting constitutional and statutory due process guarantees as placing undue burdens on school personnel. Indeed, the Supreme Court noted in 1975 that the judiciary is not imposing anything more than fair-minded school leaders have always done in ensuring fundamental fairness (*Goss v. Lopez*, 1975). School authorities will never be challenged for providing more procedural protections than legally required.

Safeguarding Individuals from Discrimination

A fundamental concept in the federal Constitution and various civil rights laws designed to enforce constitutional guarantees is that individuals are protected from governmental discrimination based on their inherent characteristics or beliefs. Thus, school policies and practices must not disadvantage selected individuals or groups. If the government creates a suspect classification, such as race or national origin, the federal judiciary applies strict judicial scrutiny in evaluating the government action. A suspect classification can be justified only if necessary to advance a compelling governmental interest, which is a difficult standard to meet unless a national emergency exists (see *Korematsu v. United States*, 1944).

Starting with the landmark decision in *Brown v. Board of Education* (1954), the Supreme Court launched a half century of school desegregation litigation based on the Fourteenth Amendment's Equal Protection Clause. During the 1970s there was at least one significant desegregation case on the Supreme Court's docket each term. However, the number of desegregation cases began to decrease in the 1980s, and in the early 1990s the Supreme Court relaxed standards to release school districts from court-ordered desegregation plans (*Board of Education v. Dowell*, 1991; *Freeman v. Pitts*, 1992). The Court has tended to decline to review desegregation cases since then, and lower federal courts have been more disposed to curtail judicial oversight by finding that school districts have eliminated the vestiges of prior discriminatory practices (see *Belk v. Charlotte-Mecklenburg*, 2001; *Manning v. School Board*, 2001; *People v. Rockford*, 2001).

Complainants also have used the Fourteenth Amendment to challenge a range of discriminatory practices beyond school segregation. Federal civil rights laws and state statutes have augmented constitutional protections afforded to groups who have been discriminated against in the past. These laws afford significant protections to shield students and school employees from discrimination based on traits such as race, national origin, gender, religion, disabilities, and age.

For example, efforts to exclude a certain class of students from public education, such as those with disabilities or whose parents entered the United States illegally, have been struck down under the Equal Protection Clause (see *Mills v. Board of Education*, 1972; *Plyler v. Doe*, 1982). Substantial litigation has focused on Title VI of the Civil Rights Act of 1964 that prohibits discrimination on the basis of race, color, or national origin by recipients of federal aid and Title IX of the Educational Amendments of 1972 that bars gender discrimination in educational institutions receiving federal funds. Also, the Equal Educational Opportunities Act of 1974 guarantees public school children equal educational opportunities without regard to race, color, gender, or national origin. School leaders and teachers should ensure that all school policies are applied in an evenhanded manner and do not impede students' rights to equal educational opportunities.

Employees similarly are protected by civil rights laws. For example, Title VII of the Civil Rights Act of 1964 is a major law offering employees significant protections against discrimination in the workforce based on race, color, gender, religion, or national origin. Title VII governs hiring, promotion, and compensation practices, and all public and private employers with fifteen or more employees must comply with Title VII regulations. Once an aggrieved employee establishes an inference of discrimination, the employer must generate a legitimate nondiscriminatory reason for the personnel action to avoid liability.

Employees with disabilities also have significant protection against discrimination. Section 504 of the Rehabilitation Act of 1973 and the Americans with Disabilities Act of 1990 prohibit discrimination against otherwise qualified disabled individuals; these laws require employers to make reasonable accommodations for individuals with disabilities. Other civil rights laws offer important protections, such as the Age Discrimination in Employment Act of 1967 that protects employees over 40 against discrimination and the Equal Pay Act that requires equal pay for men and women doing equal work (see Cambron-McCabe, McCarthy, & Thomas, 2004).

Some controversies have focused on neutral governmental policies that have a disparate impact on one or more protected groups. For example, students have challenged tracking schemes that result in the disproportionate placement of minority students in lower instructional tracks. But courts have upheld such grouping plans if not designed to segregate students by race and if the assignments are based on reasonable educational criteria to enhance student learning (see *Georgia State Conference v. Georgia*, 1985). Also, courts have upheld conditioning a high school diploma on passage of a test that a larger percentage of minority students fail, as long as the students subjected to the diploma sanction started school under desegregated conditions, were given sufficient notice of the test requirement, and were given an adequate opportunity to be prepared for the test (see *Debra P. v. Turlington*, 1984). Similarly, courts have upheld the use of licensure tests for teachers as justified to ensure a minimally competent teaching force, even though a disproportionate number of minority applicants are denied teaching licenses (see *United States v. South Carolina*, 1978).

Protections against discrimination are not confined to underrepresented groups. In a number of cases, whites have successfully challenged affirmative action plans that foreclose employment to nonminorities or disadvantage them in other ways without being narrowly tailored to achieve a compelling governmental interest (see *Richmond v. J. A. Croson*, 1989; *Wygant v. Jackson Board of Education*, 1986). Also, racial classifications in admission policies to achieve racially balanced schools have been attacked as resulting in reverse discrimination against whites. To illustrate, the Fourth Circuit ruled in favor of a white student who was denied admission to a magnet school solely on the basis of his race (*Eisenberg v. Montgomery County Public Schools*, 1999). However, in a higher education case before the U.S. Supreme Court, the Sixth Circuit held that the University of Michigan could consider race and ethnicity in its admissions decisions to advance its compelling interest in achieving a diverse student body (*Grutter v. Bollinger*, 2002).

Nondiscrimination does not mean equal outcomes or necessitate *identical* treatment of individuals (Cambron-McCabe, McCarthy, & Thomas, 2004). In fact, to be equitable, it may require different treatment of groups of students with differing needs. For example, federal and state laws, in conjunction with judicial interpretations of these provisions, require school personnel to give special assistance to students with English-language deficiencies; providing such children with the same instruction and materials as other students denies them equal opportunities (*Lau v. Nichols*, 1974).

Moreover, special education and related services must be provided for children with disabilities to address their unique needs (see *Irving Independent School District v. Tatro*, 1984). Some students' claims of disability discrimination, like those of employees, are brought under Section 504 of the Rehabilitation Act of 1973, the Americans with Disabilities Act of 1990, or state provisions. But most school litigation is brought under the Individuals with Disabilities Education Act, which provides federal aid for part of the excess costs of providing appropriate educational programs for all children with disabilities. Federal funds under the IDEA are conditioned on adherence to detailed guidelines (see Chapter 15).

Protecting Individual Liberties

A major tenet of our legal system is that individual rights must be respected by those representing the government, even if the exercise of those rights is unpopular. For example, the Supreme Court has upheld the right of the Ku Klux Klan to post a cross on a courthouse lawn (*Capitol Square v. Pinette*, 1995) and the right of protesters to burn the American flag (*Texas v. Johnson*, 1989). The government must have a compelling justification to restrict the exercise of such rights protected by the U.S. Constitution or civil rights laws. Thus, any public school policy or practice that impairs protected personal freedoms must advance legitimate educational objectives. School regulations should be widely disseminated to school staff members, students, and parents so that everyone involved understands the rationale for restrictions and the penalties for noncompliance.

The Supreme Court has recognized that teachers and students do not shed their constitutional rights at the schoolhouse door (*Tinker v. Des Moines*, 1969). When confronted with a restriction on students' or school employees' personal freedoms, courts balance the personal rights involved against the schools' interests in restricting them. Weighing the interests at stake, courts have upheld mandatory vaccination against communicable diseases as a condition of school attendance, because the personal intrusion is justified by important health concerns (see *Brown v. Stone*, 1979; *Liebowitz v. Dinkins*, 1991). The judiciary also has punished parents for disregarding compulsory education mandates, given the government's interest in ensuring an educated citizenry (see *State v. Egnor*, 1994).

In contrast, the Supreme Court found no compelling governmental interest to justify requiring students to pledge their allegiance to the American flag if they object to this observance on religious or philosophical grounds (*West Virginia v. Barnette*, 1943). The Court also has ruled that individual rights to freely exercise religious beliefs prevail over governmental interests in mandating schooling beyond eighth grade for Amish youth being prepared for a cloistered agrarian society (*Wisconsin v. Yoder*, 1972). Furthermore, the Court recognized the overriding parental interests in selecting private education for their children when it struck down state legislation requiring children to attend *public* schools (*Pierce v. Society of Sisters*, 1925).

Although teachers and students enjoy constitutional rights, the judiciary has acknowledged that the public school presents a special environment, allowing some restrictions of personal freedoms that might not be allowed in other settings. As will be discussed in the next section, lewd and vulgar student expression can be curtailed in public education, even though such expression for the general citizenry could not be censored by the government (*Bethel School District v. Fraser*, 1986), and school authorities can conduct warrantless searches of students as long as they have reasonable suspicion that the students are concealing contraband that is detrimental to the school (*New Jersey v. T.L.O.*, 1985). Also, teachers may face disciplinary action for expression that would be protected outside the school context, and as noted previously, they are held to a higher level of discretion than the general citizenry in their lifestyle choices.

Distinguishing Private Actors from Government Actors

A basic principle of our constitutional system is that the Bill of Rights and other constitutional provisions place restrictions on powers of the government. They generally do not restrict private actions. There are other remedies available to redress private wrongs such as civil suits under state tort law (e.g., seeking damages for defamation) or criminal prosecution if an individual has broken the law (e.g., seeking a conviction for statutory rape). To illustrate the distinction between private and government action, if a public school teacher searches a high school student, the teacher is acting on behalf of the state so the student's Fourth Amendment rights might be implicated. In contrast, if a classmate detains the student against his will and goes through his possessions, the Fourth Amendment does not apply, but there might be a valid tort claim or criminal charges against the aggressor.

Most private schools and other private entities are not subject to the federal Constitution, because they do not receive a sufficient amount of state aid or have enough involvement with the government to be considered *state actors*. Thus, private school teachers or students would not be entitled to Fourteenth Amendment procedural protections if facing dismissal or expulsion; they generally rely on contractual provisions or civil rights laws that apply to public and private entities in challenging private school policies or practices.

While difficult, it is not impossible to establish that private entities are state actors. For example, in most states a not-for-profit private organization regulates interscholastic sports and often has jurisdiction over other competitive activities among private and public schools. The Supreme Court ruled in 2001 that where such associations are extensively entwined with state school officials, they are considered state actors (*Brentwood Academy v. Tennessee Secondary School Athletic Association*, 2001). Under those conditions, such associations are subject to constitutional restrictions on their activities and can be liable for constitutional violations.

The distinction between private and government actors increasingly is appearing in cases involving the assertion that federal constitutional restrictions do not apply to expression or other actions of private persons. For example, as described later in this chapter, individuals are using the *private actor* justification to argue that student-initiated devotionals should be allowed in public schools. In addition, students are asserting that their private expression on the Internet does not represent the school and thus, under most circumstances, should not be subject to school censorship or disciplinary action. Similarly, employees often contend that their actions outside school are private and should not be the basis for school sanctions.

The private actor rationale also is being used to assert that the Establishment Clause does not bar government aid to religious schools as long as parents' private choices cause the public funds to flow to the sectarian entities. Illustrative are developments pertaining to the legality of voucher plans that include religious schools. In 2002, the Supreme Court in *Zelman v. Simmons-Harris* rejected an Establishment Clause challenge to the Cleveland scholarship program that allows economically disadvantaged students to use the scholarships in public or private schools. The Court ruled that the program is one of "true private choice" because parents—not the government—decide where to use the funds. The court found the use of public aid for the voucher program to be religiously neutral, even though almost all participating students attend religious schools and no public school is involved in the program. Similar to the legitimacy of using public funds to support sign-language interpreters for parochial school students (*Zobrest v. Catalina Foothills School District*, 1993), the Supreme Court in *Zelman* declared that a neutral program does not violate the Establishment Clause simply because most recipients of the aid elect to use it in sectarian schools. Given the national emphasis on providing educational options for families, the private/government distinction may become increasingly significant as a justification to allow public funds to be used in parochial schools.

Selected Substantive Aspects of the Law

This section focuses on selected substantive topics to illustrate the application of the legal principles described previously and the evolution of the law governing public schools and their students and employees. The topics addressed—search and seizure, sexual harassment, student expression rights, and religious influences in public schools—were chosen because they include some issues where the law is quite dynamic. Emerging doctrine can cause special problems for school personnel, as it is frequently impossible to know precisely what standard will be applied by courts to assess the legality of school policies and practices.

Privacy Rights: Search and Seizure

Public school students and employees are protected by the Fourth Amendment, which safeguards citizens against unreasonable searches and seizures. Along with other personal freedoms in the Bill of Rights, Fourth Amendment protections have been applied to state action through the Fourteenth Amendment and require agents of the state, such as police officers, to secure warrants before conducting most searches. To convince a judge to issue a warrant, the state agent must establish probable cause, which means that a reasonable person would conclude from the totality of evidence that a crime has likely occurred.

Reasonable Suspicion Standard.   While recognizing that public school authorities are state agents subject to Fourth Amendment restrictions, in 1985 the U.S. Supreme Court relaxed the warrant requirement in connection with some student and employee searches due to the special circumstances of the school environment. In *New Jersey v. T.L.O.* (1985), the Court held that school authorities can conduct personal searches of students (e.g., purses, pockets, book bags) based on reasonable suspicion that something detrimental to the school is concealed. An assistant principal suspected a student of smoking in the restroom in violation of school policy, and thus searched the student's purse for cigarettes. In addition to cigarettes, the administrator found drug paraphernalia, a small amount of marijuana, and other evidence implicating the student in selling drugs. The state subsequently brought delinquency charges against the student, who asserted that the items discovered could not be used against her because the search violated the Fourth Amendment.

Rejecting the student's claim, the Supreme Court ruled that the search satisfied the reasonable suspicion standard. In assessing the reasonableness of school searches, courts weigh the intrusion on the individual's privacy against the school's interests in conducting the search. Under this standard, school authorities must have reasonable grounds to suspect that the search will reveal evidence that the student has violated the law or school rules. Also, the scope of the search must be reasonable in that it is not overly intrusive given the students' characteristics and the contraband being sought.

A number of controversies has focused on what is necessary to establish reasonable suspicion to justify a warrantless search. Such suspicion can be created by a tip from a classmate, adult, or even from the police indicating that a specific student has illegal or disruptive contraband (see *In re Joseph G.*, 1995). Whereas the Seventh Circuit held that the alert of a drug-detecting dog can establish reasonable suspicion for a subsequent personal search of a student (see *Doe v. Renfrow*, 1980), most other courts have ruled that dogs can be used to establish reasonable suspicion to search lockers and cars, but have not upheld blanket sniffing of students to establish reasonable suspicion for personal searches (see *Horton v. Goose Creek*, 1982). School personnel would be wise to avoid strip searches (see *Doe v. Renfrow*, 1980; *Oliver v. McClung*, 1995), even though a few courts have upheld strip searches of students based on reasonable suspicion (see *Cornfield v. Consolidated High School District*, 1993; *Williams v. Ellington*, 1991).

The reasonable suspicion standard usually has been interpreted as requiring *individualized* suspicion of wrongdoing on the part of the student subjected to a personal search. Thus, blanket or random searches of students' clothing and possessions usually would not satisfy the *T.L.O.* standard. Courts are more likely to uphold suspicionless searches of students' lockers, because the school owns the lockers. Also, courts have condoned requiring all students to pass through metal detectors and have held that setting off the detector provides reasonable grounds for subsequent personal searches of book bags or pockets (see *Thompson v. Carthage*, 1996).

Although most controversies regarding search and seizure in public schools have focused on student searches, some cases have addressed public employees' Fourth Amendment rights. The Supreme Court recognized that public employees have a reasonable expectation of privacy in their desks and files, but held that such employees can be subjected to warrantless searches if necessary to carry out government business (*O'Connor v. Ortega*, 1987). These searches can be conducted based on reasonable suspicion that information may be discovered that is important to the operation of the government agency, such as information about a student (see *Alinovi v. Worcester*, 1985; *Shaul v. Cherry Valley-Springfield*, 2002). Reasonable suspicion can be created by informants, observations, canine sweeps of school parking lots, or actions of the targeted employees (see *Hearn v. Board*, 1999). However, a search of a school employee's workspace will not be upheld without a legitimate educational rationale. For example, the Third Circuit invalidated the search of a school counselor's desk by a school board member because the search was politically motivated and lacked a sufficient work-related justification (*Gillard v. Schmidt*, 1978).

Drug Testing.   The most contentious current strategy used to discover drug use in schools is urinalysis screening. Such drug testing constitutes a search under the Fourth Amendment, and the judiciary has upheld school authorities in subjecting individual students or employees to urinalysis with reasonable suspicion of drug possession. For example, the Eleventh Circuit upheld termination of a teacher for refusing to submit to urinalysis after marijuana was discovered in her car by drug-detecting canines in a routine sweep of the school parking lot (*Hearn v. Board*, 1999). The court concluded that the dog alert created reasonable suspicion that the teacher was using drugs, justifying the mandatory drug test.

The controversial issue is whether blanket or random drug testing can be required for all students or as a prerequisite to employment when there is no individualized suspicion. Most school districts have not implemented suspicionless drug-testing programs for the entire student body or for all newly hired employees, but there has been recent movement in this direction.

In the first Supreme Court decision addressing drug testing in schools, *Vernonia School District 47J v. Acton* (1995), the Court upheld suspicionless drug testing of students participating in athletic programs. The Court declared that "the Fourth Amendment imposes no irreducible requirement of [individualized] suspicion," reasoning that the school district's "custodial" responsibility for the welfare of children entitles school personnel to more control than would be allowed in other settings (p. 653). The Court also recognized the important government interest of deterring drug use among school children, especially among athletes, where drug use poses a significant risk of harm to others. Furthermore, the Court noted that the students' privacy interests are negligible given the "element of 'communal undress' inherent in athletic participation" (p. 657).

Following the *Vernonia* reasoning, several courts upheld drug and alcohol screening as a condition of students driving to school or participating in any extracurricular activities (see *Miller v. Wilkes*, 1999), which covers about 80 percent of high school students. While condoning such a policy, the Seventh Circuit struck down the provision requiring student drivers or other students over age eighteen to test negative for nicotine use, reasoning that the school district had not documented any serious risks associated with a student driving while using tobacco products (*Joy v. Penn-Harris-Madison*, 2000). The same court in 1999 invalidated a school district's policy requiring drug testing of all suspended students as a condition of returning to school, because the court did not find a sufficient connection between the reasons for suspension (e.g., fighting and truancy) and drug use (*Willis v. Anderson*, 1998).

The Supreme Court again addressed student drug testing in 2002 when it rendered *Board of Education v. Earls* (2002), upholding a school district's policy calling for drug testing of all student participants in extracurricular activities. Reversing the Tenth Circuit's decision, the Supreme Court emphasized that Fourth Amendment restrictions are applied differently in the school context and held that the drug-screening policy served the school board's important interests in detecting and preventing drug use among students. The Court also noted that extracurricular participants have a diminished expectation of privacy and that the urine samples were gathered in a minimally intrusive manner. Although the Supreme Court has found no federal constitutional bar to random drug testing of students who participate in extracurricular activities, states and local school districts still can go beyond the Fourth Amendment in protecting students against random or blanket drug testing (see *Theodore v. Delaware Valley School District*, 2000). Also, the significant expense of drug tests may deter many school districts from implementing such programs.

The Supreme Court has not addressed suspicionless drug testing of public educators, but a few lower courts have dealt with this issue. The New York high court struck down a blanket drug-testing program for probationary teachers because there was no individualized suspicion (*Patchogue-Medford Congress of Teachers v. Board*, 1987). However, some courts have upheld school district policies requiring employees whose duties affect student safety, such as bus drivers, to submit to drug tests as part of routine medical examinations (see *Jones v. Jenkins*, 1989). Also, the Fifth Circuit upheld suspicionless drug testing of a school custodian, reasoning that this is a safety-sensitive role because of its impact on students and staff in the building (*Aubrey v. School Board*, 1998). Two Supreme Court decisions, upholding mandatory drug testing of railroad employees involved in accidents and customs employees who carry firearms or are involved in the interdiction of illegal drugs, lend support to drug-testing requirements for public employees in safety-sensitive positions (*National Treasury Employees v. Von Raab*, 1989; *Skinner v. Railway*, 1989). In both of these cases, the Court ruled that safety and security concerns overrode the employees' privacy interests.

The Sixth Circuit expansively interpreted safety-sensitive positions by upholding a drug-testing program for public educators in *Knox County Education Association v. Knox County Board of Education* (1998), and the Supreme Court declined to review this decision. In addition to requiring employees suspected of drug use to be tested, the school district's policy requires drug testing of all new hires or transfers in safety-sensitive roles, including teachers, teaching assistants, principals, assistant principals, secretaries, and bus drivers. The appeals court reasoned that educators are on the "front line" of school security, which justifies suspicionless drug testing. Under the Sixth Circuit's logic, most school employees would occupy safety-sensitive positions, and thus most blanket or random drug-testing programs applied to school employees would seem to be permissible. Although other courts have not yet adopted this reasoning, there is some sentiment that drug testing represents a minimal impairment of individual privacy rights that might be justified to ensure that everything possible is being done to rid schools of drugs.

Concerns over student and staff safety in public schools continue to mount and are manifesting themselves not only in drug-screening policies and more stringent disciplinary practices but also in zero-tolerance policies in connection with evidence of drug use or weapon possession at school (one strike and you are out). School leaders need to be familiar with various drug-prevention programs and other strategies to combat this significant problem in our schools. Some parents fear that schools are not safe places for their children, and these anxieties are not dissipating despite their dissatisfaction with the rigidity of some zero-tolerance policies.

Sexual Harassment

Legal activity pertaining to sexual harassment is explored here in some detail to illustrate the significance of damages awards in influencing school policies and practices. Some policies evolve through periodic reviews, others through the school improvement process, and some through a concern about potential legal vulnerability because of a case reported in the media or legislation that places new requirements on the district. Changes in school practices regarding sexual harassment and penalties for employees and students engaging in such behavior have arisen primarily because of the changing legal environment governing institutional liability. Newspaper reports of large damages awards for sexual harassment have put school authorities on notice that they must take such complaints seriously. The legal dimensions of employer-to-employee harassment, employee-to-student harassment, and student-to-student harassment are briefly explored here.

Employment Harassment.   Since the 1980s, litigation pertaining to sexual harassment in employment has steadily made it easier for victims to get damages from school boards and other employers under Title VII of the Civil Rights Act of 1964, which protects employees against employment discrimination based on gender among other characteristics. If successful, aggrieved employees can get damages to compensate for the injury suffered as well as other remedies such as reinstatement and back pay.

It was well established before 1998 that employers could be liable under Title VII for negligent behavior if they were aware of, or by exercising reasonable care should have been aware of, harassing conduct and failed to take appropriate action (*Harris v. Forklift Systems,* 1993; *Meritor Savings Bank v. Vinson,* 1986). In 1998, the Supreme Court rendered three decisions, clarifying that negligence is sufficient to establish an employer's Title VII liability for sexual harassment, but is not always required for acts of supervisors who have engaged in severe or pervasive harassing conduct. The employer can in some instances be liable under Title VII without any showing of negligence or fault if, for example, the supervisor purported to act on behalf of the employer or was aided in carrying out the harassment by the employment relationship (*Burlington v. Ellerth,* 1998; *Faragher v. City of Boca Raton,* 1998). The Court also held that claims of same-sex harassment could be brought under Title VII (*Oncale v. Sundowner Offshore Services,* 1998).

The employer can assert an affirmative defense in some situations. If the victim suffers no significant change in employment status, the employer can possibly avoid liability by showing that policies prohibiting sexual harassment had been adopted and that the claimant failed to use the available grievance procedures. However, if the harassment victim suffers a tangible loss (e.g., denial of promotion), the employer cannot assert such a defense. By making it easier for aggrieved employees to get damages for sexual harassment in the workplace, these Title VII decisions have put employers on notice that their actions will be carefully scrutinized. All school employees and employers need to be aware of the legal standards and the educational implications of harassment in school settings.

Employee-to-Student Harassment.   More difficult legal issues are raised when students are the harassment victims. Title VII is an employment discrimination law, so students cannot rely on this provision to vindicate their rights. Recently, most sexual harassment cases involving students have been initiated under Title IX of the Education Amendments of 1972 that bars gender discrimination in educational institutions housing federally assisted programs. Title IX is enforced by the Office for Civil Rights (OCR) in the Department of Education; the Department can terminate federal funds to educational institutions found in violation of the law. Title IX claims are directed toward the institutional recipients of federal funds, such as schools and school districts.*

The significant upswing in sexual harassment cases involving students in the past decade does not necessarily reflect an increase in the number of incidents of harassment in schools. The growth in litigation can more likely be attributed to the 1992 decision, *Franklin* v. *Gwinnett County Public Schools* (1992), in which the Supreme Court held that individuals can use Title IX of the Education Amendment of 1972 to seek monetary damages from educational institutions for sexual harassment or abuse by school personnel. In *Franklin,* a student alleged that she was sexually harassed, including coerced intercourse by a male teacher/coach in the school district. She further alleged that the school district was aware of and investigated the employee's sexual harassment of the plaintiff and other students, but did not take action to halt it and even discouraged her from pressing charges. The school district ultimately closed the investigation after the teacher resigned. The Supreme Court held that students can use Title IX to seek monetary damages for gender discrimination in the form of sexual harassment by school employees.

The OCR issued detailed guidelines, the *Sexual Harassment Guidance* (1997), specifying that schools must have policies and procedures for responding to complaints about employee-to-student and student-to-student sexual harassment, including same-sex harassment. Judicial rulings were all across the continuum, with varying degrees of deference to the OCR standards, when the Supreme Court finally rendered decisions dealing with alleged sexual harassment of students by school employees and by peers.

In 1998, the Supreme Court in *Gebser v. Lago Vista Independent School District* clarified the Title IX standard for employee-to-student harassment by establishing a very high bar that students must cross to secure damages from school districts. The Court majority held that Title IX is violated only if school authorities who can take corrective action have actual knowledge of the harassment. Also, there must be deliberate indifference in that the recipient of federal funds makes a conscious decision not to remedy the harassment. The Court majority concluded that Title IX forms a contract in that federally assisted educational institutions promise not to discriminate based on gender and must be fully aware of any conditions that accompany federal aid.

Gebser involved a female student who sued the school district for failing to stop her long-term sexual relationship with a teacher. The student did not report the relationship to school officials, but the teacher eventually was dismissed after a policeman caught the teacher and student having sexual relations. The Supreme Court concluded that the student failed to prove that school authorities had actual

---

*Harassment victims also can bring suits against school districts and individual school authorities under 42 U.S.C. §1983 for vindication of their constitutional rights in connection with sexual harassment, although plaintiffs have been more successful bringing suits under Title VII and Title IX. For a discussion of constitutional as well as federal statutory claims, see the entire issue of the *Hastings Women's Law Journal,* vol. 12, no. 1 (2001).

knowledge of the harassment and acted with deliberate indifference. The Court further held that the school district's failure to adopt a sexual harassment policy and grievance procedure did not entitle the victim to damages under Title IX, even though the OCR requires school districts to have such policies and procedures in place. The *Gebser* dissenters and the OCR criticized this decision, asserting that it should be at least as easy to get damages from school districts for harassment of students by school personnel as for supervisor-to-employee harassment, given that students are far more vulnerable than employees.

Courts have agreed with the OCR regarding the issue of *welcomeness* if children are the harassment victims. The OCR *Guidance* states that a sexual relationship between a school employee and an elementary student can never be defended as consensual, and there is a strong presumption that such a relationship with a secondary school student is not consensual. In contrast to Title VII employment cases that can consider *welcomeness*, courts have held that there is always an element of coercion in a sexual relationship between an adult and a minor (*Mary M. v. North Lawrence*, 1997).

Peer Harassment.   The most volatile recent controversies have focused on the school district's responsibility to remedy student-to-student (peer) sexual harassment. The American Association of University Women documented disturbing statistics in 1993; four out of five students attending public schools in the United States reported that they had been victims of harassment, predominantly peer harassment, while at school (Harris et al., 1993). In a follow-up survey in 2001, students were far more likely to know what constitutes sexual harassment and to indicate that their districts had sexual harassment policies, but four fifths of the respondents still indicated that they had experienced some harassment at school (Harris Interactive, 2001). This finding is disheartening, given the efforts since 1993 to make students and staff members more aware of the harmful effects of sexual harassment on all involved. The volume of peer harassment has made courts and school personnel nervous as they contemplate the potential liability of school districts. The legal challenges focus on the school district's reactions to the harassment, rather than on the district's responsibility for the acts of third parties. In short, the district's liability is determined by its own acts or lack of action to prevent or curtail peer sexual harassment.

In *Davis v. Monroe County Board of Education* (1999), the Supreme Court ruled that school districts can be liable for damages under Title IX for student-to-student sexual harassment. The female plaintiff alleged that school authorities were indifferent when she complained that she was being sexually harassed by a male classmate. The harassment lasted for five months during fifth grade and ended after the perpetrator was charged with and pled guilty to sexual battery. During the five months of alleged indifference from school personnel, the victim's grades declined and she became so depressed that she considered suicide. She brought suit, claiming that school authorities could have stopped the inappropriate behavior but refused to act.

Building on its *Gebser* standard, the Court announced in *Davis* that school districts have an affirmative duty to protect students from peer sexual harassment if school employees with the power to curtail the harassment have actual knowledge of the behavior and exhibit deliberate indifference toward the victim. To establish a Title IX violation for peer harassment, the school district also must exercise substantial control over the harasser and the environment where the known harassment occurs. In addition, liability can be assessed against the school district only if the peer harassment is so severe, persistent, and objectively offensive that it interferes with the student victim's ability to benefit from educational opportunities reflected by declining grades or other evidence.

The Supreme Court's *Gebser* and *Davis* rulings left some issues unresolved, such as to whom notice must be given and how much notice must be provided for the school district to have "actual knowledge" of the harassment (see *Massey v. Akron*, 2000). The notice issue is more troublesome in peer harassment cases, as many employees may be empowered to take corrective action against known student harassers in contrast to the limited number of school officials authorized to stop harassment perpetrated by school personnel (see *Murrel v. School District*, 1999, p. 1247). Some fears have been voiced that school district liability for peer harassment may increase if courts broadly interpret who has authority to take corrective action as including most school employees such as coaches, teaching assistants, and bus drivers.

The OCR's 1997 *Sexual Harassment Guidance* indicated that the framework used to assess claims of sexual harassment in employment under Title VII also should be applied to students' Title IX sexual harassment claims, which conflicted with the Supreme Court's subsequent *Gebser* and *Davis* rulings. Thus, in 2001 the *Guidance* was revised to clarify the distinction between administrative enforcement of Title IX and private litigation for monetary damages. Recognizing that the Supreme Court's "actual knowledge/deliberate indifference" standard must be met in damages suits, the OCR reiterated that federal funds can be terminated in circumstances that would not give rise to claims for damages. The revised *Guidance* emphasizes that the OCR always makes schools aware of potential Title IX violations and seeks voluntary corrective action before federal aid is terminated.

The majority of student sexual harassment claims since 1999 have not succeeded in meeting the stringent Title IX standard established in *Gebser* and *Davis* (see *Davis v. DeKalb County School District*, 2000; *Oden v. North Marianas College*, 2002; *Soper v. Hoben*, 1999). But the heavy burden of proof in establishing actual knowledge and deliberate indifference can be satisfied, and some federal courts have awarded damages to student victims of employee or peer harassment (see *Massey v. Akron*, 2000; *Murrell v. School District*, 1999; *Niles v. Nelson*, 1999; *Warren v. Reading School District*, 2000).

School leaders would be wise to hold assemblies for students and inservice sessions for staff members to educate them regarding the signs of harassment and its harmful effects on all involved. It is also imperative to have clear school policies that define prohibited behavior and expression, identify penalties for engaging in the prohibited conduct, and provide grievance procedures for harassment victims. Such procedures should include two avenues to make complaints to ensure that the victim does not have to submit the complaint to the alleged perpetrator.

Students' Free Expression Rights

Until the late 1960s, it was generally assumed that school authorities could discipline students for any type of expression considered offensive, but this is no longer true. In the landmark decision, *Tinker v. Des Moines Independent Community School District* (1969), the Supreme Court ruled that students have a First Amendment right to express their political and ideological views in public schools. In *Tinker,* students planned to protest the Vietnam War by wearing arm bands to school. In anticipation of this occurrence, the principals met and adopted a policy stating that any student who refused to remove the arm band would be suspended. After three Tinker children were suspended for refusal to remove their arm bands, their parents filed suit in federal court.

The Supreme Court held that "it can hardly be argued that either students or teachers shed their constitutional rights to freedom of speech or expression at the schoolhouse gate" (p. 506). The Court, however, did not allow total freedom of student expression in the school context, holding that expression could be curtailed if reasonably calculated to cause a material or substantial disruption or invade the rights of others in the school environment. Although *Tinker* signaled an important shift in thinking about student expression and is often referred to as the Magna Carta of students' rights, it is not the only case that school leaders must consider when writing a student expression policy.

Before the mid-1980s, the category of expression *not* protected by the First Amendment entailed inflammatory, obscene, and libelous comments. In a significant 1986 decision, the Supreme Court added lewd, vulgar, and indecent expression to the unprotected category in the public school context, even though such expression may enjoy First Amendment protection elsewhere (*Bethel School District No. 403 v. Fraser,* 1986). The Court in *Fraser* upheld disciplinary action against a student for using a sexual metaphor in a nominating speech during a student government assembly, concluding that the sexual innuendos were offensive to both teachers and students. The Court majority held that the school has a legitimate interest in protecting the captive student audience from exposure to lewd, vulgar, and offensive speech, reasoning that the school board has the authority to determine what manner of student speech is appropriate to promote fundamental values of civility.

Two years later, the Supreme Court delivered another important decision, expanding the circumstances under which school authorities can censor student expression. In *Hazelwood School District v. Kuhlmeier* (1988), the Court determined that the school-sponsored newspaper was a nonpublic forum, in which articles could be censored for educational reasons. The type of forum involved is significant because this determination dictates the scope of protected expression.

Three main forum types have been recognized by the courts. In a *traditional public forum* that is reserved for assembly and expression (e.g., sidewalks, parks), speech cannot be restricted without a compelling state interest. At the other end of the continuum is a *nonpublic forum* (e.g., a public school) that is reserved for its governmental function, so viewpoint-neutral restrictions can be placed on speaker access and content. The government can intentionally create a *limited public forum* (e.g., a student activity period after school) on property generally reserved for its government use. In such a limited forum, the government can restrict the class of speakers (e.g., reserving the forum for students) and subject matter (e.g., noncommercial expression), but otherwise, the free-speech analysis is the same as in a traditional public forum. In determining the type of forum involved, courts traditionally have looked at the forum's characteristics, the usual activities that occur, and whether it historically has been designated as a place for communication (see *Cornelius v. NAACP,* 1985).

The Supreme Court in *Hazelwood* classified the school newspaper as a nonpublic forum because the school had not by policy or practice created any type of public forum in the school-sponsored paper that was produced in a class. Thus, the principal could censor the newspaper's content if the decisions were viewpoint neutral and based on pedagogical concerns. The Court found this test easily met since the principal decided to remove from the newspaper two articles dealing with teenage pregnancy and the effect of divorce on high school students for fear that individuals could be identified. The Court upheld the principal's decision and distinguished the impermissible silencing of a student's personal expression that happens to occur at school, as in *Tinker,* from "an educator's authority over school-sponsored publications, theatrical productions, and other expressive activities that students, parents, and members of the public might reasonably perceive to bear the imprimatur of the school" (*Hazelwood* v. *Kuhlmeier,* 1988, p. 217).

Hazelwood provides clear precedent that school-sponsored newspapers can be created and administered as a nonpublic forum, thereby giving schools broad control over their contents. In the wake of *Hazelwood,* schools have tended to draft policies specifying that the school-sponsored newspapers, events, and activities are nonpublic forums. There is some uncertainty, however, as to the extent of financial support, faculty involvement, student involvement, and use of school premises necessary to trigger such school-sponsorship.

Ironically, since the *Hazelwood* decision, underground student papers (student-prepared and not representing the school) have more protection than do school-sponsored publications, unless a state has enacted a law to give students editorial control of school-sponsored papers. These underground publications, even though distributed at school, are considered private expression in contrast to papers that students write as part of a journalism class for academic credit or as an extracurricular noncredit activity under a faculty sponsor. Underground newspapers may be regulated for content only when the regulation serves a compelling state interest (e.g., avoiding a substantial disruption of the educational process), which is a more stringent standard than applied to school-sponsored papers that can be censored for pedagogical reasons (*Hazelwood,* 1988). Underground newspapers cannot be kept out of the school because of the viewpoint of the writer, but distribution can always be stopped after the fact if the content is disruptive, libelous, lewd, or vulgar.

Also, schools can apply reasonable restrictions on the time, place, and manner that both underground as well as school-sponsored papers are distributed at school. These regulations have traditionally been viewed by the courts as a vehicle to monitor that the distribution does not create a disruption rather than a strategy to curtail students' free expression rights. Such restrictions on how, where, and when materials are distributed must be reasonable and viewpoint neutral.

Electronic Expression.   Substantial current controversy pertains to students' expression rights on the Internet. Students have challenged school disciplinary action for materials they prepared and disseminated on the world wide web from their homes. The guiding legal principles are evolving, so it is important for school leaders to stay abreast of developments.

To date, most courts have applied the *Tinker* disruption standard to assess whether students can be disciplined for web pages created at home (see *Emmett v. Kent School District*, 2000; *Killion v. Franklin Regional School District*, 2001). For example, a student received a preliminary injunction blocking his suspension for using his home computer to create a home page that criticized school administrators, because of insufficient evidence linking the web site to any negative impact on the school (*Beussink v. Woodland R-IV School District*, 1998).

However, if evidence shows that the expression interferes with management of the school or threatens a disruption, disciplinary action will be upheld. To illustrate, the Pennsylvania Supreme Court approved a student's expulsion because he created on his home computer a web site ("Teacher Sux") that contained disparaging comments about teachers and administrators and depicted the algebra teacher's death, causing her to take a leave of absence (*J. S. v. Bethlehem Area School District*, 2002). The central consideration in determining the validity of disciplinary action against students appears to be whether the material created off-campus and disseminated on the Internet has a harmful impact on the school. Of course, school personnel can place restrictions on students' use of *school* computers and networks, and most school districts have adopted *acceptable use* policies that specify penalties for infractions.

In addition to sanctions against students for their expression on the web, federal laws also have been enacted to protect minors from harmful materials transmitted on the Internet (see *Children's Internet Protection Act*, 2002; *Child Online Protection Act*, 2002), even though the constitutionality of these measures is being questioned (see Cambron-McCabe, McCarthy, & Thomas, 2004). Also, school districts are placing restrictions on web sites that can be visited by students at school and are monitoring the use of school equipment and networks by staff members (see *Urofsky v. Gilmore*, 2000). Some educators are concerned that such measures may have a chilling effect on their efforts to use computer networks to enhance instructional experiences for students.

Student Attire.   Students' expression rights often are raised in cases challenging restrictions on their appearance. Student hair length that was quite controversial in the 1960s and 1970s has declined as a major subject of litigation, but other student appearance fads have become controversial. Students have asserted a First Amendment right to express themselves through their attire at school, and school authorities have argued that student attire can be restricted to advance the educational mission. And courts consistently have recognized that schools can prohibit attire that is immodest, lewd, vulgar, disruptive, or unclean, or if it conflicts with the school's objectives (Cambron-McCabe, McCarthy, & Thomas, 2004).

For example, a federal district court ruled that students could be prevented from wearing a t-shirt that depicted three high school administrators drunk because the shirt undermined school authorities and hampered their efforts to educate students about the dangers of alcohol (*Gano v. School District*, 1987). Similarly, a Virginia federal court upheld a student's one-day suspension for refusing to change her shirt printed with the words "Drugs Suck," which the court found to be vulgar (*Broussard v. School Board*, 1992). Several courts have upheld dress codes that prohibit male students from wearing earrings, rejecting the assertion that jewelry restrictions must be applied equally to male and female students and noting that community norms and concerns about gang influences can be considered (see *Barber v. Colorado Independent School District*, 1995; *Hines v. Caston School Corporation*, 1995).

Student attire does not have to be disruptive to be barred from public schools. The Sixth Circuit upheld a school district's decision to prohibit students from wearing Marilyn Manson t-shirts, reasoning that the shirts were offensive and promoted behavior that conflicted with the school's efforts to deter drug use and promote human dignity (*Boroff v. Van Wert City Board of Education*, 2000). This court also upheld a restrictive student dress code (limiting the colors, materials, and types of clothing) that was devised by a Kentucky school-based council to reduce gang influences and student conflicts over clothing and was *not* adopted to suppress student expression (*Long v. Board of Education*, 2001). An Illinois court also upheld a dress code that allowed students to wear only black and white clothing and prohibited logos, patches, imprinted words, and designs (*Vines v. Board of Education*, 2002). Educational justifications, beyond the prevention of a disruption, increasingly are being used to justify attire restrictions in public schools as long as the policies are not intended to curtail expression.

The line is somewhat blurred between a restrictive dress code and a student uniform policy. Courts to date have upheld uniform policies as justified by substantial government interests in improving safety, reducing gang-related attire and violence, decreasing socioeconomic tensions, increasing attendance, and reducing dropouts (see *Canady v. Bossier Parish School Board*, 2001; *Littlefield v. Forney Independent School District*, 2001). Those supporting uniforms also contend that they improve school climate by placing the emphasis on academics rather than fashion. Student uniforms are gaining popularity, particularly in urban school districts. In most instances, students can opt out of the uniform requirements for religious or philosophical reasons, and provisions are made for children who cannot afford the uniforms.

The judicial trend is to uphold constraints on student attire and hairstyles, but the restrictions will be invalidated if they lack an educational rationale (see *Jeglin v. San Jacinto Unified School District*, 1993). For example, a Texas federal district court ruled in favor of two students who had been told they could not wear rosaries out-side their shirts because of the school's dress code that prohibited any gang-related apparel (*Chalifoux v. New Caney Independent School District,* 1997). In addition, the general principle that school policies cannot be discriminatory applies to the en-forcement of dress codes (see *Castorina v. Madison County School Board,* 2001).

Dress codes or uniform policies should be included in student handbooks and disseminated to all students and their parents. Any such policies should be based on a sound educational rationale. Litigation dealing with student appear-ance in public schools will likely continue, given the friction between school au-thorities' concerns about attire linked to gangs and violence and students' interests in expressing themselves through tattoos, body piercing, and various types of clothing.

Antiharassment Policies.   Another area of emerging legal doctrine involves an-tiharassment policies. During the past few years of heightened political aware-ness, many school districts have adopted policies for their elementary and secondary schools that prohibit harassing expression and behavior based on race, religion, color, national origin, gender, sexual orientation, disability, or other per-sonal characteristics. These policies have become controversial because they pit the legitimate governmental interest in instilling civil behavior and respect for others against the fundamental right to express views, even if unpopular. Al-though expression that is protected in an open forum includes "offensive speech" (see *Dambrot v. Central Michigan University,* 1995; *R.A.V. v. St. Paul,* 1992), the appli-cability of that principle to student expression in the public school's limited or nonpublic forum is much less clear. Until recently, it was generally assumed that public schools are a special environment, because part of their mission is to instill basic democratic values, including civility and respect for diversity.

For example, the Tenth Circuit upheld disciplinary action against a middle school student for violating the school district's antiharasssment provision by drawing a Confederate flag during math class (*West v. Derby Unified School Dis-trict,* 2000). The court agreed with the school district that the student's drawing might cause a disruption and interfere with the rights of others, given prior racial incidents related to the Confederate flag. Also recognizing that students can be disciplined for expression that intrudes on the school's legitimate function of in-culcating manners and habits of civility, the Eleventh Circuit observed: "Racist and other hateful views can be expressed in a public forum. But an elementary school under its custodial responsibilities may restrict such speech that could crush a child's sense of self-worth" (*Denno v. School Board,* 2000, p. 1273).

Departing from the general judicial trend, the Third Circuit in 2001 struck down a Pennsylvania school district's antiharassment policy (*Saxe v. State College Area School District,* 2001). The policy provided specific examples of what would be considered harassment (e.g., demeaning comments, graffiti, gestures) and set forth punishments for violating its provisions. The Third Circuit found the policy uncon-stitutionally overbroad, disagreeing with the district court's conclusion that the policy simply curtailed expression already prohibited under federal and state antidiscrimination laws. Reasoning that the policy went beyond expression that could be prohibited under the *Tinker* disruption standard, the court found no evidence that the policy was necessary to advance the compelling government interests of maintaining an orderly school environment and protecting the rights of others.

Subsequently, the same court upheld a district's antiharassment policy that was narrowly designed to respond to incidents of race-based conflicts. However, the court ruled that the policy's phrase banning speech that "creates ill will or hatred" had to be eliminated, as this restriction would allow some protected expression to be curtailed (*Sypniewski v. Warren Hills*, 2002). Questions remain regarding the legality of such antiharassment policies, especially those adopted in the absence of disruptive incidents, so additional challenges seem assured. School authorities would be wise to review carefully all policies that restrict students' rights to freely express their views and be certain that such restrictions are necessary to advance legitimate school objectives.

Religious Activities and Observances in Public Schools

The First Amendment provides in part that "Congress shall make no law respecting an establishment of religion, or prohibiting the free exercise thereof," and these restrictions on congressional action are applied to the states and their subdivisions through the Fourteenth Amendment. The Supreme Court settled in the early 1960s that public school personnel cannot lead devotional activities, such as reading Bible passages or saying the Lord's Prayer; school sponsorship of such observances abridges the Establishment Clause (*School District v. Schempp*, 1963; *Engle v. Vitale*, 1962). It was immaterial that students could be excused from the exercises or that the activities were relatively minor encroachments on religious liberties. But the precise meaning of the religion clauses has been the source of considerable litigation and numerous Supreme Court opinions, and the scope of religious accommodations allowed in public education is still evolving.

In reviewing the school prayer decisions, Carter (1994) addressed the public dissatisfaction with the long line of school prayer cases, observing that "not every legal funeral leads to a political burial" (p. 60). Unlike many areas of constitutional law that were broadly criticized at the time of Supreme Court action (e.g., *Brown v. Board of Education*, 1954, striking down state-sanctioned school segregation) and then generally settled into the nation's moral and political conscience, school prayer cases have been unpopular with a large segment of the population for forty years. The Supreme Court continues to be split in interpreting the Establishment Clause, although recent decisions lean more toward governmental accommodation of religion.

About half of the states have enacted laws authorizing a "moment of silence" at the beginning of school, and some of these provisions have been contested under the Establishment Clause. These statutes vary, with some specifying that the moment of silence may be used for prayer, whereas others mention only meditation. In *Wallace v. Jaffree* (1985), the Supreme Court invalidated an Alabama statute that authorized a period of silence "for meditation or voluntary prayer," finding that its intent was to encourage children to pray as the state already had a silent meditation law. Thus, the addition of *prayer* to the law coupled with the provision's legislative history convinced the Court that it was designed to advance religion.

But more recently, federal appellate courts have endorsed Virginia and Georgia laws calling for a moment for silent meditation or prayer in public schools (*Bown v. Gwinnett*, 1997; *Brown v. Gilmore*, 2001). These courts recognized the secular purpose of using a moment of silence to settle students at the beginning of the school day and found no evidence that students were encouraged to pray during the moment of silence. An assessment of legislative intent is crucial in determining the constitutionality of such provisions.

State laws and school board actions pressing the limits of the Establishment Clause and judicial responses have increased since the Supreme Court's 1992 decision, *Lee v. Weisman*. The divided Supreme Court in *Weisman* struck down a school district's policy allowing principals to invite clergy members to deliver nonsectarian invocations and benedictions at middle and high school graduation ceremonies. The Court majority concluded that the policy entailed indirect coercion in that students felt peer pressure to participate in the graduation devotionals; students should not have to choose whether to respect their religious beliefs or attend this important event.

Some school districts have responded to *Weisman* by reinstating baccalaureate services sponsored by outside groups that rent school facilities for a nominal fee (see *Shumway v. Albany County*, 1993; *Verbena v. Chilton County*, 1991). Others have authorized student-led religious messages at graduation ceremonies and other school-related events, contending that school sponsorship is eliminated because students initiate and lead the religious activities.

Student-Initiated Devotionals.   Recent litigation has addressed competing claims that the First Amendment demands equal treatment of religious and secular expression in public schools and that the Establishment Clause requires differential treatment. Illustrative are controversies over students' religious messages in graduation ceremonies.

Two Ninth Circuit rulings portray how the same court can reach different conclusions regarding the constitutionality of religious graduation messages, because the factual situations differ. In the first case, the court upheld an Idaho school district's policy that created a forum for student expression in the graduation ceremony. Under the policy, student graduation speakers were selected by academic standing and could choose any type of message, including prayers, but they were not advised to select religious content (*Doe v. Madison School District*, 1998). The policy prohibited school authorities from censoring students' graduation speeches, and the court considered the ceremony a forum for student expression. However, in the second case, the school district retained control over the graduation exercises, and the principal reviewed graduation speeches before their delivery. Finding the graduation ceremony in this situation to be a nonpublic forum, the appeals court upheld the school district's decision to prohibit students from making proselytizing speeches as necessary to avoid an Establishment

Clause violation (*Cole v. Oroville*, 2000). The primary distinction between these two cases was the status of the graduation ceremony—it was designated a forum for student expression in one case and a nonpublic forum under the school's control in the other.

In some situations, school districts have allowed students to vote whether to have nonsectarian graduation prayers delivered by students, and this practice has generated a number of legal challenges. The Fifth Circuit ruled that the student election removed school sponsorship, and thus, there was no Establishment Clause infraction (*Jones v. Clear Creek*, 1992). However, the Third and Ninth Circuit appellate courts conversely held that school authorities could not delegate decisions to students that the Establishment Clause forbids school districts from making in the first place (*ACLU v. Black Horse Pike*, 1996; *Harris v. Joint School District*, 1994).

The Supreme Court has not clarified the legal status of student-initiated graduation devotionals, but it did render a decision pertaining to student-led devotionals before public school football games. In *Santa Fe Independent School District v. Doe* (2000), the Court struck down a school district's policy authorizing students to decide by election to have invocations at the athletic events and to identify a classmate to lead the devotionals. The Court majority held that student-led expression at a school event on school property under the supervision of school personnel cannot be considered private speech; the policy was designed to promote Christian observances in school-related activities. Recognizing that the purpose of the Bill of Rights is to remove certain topics from majority rule, the court concluded that the student elections guarantee that minority views will be silenced. But the Court also emphasized that the Constitution does not prohibit public school students from engaging in voluntary prayer at school—only state sponsorship of devotionals violates the Establishment Clause.

Although school-prayer advocates viewed the *Santa Fe* ruling as a setback, subsequent federal appellate rulings have upheld students' free speech rights to express religious views in public schools. After *Santa Fe*, the Eleventh Circuit reaffirmed a Florida school district's policy that authorizes public school seniors to select classmates to give graduation messages and allows the speakers to choose the content (*Adler v. Duval County*, 2001). The court emphasized that the student elections are not tied to delivering prayers, as the content of the speakers' messages is not specified. The same court in an Alabama case reinstated its earlier decision (remanded for reconsideration in light of *Santa Fe*), in which it had lifted part of a court injunction prohibiting all student religious expression during school (*Chandler v. Siegelman*, 2000). The appeals court declared that the Establishment Clause does not require and the Free Speech Clause does not allow a ban on student-initiated religious expression in public schools. The Eleventh Circuit reasoned that both school-sponsored student prayer and school censorship of private student religious expression are unconstitutional. The appeals court emphasized that all student religious speech in a public school is not *sponsored* by the school.

It appears that student religious expression may be considered private, and thus constitutionally protected, if clearly student-initiated and not viewed as representing the public school. However, given the *Santa Fe* decision, it is doubtful that student elections to authorize student-led devotionals in school-sponsored activities will be upheld.

Some of the controversies over student-initiated religious expression have involved class assignments. Given the school's control over the classroom, which is a nonpublic forum, most courts have upheld school personnel in curtailing students' proselytyzing activities in presentations or other displays (see *DeNooyer v. Merinelli*, 1993; *Settle v. Dickson County School Board*, 1995). But if an assignment is couched in terms of students expressing their own views, teachers might impair free speech rights if religious submissions are rejected.

Equal Access and Treatment of Religious Expression and Groups. The current focus on equal access for religious groups and equal treatment of religious expression can be traced to a higher education case, *Widmar v. Vincent* (1981), in which the Supreme Court ruled that a state university could not deny use of its facilities to a student religious club since it had created a forum for student groups to meet. This *equal access* notion has been applied to the secondary school level in First Amendment cases where courts have concluded that student distribution of religious and secular materials must be treated the same (*Hedges v. Wauconda Community Unit School District No. 118*, 1993; *Thompson v. Waynesboro*, 1987).

In 1984, Congress codified the equal access concept for student-initiated clubs in secondary schools when it passed the Equal Access Act (EAA). This law stipulates that secondary schools receiving federal funds and allowing noncurriculum-related student groups to meet on school premises during noninstructional time may not deny access to any group based on the religious, political, philosophical, or other content of its meetings. The EAA was enacted to allow student religious groups to meet in public high schools, but it protects other student expression as well.

In 1990, the Supreme Court rejected an Establishment Clause challenge to the EAA, finding no advancement of religion in the neutral law designed to protect student expression on a range of topics (*Board of Education v. Mergens*, 1990). The Court held that if a secondary school receiving federal aid allows one noncurriculum group to use school facilities during noninstructional time, it has created a forum for student groups and must comply with the EAA.

The critical phrase in applying the statute is "noncurriculum-related student group." The Court majority interpreted this term as applying to any student groups "that are not related to the body of courses offered by the school" (p. 237). Four factors are important in determining whether the group directly relates to the school's curriculum: (1) if its subject matter is actually taught, or will soon be taught, in a regularly offered course; (2) if that subject matter concerns the body of courses as a whole; (3) if participation in the group is required for a particular course; and (4) if participation in the group will result in academic credit. Where one noncurriculum student club is allowed public school access, the school has created a limited forum and cannot discriminate against students desiring to use school facilities for religious or other nondisruptive meetings. Student religious groups also can require certain officers to be Christians to safeguard the spiritual content of their meetings (*Hsu v. Roslyn Union School District*, 1996).

The Ninth Circuit has delivered several decisions broadly interpreting the reach of the EAA. In *Garnett v. Renton School District No. 403* (1993), it held that a state constitutional provision more restrictive than the Establishment Clause must yield to the federal right created by the EAA. The appeals court subsequently held that the "no religious preference clause" in the California Constitution, even though more stringent than the Establishment Clause, cannot limit students' rights under the EAA; thus, student religious groups could meet during lunch when no classes are in session if other student meetings are allowed at this time (*Ceniceros v. Board of Trustees of San Diego Unified School District*, 1997). The court showed no concern about peer pressure on other students during the lunch hour. More recently, the Ninth Circuit delivered its most expansive interpretation of the EAA by requiring student religious groups to be provided equal access as other student groups to school equipment, vehicles, and funds (*Prince v. Jacoby*, 2002). The court also held that it would be viewpoint discrimination under the First Amendment's Free Speech Clause to treat the religious group differently from other student clubs as to meeting times and use of school supplies.

As secondary schools cope with EAA compliance, they must first assess whether they allow any noncurriculum-related student groups to meet on school premises during noninstructional time. If they do, these schools must allow access to all nondisruptive student groups. This applies not only to religious groups, such as the Fellowship of Christian Athletes, but also to student groups that want to discuss topics that may be viewed unfavorably by large segments of the community, such as homosexuality. Indeed, the Gay/Straight Alliance has been involved in a number of cases, and most courts have concluded that the EAA entitles the Alliance to meet in public secondary schools if other noncurriculum groups are allowed such access (see *Colin v. Orange Unified School District*, 2000).

Because the EAA covers only student groups, community groups seeking access to public school facilities must rely on the First Amendment. Where public schools allow community groups to meet after school hours, controversies have arisen if religious groups have been denied access to hold devotional meetings. In *Lamb's Chapel* v. *Center Moriches Union Free School District* (1993), the Supreme Court ruled that a school district could not deny school access to an evangelical church that wanted to show a film series on family relationships, because religious perspectives on this subject must be treated the same as other perspectives. In essence, the Court ruled that school-district enforcement of school-facility use policies cannot discriminate against a specific community group's viewpoint.

The Supreme Court in 2001 delivered a significant decision, upholding the Good News Club's free speech right to meet in a New York public school after school hours to hold clergy-led meetings targeting elementary school children, because other community groups were allowed school access (*Good News Club v. Milford Central School*). Reversing the lower courts' conclusion that the club was engaging in religious worship in violation of the Establishment Clause, the Supreme Court ruled that denying the club access would violate the Free Speech Clause by discriminating against religious viewpoints. The Court rejected the distinction between meetings of the Good News Club and the showing of films primarily to adults (that was upheld in *Lamb's Chapel*), reasoning that whether moral lessons are taught through live storytelling and prayers or through films is constitutionally insignificant.

This decision will likely encourage sectarian groups to seek greater religious accommodations—perhaps even weekly services—in public schools if other community groups are allowed school access for meetings (see *Bronx Household of Faith v. Board of Education,* 2002). It may portend that the Supreme Court will expand what is considered *private* religious expression protected by the Free Speech Clause in contrast to *government-sponsored* religious expression prohibited by the Establishment Clause.

There has been a shift away from Establishment Clause analysis to Free Speech Clause analysis if the controversy involves religious expression, and a hierarchy of First Amendment rights seems to be emerging, with Free Speech Clause protections trumping Establishment Clause restrictions (McCarthy, 1996). Also, the federal government is championing more religious accommodations in public schools, as reflected in the *Guidance on Constitutionally Protected Prayer in Public Elementary and Secondary Schools* (2003) accompanying the No Child Left Behind Act of 2001. These developments have significant implications regarding how school leaders deal with student, staff, and community requests to allow religious practices in public education.

Legal Liability

Fear of potential liability is a powerful motivation to comply with legal standards. This fear extends to public-school teachers and administrators, many of whom worry about personal and school district liability and communicate such apprehension to other staff members and possibly to students. This section briefly explores selected aspects of educators' and school districts' legal liability.

Liability generally refers to the negative consequences that can result from failure to satisfy a legal obligation, but it is especially concerned with the narrower topic of monetary consequences. Standards of liability differ markedly from one area of law to another. In the remainder of this section, potential liability is explored in connection with negligence under state law and with impairments of federally protected rights under federal civil rights laws.

Liability for Negligence

As mentioned in the first section of this chapter, negligence is a branch of tort law that affords a damages remedy when an individual causes harm to another's person, property, or reputation. Tort law defines a particular level of conduct that individuals owe one another, and tort suits are important because they provide a remedy for actions that might not evoke criminal charges. Although torts include negligence, defamation (libel and slander), assault and battery, false imprisonment, and intentional infliction of emotional distress, school personnel and districts are most likely to be defendants in negligence actions.

Four basic elements must be present to establish negligence. First, there must be a *duty* to protect others from harm. In school cases, educators have a duty to protect the health and safety of the students in the custody of the school. Once such a duty is legally established, tort law requires a certain standard of conduct to protect others against unreasonable risks. A *breach of the duty* amounts to a failure of one party to conform to the standard of care required toward another. Such a breach can occur from either an action (e.g., sending a child on an errand) or an omission (e.g., failure to supervise students) showing that the defendant acted unreasonably. The third element is *causation;* there must be a reasonably close causal connection between the alleged misconduct and the resulting injury. In essence, the injury would not have occurred without the negligent behavior. And finally, there must be an *injury;* the plaintiff must show an actual loss or real damages. The amount of damages awarded depends on the particular circumstances of the person injured and the amount of money it will take to make that person whole.

Schools and their employees are not responsible for all injuries that occur. In assessing whether there is legal liability for negligence, foreseeability is a key consideration, which means that the defendant could or should have seen the potentially dangerous consequences of the action when it was taken. The defendant is presumed to be an ordinary, prudent, *reasonable person* under the circumstances, and the jury then determines foreseeability. When the defendant is an educator, he or she is expected to exhibit behavior of a reasonable educator with the training and experience that licensed individuals usually possess. Reasonable actions in one situation may be viewed as unreasonable under other conditions.

The application of these legal standards depends on the particular set of facts involved. The jury usually plays the central role as fact finder for all the elements of the case. Still, the judge controls, as a matter of law, which cases involve factual allegations sufficient to go to the jury.

Until the 1950s, most school districts still enjoyed governmental immunity from damages for negligence. This doctrine originated in the Middle Ages ("the king can do no wrong") and evolved into the common law doctrine that government agencies cannot be held liable for their employees' negligent actions. Although this common law doctrine still exists, most states have limited its use by allowing damages for known dangerous conditions in school buildings (see *Velmer v. Baraga Area School,* 1988), for proprietary functions that could be provided by private corporations (see *Genao v. Board of Education,* 1995), or for ministerial duties in carrying out directions (in contrast to activities requiring the exercise of discretion, see *Pauley v. Anchorage School District,* 2001). The availability of governmental immunity as a defense in negligence cases varies widely across states.

Public school employees, like other citizens, cannot insulate themselves from being sued for negligence. However, they can take steps to protect themselves against successful claims even in locales where governmental immunity has been abrogated. Several defenses are available that provide a total or partial bar to recovery by the injured party. Assumption of risk is one affirmative defense that can be used when the injured plaintiff, through actual knowledge or extreme recklessness, knew that the action engaged in could cause the injury suffered. A student can assume reasonable risks for a given activity, such as the potential for injury from playing football (see *Hammond v. Board of Education*, 1994). But the student athlete does not assume the risk of faulty equipment.

Another affirmative defense is contributory negligence, where the injured plaintiff's conduct was unreasonable or negligent under the circumstances, which led to the resulting injury. The rationale is that the injured plaintiff should not be rewarded for an injury that at least partially is caused by his or her own negligence. If contributory negligence is established, the injured plaintiff would receive no compensation for the injuries sustained. Many states have replaced contributory negligence with the defense of comparative negligence. Whereas contributory negligence is an all-or-nothing determination, using comparative negligence, liability is distributed according to fault. For example, where a teacher on playground duty breaks up a fight that has been taking place for several minutes, the injured plaintiff may be found 20 percent negligent for engaging in the fight, the teacher may be found 30 percent negligent for not supervising more closely, and the intervening student who initiated the fight may be 50 percent negligent.

Even if an educator is found to be negligent, many states by law protect district employees from personal liability if their negligence occurred within the scope of employment. These statutes effectively make the school district financially responsible for employees' tortious acts committed in performing their jobs and often obligate the district to provide legal defense for the employees being sued. The school district can cover these potential liabilities through its insurance policy. But the school district is not financially responsible when an employee's misconduct occurs outside the scope of employment.

Liability for Impairments of Federally Protected Rights

Negligence cases are handled on the basis of state law, but school districts and school authorities also can face liability for damages based on the impairment of federally protected rights. A number of federal laws explicitly provide or have been judicially interpreted to provide a private right for individuals to initiate lawsuits for damages to vindicate their rights. As noted previously, employees have relied primarily on Title VII of the Civil Rights Act of 1964 to challenge discriminatory employment policies and practices. If successful, aggrieved employees can get damages to compensate for the injury suffered as well as other remedies such as reinstatement and back pay. Successful plaintiffs can also get attorneys' fees, which often are substantial.

Some federal laws have been interpreted as precluding such private suits for damages. For example, the Supreme Court in 2002 ruled that the Family Educational Rights and Privacy Act does not allow private suits for damages as the law contains no rights-creating language (*Gonzaga v. Doe*, 2002). The remedy for recordkeeping violations under the law is for the Secretary of Education to withdraw federal aid from noncomplying educational institutions. If the Court instead had allowed private damages suits in *Gonzaga*, litigation over recordkeeping practices would have escalated. Parents would be far more motivated to challenge practices if they could receive monetary awards than if the only relief is to punish the school district by withholding its federal aid—a penalty that no school district has yet suffered.

In addition to liability under specific federal laws, the Civil Rights Act of 1871, enacted to protect the rights of African Americans, provides a vehicle for individuals to secure damages for impairments of constitutional and certain other federally protected rights (see *Maine v. Thiboutot*, 1980). A number of federal damages suits have been initiated under this law, referred to as Section 1983, which stipulates:

> Every person who, under cover of any statute…of any State…subjects…any citizen of the United States or any person within the jurisdiction thereof to the deprivation of any rights, privileges, or immunities secured by the Constitution and laws, shall be liable to the party injured in an action at law, suit in equity, or other proper proceeding for redress.

Section 1983 is a popular cause of action, because of the robust remedies available—injunctive relief as well as monetary damages. Injunctive relief provides the court authority to order parties to take certain actions separate from the payment of fines. Liability is assessed against the state actor only if the federally protected right was clearly established at the time the alleged improper conduct occurred (*Harlow v. Fitzgerald*, 1982; *Wood v. Strickland*, 1975). The Supreme Court has broadly interpreted "persons" under Section 1983 to include local governments, including school districts, so these entities can be assessed damages for federal impairments based on official policy (*Monell v. New York City Department of Social Services*, 1978). Although school officials can plead good faith immunity for their actions, ignorance of clearly established law would be evidence of bad faith. The good-faith defense is not available to school districts, which can be liable for violations of constitutional rights resulting from official policies (*Owen v. City of Independence*, 1980). But school districts are not responsible for the isolated, insubordinate acts of their employees.

Section 1983 claims often are referred to as constitutional torts because the primary remedy is a damages award similar to awards in tort cases under state law. The measure of compensatory damages awarded by the jury needs to be based on the actual deprivation of federal rights and what it will take to restore the person to the position enjoyed before the deprivation; the individual is not entitled to be compensated for the abstract value placed on the impairment of a constitutional right (*Memphis Community School District v. Stachura*, 1986). Where no injuries are involved, the court may award nominal damages of one dollar, recognizing the deprivation of a constitutional right but no injuries meriting compensation. In the case of nominal damages, however, attorney fees could be awarded to the plaintiffs.

Punitive damages, designed to punish the wrongdoer, are not available against school districts (*City of Newport v. Fact Concerts*, 1981). However, punitive damages may be assessed under Section 1983 against an individual whose conduct is shown to be motivated by "evil intent" or when it involves "reckless indifference" toward others' federally protected rights (*Smith v. Wade*, 1983, p. 43).

As mentioned in Chapter 15, the Eleventh Amendment has been interpreted as barring citizens from initiating federal lawsuits against a state without its consent, and this affects school districts only if they are considered an arm of the state. Congress can abrogate state immunity through laws designed to enforce the Fourteenth Amendment, but the Supreme Court recently has strengthened states' Eleventh Amendment immunity. The Court has required explicit language in federal legislation in order to eliminate states' immunity, and only federal laws intended to enforce constitutional rights can do so. For example, the Court has ruled that neither the Americans with Disabilities Act nor the Age Discrimination in Employment Act satisfy these conditions for abrogating immunity (*Board of Trustees v. Garrett*, 2001; *Kimel v. Florida Board of Regents*, 2000). Although citizens cannot sue states under these laws, they still can sue school districts that function like municipalities rather than an extension of the state (see *Mt. Healthy City School District v. Doyle*, 1977).

Judicial Deference

Most school controversies do not result in litigation; they are handled through administrative appeals. Indeed, litigated controversies are like the tip of the iceberg, with the vast majority of disputes being addressed through other means. For example, requests for students to be excused from specific assignments or activities for religious reasons are usually handled at the classroom or school level. If controversies are appealed to the judiciary, a court often will refuse to review the case until appropriate administrative remedies have been exhausted. Courts are hesitant to interfere with judgments of school personnel and school boards who have educational expertise.

The Supreme Court has recognized that in controversies over educational policies, the judiciary's "lack of specialized knowledge and experience counsels against premature interference with the informed judgments made at the state and local level" (*San Antonio v. Rodriguez*, 1973, p. 42). Although the judiciary will defer to decisions of school policy makers whenever possible, it will intervene if protected rights hang in the balance. And it is somewhat sobering to realize that the scope of our protected rights might be determined by one vote in a given decision.

School leaders are expected to stay abreast of established legal principles (*Wood v. Strickland*, 1975) and to understand the basic values underlying the legal system in the United States. If school leaders make every effort to exhibit reasonable behavior and act in an equitable, fair, and just manner, their decisions are likely to be upheld if legally challenged. And more importantly, a legal perspective can be helpful in their efforts to maintain an appropriate educational environment for students and staff members.

REFERENCES

ACLU of New Jersey v. Black Horse Pike Regional Board of Education, 84 F.3d 1471 (3d Cir. 1996).

Adler v. Duval County School Bd., 250 F.3d 1330 (11th Cir. 2001), *cert. denied*, 534 U.S. 1065 (2001).

Age Discrimination in Employment Act of 1967, 29 U.S.C. §621 et seq. (2002).

Alexander, S. K., & Alexander, D. (2001). *American public school law*. St. Paul: West.

Alinovi v. Worcester School Community, 777 F.2d 776 (1st Cir. 1985).

Americans with Disabilities Act of 1990, 42 U.S.C. §12101 et seq. (2002).

Aubrey v. School Board, 148 F.3d 559 (5th Cir. 1998).

Barber v. Colorado Independent School District, 901 S.W.2d 447 (Tex. 1995).

Belk v. Charlotte-Mecklenburg Board of Education, 269 F.3d 305 (4th Cir. 2001).

Bethel School District Number 403 v. Fraser, 478 U.S. 675 (1986).

Beussink v. Woodland R-IV School District, 30 F. Supp. 2d 1175 (E.D. Mo. 1998).

Board of Education of Oklahoma City Public Schools v. Dowell, 498 U.S. 237 (1991).

Board of Education of Westside Community Schools v. Mergens, 496 U.S. 226 (1990).

Board of Education v. Dowell, 498 U.S. 237 (1991).

Board of Education v. Earls, 536 U.S. 822 (2002).

Board of Trustees v. Garrett, 531 U.S. 356 (2001).

Boring v. Buncombe County Board of Education, 136 F.3d 364 (4th Cir. 1996).

Boroff v. Van Wert City Board of Education, 220 F.3d 465 (6th Cir. 2000), *cert. denied*, 532 U.S. 920 (2001).

Bown v. Gwinnett County School District, 112 F.3d 1464 (11th Cir. 1997).

Brantley v. District of Columbia, 640 A.2d 181 (D.C. Ct. App. 1994).

Brentwood Academy v. Tennessee Secondary School Athletic Association, 531 U.S. 288 (2001).

Bronx Household of Faith v. Board of Education, 226 F. Supp. 2d 401 (S.D.N.Y. 2002).

Broussard v. School Board of Norfolk, 801 F. Supp. 1526 (E.D. Va. 1992).

Brown v. Board of Education of Topeka, 347 U.S. 343 (1954).

Brown v. Gilmore, 258 F.3d 265 (4th Cir. 2001), *cert. denied*, 533 U.S. 1301 (2001).

Brown v. Stone, 378 So.2d 218 (Miss. 1979).

Burlington Industries v. Ellerth, 524 U.S. 742 (1998).

Cambron-McCabe, N., McCarthy, M., & Thomas, S. (2004). *Public school law: Teachers' and students' rights* (5th ed.). Boston: Allyn and Bacon.

Canady v. Bossier Parish School Board, 240 F.3d 437 (5th Cir. 2001).

Capitol Square Review and Advisory Board v. Pinette, 515 U.S. 753 (1995).

Carter, S. (1994, December 5). Let us pray. *The New Yorker*, 60–74.

Castorina v. Madison County School Board, 246 F.3d 536 (6th Cir. 2001).

Ceniceros v. Board of Trustees of San Diego Unified School District, 106 F.3d 878 (9th Cir. 1997).

Chalifoux v. New Caney Independent School District, 976 F. Supp. 659 (S.D. Tex. 1997).

Chandler v. Siegelman, 230 F.3d 1313 (11th Cir. 2000), *cert. denied*, 533 U.S. 916 (2001).

Children's Internet Protection Act, 20 U.S.C. §9134(f) (2002); 47 U.S.C. §254(h)(5) (2002).

Child Online Protection Act, 47 U.S.C. §231 (2002).

City of Newport v. Fact Concerts, 453 U.S. 247 (1981).

Civil Rights Act of 1871, 42 U.S.C. §1983 (2002).

Cole v. Oroville Union High School District, 228 F.3d 1092 (9th Cir. 2000).

Colin v. Orange Unified School District, 83 F. Supp. 2d 1135 (C.D. Cal. 2000).

Cornelius v. NAACP Legal Defense and Education Fund, 473 U.S. 788 (1985).

Cornfield v. Consolidated High School District No. 230, 991 F.2d 1316 (7th Cir. 1993).

Dambrot v. Central Michigan University, 55 F.3d 1177 (6th Cir. 1995).

Davis v. DeKalb County School District, 233 F.3d 1367 (11th Cir. 2000).

Davis v. Monroe County Board of Education, 526 U.S. 629 (1999).

Debra P. v. Turlington, 730 F.2d 1405 (11th Cir. 1984).

Denno v. School Board of Volusia County, 218 F.3d 1267 (11th Cir. 2000).

DeNooyer v. Merinelli, 12 F.3d 211 (6th Cir. 1993).

Doe v. Madison School District No 321, 147 F.3d 832 (9th Cir. 1998), *vacated and remanded en banc*, 177 F.3d 789 (9th Cir. 1999).

Doe v. Renfrow, 631 F.2d 91 (7th Cir. 1980).

Eisenberg v. Montgomery County Public Schools, 197 F.3d 123 (4th Cir. 1999).

Emmett v. Kent School District No. 415, 92 F. Supp. 2d 1088 (W.D. Wash. 2000).

Engle v. Vitale, 370 U.S. 421 (1962).

Equal Access Act, 20 U.S.C. §§4071-4074 (2002).

Equal Educational Opportunities Act, 20 U.S.C. §1701 et seq. (2002).

Equal Pay Act, 29 U.S.C. §206(d) (2002).

Family Educational Rights and Privacy Act, 20 U.S.C. §1232g (2002).

Faragher v. City of Boca Raton, 524 U.S. 775 (1998).

Fowler v. Board of Education, 819 F.2d 657 (6th Cir. 1987).

Franklin v. Gwinnett County Public Schools, 503 U.S. 60 (1992).

Freeman v. Pitts, 503 U.S. 467 (1992).

Gano v. School District 411, 674 F. Supp. 796 (D. Idaho 1987).

Garnett v. Renton School District No. 403, 987 F.2d 641 (9th Cir. 1993).

Gebser v. Lago Vista Independent School District, 524 U.S. 274 (1998).

Genao v. Board of Education of City of New York, 888 F. Supp. 501 (S.D.N.Y. 1995).

Georgia State Conference of NAACP v. Georgia, 775 F.2d 1403 (11th Cir. 1985).

Gillard v. Schmidt, 579 F.2d 825 (3d Cir. 1978).

Girard, K., & Koch, S. J. (1996). *Conflict resolution in the schools: A manual for educators.* San Francisco: Jossey-Bass.

Gonzaga University v. Doe, 536 U.S. 273 (2002).

Good News Club v. Milford Central School, 533 U.S. 98 (2001).

Goss v. Lopez, 419 U.S. 565 (1975).

Grutter v. Bollinger, 288 F.3d 732 (6th Cir. 2002), *cert. granted,* 2002 U.S. LEXIS 8677 (Dec. 2, 2002).

Guidance on constitutionally protected prayer in public elementary and secondary schools (2003). Washington, DC: U.S. Department of Education.

Hall v. Tawney, 621 F.2d 607 (4th Cir. 1980).

Hammond v. Board of Education, 639 A.2d 223 (Md. Ct. App. 1994).

Harlow v. Fitzgerald, 457 U.S. 800 (1982).

Harris v. Forklift Systems, 510 U.S. 17 (1993).

Harris v. Joint School District Number 241, 41 F.3d 447 (9th Cir. 1994), *vacated,* 515 U.S. 1154 (1995).

Harris Interactive. (2001). *Hostile hallways: Bullying, teasing, and sexual harassment in school.* Washington, DC: American Association of University Women Educational Foundation.

Harris, L., & Associates (1993). *Hostile hallways: The AAUW survey on sexual harassment in American schools.* Washington, DC: American Association of University Women Educational Foundation.

Hazelwood School District v. Kuhlmeier, 484 U.S. 260 (1988).

Hearn v. Board of Public Education, 191 F.3d 1329 (11th Cir. 1999).

Hedges v. Wauconda Community Unit School District Number 118, 9 F.3d 1295 (7th Cir. 1993).

Hines v. Caston School Corporation, 651 N.E.2d 330 (Ind. Ct. App. 1995).

Hoffman v. Board of Education, 424 N.Y.S.2d 376 (1979).

Honig v. Doe, 484 U.S. 305 (1988).

Horton v. Goose Creek Independent School District, 693 F.2d 524 (5th Cir. 1982).

Hsu v. Roslyn Union Free School District, 85 F.3d 839 (2d Cir. 1996).

In re Joseph G., 38 Cal. Rptr.2d 902 (Cal. Ct. App. 1995).

Individuals with Disabilities Education Act, 20 U.S.C. §1401 et seq. (2002).

Irving Independent School District v. Tatro, 468 U.S. 883 (1984).

J. S. v. Bethlehem Area School District, 807 A.2d 847 (Pa. 2002).

Jeglin v. San Jacinto Unified School District, 827 F. Supp. 1459 (C.D. Cal. 1993).

Johnson, D. W., & Johnson, R. T. (1995). Teaching students to be peacemakers: Results of five years of research. *Peace and Conflict: Journal of Peace Psychology, 1*(4), 417–438.

Joint Anti-Fascist Refugee Committee v. McGrath, 341 U.S. 123 (1951).

Jones v. Clear Creek Independent School District, 977 F.2d 963 (5th Cir. 1992).

Jones v. Jenkins, 878 F.2d 1476 (D.C. Cir. 1989).

Joy v. Penn-Harris-Madison School Corporation, 212 F.3d 1052 (7th Cir. 2000).

Killion v. Franklin Regional School District, 136 F. Supp. 2d 446 (W.D. Pa. 2001).

Kimel v. Florida Board of Regents, 528 U.S. 62 (2000).

Knox County Education Association v. Knox County Board of Education, 158 F.3d 361 (6th Cir. 1998).

Korematsu v. United States, 323 U.S. 214 (1944).

Lamb's Chapel v. Center Moriches Union Free School District 508 U.S. 384 (1993).

Lau v. Nichols, 414 U.S. 563 (1974).

Lee v. Weisman, 505 U.S. 577 (1992).

Liebowitz v. Dinkins, 575 N.Y.S.2d 827 (1991).

Littlefield v. Forney Independent School District, 268 F.3d 275 (5th Cir. 2001).

Littlejohn v. Rose, 768 F.2d 765 (6th Cir. 1985).

Long v. Board of Education, 121 F. Supp. 2d 621 (W.D. Ky. 2000), *aff'd mem.,* 21 Fed. Appx. 252 (6th Cir. 2001).

Maine v. Thiboutot, 448 U.S. 1 (1980).

Manning v. School Board, 244 F.3d 927 (11th Cir. 2001), *cert. denied,* 534 U.S. 824 (2001).

Mary M. v. North Lawrence Community School Corporation, 131 F.3d 1220 (7th Cir. 1997).

Massey v. Akron Board of Education, 82 F. Supp. 2d 735 (N.D. Ohio 2000).

McCarthy, M. (1996). Free speech versus anti-establishment: Is there a hierarchy of First Amendment Rights? *Education Law Reporter, 108,* 475–488.

Melzer v. Board of Education, 196 F. Supp. 2d 229 (E.D.N.Y. 2002).

Memphis Community School District v. Stachura, 477 U.S. 299 (1986).

Meritor Savings Bank v. Vinson, 477 U.S. 57 (1986).

Miller v. Wilkes, 172 F.3d 574 (8th Cir. 1999).

Mills v. Board of Education, 348 F. Supp. 866 (D.D.C. 1972).

Monell v. New York City Department of Social Services, 436 U.S. 658 (1978).

Mt. Healthy City School District v. Doyle, 429 U.S. 274 (1977).

Murrell v. School District Number 1, Denver, 186 F.3d 1238 (10th Cir. 1999).

National Gay Task Force v. Board of Education, 729 F.2d 1270 (10th Cir. 1984), *aff'd by equally divided Court*, 470 U.S. 903 (1985).

National Treasury Employees Union v. Von Raab, 489 U.S. 656 (1989).

New Jersey v. T.L.O., 469 U.S. 325 (1985).

Niles v. Nelson, 72 F. Supp. 2d 13 (N.D.N.Y. 1999).

No Child Left Behind Act of 2001, 20 U.S.C. §6301 et seq. (2002).

O'Connor v. Ortega, 480 U.S. 709 (1987).

Oden v. North Marianas College, 284 F.3d 1058 (9th Cir. 2002).

Office for Civil Rights (1997, 2001). *Sexual harassment guidance: Harassment of students by school employees, other students, and third parties.* Washington, DC: Department of Education.

Oliver v. McClung, 919 F. Supp. 1206 (N.D. Ind. 1995).

Oncale v. Sundowner Offshore Services, 523 U.S. 75 (1998).

Owen v. City of Independence, 445 U.S. 622 (1980).

Palmer v. Board of Education of Chicago, 603 F.2d 1271 (7th Cir. 1979).

Patchogue-Medford Congress of Teachers v. Board of Education, 510 N.E.2d 325 (N.Y. 1987).

Pauley v. Anchorage School District, 31 P.3d 1284 (Alaska 2001).

People Who Care v. Rockford Board of Education, 246 F.3d 1073 (7th Cir. 2001).

Pierce v. Society of Sisters, 268 U.S. 510 (1925).

Plyler v. Doe, 457 U.S. 202 (1982).

Prince v. Jacoby, 303 F.3d 1074 (9th Cir. 2002).

R.A.V. v. City of St. Paul, 505 U.S. 377 (1992).

Rehabilitation Act of 1973, Section 504, 29 U.S.C. §794 et seq. (2002).

Richmond v. J. A. Croson, 488 U.S. 469 (1989).

Roberts v. Madigan, 921 F.2d 1047 (10th Cir. 1990).

Robinson, T. R., Smith, S. W., & Daunic, A. P. (2000). Middle school students' views on the social validity of peer mediation. *Middle School Journal*, *31*(5), 23–29.

Rowland v. Mad River Local School District, 730 F.2d 444 (6th Cir. 1984).

San Antonio Independent School District v. Rodriguez, 411 U.S. 1 (1973).

Santa Fe Independent School District v. Doe, 530 U.S. 290 (2000).

Saxe v. State College Area School District, 240 F.3d 2000 (3d Cir. 2001).

School District of Abington School District v. Schempp, 374 U.S. 203 (1963).

Settle v. Dickson County School Board, 53 F.3d 152 (6th Cir. 1995).

Shaul v. Cherry Valley-Springfield Central School District, 218 F. Supp. 2d 266 (N.D.N.Y. 2002).

Sherburne v. School Board of Suwannee County, 455 So. 2d 1057 (Fla. Dist. Ct. App. 1984).

Shumway v. Albany County School District, 826 F. Supp. 1320 (D. Wyo. 1993).

Skinner v. Railway Labor Executives Association, 489 U.S. 602 (1989).

Smith v. Wade, 461 U.S. 30 (1983).

Soper v. Hoben, 195 F.3d 845 (6th Cir. 1999).

State v. Egnor, 443 S.E.2d 193 (W. Va. 1994).

Suriano v. Hyde Park, 611 N.Y.S.2d 20 (1994).

Sypniewski v. Warren Hills Regional Board of Education, 307 F.3d 243 (3d Cir. 2002).

Texas v. Johnson, 491 U.S. 397 (1989).

Theodore v. Delaware Valley School District, 761 A.2d 652 (Pa. Commw. 2000).

Thompson v. Carthage School District, 87 F.3d 979 (8th Cir. 1996).

Thompson v. Waynesboro Area School District, 673 F. Supp. 1379 (M.D. Pa. 1987).

Tinker v. Des Moines Independent Community School District, 393 U.S. 503 (1969).

Title VI of the Civil Rights Act of 1964, 42 U.S.C. §2000d et seq. (2002).

Title VII of the Civil Rights Act of 1964, 42 U.S.C. §2000e et seq. (2002).

Title IX of the Education Amendments of 1972, 20 U.S.C. §1681 et seq. (2002).

United States v. South Carolina, 445 F. Supp. 1094 (D.S.C. 1977), *aff'd*, 434 U.S. 1026 (1978).

Urofsky v. Gilmore, 216 F.3d 401 (4th Cir. 2000), *cert. denied*, 531 U.S. 1070 (2001).

Valente, W., & Valente, C. (2001). *Law in the schools.* Columbus: Merrill/Prentice Hall.

Velmer v. Baraga Area School, 424 N.W.2d 770 (Mich. 1988).

Verbena United Methodist Church v. Chilton County Board of Education, 765 F. Supp. 704 (M.D. Ala. 1991).

Vernonia School District 47J v. Acton, 515 U.S. 646 (1995).

Vines v. Board of Education, No. 01 C 7455, 2002 U.S. Dist. LEXIS 382 (N.D. Ill. Jan. 10, 2002).

Wallace v. Jaffree, 472 U.S. 38 (1985).

Warren v. Reading School District, 82 F. Supp. 2d 395 (E.D. Penn. 2000).

Weaver v. Nebo School District, 29 F. Supp. 2d 1279 (D. Utah 1998).

West v. Derby Unified School District, 206 F.3d 1258 (10th Cir. 2000).

West Virginia State Board of Education v. Barnette, 319 U.S. 624 (1943).

Widmar v. Vincent, 454 U.S. 263 (1981).

Williams v. Ellington, 936 F.2d 881 (6th Cir. 1991).

Willis v. Anderson Community School Corporation, 158 F.3d 415 (7th Cir. 1998), *cert. denied,* 526 U.S. 1019 (1999).

Wisconsin v. Yoder, 406 U.S. 205 (1972).

Wood v. Strickland, 420 U.S. 308 (1975).

Wygant v. Jackson Board of Education, 478 U.S. 1014 (1986).

Zelman v. Simmons-Harris, 536 U.S. 639 (2002).

Zobrest v. Catalina Foothills School District, 509 U.S. 1 (1993).

17

School Finance*

Schools are big business in the United States. Estimated current expenditures for public elementary and secondary education nationally were about $358 billion for fiscal year 2002, ranging from a high of almost $43 billion in California to a low of $720 million in Wyoming (National Center for Education Statistics [NCES], 2002). Public elementary and secondary schools employ almost 3 million teachers and enroll more than 47 million students (NCES, 2002). Indeed, 20 percent of the population either attends or is employed by public schools (Webb, Metha, & Jordan, 2003). The average per-pupil expenditure nationally is over $8,000 (NCES, 2002), and support for public schools is the largest item in the budgets of many local and state governments (Webb, Metha, & Jordan, 2003).

Determining the appropriate spending level for public education is a fundamental policy question as well as a continuing political issue at the national, state, and local levels. It involves complex choices that are inextricably intertwined with demographic conditions, competition for tax revenues among various public services, the general health of the economy, the state's political context, and other factors. This chapter reviews the revenue sources that support public education and how education funds are distributed, with a focus on revenue for school operations rather than capital improvements. The chapter also explores marketplace delivery systems, litigation addressing alleged inequities and inadequacies in state funding systems, and challenges facing policymakers and school leaders in linking school funding to student performance measures.

Revenue Generation

Public schools are funded primarily through a combination of state, local, and federal aid. The level of state funding jumped from around 40 percent to about 47 percent during the 1970s, and it stayed at this level through the early 1990s. By

*The author wishes to thank L. Dean Webb, Arizona State University; John Dayton, University of Georgia; and Barry Bull, Charles Little, and Ran Zhang from Indiana University for their thoughtful suggestions regarding this chapter.

2000 to 2001, states provided about half of public school revenues (50.2 percent; Figure 17.1), with a range from almost 90 percent in Hawaii to 30 percent in Nevada (National Education Association [NEA], 2002).* Local support has steadily declined since the 1950s, but still accounted for 42.5 percent of public school revenues in 2000 to 2001. The percentage of support from the local level (excluding Hawaii, which has no local districts) varied from under 13 percent in New Mexico to 65 percent in Nevada (NEA, 2002).

Federal aid for education increased through the 1950s, 1960s, and 1970s with declining levels of funding in the 1980s and a slight increase since the early 1990s. In 2000 to 2001, the federal government contributed 7.3 percent of education revenues nationally, ranging from over 14 percent in Mississippi to 3 percent in New Jersey (NEA, 2002). The overall federal share is expected to increase with implementation of the No Child Left Behind Act (2002) and the upcoming reauthorization of the Individuals with Disabilities Education Act.

The changing pattern in the proportion of revenue from the different levels of government also reflects changes in the sources of taxes used for school purposes. Local school revenues are principally from property taxes, the federal government relies to a large extent on income taxes, and the state government relies primarily on income and sales tax revenues to support schools. The remainder of

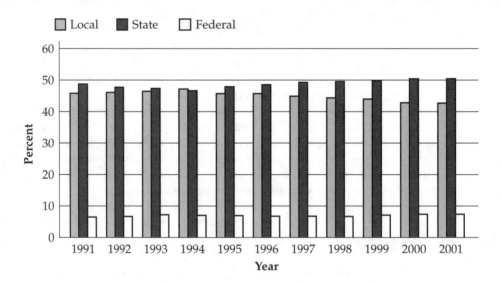

FIGURE 17.1   Annual School Revenue by Source, 1991 to 2001

Source: National Education Association, *Rankings & Estimates: Rankings of the States 2001 and Estimates of School Statistics 2002.* © 2002, NEA; used by permission of the NEA.

---

*All NEA data used here represent projections by state education agencies and NEA research as of February 2002.

this section provides an overview of criteria to assess various taxes, the major sources of taxes, and nontax sources of funds to support public education.

Criteria for Evaluating Taxes

Advantages and disadvantages of various taxes can be analyzed along several dimensions. A crucial consideration is whether the tax yields sufficient resources to fund government services, so the tax revenues need to be dependable or predictable in matching projected expenditures. One index of dependability is *elasticity,* which is assessed by changes in tax yield in relation to changes in the gross national product or total personal income. A tax is said to be elastic if the yield from the tax grows at a greater rate than the rate of the nation's economic growth. Whereas an elastic tax has superior yields when the economy is good, its yield may fall faster during downturns, so an inelastic tax with predictable yields regardless of the economic conditions is preferred.

It is usually desirable for taxes also to be *efficient* (neutral) in that they do not have negative side effects on the overall economic system. Efficient taxes do not change the spending patterns, work incentives, or other behavior of individuals or businesses. At times, however, nonneutral taxes are adopted specifically to affect consumption in ways considered socially desirable (e.g., taxes on alcohol).

A fundamental principle is that tax policy should be fair or equitable to those being taxed. *Equity* can be gauged in terms of the benefits the taxpayers receive, but such an assessment usually focuses on the taxpayer's ability to pay the tax. Horizontal equity is concerned with the equal tax treatment of equals. In essence, people in similar economic circumstances should pay the same tax. This rather straightforward proposition becomes difficult when trying to identify a measure of one's "ability to pay." Monk (1992) identified three different measures of ability to pay: income-based measures, consumption-based measures, and wealth-based measures. Obviously, different taxes are keyed to different measures of ability to pay. Horizontal equity problems arise because of the variety of resources people have. For example, there may appear to be equity because two taxpayers with equal property wealth are taxed at the same level. Yet, because of quite different levels of income, each taxpayer's ability to pay the property tax may differ markedly. Taxing decisions are often made by different levels of government, using different measures of resources, and there is little systematic, overall attention to horizontal equity.

Vertical equity calls for different tax payments from individuals with different abilities to pay (i.e., people in different financial circumstances should be treated in appropriately different ways). Vertical equity is based on the assumption that ability to pay can be used to equalize the taxation load in that those with higher incomes have more discretionary funds that are not needed to purchase essential goods. The debate with regard to vertical equity turns on the meaning to be given to "appropriately different" treatment. For example, should a person who has twice the ability to pay be required to pay twice as much tax? Vertical equity is often considered in terms of the *regressivity* or *progressivity* of a tax. If the percentage of income paid in taxes increases as income increases, the tax is progressive; if

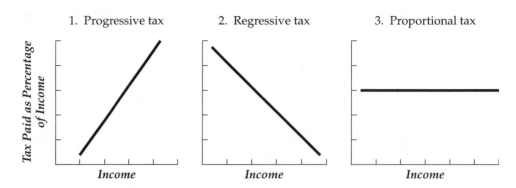

FIGURE 17.2   **Relationship between Tax Rate and Income for Progressive, Regressive, and Proportional Taxes**

this percentage decreases as income increases, the tax is regressive. A tax is proportional if the amount paid as a percentage of income remains the same as income increases (Figure 17.2).

In addition to equity, dependability (elasticity), and efficiency, other criteria are also used in assessing the merits of taxes. For example, they are evaluated based on their *simplicity* or ease of administration and the *absence of loopholes* that would allow the taxes to be evaded.

Tax Sources

As noted, the three most significant taxes in terms of generating revenues are income, sales, and property taxes. Each has advantages and disadvantages, and all provide major funding sources for elementary and secondary education. In addition, some revenues from lotteries and other types of taxes are earmarked for education.

Income Tax.   The Sixteenth Amendment, ratified in 1913, authorized Congress to collect taxes on individual incomes. Since then, income taxation has become a significant source of revenue for the federal government and most state governments. In 2000, individual and corporate income taxes generated almost 49 percent of the tax revenue collected by the federal government (King, Swanson, & Sweetland, 2003). Almost all federal education aid comes from income taxes. The income tax is based on the principle that income earned—rather than wealth as measured by currently held property assets—is subject to taxation. That is why interest earned on money in a savings account is taxed, whereas the principal in the account is not.

The concept of income tax is quite simple; however, the mechanism developed to determine one's income-tax liability is complicated because of tax and social policy considerations. A detailed examination of these complicating considerations is beyond the scope of this chapter, but it is important at least to note that a number of deductions and tax credits are provided for expenditures ranging from business expenses to child-care costs. Each of these deductions or credits is based on the general principle that certain expenses are incurred as necessary in working and generating income. Other incentives are provided to encourage certain types of expenditures, such as the purchase of municipal bonds because the interest on such bonds is not subject to federal income tax.

Federal income-tax rates increase as income increases. This graduated income-tax system is considered progressive, because the tax increases are correlated with ability to pay. But, income taxes are relatively elastic; income-tax revenues lack predictability as they fluctuate with economic conditions. Also, income taxes are not easy to pay, and there are significant costs associated with administering the tax.

States' use of income taxes for revenue has steadily increased, recently changing the traditional trend of states' relying primarily on sales taxes. Whereas in 1970, revenues across states were 10 percent higher from sales taxes than from income taxes, by 2000, 32 percent of the revenue across states was from sales taxes compared with 36 percent from income taxes (King, Swanson, & Sweetland, 2003). This shift reflects a current policy preference for taxing earnings rather than consumption.

Although most states impose income taxes on both individuals and corporations, states differ as to the existence of a constitutional limit on the extent to which the corporate tax rate can exceed the personal income-tax rate. States also differ regarding how state income-tax rates are calculated. About three fourths of the forty-four states with income taxes have a graduated system in that they collect a higher percentage of income from those earning more, similar to the federal government. Five states apply a flat rate to all incomes, and the remaining states tax a percentage of taxable income or tax limited types of earnings (King, Swanson, & Sweetland, 2003). In addition, some states give special income-taxing authority to municipalities or county governments, so residents are subject to federal, state, and local income taxes.

Sales Tax. A significant source of financial support for public education is the state sales tax, which is based on the sale of a good or commodity at the retail level. The purchaser pays the sales tax, and the seller is responsible for transferring the tax revenues to the governmental taxing authority. All but five states collect a general sales tax, and quite a range exists in the portion of state revenues generated by this tax. In 2001, the spread was from under 14 percent of total tax revenues in Vermont to almost 64 percent in Washington (Bureau of the Census, 2001). States vary in what they include as taxable. Most states do not tax medicines and food, and some states exempt clothing or other necessities. In addition to the general sales tax, most states permit local governments to levy a local sales tax. New York City, for example, has a higher sales tax than the state of New York.

Excise taxes are a type of sales tax, with direct charges levied on particular items. Some of these taxes are imposed to affect consumption habits by raising the price of selected items, and they may be designed to raise revenues for targeted purposes. The best-known excise taxes are those charged for gasoline, cigarettes, customs duties, and liquor. Gasoline taxes are presently used to provide maintenance and construction money for highways and are not usually earmarked for education. With increased pressure for new revenue sources, more attention has been given to excise taxes. The federal government has increased excise taxes on several products, and many states have raised tax rates on liquor and cigarettes.

Historically, the costs of services, such as those provided by lawyers and doctors, have not been taxed. However, some states are extending the sales tax to certain services, such as the costs of dry cleaning clothes. A number of states have placed excise taxes on other types of consumption (e.g., long-distance telephone charges). It is argued that taxes on services achieve more vertical equity, because people use more services as their income increases (Howard, 1989).

Sales and excise taxes are easy to pay and relatively simple to administer. However, they are more regressive than income taxes in that individuals pay the same sales tax on a given item, regardless of their ability to pay the tax. The yield from sales taxes is less predictable with changing economic conditions than the yield from property taxes, but it is more predictable than the yield from income taxes.

Property Tax.   The property tax is a form of taxation on one specific classification of wealth. The federal government collects no property taxes, and state revenue from property taxes is negligible. However, property taxes remain important at the local level and continue to provide substantial support for public education, even though there has been a slow, but steady, decline in local governments' reliance on property taxes since the mid-1950s (American Council on Intergovernmental Relations, 1998).

A legal distinction exists between real property, which includes the land and any physical improvements on it, and personal property, which includes any personal belongings, such as checking accounts or animals that are not attached to the land and can be easily moved. In some locales, individual and corporate properties are treated differently. A state may assess and tax corporate personal property but not individual personal property. Even though states vary considerably in what is included in their property tax system, a significant source of revenue comes from the individual property tax.

The principle of taxing the value of real property is simple, but implementation of the principle is more difficult. Assessment provides the greatest problem. All real property has to be given an assessed valuation, which necessitates the use of judgment. The touchstone in valuing property is its real market value—the value of this property if it were to be sold today. Real market value is easier to determine when dealing with types of property that are sold frequently. Some items, such as large industrial plants, are hard to value because the market for them is very specialized. In certain circumstances, the determination of replacement cost can be used as an alternative method of valuation. With this method, the assessor asks what it would cost to build the property in question today. The assessed value of property is usually pegged at a certain percentage of its real market value or replacement cost, and the percentage used varies greatly across states. Some states also allow property of various types to be classified at different rates of full market value. Properties used for utilities, commercial, and industrial activities are often taxed at a higher rate than agricultural and residential properties.

Uniformity of assessment is a central concern with property taxes. The lack of uniformity is partly the result of the fact that many assessors are elected officials and are therefore anxious to avoid increasing assessments for fear of political reprisal. Consequently, assessed valuations tend to lag behind increases in real market values associated with inflation. If a state requires a standard property tax rate, it becomes imperative that assessment practices be standardized statewide. One proposal to address assessment and other equity issues is to give the state access to all property wealth, so that property taxes are locally gathered but considered state—not local—revenue (akin to the sales tax). Although this would reduce revenue disparities tied to property values across school districts, it is not likely to receive support, given the strong tradition of using property tax revenues in the jurisdiction where they are collected.

The high rates of inflation in the late 1960s and 1970s caused property values and property taxation to increase at a much faster rate than other forms of wealth, such as personal income. As a consequence, taxpayer revolts occurred in some states. In Arizona, California, and Massachusetts, constitutional amendments were passed to limit the increased value of property to a certain annual maximum level, unless the property was transferred. The California measure, Proposition 13, froze ad valorum property tax rates on individual properties at 1 percent and rolled back property tax assessments to the 1975 levels. Circuit-breaker provisions have been passed in other states to relieve the regressive effect of a high property tax on persons with fixed incomes. Under such provisions, persons with fixed incomes pay a reduced or possibly no income tax when their property taxes reach a certain proportion of their personal income.

A dramatic response to dissatisfaction with property taxes occurred in Michigan, when the legislature in 1993 reduced the role of local property taxes in financing public schools. In a 1994 referendum, Michigan voters selected the sales tax to compensate for the lost revenue for education, and the state continues to raise some education funds from a state property tax and local levies on nonhomestead property (Drake, 2002).

The tax rate applied to the assessed value of property for school operating levies is determined by state law, school board decision, voter referendum, or a combination of all three. School districts are allowed to tax at a rate equal to or lower than the maximum allowed by law, and they must get approval of the district's voters to exceed this limit. Determination of a school district's tax rate (t) is calculated by dividing the amount of money needed from local property taxes (Mn) by the local tax base (B), which is the total assessed valuation of the district [t = Mn/B]. If this calculation results in a tax rate higher than the maximum rate allowed by law, the district must revert to the legal maximum. This tax rate is added to tax rates for other services, such as fire and police protection, and then charged against the property owners. The tax rate is usually described as either a percentage or a millage. One mill equals 0.1 percent. Therefore, a tax rate of 245 mills is the same as a rate of 24.5 percent.

Despite substantial criticism, property taxes remain a significant source of school revenue, and thus it is difficult to imagine a state income or sales tax generating sufficient funds to replace the property tax as a central source of school revenues. Property taxes, being relatively stable, also serve to buffer school budgets during periods of recession, when shortfalls occur from projected sales and income-tax revenues. Of course, certain types of real property can decrease in value when the rate of inflation decreases, with negative consequences for governmental bodies that rely on property-tax revenue. Property taxes require more resources to administer than income or sales taxes—there are significant costs in assessing property, maintaining the property tax rolls, and collecting the revenues.

Other Taxes.   A number of other taxes are used in varying degrees across states. For example, states increasingly are using casinos and games of chance to raise government revenues. Although lotteries were used by churches and governments before the Civil War, this revenue source fell into disrepute in the late 1800s because of concerns about corruption and the encouragement of immoral behavior (King, Swanson, & Sweetland, 2003). Since the 1960s, this revenue source has been revived, and by 2002 most states had lotteries or other games of chance to raise some government funds. Of the states with lotteries, twenty-two earmark some of the proceeds for education (King, Swanson, & Sweetland, 2003). Advantages of this tax are that payment is completely voluntary in that only those electing to participate pay the tax, and it is relatively easy to administer. However, moral concerns continue to be raised about the government encouraging gambling and using such funds to support government services.

States yield some funds from gift and estate taxes and taxes on various licenses, but most of these provide minimal support for education. Also, some states impose taxes on coal, oil, gas, and other materials extracted from the earth, but only a few states yield much revenue from these severance taxes (Brimley & Garfield, 2002). Some support exists for adopting a value-added tax, which is popular among European nations. This tax is similar to a sales tax, but is imposed on the value added to a good or service at each stage of its development. If such a value-added tax were adopted, other taxes would have to be reduced so as not to overburden taxpayers.

Nontax Sources of Revenue

School leaders and policymakers are always searching for new sources of school revenues. Administrators no longer passively wait to see how much money is allocated to their district through the traditional revenue channels. Rather, like their private-sector counterparts always have done, public school leaders increasingly are seeking creative revenue sources. For example, some school districts are raising revenue or reducing costs by selling items to individuals and organizations, charging tuition for nonresident students, renting some facilities, participating in business/school partnerships, seeking grants from philanthropic foundations, and contracting for services from private vendors who can provide the services at lower costs. In a number of states since 1998, school districts have benefited from funds earmarked for education in the twenty-five-year settlement with major tobacco companies. This settlement is intended to help states recoup some of the costs of treating tobacco-related diseases that precluded states from funding other services (Sandham, 2000). Also, many school districts are trying to pass certain expenses on to the students in the form of student fees for various activities and materials; this practice has been characterized as a hidden tax (Bouman & Brown, 1996). In addition, some school districts are establishing tax-exempt foundations that solicit donations for school innovations and other educational activities.

Public schools increasingly are looking to the corporate world as a revenue source, and businesses are eager to enter into a variety of contractual arrangements with school districts. For example, corporations are interested in arrangements that allow them to advertise in public schools because of the large, captive audience to receive the sales pitches. Channel One, the brainchild of Christopher Whittle, combines a ten-minute news program with two minutes of advertisements, and this program is viewed by secondary students nationwide. If schools agree to show the program to students on a daily basis, they receive free televisions and other equipment in return. Other contractual arrangements with businesses provide money or services to schools in return for print or media advertisements. For example, schools can receive computers and high-speed Internet access for subjecting students to advertisements when they use the Internet. Although the commercialization of public schools has been controversial (Kozol, 1992; Molnar & Morales, 2000), such arrangements are enticing to administrators in financially strapped school districts.

Distribution of School Revenues

Three basic concerns in distributing funds for public schools are: equity, adequacy, and choice (Webb, Metha, & Jordan, 2003). One way to evaluate equity in distribution plans is by a standard of fiscal neutrality. This means that the distribution of educational services may be determined by educational preferences of the taxpayers, needs of students, and other factors that do not relate to taxpayers' ability to pay based on property wealth of the district or some other measure. If a system is fiscally neutral, the only wealth determinant of education revenues is the wealth of the state as a whole. Also, equity in distribution plans, similar to taxation systems, can be viewed horizontally (treating similar students and districts the same in the distribution of resources) and vertically (recognizing that some students/districts deserve more resources and services because of their special needs) (Odden & Picus, 2000).

Adequacy is more difficult to define as it necessitates identifying the components of an adequate education. Clune (1995) has defined adequacy as "resources which are sufficient to meet defined or absolute, rather than relative, output standards" (p. 481). Currently, adequacy in distribution plans is often measured by calculating the costs of providing particular services considered essential, and in some instances adequacy is gauged by determining what resources are necessary to ensure that all students perform satisfactorily on tests of basic academic skills (Reschovsky & Imazeki, 2000).

The concern for choice essentially means that the wishes of parents or other school patrons should be considered, whether in selecting a tax rate (effort) to determine how much money their school district will have or in deciding where their children will attend school. Providing educational options for families is an important theme in school reform strategies at the federal level and across many states. Choice is the overriding concern in voucher systems, in which parents are allocated a designated amount of money that they can spend at public or private schools. No state currently is distributing educational funds primarily through voucher plans, which are discussed in the next section with other marketplace delivery systems.

Many other options for disbursing revenues to local school districts are available to states. These options include full-state funding, flat grants, categorical aid, minimum foundation programs, and power-equalization formulas. The selection of a distribution mechanism has a profound effect on sufficiency of funds and on the degree of equity achieved. For example, *flat grants* provide a designated amount of financial support at a per-pupil level and often include weighting factors for different levels of schooling. Such flat grants, if extremely large, can have an equalizing effect, but only if weighting factors are used to adjust allocations based on student needs in addition to level of schooling. *Categorical grants* provide money according to specific program categories (e.g., special education, vocational education, and summer school). Such categorical grants do not equalize the distribution of school funds, but they do address special needs of students and thus can improve educational opportunities for targeted populations and can compensate school districts for students with special needs. The remainder of this section addresses equalization models to distribute school funds and methods used to reflect differences among students and school districts in distribution plans.

Equalization Models

Several strategies have been implemented to equalize resources across school districts in a state. The central models include *full-state funding, minimum-foundation programs,* and *power-equalization formulas.* A state using full-state funding would assume primary responsibility for funding the education for all children in the state at the same level. This plan, by definition, would guarantee equity in resources throughout the state. Allocations could be distributed based on student or district needs or other factors such as local cost variations in providing educational services, but the allocations would not be contingent on local district wealth. Several states approach full-state support but still allow some local leeway (e.g., New Mexico, Washington). Hawaii, which has no local school districts, essentially has full-state funding for public education.

Formula-distribution systems (foundation programs or power equalizing) are the most popular strategies to enhance equalization in the distribution of school funds. Equalization formulas can be used to allocate state monies to supplement locally generated taxes. By providing more state support to property-poor school districts, the formula equalizes support for students, thereby minimizing the effects of wide disparities in property wealth across districts.

The basic principle of a minimum foundation plan is that a certain minimal level of support, or foundation, will be provided each student in the state as long as the taxpayers are willing to be taxed at a specified minimum level. The state will make up the difference between what the district can raise by taxing at the designated rate and the guaranteed foundation level. Assume that a state has set a foundation level of $500 per pupil and a qualifying tax rate of 10 mills (1 percent) and that two districts, A and B, each have 1,000 students. District A has a tax base of $20 million and district B has a tax base of $40 million. Both districts will receive a total of $500,000, although the amounts from state and local sources will differ. District A will receive $200,000 from local and $300,000 from state sources, and district B will receive $400,000 from local and $100,000 from state sources.

Under most foundation formulas, school districts can generate additional money by taxing at rates higher than the qualifying tax rate, which has a differential impact on districts with different tax bases. Using the same districts A and B, assume they are both taxing at 15 mills (1.5 percent). District A will receive $600,000 ($500,000 from the foundation computation plus $100,000 from additional 5 mills—0.5 percent times $20 million), whereas district B will receive $700,000 ($500,000 as figured previously plus $200,000 from additional 5 mills—0.5 percent times $40 million). As this example shows, considerable disparity can exist between wealthy and poor districts (measured by property wealth) under a foundation program, particularly when the foundation level and the required tax rate are kept relatively low and the leeway allowed above the foundation tax effort is large.

By the late 1970s, thirty-four states were using some type of foundation plan to distribute school revenues, and only two additional states adopted foundation plans by 2000 (King, Swanson, & Sweetland, 2003). Originally, local districts were granted considerable leeway to tax above the level of effort required for the minimum foundation program. As noted previously, this resulted in inequities among school districts in per-pupil expenditures because of the ability of citizens in property-wealthy districts to supplement school revenues with minimal increases in their tax effort. If the foundation level is kept at a reasonably high level with a small amount of leeway above the foundation, this equalizing plan is attractive because it ensures sufficient funds for all districts, but still allows some local initiative in providing more resources for education than the state provides. The value placed on local discretion determines the amount of leeway. Assuming that uniformity is the overriding value, then it is difficult to justify allowing local districts to choose to tax themselves at a higher rate to provide more educational resources for their students, because property-poor districts would have to expend much greater effort than property-rich districts to generate similar revenue. But, if preserving local discretion is the dominant value, such leeway is encouraged.

Foundation programs have been criticized for how the minimum guaranteed level is identified. There is considerable sentiment that the foundation level selected is based on political and budgetary considerations rather than on data regarding the amount that an adequate education actually costs. Expert testimony in litigation challenging Ohio's school funding system indicated that the foundation formula amount "has no real relation to what it actually costs to educate a pupil" but instead "is a budgetary residual, which is determined as a result of working backwards through the state aid formula after the legislature determines the total dollars to be allocated to primary and secondary education" (Howard Fleeter quoted in *DeRolph v. State I*, 1997, p. 199).

Unlike a foundation program, the use of power-equalizing formulas guarantees all districts, regardless of the variation in property wealth, equalized yields for a given tax rate. Under this guaranteed-tax base system, different tax rates will generate different levels of support, but a specific tax rate will generate the same revenue regardless of the property wealth of the districts. School districts can reflect different commitments to education by selecting different tax *rates*. For example, under this distribution plan, if districts A and B, discussed previously, agree to a 15 mill tax for education, this rate will result in the same amount of revenue in both school districts, even though the actual yields are different. The state supplies the difference to equalize the revenue generated by a given tax rate. Under a power-equalizing formula, differences in effort (tax rates) will determine differences in resources, but variations in the property tax base will not.

Equalization is encouraged when large amounts of money are injected at the state level, with a general leveling up of all districts. But with stiff competition for additional resources, this leveling up is difficult to accomplish. Thus, identification of the amount of money necessary to provide a minimally adequate education for all children becomes critical in a period when budget deficits are common and the political will to provide new funds for education is not forthcoming. A fundamental question facing state policymakers is whether their aspiration is to provide either an adequate or an equitable education for every student in the state or whether they strive to provide both.

Adjustments to Recognize Students' and School Districts' Needs

School funding formulas have become quite complicated in many states. The increased complexity is due in part to efforts to allocate school funds based on an assessment of students' differing educational needs and differences across school districts.

Students' Needs. States use some measure of average daily membership or average daily attendance in distributing school funds, and they generally make adjustments for the needs of specific groups of children. Most states use weighted pupils or classroom units to calculate how funds will be distributed. In an illustrative system, the base weight of 1.0 would be assigned to regular education students in grades 4 through 8. Students in primary grades would be assigned a higher weight (e.g., 1.3), indicating that each student at that level is more costly to educate (usually because of lower class size). High school students might also carry a weight of 1.3, because of more costly instruction in high school courses. Various categories of students with disabilities, vocational education students, and students with English-language deficiencies would also have different weights that might range from 1.3 to 4.0.

Determining pupil or classroom unit weights has been controversial. Some systems use weights determined by what *best practices* cost. Other states have calculated weights based on actual amounts spent for the different types of instruction rather than on a measure of student need. Chaikind, Danielson, and Brauen (1993) reported that student weights were often based on surveys of special education expenditures rather than on any measures of student outcomes. Weighting systems also have been criticized for providing an incentive for school districts to misclassify students in order to receive larger state allocations.

Another method to recognize students' needs in allocation formulas is for the state to reimburse local districts for the excess costs associated with providing appropriate educational programs for special student populations. In essence, all students are funded through regular sources up to a specified amount, and the amount above this level required to provide special education, vocational education, and other more costly programs is provided by the state in a special allocation.

School Districts' Needs.   In addition to adjustments for students' characteristics, distribution schemes often include adjustments for school districts' characteristics. For example, there may be a weighting factor reflecting special costs associated with density or sparsity of the population. Larger school districts up to a point may be able to offer education more economically because of economies of scale. But very densely populated urban districts and sparsely populated rural districts have additional costs. Rural districts suffer from diseconomies of scale due to smaller schools and classes. Urban districts have higher costs due to the concentration of students with special needs.

Most funding formulas make adjustments for at least some characteristics of school personnel, since the vast majority of the school's budget is earmarked to pay personnel. A few states have adopted cost-of-living adjustments for personnel based on the comparative prices of consumer goods, but a more common adjustment in determining allocations is an index that incorporates differences in teachers' education and experience, which directly affect salary.

Because most approaches being used do not link the expenditures for educational services to outcome measures in terms of student performance, alternative strategies to account for student and district needs are being pursued. Some researchers are developing sophisticated education cost indices to estimate the amount of money required to achieve student performance goals in districts with varying characteristics. Such an index is developed using regression equations to account for variations in input prices (e.g., teacher salaries) and differences in student characteristics (e.g., need for special education services) that affect educational costs to meet a given standard. The purpose of a cost index is to measure the fiscal effects of factors beyond school officials' control (see Duncombe & Yinger, 1999; Reschovsky & Imazeki, 2000).

Market-Driven Delivery Systems

Increasing attention is focusing on models to deliver education and to allocate resources that give families more educational choices. Indeed, one of the central themes of the federal No Child Left Behind Act (2002) is to increase educational options for students attending schools that are not making adequate yearly progress toward their objectives. Given that private options may become important in determining the composition of schooling in our nation, this section provides a brief overview of three strategies that open education at least in part to market forces: voucher systems, charter school legislation, and contractual arrangements with private companies to manage public schools.

Voucher Systems

Voucher systems have been discussed in the educational literature for several decades (see Coons & Sugarman, 1978), and states traditionally have authorized school districts without high schools to provide a stipend for their resident high school students to attend neighboring public schools or nonreligious private schools. Other than such tuition reimbursement plans, which have been popular in New England states, no significant voucher experiments were implemented in the United States until the 1990s.[*] In fact, not until 1999 did Florida become the first state to adopt a statewide voucher system, and this program targeted only students attending public schools rated as deficient. Publicly funded voucher programs are operating in Cleveland and Milwaukee for disadvantaged youth, and privately funded scholarship programs to support private school tuition are available in a number of cities nationwide.

Under a basic voucher proposal, a designated amount would be available per child that could be used in a private or public school of the family's choice. Families could supplement the voucher for the child to attend private schools that charge more for tuition than the voucher amount. Several variations are possible, such as restricting participation to those private schools that agree to limit the co-pay amount charged to parents. Also, the vouchers can be made available only to specific student populations, such as children with disabilities, economically disadvantaged students, or those attending schools rated as deficient on various criteria.

As addressed in Chapter 16, the Supreme Court has removed the Establishment Clause barrier to voucher programs that include sectarian schools (*Zelman v. Simmons-Harris*, 2002), and about half of the states currently are considering some

---

[*]There was a brief federally supported voucher experiment in the 1970s, but the Alum Rock School District in California ended up being the only demonstration site.

type of voucher program to provide educational options for specific groups of students. However, it appears unlikely that a state will convert its entire school funding system to vouchers in the near future, because of the fiscal implications. If all students were eligible for vouchers, the students currently supported by parents in private schools or home education programs (about 12 percent of the students nationally) would receive state support. This would carry a high price tag for financially strapped state and local governments, so it is not surprising that voters have rejected proposals for statewide voucher systems to fund education. During the past decade, voucher initiatives on state ballots in California, Colorado, Michigan, and Washington have been soundly defeated.

Nonetheless, voucher plans targeting economically disadvantaged students or those attending failing public schools are likely to increase during the next decade. Such limited voucher plans are viewed as less costly than some other reform strategies (e.g., reducing class size in public schools). Also, proponents contend that such programs can give poor children options that only the wealthy traditionally enjoyed (see Chubb & Moe, 1990; Cookson, 1994). But critics are concerned that voucher programs will have a negative impact on the democratizing function of public schools and will increase economic and racial segregation (see Fowler, 1991; Goodlad, 1997).

Charter Schools

Charter schools remain public schools but are exempt from many state regulations based on a charter with state or local education agencies or with universities. Unlike the fiscal impact of a large-scale voucher program, charter schools are viewed by many policymakers as a relatively inexpensive school reform strategy. Given its political popularity, it is not surprising that the majority of the states have enacted charter school legislation. As reported in Chapter 15, within the past decade, most states have adopted charter school legislation. States vary greatly as to whether they cap the number of charters that can be granted, and they also differ regarding the scope of the exemptions granted from state regulations.

About 10 percent of the charter schools nationally are managed by private companies, and the corporate world sees exciting financial prospects in opening education to the marketplace. Also, several virtual charter schools have been established, which raise questions about the participation of students from different states. Incentive funds are available in some states to start charter schools, and the federal government also has supported charter schools by providing grants to help offset some of the start-up costs. If the number of charter schools continues to increase as rapidly as it has during the past decade, implications for funding, organizing, and administering schools in our nation may be significant.

Private Management of Schools

As noted, some charter schools currently are operated by private companies. Even in states that preclude private corporations from chartering schools, school districts can enter into contracts for companies to offer instructional services, to operate specific schools, or perhaps to manage the entire district. Although large-scale private management experiments involving Education Alternatives, Inc., in Baltimore and Hartford were not successful (see McCarthy, 2000), and the Edison Project's contract to manage twenty low-performing schools in Philadelphia is plagued with controversy (see Rimer, 2002), private companies continue to seek public school contracts. These companies view charter schools as particularly attractive because they are exempt from some of the restrictive state regulations that might interfere with implementation of innovative staffing and instructional practices.

Corporate involvement in education is not limited to the companies that want to manage schools or districts. More targeted corporate involvement is quite common and less controversial. For example, Kaplan Educational Centers, Sylvan Learning Systems, Berlitz Language Schools, and similar companies are providing instructional services to students in school districts across the nation. Given the widespread adoption of high-stakes testing programs, targeted tutoring in specific areas under contractual arrangements is becoming increasingly popular.

Constitutional Challenges to State School Finance Systems

School finance litigation has addressed a range of issues such as tax relief measures, spending restrictions, reductions in state aid, property tax exemptions, school bond referenda, the provision of services for children with disabilities, the distribution of funds to students in religious schools, and a host of other issues. Some of the most significant school finance litigation has entailed challenges to state school funding systems, and since the early 1970s, litigation has been a popular vehicle to effect school finance reform. More than four fifths of the states have experienced challenges to their school funding systems, and the judicial scoreboard is mixed.

Equity Litigation

Challenges to state funding systems have gone through several phases, beginning with Fourteenth Amendment challenges to resource disparities among districts within a state (Thro, 1990). Such constitutional challenges focusing on the federal Equal Protection Clause were short lived, starting with the California case, *Serrano v. Priest* (1971), and culminating with the Supreme Court's ruling in *San Antonio Independent School District v. Rodriguez* (1973).

Many view the *Serrano* decision as marking the beginning of the judicial role in school finance reform. California's system of financing public schools, with its heavy reliance on property wealth, was challenged under the equal protection clauses of both the U.S. and California Constitutions. Because of the tremendous disparity in property values among districts, residents of a wealthy district could tax themselves at about one third the rate that residents of a property-poor district could tax themselves, and the former would still receive about three times the yield of the poorer district. The constitutional challenge in *Serrano* focused on these disparities in per-pupil expenditures and their significant impact on the quality of students' education. In *Serrano I* (1971), the California Supreme Court ruled as a matter of law that reliance on a property tax with such a disparate effect on per-pupil expenditures violated both the U.S. and California Constitutions.

The *Serrano I* decision had ripples throughout the United States, because all states except Hawaii relied on property taxes in basically the same fashion as did California. A flurry of cases followed, using the arguments endorsed in *Serrano I* to challenge state finance formulas. But this activity was stymied after the United States Supreme Court agreed to review a Texas case, *San Antonio Independent School District v. Rodriguez,* based exclusively on the Fourteenth Amendment Equal Protection Clause. The Supreme Court reversed the federal district court's decision and rejected the federal constitutional challenge to the Texas school finance system, finding neither a suspect classification nor a fundamental interest at stake. Disagreeing with the district court's conclusion that the large variations in school-district property wealth created a suspect classification, the Supreme Court could not find a connection between the property wealth of the district and the individual wealth of persons living in the district. The Court majority also refused to consider education a fundamental interest since it is not explicitly mentioned in the Federal Constitution, and it found no basis for making education an implied fundamental right. Despite the claim's focus on equal protection grounds, the *Rodriguez* majority seemed to rely on the fact that the state's foundation program ensured at least a minimum education for all students in the state. The majority also was supportive of local districts having the discretion to provide additional funds for education, even though it would take a far higher tax rate in property-poor districts than in property-wealthy districts to raise comparable funds.

The *Rodriguez* decision was a setback for those viewing the courts as the major vehicle to effect changes in school funding systems. Indeed, some had hoped *Rodriguez* would do for school finance reform what *Brown v. Board of Education* (1954) had done for school desegregation. But instead of establishing a national standard, the effect of the *Rodriguez* decision was to make state courts the principal venue for school-finance challenges. Since 1973, comparable numbers of state high courts have upheld and invalidated school funding systems (see Wood & Dayton, in press). Early cases focused on state equal protection provisions, but some claims also were based on state constitutional provisions directing legislatures to provide for public education in the state.

Unlike the Federal Constitution, all state constitutions place a duty on the legislature to provide for some variant of a thorough and efficient, ample, adequate, uniform, common, or basic education for all children. Given the explicit duty, one might assume that state courts reviewing challenges to funding systems would declare education to be a fundamental right under state constitutions. But this has not always happened. Some state courts have followed the Supreme Court's lead by adopting the *Rodriguez* reasoning in interpreting their state constitutions. In short, they have reasoned that provision of a minimum level of education through foundation support satisfies state as well as federal constitutional requirements (see *McDaniel v. Thomas*, 1981; *Thompson v. Engelking*, 1975). Although the Arizona Supreme Court in 1973 found education to be a fundamental right in the state, it nonetheless declined to apply strict judicial scrutiny and ruled that the inequities in resources across districts did not violate the state constitution as long as all students had access to a minimum education (*Shofstall v. Hollins*, 1973).

In spite of the state constitutional duty to provide for education, several state courts have continued to mirror the Supreme Court's reasoning, such as the highest courts in Rhode Island (*Pawtucket v. Sundlun*, 1995) and Virginia (*Scott v. Commonwealth*, 1994). Rejecting an equal protection claim to its state school funding system, the Illinois Supreme Court noted that "not every right secured by our state constitution is 'fundamental'" (*Committee v. Edgar*, 1996, p. 1194). An equity claim was not successful in Alaska because the state high court found no evidence of an overall disparity in state aid across districts (*Matanuska-Susitna v. State*, 1997).

Other state courts, however, have struck down funding systems under state equal protection provisions or state education clauses. The West Virginia Supreme Court, for example, in 1979 held that education is a fundamental right guaranteed by the West Virginia Constitution and that any discriminatory classification found in the educational financing system would be reviewed under the strict scrutiny standard (*Pauley v. Kelly I*). Also, the Wyoming Supreme Court in *Washakie County School District v. Herschler* (1980) found education to be a fundamental interest under the Wyoming Constitution's Equal Protection Clause and struck down the school funding system because of inequities across districts.

More than fifteen years after the landmark *Rodriguez* (1973) decision, the Texas Supreme Court invalidated the state's funding system under the state constitution (*Edgewood v. Kirby*, 1989). The Texas Supreme Court opined that "the legislature must establish priorities according to constitutional mandates; equalizing educational opportunity cannot be relegated to an 'if funds are left over' basis" (pp. 397–398). The court concluded that given the financial disparities across districts, the state was not providing the constitutionally mandated efficient education for all students. More recently, the Vermont Supreme Court in *Brigham v. State* (1997) held that the state's school finance system was unconstitutional because of unequal spending and tax rates.

Other than full-state funding, recapture provisions would be the most effective strategy to equalize resources across school districts. Under such a provision, property taxes would still be collected locally, but would be centrally distributed to compensate for differences in property wealth. Such recapture proposals have been controversial and not widely adopted. In an early case, the Wisconsin Supreme Court struck down a recapture provision under the state constitutional mandate of a uniform system of taxation (*Buse v. Smith*, 1976). Noting the "worthiness of the cause," the court nonetheless held that "the state cannot compel one school district to levy and collect a tax for the direct benefit of other school districts" (p. 155). However, the Kansas Supreme Court in 1994 upheld state legislation intended to remedy existing inequities in part by redistributing revenues gathered in wealthy districts to support programs in poorer districts. The court reasoned that this recapture provision did not violate the state constitutional prohibition on taking private property for public use without just compensation (*Unified School District v. State*, 1994).

Adequacy Litigation

A subtle, but significant, shift has occurred in the focus of school finance cases in that challenges are focusing increasingly on the adequacy of resources to reach school goals and objectives and not simply on resource disparities across districts. These cases are based primarily on education clauses in state constitutions. Some state courts are not accepting the assertion that the establishment of a minimum foundation program with a guaranteed base of funding for each district assures adequate educational resources. In essence, courts are being asked to assess whether available resources are *sufficient* to satisfy statutory requirements in terms of all students receiving an appropriate education so they can meet academic and other performance standards. Whereas inequities can be reduced by leveling down spending in all districts, educational inadequacies can be remedied only by ensuring sufficient funds to meet the state's specifications of what an adequate education entails.

One of the first cases to address the elements of an adequate education that must be provided to all children within the state was a 1978 Washington Supreme Court decision. Four years after the court rejected allegations that the school funding system's reliance on property taxes did not make ample provision for a basic education in the state (*Northshore School District v. Kinnear*, 1974), the court was again called on to review the funding system. In 1978, the court ruled that the state was not fulfilling its constitutionally mandated "paramount duty" to make ample provisions for a basic education by relying on excess local levies to generate school revenues (*Seattle School District v. State*, 1978). The court held that the legislature was obligated to identify the specific components of the basic education program and to assure full support from dependable tax sources.

Also, litigation in West Virginia broke new ground, because after the state high court invalidated the school funding system, the trial court on remand announced standards for a "high quality" education in terms of curriculum, personnel, facilities, materials, and equipment (*Pauley v. Bailey*, 1982). Finding the West Virginia school finance system inadequate, the court departed from the usual judicial deference to legislatures in defining the components of the constitutionally required basic education. The court specified requirements such as student–teacher ratios, the number of minutes of instruction required in specified subjects, and square footage per pupil for facilities. Reasoning that property-poor districts were not able to offer high-quality educational programs, the judge appointed an agent of the court ("special master") to work with the legislative and executive branches to develop a master plan in accordance with the court's standards. The court also concluded that the state tax system was unconstitutional, because it allowed substantial variations in property valuations among counties, and ordered the state tax commissioner to use full value assessments in developing a plan to correct the assessment deficiencies. In 1984, the West Virginia Supreme Court supported the trial court's authority, declaring that the state has a duty to ensure delivery and maintenance of a thorough and efficient system of public schools as embodied in the master plan (*Pauley II,* 1984).

A significant adequacy case, *Rose v. Council for Better Education,* was decided in 1989 by the Kentucky Supreme Court and effectively shifted the nature of the debate about the constitutionality of school finance systems across the country. The Kentucky high court struck down the state's school funding scheme as not providing the constitutionally mandated efficient system of common schools, because the schools were underfunded and plagued with inequities, ranked poorly in the nation, and were not uniform in the educational opportunities provided.

The Kentucky Supreme Court provided a rich description of what is included in the meaning of an "efficient system," thereby articulating a standard for the legislators in remedying the deficiencies. First, the court opined that an efficient system must provide an equal opportunity for every child in the state to have an adequate education to achieve the state's goals. Local tax initiatives designed to supplement state resources for education were deemed acceptable so long as they provided funds above resources necessary for the provision of an adequate education. The court went further by directing the legislature to "recreate and redesign" a new educational system to guarantee an adequate education throughout the state. The court then described the elements of a minimally adequate education (e.g., it should provide all children with sufficient oral and written communication skills to function in a complex and changing world). The court concluded that Kentucky's entire educational system—not merely how it was funded—was unconstitutional, and that legislation would have to be used to develop a new system of public schools. The opinion called for the broadest overhaul to date of any state educational system.

One major attraction of the adequacy school finance litigation is its potential to force states to provide significant amounts of new money for public elementary and secondary education. The Kentucky Education Reform Act (1990), passed to remedy the constitutional infirmities identified in *Rose,* provided an increase of 38 percent in combined state and local support for public schools between fiscal years 1990 and 1992. All Kentucky school districts experienced a significant increase in spending during this period. The legislation put $490 million in new funds into local school districts in fiscal year 1991, 77 percent of which came from state funds (Trimble & Forsaith, 1995).

As noted, the *Rose* decision proved to be a turning point in conceptualizing and arguing school finance cases with a focus on educational adequacy (Grossman, 1995). Until 1990, claims were fairly evenly initiated under state constitutions' equal protection mandates or education clauses or both. Since 1990, education clauses are clearly the dominant grounds for challenges to state school funding systems (Odden & Picus, 2000). Plaintiffs have been successful in getting courts to invalidate school funding systems in about a dozen states since the *Rose* decision, and most of these cases have focused primarily on funding adequacy or at least have included a major adequacy component.

For example, Ohio's school funding system has generated four Ohio Supreme Court decisions since 1997 as well as a number of supplemental orders. In 1997, the state's funding system was found unconstitutional for not providing sufficient funds to provide students a safe and healthy learning environment (*DeRolph v. State I*, 1997). In reviewing the revised system in 2000, the court ruled that despite the efforts, the constitutional mandate of a thorough and efficient system was still not fulfilled (*DeRolph II*, 2000). The following year the court rendered a ruling with which none of the justices felt "completely comfortable," recognizing that the foundation program would be upheld if implemented with certain modifications (*DeRolph III*, 2001). The court agreed to reconsider this decision and vacated the 2001 opinion in *DeRolph IV* (2002). The court in 2002 acknowledged the difficulties facing the Ohio General Assembly, but noted that such difficulties "cannot trump the constitution" (p. 530). Again finding the school funding system unconstitutional, the court ordered the General Assembly to engage in a complete and systematic overhaul of the funding system to ensure that it is thorough and efficient as constitutionally required.

The emphasis on educational adequacy, however, has not assured that lawsuits challenging funding systems will succeed. Some state high courts have continued to interpret state constitutional mandates pertaining to public education as not prescribing a specific level of education that must be provided and have deferred to legislatures to make such determinations. More than a dozen state high courts have rejected challenges to their state school funding systems since 1990 (see Wood & Dayton, in press). For example, the Supreme Court of Nebraska noted that the plaintiffs failed to allege that the disparities among school districts in expenditures and property tax rates produced inadequate schooling (*Gould v. Orr*, 1993). Subsequently, the South Carolina Supreme Court in a case focusing directly on educational adequacy, held that the constitutional duty to ensure a minimally adequate education for each South Carolina student rests with the legislature, and it is not the role of the courts "to become super-legislatures or super-school boards" (*Abbeville v. State*, 1999, p. 541).

In some recent educational adequacy cases, the judiciary seems to be focusing on school accountability for student academic performance to assess whether education funding is adequate or not. For example, the New Hampshire Supreme Court in *Claremont v. Governor III* (2002) held that accountability is an essential aspect of the state's duty, noting that the state must define a constitutionally adequate education, including standards and reasonable assessments, so it is possible to determine whether the state's obligation has been fulfilled. The Ohio Supreme Court similarly indicated that accountability for fully developed statewide standards is an important feature of the state's constitutional obligation to provide an effective educational system (*DeRolph v. State II*, 2000). The detailed accountability laws enacted across states are likely to become more significant in future school funding litigation.

Special Urban and Rural Issues

Some school finance cases have included claims that urban school districts are disadvantaged because they have to compete with other government services for the tax base (municipal overburden) and have a higher concentration of students with special needs (educational overburden). In an early New York case, the state high court denied relief for such claims (*Board of Education v. Nyquist*, 1982). More recently, however, the New Jersey Supreme Court found that one of the deficiencies in the state school funding system was that it did not adequately respond to the special needs of urban districts (*Abbott v. Burke*, 1998).

In a somewhat unusual case, the Connecticut Supreme Court was asked to decide whether the state satisfied its constitutional duty to provide equal educational opportunities if it substantially equalized funding, while racial and ethnic isolation continued to exist in the Hartford public schools. The court reasoned that the state constitution imposed on the legislature an affirmative obligation beyond mandates of the Federal Constitution to provide minority children with educational opportunities substantially equal to opportunities enjoyed by other children in the state. Finding that the combination of unequal resources and racial isolation denied equal educational opportunities to children in the Hartford school district, the court limited its judgment to declaratory relief, instructing the legislature to remedy the situation and retaining jurisdiction to grant further relief if needed (*Sheff v. O'Neill*, 1996). In 1999, a Connecticut superior court ruled that the state had taken sufficient actions to address white flight and de facto segregation, rejecting a claim that the state's response to the earlier ruling had been inadequate (*Sheff v. O'Neill*, 1999), but legal controversies continued. In 2003, after months of negotiations, a settlement was signed in which the state agreed to spend $45 million over four years to facilitate integration of Hartford's schools, including the creation of two magnet schools each of the four years (Bonan, 2003).

New York litigation also has focused in part on the education provided for minority children in New York City. Plaintiffs produced statistical evidence of the disparity between resources for minority and nonminority students and resulting gross educational inadequacies. In 1995, the state high court reinstated claims that the funding system violated the implementing regulations of Title VI of the Civil Rights Act of 1964 (barring discrimination on race, color, or national origin in federally assisted programs) and did not provide the sound basic education required under the state constitution (*Campaign for Fiscal Equity v. State*, 1995). But in 2002, a state appeals court found insufficient evidence that New York City students were not acquiring basic skills or in other ways being denied the opportunity for a sound basic education (*Campaign v. State*, 2002).

Several cases have focused on special needs of rural districts. The Supreme Court of Alabama dismissed a claim that inequities involving rural districts had to be remedied (*Ex parte James*, 2002). In contrast, the Supreme Court of Tennessee ruled in favor of rural plaintiffs who successfully argued that resource inequities disadvantaging small, rural school districts abridged the state constitution (*Tennessee Small School Systems v. McWherter I*, 1993; *McWherter II*, 1995; *McWherter III*,

2002). The court found no rational basis for excluding from the equalization plan an adjustment for differences in the costs of hiring teachers across rural, urban, and suburban districts.

Does Litigation Make a Difference?

After a state high court invalidates the school funding system and the legislature attempts to remedy the deficiencies, often the legislative response is again challenged as being insufficient to meet the judicial standards. This has resulted in some tension between judicial and legislative bodies and has raised questions about the impact of court rulings on school funding methods and levels. Consensus has not been reached as to whether school finance litigation has had a positive impact on finance reform despite the implicit assumption that judicial intervention will lead to a remedy that provides more money for schools. This assumption is hard to test empirically because it is difficult to know what the state's level of school funding would have been if the judicial decree had not been issued. Also, some state legislatures have revised funding systems to avoid lawsuits, which further complicates an assessment of judicial impact (Guthrie & Rothstein, 1999).

The limited amount of research that does exist on the impact of school finance cases is mixed. A 1992 study by Hickrod and colleagues supports the assumption that increases in the growth of educational spending are correlated with state supreme court decisions invalidating state school finance systems. But Heise (1995) used a time-regression model to test this assumption for Wyoming and Connecticut, and he challenged the conventional wisdom by concluding that "court decisions in both states are associated with declines in educational funding" (p. 1761).

Joondeph (1995) analyzed per-pupil expenditures in Arkansas, California, Connecticut, Washington, and Wyoming where the states' highest courts found the school financing schemes unconstitutional before 1984. In all five states, a more equitable distribution of educational resources was achieved. However, in each of these states except Connecticut, educational funding grew at a lower rate than the national average. Joondeph also found that "as a general matter, those states that reduced disparities the most, increased educational funding the least" (p. 774). The results from California were most disturbing; despite improved equalization between poor and wealthy districts, the per-pupil expenditures in the poorest districts grew more slowly than the national average.

In a subsequent study, Manwaring and Sheffrin (1997) found evidence that extensive judicially ordered reforms had a depressing effect on spending. But Goertz and Natriello (1999) reported that Kentucky, New Jersey, and Texas all changed their distribution schemes after litigation to target more money to low-wealth districts. Also, Evans, Murray, and Schwab (1999) concluded from their review of studies in this area that court-ordered reforms have resulted in more equitable distribution of resources. They reported that in most states, except for California, resources have been leveled up with additional state aid provided to poor school districts so that wealthy districts are not negatively affected. Clark (2003) subsequently affirmed that Kentucky's school finance system had become much more equitable in terms of reducing financial disparities among school districts since the *Rose* decision, but she did not find evidence that the reforms had narrowed the gap in student test scores between wealthy and poor school districts.

No state high court has required precise equality in per-pupil expenditures, recognizing that different student needs require different levels of spending. And courts have differed as to whether they have accepted the premise that the amount of school funding affects the quality of educational opportunities. Dayton (2001) has reported that judicial decisions in more than one third of the states have accepted a positive correlation between education expenditures and the opportunities provided, but several other high courts have noted that the correlation between money and educational opportunities has not been proven.

In a few states, such as Idaho, Oregon, and Wisconsin, more than one challenge to the state funding system has been unsuccessful. In other states, such as Arizona, Connecticut, Ohio, New York, Texas, and Washington, after an initial decision upholding the finance plan, a subsequent challenge has resulted in the funding system being struck down (see Wood & Dayton, in press, for a chronological summary of school finance cases). Typically, once a state constitutional violation is found, the funding system returns to court several times as legislatures attempt to remedy the constitutional defects, and the new plans are challenged as not satisfying the judicial mandate. New Jersey, for example, has experienced numerous state high court decisions regarding the legality of its school funding system and has been in litigation for thirty years.

The explanation for the range of judicial opinions lies not so much in significant differences in the constitutional provisions among the states as in differences in attitudes about the extent to which changes in the funding formula are appropriately resolved by judicial decree rather than through the political system. As noted in Chapter 14, judges have biases and political leanings as do other individuals. Also, the severe budget deficits in some states are undoubtedly influencing judicial rulings, because courts are not as motivated to order massive reforms when the likelihood of appropriate legislative responses is remote. Nonetheless, there are no signs that challenges to state school funding systems will slow down in the near future.

Adequately Financing Schools in an Era of Accountability

School finance litigation has provided an impetus to reform school funding systems in many states, but it remains clear that meaningful school finance reform is basically a political matter. Litigation may be one avenue to leverage public and legislative attention, but it by no means guarantees an optimal solution for public education. Tax policy and the citizenry's commitment to public education need to be addressed to a large extent in the political arena.

The current education policy focus in Congress and across states concerns standards-based reforms. Indeed, standards and assessments to ascertain that the standards are met are affecting all levels of the educational enterprise. The federal No Child Left Behind Act (NCLB) (2002) reflects a conceptual shift in holding states, school districts, and schools more accountable for increasing student achievement and implementing annual testing based on academic standards in certain areas (see Chapter 15). Not only are schools accountable for making adequate yearly progress toward proficiency in basic skills for all students, but also they must ensure that all teachers are of high quality. Test scores are being used to identify schools that need additional assistance, and educational options must be provided for students attending Title I schools that do not make adequate progress for two consecutive years. Increasing options for families is one of the NCLB's central themes.

Most states have adopted similar provisions, placing greater responsibilities on school district administrators—especially school building leaders—to effect school improvements. Accountability mandates across states focus on aligning curriculum and assessments to rigorous academic standards, using high-stakes testing, and publicly reporting test results by school and grade level. Indeed, high-stakes tests in basic skills are at the center of most of the state and federal accountability mandates. Based on test scores, students are denied promotion and graduation, schools are ranked and perhaps penalized, and in some locales teachers and administrators can lose their jobs due to inferior student performance. The stakes are indeed high for all involved, so an overemphasis on teaching to the tests is understandable.

The widespread support among policymakers regarding academic standards for student performance has been truly remarkable. But use of test scores to assess that the standards are met is not as universally endorsed. Identifying the measures of student performance is critically important, as they *will* drive the educational system. Researchers often argue for multiple measures to be selected to reflect the range of educational activities considered important for an educated citizen. Some have faulted the reliance on statewide tests in reading and mathematics as being too narrow and neglecting many important aspects of the instructional program, such as creativity and higher level thinking skills (Bracey, 2000; Kohn, 2002; Merrow, 2001). Efforts have been made to include dropout rates and other student performance measures beyond test scores, but such alternatives have not been widely adopted.

Thus, despite some vocal critics, educational adequacy is being defined in terms of students satisfying academic standards as measured by statewide tests. Yet, translating such performance standards into resource distribution plans has been problematic. Current state funding systems do not "link the availability of funds and the educational performance of students" (Reschovsky & Imazeki, 2000, p. 1), and consensus has not been reached as to how this should be accomplished. Several strategies are being discussed, and some implemented, to determine the funds necessary for the academic standards to be met.

An approach used in several states entails identifying school districts where students are meeting the standards based on test scores and calculating the average spending per pupil in these districts as a measure of funding adequacy. This approach can provide an average per-pupil expenditure but does not account for variations in the cost of meeting the standards across districts with different types of students. Thus, some researchers have developed elaborate education cost indices to account for various characteristics of school districts and their students that affect the resources necessary to satisfy the standards (see Ladd & Hansen,1999; Reschovsky & Imazeki, 2000). Duncombe and Yinger (1999) have observed that if a funding system does not account for differences in the educational environment across districts (e.g., poverty rates and single-parent families), it would be similar to not accounting for different winter weather conditions in Minnesota and Alabama in calculating heating costs for the two states.

And even if such population and environmental differences are accounted for in determining adequate resources, there are no assurances that the funds will be used effectively. Thus, accountability mandates are becoming increasingly explicit in requiring districts to justify how resources are being used. King, Swanson, and Sweetland (2003) have placed "the concerns of equity and adequacy second to that of efficiency" (p. 504); they contend that developing systems to improve efficiency is the greatest challenge facing school finance reformers. States are attempting to better evaluate how schools and school districts are using their financial resources and to link resources with student outcomes, but much work remains to be done in this arena. Some researchers are developing complex statistical techniques to measure efficiency by identifying districts where spending is low and high compared with other districts with similar student performance and educational costs (see Duncombe & Yinger, 1999; Swanson & Engert, 1999). The low-spending districts attaining similar outcomes as the high-spending districts would be considered more efficient in using their resources.

In enacting school accountability mandates, policymakers must consider a number of issues. For example, should there be incentives in terms of state support for demonstrated improvements in student performance? Do fiscal rewards result in school improvements? Should there be fiscal consequences for poor performance? How should the special needs of students and districts be accounted for in standards-driven distribution plans? How can schools be held accountable for meeting statewide standards and at the same time enjoy some discretion in selecting strategies to attain them? How can states avoid negative side effects of reliance on high-stakes student assessments to rate schools and districts (e.g., teachers overemphasizing test preparation)? If equity across school districts is still an important concern, how is it advanced in an era of accountability?

A number of challenges face those interested in reforming school funding systems in addition to those mentioned previously. Policymakers need to be convinced that money well spent does make a difference in student performance. This is particularly difficult to do in a time of severe budget deficits across states and increasing competition for tax dollars (e.g., to provide services for the elderly).

Starting with the landmark *Coleman Report* (Coleman et al., 1966) and its questions about the impact of money on improving student achievement, this connection has been hotly debated and has generated a large volume of educational production function studies to delineate how various features affect educational outcomes. Some widely cited studies have found little impact of various school inputs on student performance on standardized tests (see Hanushek, 1986, 1991, 1995). However, other researchers have documented that certain variables, such as class size, after-school and summer programs, early intervention programs, and especially teacher quality variables (e.g., academic ability, pedagogical preparation, education, experience) have an important impact on student performance (Ferguson, 1998; Goldhaber, 2002). Even if the impact of certain variables on student learning is clearly identified, linking resource levels to those variables is not easy to do. For example, research clearly supports that teacher quality has a crucial impact on student learning, but identifying the specific influential characteristics and translating them into resources to ensure that teachers have or acquire these characteristics has been more elusive (Goldhaber & Anthony, 2003).

Another challenge of school finance reform and education reform in general in the twenty-first century is to address how to capitalize on the escalating pace of technological advances. For example, policymakers must address whether it is more efficient to put money into building more schools or to providing computers so students can be connected from home to learning activities. Some modes of communication that are now routine were unheard of only a decade ago, and the concept of education—particularly where learning takes place—is clearly being transformed.

A cluster of challenges are also presented by the strong movement nationally to provide educational options for students, including private options in the form of voucher programs or privately operated charter schools. If public aid for nonpublic education continues to increase, the ratio of private to public school enrollments could shift, which would mean that significant school governance changes could be on the horizon. Hess (2002) recently observed that "the hard-and-fast lines we have drawn between *public* and *private* are much more blurry and less useful than we pretend" (p. 1). Decisions made during the next decade regarding the use of public funds to support educational options for families could influence state school funding systems and ultimately the character of education in our nation.

REFERENCES

Abbeville County School District v. State, 515 S.E.2d 535 (S.C. 1999).

Abbott v. Burke, 710 A.2d 450 (N.J. 1998).

American Council on Intergovernmental Relations. (1998). *Significant features of fiscal federalism*, vol. 2. Bethesda, MD: ACIR.

Board of Education, Levittown Union Free School District v. Nyquist, 439 N.E.2d 359 (N.Y. 1982).

Bonan, D. (2003, January 27). *Sheff v. O'Neill* settled!—Landmark Connecticut school desegregation case. Danbury, CT: Independent Media Center. *www.madhattersimc.org/print.php?sid=1356.*

Bouman, C. E., & Brown, D. J. (1996, December). Public school fees as hidden taxation. *Educational Administration Quarterly, 32,* 665–685.

Bracey, G. (2000). *High stakes testing.* Education Policy Project, Center for Education Research, Analysis, and Innovation (00–32). Milwaukee: University of Wisconsin-Milwaukee. *www.uwm.edu/Dept/CERAI/.*

Brigham v. State, 692 A.2d 384 (Vt. 1997).

Brimley, V., & Garfield, R. (2002). *Financing education in a climate of change* (8th ed.). Boston: Allyn & Bacon.

Brown v. Board of Education of Topeka, 347 U.S. 343 (1954).

Bureau of the Census. (2001). *State government tax collection 2001.* Washington, DC: U.S. Department of Commerce.

Buse v. Smith, 247 N.W.2d 141 (Wis. 1976).

Campaign for Fiscal Equity v. State of New York, 655 N.D.2d 661 (N.Y. 1995).

Campaign for Fiscal Equity v. State of New York, 719 N.Y.S.2d 475 (Sup. Ct. 2001), *rev'd*, 744 N.Y.S.2d 130 (App. Div. 2002).

Chaikind, S., Danielson, L. C., & Brauen, M. L. (1993). What do we know about the costs of special education? A selected review. *The Journal of Special Education, 26*, 344–370.

Chubb, J., & Moe, T. (1990). *Politics, markets, and America's schools.* Washington, DC: Brookings Institute.

Claremont School District v. Governor III, 794 A.2d 744 (N.H. 2002).

Clark, M. A. (2003, January 8). Education reform, redistribution, and student achievement: Evidence from the Kentucky Education Reform Act. Princeton, NJ: Princeton University.

Clune, W. (1995). Accelerated education as a remedy for high-poverty schools. *University of Michigan Journal of Law Reform, 28*, 481–491.

Coleman, J. S., Campbell, E. Q., Hobson, C. J., McPartland, J., Mead, A. M., Weinfeld, F. D. (1966). *Equality of educational opportunity.* Washington, DC: U.S. Department of Health, Education & Welfare.

Committee v. Edgar, 672 N.E.2d 1178 (Ill. 1996).

Cookson, P. W. (1994). *School choice: The struggle for the soul of American education.* New Haven, CT: Yale University Press.

Coons, J. E., & Sugarman, S. D. (1978). *Education by choice: The case for family control.* Berkeley, CA: University of California Press.

Dayton, J. (2001). *Serrano and its progeny: An analysis of 30 years of school funding litigation. Education Law Reporter, 157*, 447–464.

DeRolph v. State I, 677 N.E.2d 733 (Ohio 1997).

DeRolph v. State II, 728 N.E.2d 993 (Ohio 2000).

DeRolph v. State III, 754 N.E.2d 1184 (Ohio 2001).

DeRolph v. State IV, 780 N.E.2d 529 (Ohio 2002).

Drake, D. (2002). *A review and analysis of Michigan tax policies impacting K–12 finances.* Lansing, MI: Michigan Association of School Administrators.

Duncombe, W., & Yinger, J. (1999). Performance standards and educational cost indexes: You can't have one without the other. In H. F. Ladd, R. Chalk, & J. Hansen (Eds.), *Equity and adequacy in education finance: Issues and perspectives* (pp. 260–297). Washington, DC: National Research Council/National Academy Press.

Edgewood v. Kirby, 777 S.W.2d 391 (Tex. 1989).

Evans, W., Murray, S., & Schwab, R. (1999). The impact of court-mandated school finance reform. In H. Ladd, R. Chalk, & J. Hansen (Eds.), *Equity and adequacy in education finance: Issues and perspectives* (pp. 72–98). Washington, DC: National Research Council/National Academy Press.

Ex Parte James, No. 1950030, 2002 Ala. LEXIS 1656 (Ala. May 31, 2002).

Ferguson, R. F. (1998). Can schools narrow the black-white test score gap? In C. Jencks & M. Phillips (Eds.), *The black-white test score gap* (pp. 318–374). Washington, DC: Brookings Institute.

Fowler, F. (1991). The shocking ideological integrity of Chubb and Moe. *Journal of Education, 173*, 119–129.

Goertz, M., & Natriello, G. (1999). Court-mandated school finance reform: What do the new dollars buy? In H. Ladd, R. Chalk, & J. Hansen (Eds.), *Equity and adequacy in education finance: Issues and perspectives* (pp. 99–135). Washington, DC: National Research Council/National Academy Press.

Goldhaber, D. (2002). The mystery of good teaching: Surveying the evidence on student achievement and teachers' characteristics. *Education Next, 2*(1), 50–55.

Goldhaber, D., & Anthony, E. (2003). *Teacher quality and student achievement.* New York City: Teachers College Institute for Urban and Minority Education, ERIC Clearinghouse on Urban Education.

Goodlad, J. (1997, July 9). Making democracy safe for education. *Education Week, 40*, 56.

Gould v. Orr, 506 N.W.2d 349 (Neb. 1993).

Grossman, M. S. (1995). Oklahoma school finance litigation: Shifting from equity to adequacy. *University of Michigan Journal of Law Reform, 28*(3), 521–557.

Guthrie, J., & Rothstein, R. (1999). Enabling "adequacy" to achieve reality: Translating adequacy into state school finance distribution arrangements. In H. Ladd, R. Chalk, & J. Hansen (Eds.), *Equity and adequacy in education finance* (pp. 209–259). Washington, DC: National Research Council/National Academy Press.

Hanushek, E. A. (1986, September). The economics of schooling: Production and efficiency in public schools. *The Journal of Economic Literature, 24*, 1141–1173.

Hanushek, E. A. (1991). When school finance "reform" may not be good policy. *Harvard Journal on Legislation, 28*, 423–456.

Hanushek, E. A. (1995). The quest for equalized mediocrity: School finance reform without consideration of school performance. In L. O. Picus (Ed.), *Where does the money go: Resource allocation in elementary and secondary schools* (pp. 20–43). Newbury Park, CA: Corwin Press.

Heise, M. (1995). State constitutional litigation, educational finance, and legal impact: An empirical analysis. *The University of Cincinnati Law Review, 63,* 1735–1765.

Hess, F. (2002, November). Making sense of the "public" in public education (Policy Report). Washington, DC: Progressive Policy Institute.

Hickrod, G. A., Hines, E. R., Anthony, G. P., Dively, J. A., & Pruyne, G. B. (1992). The effect of constitutional litigation on education finance: A preliminary analysis. *Journal of Educational Finance, 18*(2), 180–210.

Howard, M. A. (1989). State tax and expenditure limitations: There is no story. *Public Budgeting and Finance, 9,* 83–90.

Individuals with Disabilities Education Act, 20 U.S.C. §1401 et seq. (2002).

Joondeph, B. W. (1995). The good, the bad, and the ugly: An empirical analysis of litigation-prompted school finance reform. *Santa Clara Law Review, 35*(3), 763–824.

Kentucky Education Reform Act of 1990, Kentucky Revised Statutes Annotated (KRS ANN. ch. 476 (2002).

King, R., Swanson, A., & Sweetland, S. (2003). *School finance* (3rd ed.). Boston: Allyn & Bacon.

Kohn, A. (2002, January 24). Measures fall short. *USA Today,* 12A.

Kozol, J. (1992, September 21). Whittle and the privateers. *The Nation, 272, 274, 276–278.*

Ladd, H. F., & Hansen, J. S. (Eds.) (1999). *Making money matter: Financing America's schools.* Committee on Education Finance. Washington, DC: National Research Council/National Academy Press.

Manwaring, R., & Sheffrin, S. (1997, May). Litigation, school finance reform and aggregate educational spending. *International Tax and Public Finance, 4,* 107–127.

Matanuska-Susitna v. State, 931 P.2d 391 (Alaska 1997).

McCarthy, M. (2000). Privatization of education: Marketplace models. In B. Jones (Ed.), *Educational administration: Policy dimensions in the twenty-first century* (21–40). Greenwich, CT: Ablex.

McDaniel v. Thomas, 285 S.E.2d 156 (Ga. 1981).

Merrow, J. (2001). Undermining standards. *Phi Delta Kappan, 82,* 653–659.

Molnar, A., & Morales, J. (2000). *The third annual report on trends in schoolhouse commercialism.* Arizona State University: Commercialism in Education Research Unit.

Monk, D. H. (1992). Education productivity research: An update and assessment of its role in

education finance reform. *Educational Evaluation and Policy Analysis, 14,* 307–332.

National Center for Education Statistics. (2002, April). U.S. Department of Education. *Early estimates of public elementary and secondary education statistics: School year 2001–2002.* Washington, DC: U.S. Government Printing Office.

National Education Association. (2002). *Rankings and estimates.* Annapolis: NEA.

No Child Left Behind Act, 20 USC §6301 et seq. (2002).

Northshore School District N. 417 v. Kinnear, 530 P.2d 178 (Wash. 1974).

Odden, A., & Picus, L. (2000). *School finance: A policy perspective.* Boston: McGraw-Hill.

Pauley v. Bailey, No. 75–126 (Cir. Ct. Kanawha County, 1982), *remanded (for monitoring),* Pauley II, 324 S.E.2d 128 (W.V. 1984).

Pauley v. Kelly (Pauley I), 255 S.E.2d 859 (W.V. 1979).

Pawtucket v. Sundlun, 662 A.2d 40 (R.I. 1995).

Reschovsky, A., & Imazeki, J. (2000, October). *Achieving educational adequacy through school finance reform.* CPRE Research Report Series RR-045. Philadelphia: Consortium for Policy Research in Education.

Rimer, S. (2002, December 15). Philadelphia school's woes defeat veteran principal. *The New York Times,* YNE 25.

Rose v. Council for Better Education, Inc., 790 S.W.2d 186 (Ky. 1989).

San Antonio Independent School District v. Rodriguez, 411 U.S. 1 (1973).

Sandham, J. (2000, June 21). States devoting tobacco money to education. *Education Week,* 19.

Scott v. Commonwealth, 443 S.E.2d 138 (Va. 1994).

Seattle School District No. 1 v. State, 585 P.2d 71 (Wash. 1978).

Serrano v. Priest, 487 P.2d 1241 (Cal. 1971).

Sheff v. O'Neill, 678 A.2d 1267 (Conn. 1996).

Sheff v. O'Neill, 733 A.2d 925 (Conn. Super. Ct. 1999).

Shofstall v. Hollins, 515 P.2d 590 (Ariz. 1973).

Swanson, A. D., & Engert, F. (1999). *Benchmarking: A study of school and school district effect and efficiency.* Buffalo, NY: SUNY-Buffalo Graduate School of Education Publications.

Tennessee Small School Systems v. McWherter I, 851 S.W.2d 139 (Tenn. 1993).

Tennessee Small School Systems v. McWherter II, 894 S.W.2d 734 (Tenn. 1995).

Tennessee Small School Systems v. McWherter III, 91 S.W.3d 232 (Tenn. 2002).

Thompson v. Engelking, 537 P.2d 635 (Idaho 1975).

Thro, W. E. (1990). The third wave: The implications of the Montana, Kentucky, and Texas decisions for the future of public school finance reform litigation. *Journal of Law and Education, 19*(2), 219–250.

Title VI of the Civil Rights Act of 1964, 42 U.S.C. §2000d et seq. (2002).

Trimble, C. S., & Forsaith, A. C. (1995, Spring). Achieving equity and excellence in Kentucky education. *University of Michigan Journal of Law Reform, 28,* 599–653.

Unified School District v. State, 885 P.2d 1170 (Kan. 1994).

Washakie County School District v. Herschler, 606 P.2d 310 (Wyo. 1980).

Webb, L. D., Metha, A., & Jordan, K. F. (2003). *Foundations of American education* (4th ed.). Upper Saddle River, NJ: Prentice Hall.

Wood, R. C., & Dayton, J. (in press). *Education funding litigation: Education policy and the courts.* Norwood, MA: Christopher–Gordon.

Zelman v. Simmons-Harris, 536 U.S. 639 (2002).

INDEX